D0197439

The Autobiography
of William Carlos Williams

Books by William Carlos Williams

1909 Poems
1913 The Tempers
1917 Kora in Hell: Improvisations
1920 Al que quiere!
1921 Sour Grapes
1922 Spring and All
1923 The Great American Novel
1925 In the American Grain
1928 A Voyage to Pagany
1932 A Novelette and Other Prose
      The Knife of the Times
      The Cod Head
1934 Collected Poems, 1921-1931
1935 An Early Martyr
1936 Adam and Eve & The City
1937 White Mule
1938 The Complete Collected Poems of William Carlos Williams
      Life Along the Passaic River
1940 In the Money
1941 The Broken Span
1944 The Wedge
1946 Paterson, Book I
      First Act
1948 Paterson, Book II
      A Dream of Love
      The Clouds
1949 The Pink Church
      Paterson, Book III
1950 A Beginning on the Short Story
      Make Light of It: Collected Stories
      Collected Later Poems
1951 Paterson, Book IV
      Collected Earlier Poems
      The Autobiography of William Carlos Williams
1952 The Build-Up
1954 The Desert Music
      The Dog and The Fever (Tr. of Quevedo)
      Selected Essays
1955 Journey to Love
1957 Selected Letters
1958 I Wanted to Write a Poem
      Paterson, Book V
1959 Yes, Mrs. Williams
1961 The Farmers' Daughters (Collected Stories)
      Many Loves (Collected Plays)
1962 Pictures from Brueghel
1966 The William Carlos Williams Reader

THE AUTOBIOGRAPHY
OF WILLIAM CARLOS WILLIAMS

A NEW DIRECTIONS BOOK

Copyright 1948, 1949, 1951, by William Carlos Williams.

All rights reserved. Except for brief passages quoted in a
newspaper, magazine, radio, or television review, no part of
this book may be reproduced in any form or by any means,
electronic or mechanical, including photocopying and
recording, or by any information storage and retrieval system,
without permission in writing from the Publisher.

In June and August, 1948, and May, 1949, the magazine
Poetry published an earlier version of the first twenty or
thirty pages of this autobiography. I am grateful to them for
the suggestion that the task be undertaken and for their kind
permission to include much of this earlier material.
Thanks are also due to Charles Olson and *Poetry New York*
for permission to reprint part of Mr. Olson's essay,
"Projective Verse," copyright 1950 by *Poetry New York*.

First published as New Directions Paperbook 223 in 1967.

Manufactured in the United States of America.

Designer: Ernst Reichl

New Directions Books are published for James Laughlin
by New Directions Publishing Corporation,
333 Sixth Avenue, New York 10014.

To F.H.W.

Contents

Foreword

Nine-tenths of our lives is well forgotten in the living. Of the part that is remembered, the most had better not be told: it would interest no one, or at least would not contribute to the story of what we ourselves have been. A thin thread of narrative remains—a few hundred pages—about which clusters, like rock candy, the interests upon which the general reader will spend a few hours, as might a sweet-toothed child, preferring something richer and not so hard on the teeth. To us, however, such hours have been sweet. They constitute our particular treasure. That is all, justly, that we should offer.

I can't tell more than I know. I have lived, somehow, from day to day; and so I describe it, from day to day, as I have struggled to get a meaning from my failures and successes. Not that my conclusions have been profound. But even the most trivial happenings may carry a certain weight.

I do not intend to tell the particulars of the women I have been to bed with, or anything about them. Don't look for it. That has nothing to do with me. What relations I have had with men and women, such encounters as have interested me most profoundly, have not occurred in bed. I am extremely sexual in my desires: I carry them everywhere and at all times. I think that from that arises the drive which empowers us all. Given that drive, a man does with it what his mind directs. In the manner in which he directs that power lies his secret. We always try to hide the secret of our lives from the general stare. What I believe to be the hidden core of my life will not easily be deciphered, even when I tell, as here, the outer circumstances.

Such an autobiography as this could stretch into a thousand pages. All I should have to do would be to keep on writing. No doubt I could hold the general interest even so. But stretching the story out, padding it up a bit, putting in a few more stories of some of my contemporaries wouldn't help much to clarify it. It might make a far more amusing book than it is likely to be in its present proportions, but nothing thereby would be added to its worth—if it has any worth beyond that lent to it by the interest of a few friends.

I have not even attempted to include a full list of my friends. I have paid no attention to lists of any kind. All that I have wanted to do was to tell of my life as I went along practicing medicine and at the same time recording my daily search for . . . what? As a writer, I have been a physician, and as a physician a writer; and as both writer and physician I have served sixty-eight years of a more or less uneventful existence, not more than half a mile from where I happen to have been born.

Because Flossie, my wife, and I have never moved, Nine Ridge Road has become a landmark for many friends who, though they have seldom or never visited us, have at least known where we lived. They have written many letters, all of which I have answered; that has been one of my major occupations over the years. I am surprised that I have not mentioned such names as Ed Corson, Arthur Noyes and Bert Clark, among my classmates at medical school; they are old friends. Wallace Stevens is another scarcely mentioned, though he is constantly in my thoughts. And the late Alfred Stieglitz. None of these ever has been to see me in Rutherford. There is a great virtue in such an isolation. It permits a fair interval for thought. That is, what I call thinking, which is mainly scribbling. It has always been during the act of scribbling that I have gotten most of my satisfactions.

For instance, I'd go to see Alfred Stieglitz. I did this fairly regularly at one time. There'd be no one at all in the gallery. He'd recognize me, and after I had had a chance to look around he'd come out from behind his partition and we'd begin to talk.

We'd talk about the pictures, about John Marin and what he was doing then. Or another day it would be a Hartley show or a visit to the Portinari show at the Modern Museum. Or we'd have been to hear Pablo Casals. Or we'd visit the tapestries at The Cloisters. After that, I'd come home and think—that is to say, to scribble. I'd scribble for days, sometimes, after such a visit, or even years, it might be, trying to discover how my mind had readjusted itself to its contacts.

Or sometimes, not often enough, we'd get in the car and go forty miles into the country to visit my fellow Jerseyite, Kenneth Burke, and his family. The life he has led on his old abandoned farm in Andover has always fascinated me. I approve of it. I admire the mind that conceived and carried out such a life. We'd meet there Peggy Cowley who'd be bitten by a rattlesnake and yell for me before she'd be taken to the hospital to be cured, Mattie Josephson, Malcolm Cowley, Gorham Munson, in striped pants and carrying a cane in that country place. All afternoon would be spent in argument, we hugging our glasses of apple-jack. Reactivated, I'd go home to the eternally rewarding game of scribbling. Thought was never an isolated thing with me; it was a game of tests and balances, to be proven by the written word. Then would come the trial. The poem would be submitted to some random editor, or otherwise meet its fate in the world. I would observe that fate and so come to judge the intelligence of my contemporaries. Once, in great excitement, we took the train for Philadelphia late in the day to be present at a performance of *Lysistrata* before it could be censored.

When and where, after such forays, did I or could I write? Time meant nothing to me. I might be in the middle of some flu epidemic, the phone ringing day and night, madly, not a moment free. That made no difference. If the fit was on me— if something Stieglitz or Kenneth had said was burning inside me, having bred there overnight demanding outlet—I would be like a woman at term; no matter what else was up, that demand had to be met.

Five minutes, ten minutes, can always be found. I had my typewriter in my office desk. All I needed to do was to pull up the leaf to which it was fastened and I was ready to go. I worked at top speed. If a patient came in at the door while I was in the middle of a sentence, bang would go the machine—I was a physician. When the patient left, up would come the machine. My head developed a technique: something growing inside me demanded reaping. It had to be attended to. Finally, after eleven at night, when the last patient had been put to bed, I could always find the time to bang out ten or twelve pages. In fact, I couldn't rest until I had freed my mind from the obsessions which had been tormenting me all day. Cleansed of that torment, having scribbled, I could rest.

We have lived by the seasons. It is in winter that illness occurs here, mostly. It is then that a physician's services are in greatest demand. But it is then that the going is hardest. I have never taken a winter vacation. Perhaps the time is coming when that will have to be changed. Winter is a tough time for a doctor. But in spring the world is altered for us. The small world of the patch of ground that I call my yard has always been of tremendous importance to me. Henri Fabre has been one of my gods. Not that I have followed his scientific example, though at one time I might have done so and perhaps have been a happier man, but his example has always stood beside me as a measure and a rule. It has made me quiet and induced in me a patient industry, and in spite of my insufficiencies, a long-range contentment. What becomes of me has never seemed to me important, but the fates of ideas living against the grain in a nondescript world have always held me breathless.

William Carlos Williams

Part One

Chapter 1

First Memories

I was an innocent sort of child and have remained so to this day. Only yesterday, reading Chapman's *The Iliad of Homer*, did I realize for the first time that the derivation of the adjective venereal is from Venus! And I a physician practicing medicine for the past forty years. I was stunned!

Terror dominated my youth, not fear. I was not afraid. I had the normal fears, naturally, but they could be condoned, not the terror that flared from hidden places and all "heaven."

My first definable memory is of being put outdoors after the blizzard of '88 and yelling to be taken in again away from the cold and the wind. And they did say that that same spring I went out with a handful of salt to try to catch sparrows by putting it on their tails as my Uncle Godwin had told me to do.

Earlier, though I do not remember it, Mother was impressed by the accuracy with which I beat the drum at my Uncle Irving's instigation: he would hit the big drum (it comes to mind as I write this), Bam! Bam! slowly. Then there would be a one-beat interval after which I would come in rapidly on the little drum, Bam bam! They say my time was perfect.

And the first time I ever laughed out loud, Mother says, was when I must have been under a year (for it was in the old house even before Ed my brother was born). Pop was chopping down a small tree. Each time he'd swing the axe and I heard it wham into the wood, I'd let out a wild cackle of delight.

3

But my second placeable recollection after the snow scene—
it must have been the April or May following the blizzard—
was of the great swings in the Janeses' side yard under the oaks.
They were marvelous, those swings, and especially I remember
the little one for babies with four ropes, to steady it! But we
older kids—I was four and a half—sat on the two-rope swings
and would let the other children run all the way under us and
out the other side—pushing us up and up at arms' length. Back
and forth, back and forth.

Pop was away a good deal in those days on business in South
and Central America, so that my uncles, Godwin and Irving,
my father's half-brothers, were closely associated with my upbringing. Poor Godwin, a fatal name in our family, he was never
quite right in the head. He taught me one rhyme I have never
forgot:

> Oh boys keep away
> From the girls I say
> And give them plenty of room
> For when you come to wed
> They'll bang you on the head
> With the bald-headed end of a broom.

He never married but died insane at Morris Plains many years
later. He was a grand rouser of a child's imagination.

Irving, the other uncle, was musical and had a beautiful
baritone voice. Sometimes Mother would sing duets with him.
Pop and he would play the flute to Mother's accompaniment.
But Pop was never very good. He had other talents.

There was Mother, of course, and Grandma Wellcome, my
father's mother, the Englishwoman who still sometimes dropped
her aiches like any Cockney. Grandma remembered more than
she would tell of her girlhood in London in the home of the
Godwins whose ward she was—the William Godwins, perhaps,
who knows? A dark chapter. Ed, my only brother, was born when
I was thirteen months old. Grandma took me over from that
time on. I was in a great measure *her* boy.

I never had a sister, no aunts and no female cousins, at least
within striking distance. So that aside from Mother and Grandma

I never knew a female intimately for my entire young life. That was very important. It generated in me enough curiosity to burn up fifty growing boys.

Grandma took me over or tried to. But once Mother lost her temper and laid the old gal out with a smack across the puss that my mother joyfully remembered until her death. Her Latin blood got the best of her that day. Nor was she sorry; it did her more good, in fact, than anything that had happened to her since her coming to the States from Santo Domingo to be married. I think that one of the most potent forces that kept my mother going to the age of ninety-two was a malign determination to out-live her mother-in-law, who died at eighty-three in 1920. I hope I take after my female ancestors.

Chapter 2
The Bagellon House

The Bagellon house! It is impossible for me to pass it by without one last look at all the thronging memories. The apples that grew in the orchard next to Charlie Wadsworth's print shop beyond the fence in the rear of the big house are still my favorites and must always remain so: Baldwins! As I speak of them I immediately recall also the birds that lived in a hole in one of those trees, pale blue birds that flitted quietly away as we approached under the green foliage.

One day Ed and I, having removed our shoes and stockings against orders, were sitting with our feet in a little pool of water we had found there. Suddenly Godwin pounced upon us and dragged us away. We were whaled properly for it. The pool was a deep well from which the cover had been inadvertently removed. But that must have been the second year. For before Charlie Wadsworth set up his shop in the little one-room shack, some poor people lived there whom I recall for a special reason.

I don't remember whether Ed was with me that day or not. But there were some boys about my age or a little older, semi-clad in rags, squirting around the place and I along with them. But one didn't seem to have the same equipment—a very small one with clothes held above the waist. I was amazed and puzzled. But when I told my mother about it later I was warned never to mention such things again and not to play with those dirty children any more.

Another day I watched Uncle Irving shooting with an air gun of unusual power, such a gun as I have never seen since, at a red squirrel at the top of a pine tree in the front yard. At last the squirrel fell, all bloody, at our feet. Another day, having left my rubber boots outdoors and putting them on the next morning, after they had been brought in to me, I found one of them to be wet inside. I had killed a toad which had crept in for its night's rest.

Once they were digging a post-hole and turned up a large red snake. I remember as though it were yesterday that Godwin said it would not die until sunset though its head had been completely crushed, for its tail was still wriggling.

In the barnyard Godwin put a needle hole in a fresh laid egg and made me suck out the contents. It was also he who told me that if I put a horsehair in the water trough by the well in the barnyard it would turn to an eel by morning. I went to look and did see some slender black worms wriggling at the bottom.

Once I found a dime in the dirt path that ran around the east side of the house and came tearing around to the front again to tell everyone about it. "Go back and maybe you'll find another," said Irving. I went back and did find another. "Try it again," said Irving. "Maybe it's a money mine." I did and found a third dime. By this time everyone came. We dug and Ed, I think, found an additional nickel but that was all!

The Norsworthys would arrive on Saturdays to visit us, and we would jump from the barn door to the manure heap where Godwin told us the Germans always buried Limburger cheese to ripen it. He loved Limburger cheese and it also afforded him his favorite joke.

Men would come to hunt rabbits in the open fields back of the orchard. There I saw some hunter who had killed a rabbit take a sharp knife and laughing stab it into the poor creature's body just under the tail. It made me ill.

And there, in those fields, I remember one day when Ed and I were watching an old colored man spading up the ground, we noticed that the palms of his hands were as white as our own. He was a wonderful person to us and gave us a drink out of the tin water-pail he had in the grass near him as he worked. It was a little rusty on the bottom as we drank, looking in. When we told all these discoveries to the people at home we were threatened with terrible things if we ever wandered off that way again.

And the horses! Big Billy and Little Billy. The latter, which Godwin bought from the gypsies, damn near finished him later on. And the men crawling under the freight cars stalled at the railroad crossing!

Those were lyrical years. Pop was away most of that time but there is one memory with which he is still intimately associated: the kite—and the stories of kites and his own childhood in the West Indies. It was a kite, featuring upon it the heads of three horses racing neck and neck, a kite taller than I, made from one of the posters Charlie Wadsworth printed in his shop advertising the cards at the Clifton track where Godwin would go regularly to lose whatever little change he could rake up. Pop made the kite as only Pop could make things. He flew it from the yard one day after readjusting the rag-tail a few times and lashed it that night to the rail of the back porch. In the morning, on a southern breeze, it was still magnificently flying, the cord as tense as a fiddle string. I remember holding it in my hand and feeling the tug and vibration.

From the glassed-in cupola atop that old house, through a telescope someone had placed there, we once looked fearfully at the moon. I remember also the arrow Irving shot through the front of the barn just above the big door! There it remained winter and summer for the following two years or until we left the Bagellon house and returned to civilization.

Chapter 3

At the Shore

Another and different memory of those early days is of the summers we spent at "the shore" or at Munger's in the Catskill Mountains. It was there at Munger's that we hunted chipmunks in the stone walls with Pop and Irving, though the latter would more often be playing croquet or lawn tennis with the ladies. Once we children went for a long drive with the others behind a team of horses to the top of some high place nearby. When I alighted, I started immediately to run and fell, my chin hitting the rocky ground—a thundering whack. I remember that well.

On another day I watched the men in striped jackets and the women in long skirts fishing in a fast-running and shallow stream. The fish were thick in the water, of a good size, and sluggish enough to be caught with a noose of copper wire.

They had long poles to which were attached the usual line at the end of which was a wire noose. The trick was to drop the noose into the water upstream—where the fish were heading—slip it cautiously down over the fish's head, and with a jerk the thing would be done. What else could they have been but suckers clinging fast to the stones? I didn't see any caught, so perhaps the trick was harder to accomplish than it looked.

A year later when Ed had whooping cough, I traveled to Connecticut alone with Grandma on the New Haven boat. I must have been nearly six at the time and yet was taking the

9

bottle. Grandma had one with her. Ashamed to be seen, I crouched against the old lady's skirts on deck to suck it, but being observed by others about us I refused the favor. That ended my addiction.

In West Haven she and I stayed with Mrs. Forbes, wife of an old sea-captain friend Grandma had known from her Saint Thomas days. There I went swimming for the first time, or rather had a bucket of salt water poured over my head when I was too timid to adventure into the sea.

Most vivid of the adventures of that summer was the day when one of the older boys took me to see his father's street-watering wagon, a one-horse affair with a high seat behind which in a wooden tank the water was carried for use on days when the dust in the streets was troublesome. It seemed enormous to me, that apparatus, and when I was lifted to the driver's seat, I thought I would never be able to get down again.

The next summer we went to Long Island where Ed, because of whooping cough, had gone alone the year before. Mother was still doing a little painting. An outdoor study of a twig of yellow and red crab-apples hanging from a nail is the last thing I ever saw her actually painting. That summer while I was up a small cherry tree I happened to look toward the barn, my attention attracted by the violent bleating of a lamb. As I turned my head toward the sound, one of the men drew a knife across the beast's throat. As the blood gushed out, my head swam though I managed somehow to get to the ground and run off.

At Goodale's boarding house in the evening we'd sit and sing:

> There is a boarding house
> Just 'cross the way
> Where they have ham and eggs
> Three times a day.
>
> Oh how the boarders yell
> When they hear the dinner bell
> Oh how the eggs do smell
> Ten miles away.

George Goodale was sent one evening to fetch in the cow who had jumped the fence and run off into an adjoining pasture. We found her but couldn't catch her—she was running wild, jumping fences as we followed. It was milking time and I can remember as she went over the fence, the milk flying out behind her in our faces.

That summer I fell in love—with a girl up the road who was said to have heart disease. I was so sorry for her. She was a quiet little girl but very attractive to me; it was her sorrowful isolation, I suppose, that found in me an ally.

There were many other summers and many other loves but those were the first summers and that as far as I know was the first love.

From that time on, going to school, Ed and I grew up together to become as one person. All that I experienced as a growing child and up to the time of my marriage was shared with him. We were constantly together for nearly twenty years. We were on the same teams; he caught and I pitched and so forth. I can remember later, how sometimes we would stand not more than eight to ten feet apart and I would shoot the ball with almost all my speed into his catcher's mitt, never missing. That's how much confidence we had in each other.

After the farm and all its fascinations were left behind, the bitch, Norma—whose puppies I once kicked around thinking they were rats that were biting her—the horses, the rabbits, the chickens with their nests among the burdocks—a book in itself—one day, we were at table with Pop and Mom. I suppose I had been tormenting Ed, but he picked up a silver teaspoon and hit me with it, from across the table, right between the eyes. I was superior to such childishness—it didn't hurt much —and I just brushed it off without allowing my spirits to be ruffled. That's how much we loved each other.

At another time, I hit him in the middle of the back with a table knife as he was running upstairs away from me.

Poor Mother, sometimes she'd whale hell out of us with anything she could lay her hands on. It was a piece of cord wood once. She laid it on good, too, and later took me upstairs to bathe the place with witch hazel.

Did I say I grew up with no young females about me? No, there were the servant girls, Irish, Finnish (I know one Finnish word still from Anna, "hamahakquivergo," meaning, I think, cobweb). I'll never forget them, especially Georgie, from Georgia, who could peg a rock left-handed over the top of the chestnut tree two doors down from where we lived along the back fence —which was more than we could ever do. What a wing that woman had!

I saw Georgie naked once taking a bath in a basinful of water on the floor before her. We kids all took turns peeking through a hole in the wall of her attic bedroom. I had seen Grandma in the same way through a hole in the coverlet she had told me to draw up over my head while she dressed. I remember one of Grandma's naughty stories: If a lady were just about to take a bath and a man came suddenly into the room, where should she put her hands? Over his eyes, of course.

But athletics, as Ed and I grew older, was our entire life. I played everything, though I was never very good at anything, with a wild abandon which gave me the only ecstasy I ever knew in those days. I would go insane over the battles but, as I remember, it always ended in a feeling of sorrow when we had won. I never was a sadist. One of the best and earliest games was shinny played in the street using for puck a wooden top from which the peg had been lost. That was a game! The sweat, the breathlessness, the injuries—that's what sport is.

It's the feeling of walking out onto the field, the turf springy under the feet, that is the big moment. Then the ball is kicked or the first pitch is thrown and you begin to run. That's the secret.

But the best game I can remember was hares and hounds. It didn't often come up, but when it did I used to imagine that I could keep on forever. One day I was one of the hounds, not one of the oldest or best, but I had my own ideas. After giving the hares ten minutes' start with their bags of torn newspaper on their shoulders, we set out after them. We knew they'd cheat, not drop any tracers at important places, but that was part of it.

Two of the hares were the toughest fighters in the neighborhood and those were the ones we knew we'd be stuck with in the end.

I thought I could run, though none of the others considered me especially good. We ran all Saturday morning until, the easy ones having been picked up and all traces of those last two lost, a few of us decided, or maybe some of their own side told us, that Dago and Jo had last been seen headed for the Cedar Swamps beyond the copper mines. What a spot! It was already past noon but that's where we headed and sure enough, as we got to the top of the hill overlooking the mines, we saw them, out along the old wood road into the marshes between the cedars and swamp maples.

Those are the days and the excitement that I remember! How we went in after them, and how they eluded us. We had to capture them, not just sight them, and bring them out. We did it, too, but not easily. They fought to the bitter end through mud, brambles, fallen trunks and bog up to our middles after most of the gang had gone home in disgust. But a few of us kept on, in a sort of frenzy, for no reason at all except that we weren't going to let them beat us.

And when it was over, even to a fist fight during which they were overpowered—one even climbed a tree—we all walked out together, talking and laughing, delighted with ourselves, bruised, scratched and mud-caked. That was fun.

Chapter 4

Pop and Mother

My father was an Englishman who lived in America all his adult years and never became a citizen. He said it was more convenient for him to carry British than American papers on his frequent and prolonged trips to South America. He was probably right.

I'll never forget the dream I had a few days after he died, after a wasting illness, on Christmas Day, 1918. I saw him coming down a peculiar flight of exposed steps, steps I have since identified as those before the dais of Pontius Pilate in some well-known painting. But this was in a New York office building, Pop's office. He was bare-headed and had some business letters in his hand on which he was concentrating as he descended. I noticed him and with joy cried out, "Pop! So, you're *not* dead!" But he only looked up at me over his right shoulder and commented severely, "You know all that poetry you're writing. Well, it's no good." I was left speechless and woke trembling. I have never dreamed of him since.

Our household always, as I remember, included guests, guests who stayed sometimes for weeks and months or even all winter, people like poor old Mrs. Forbes who got lost once between her bedroom and the bathroom in the night and yelled for help so that Mom had to rush out and rescue her. Our guests were either Grandma's English friends or Mother's friends and relatives from the West Indies.

Spanish and French were the languages I heard habitually while I was growing up. Mother could talk very little English when I was born, and Pop spoke Spanish better, in fact, than most Spaniards. But Pop spoke English too, and as time went on one of my happiest memories of him was when he would sometimes read to us in the evening. Those were the marvelous days!

I remember now his readings of the poems of Paul Laurence Dunbar, and I can.to this day repeat many of the refrains he made familiar to me then. It was he who introduced me to Shakespeare, whom I read avidly, practically from beginning to end.

Poor (or rich) Pop (he was a single-taxer) once offered me a dollar apiece if I would read *The Origin of Species* and *The Descent of Man*. I took him up. It was well-earned cash.

But I remember also the three volumes of the famous illustrated translation of Dante's *Divine Comedy*. I'll never forget how I studied Gustave Doré's pictures of those beautiful but damned ladies and with what profound disappointment I failed to discover from them the anatomical secrets which so fascinated me at the time. The text escaped me.

Up to then, neither Mother nor Pop had any immediate church connections, but used to meet with a few others at spiritualistic seances, sometimes at home, sometimes elsewhere around the block. A prime mover in this form of religious service was old man Demarest, a devout believer. The chief tenet of these earnest persons was that the dead did live as spirits about us and would come or could be called to us at certain times by prayer or otherwise. There were curious consequences.

One evening at the Bagellon house, where we lived, at supper, Mother, who was known among her intimates as a medium, suddenly said to my father, looking right and left at Ed and me, "So these are the boys. How they have grown. Come here, my dears," she said to us, reaching out her hands, "and let me see you!" This to her own children whom she had been caring for all day.

Pop, who was accustomed to such occasions, told us gently, bewildered as we must have been, to do as we were bid—to go to

Mother, which we did, one on either side. She put her hands on each of our heads and patted us with smiles of approval and loving affection. "How well they look. I am so happy."

At this Pop said to her, to his own wife, "Who is this we have the pleasure of talking to?"

"Don't you know me?" Mother answered. "Why I'm Lou Paine." With that the seizure passed and Mother was herself again. Everything went on as before.

Pop told me many times after that that he had sent a wire forthwith to Jesse Paine, an old friend and neighbor of ours from Passaic Avenue, then residing in Los Angeles, asking what, if anything, had happened to Lou, his wife.

Two weeks later he received a letter saying that Jesse was sorry not to have been able to answer the telegram sooner, the reason being that Lou had been ill; in fact at the time the telegram had arrived, she was in the hospital where, that day, she had been given up for dead, following a serious abdominal operation. Now, however, she was sufficiently recovered so that he could say that she was safe and that he could resume his regular life —and so forth.

These meetings of the spiritualists, preceding the organization of the Unitarian Church and Sunday School in Rutherford, went on for years. One night, very early in the history of the thing, when Mother was still a good deal of an outsider because of the language difficulty, she was sitting a little apart from the others, merely listening in on the proceedings, when Grandma held up her closed fist and asked to speak to whoever it was, unstated, that was represented by what she held in her hand.

Immediately Mother, insane to all appearances, went out of her head. Unable to bring her to, old man Demarest fell upon his knees to implore God to return this woman to her senses.

So intense was the appeal and so impressed were all those present by the seriousness of the situation that Mother did, after a moment, come to herself and once more act normally among them—for which Mr. Demarest gave thanks to God—and Grandma was properly reprimanded for her part in the affair.

It appears that what she had wanted was to speak to her dead daughter Rosita, whom Mother had known well, an epileptic recently dead. To achieve this, she had taken, unknown to the others, a lock of the dead girl's hair, hiding it in her fist, asking only that the spirit, unidentified, speak and say she was present. Mother, her girlhood friend, was the medium upon whom the poor girl had seized for her approaches.

Mother would be possessed at such times—and it went on for years—by an uncontrollable shaking of the head. It would happen anywhere and at any time. I even saw it happen once while she was playing the piano at Sunday School. Ed and I were horribly embarrassed. But most often it would be at home primarily under strained emotional circumstances as after the death of some friend or intimate, but not necessarily involving the appearance of that particular person.

We'd all know at once what was about to take place—Mother's look would become fixed, her face would flush, and she'd reach out her hand and grasp the hand of one of us. Sometimes she'd indicate that she wanted Ed or me or anyone. Then someone would say, Is it this one? or that one? and she would try against heavy restraints to put her hand forward, but it would be impossible for her to do it. She'd struggle to try to clasp the hand offered her, but if this were not the one she wanted, she'd recoil, violently, unable to seize it. Her face would be red, contorted, she couldn't talk, her whole body seized by some inscrutable violence.

A name would be offered. No. Then another. She would shake her head violently, her cheeks flaming, her eyes like those of a person in violent effort of any sort. Finally Pop might say, "Is it Carlos?" meaning her brother, and she'd grasp the hand offered in both hers, and the presence would leave her.

How Ed and I dreaded these occasions! Pop believed literally, I think, in their authenticity: that the spirits of the dead did materialize through her and did try to reach us. But why they should want to come I never could understand.

Once after Pop died, Mother, in one of these seizures, asked for a pencil and tried to write, but her movements were too violent. Nothing came of it.

Chapter 5

In My Early Teens

One Fourth of July, when Uncle Carlos and my cousins Carlito and Raquel were here on a visit—I was nine or ten years old—we children were playing with a toy cannon, loading it with black powder, hammering a wad of damp paper down the muzzle, then putting the fuse from a firecracker into the touch hole to set it off. It made a very satisfactory *wham*! and we were delighted. We had done this several times but once the discharge didn't come off as planned. We had rammed the charge home with a hammer and a ten-penny nail as usual—in fact we had rammed it down extra hard for a good blast—the fuse was lit, but nothing happened. We waited a few moments to see that the fuse had burnt itself out, then I went forward to look. I leaned my face down to see why the fuse had expired. Instead of the charge exploding out of the muzzle of the cannon which, apparently, it couldn't do, we had packed it so hard, it flared up out of the touch hole right into my face and eyes!

I screamed that I was blind! My face was peppered with powder burns but, by the greatest of good luck, only the whites of my eyes were affected. No infection ensued. For weeks after I lay with bandages about my face while Raquel with a needle picked the powder grains from my cheeks, nose and forehead. For years there was one black spot on the sclera of my left eye between the iris and the inner canthus, but this too finally disappeared.

Kipp's woods, just over the back fence, was our wilderness. The fence itself was an object of delight to us with its wooden gate into the paths among the weeds. We seldom went through, however—but over it. You could sit on top with your feet on the upper rail and talk by the hour. I knew every tree in that wood, from the hickory where a squirrel had its hole to the last dogwood where in the fall the robins would gather for the red berries they are so fond of. We would hunt them with our BB rifles. They were not bad eating at that, though we were never good enough shots to get many.

But that wasn't what interested me most, nor was it the chestnuts we'd find about the big trees that were beginning to die of the blight. I saw Mr. Kipp and his colored man and dog take a wooden maul to the hickory of which I have spoken. They struck that tree with the maul until the squirrel appeared, then, at the right moment, hit the tree again so that the squirrel fell to the ground and the dog killed it. One day out behind the fence Charlie Newland had a little bitch on which someone else's dog was mounted and working. That wasn't it either.

What I learned was the way the moss climbed about a tree's roots, what growing dogwood and iron wood looked like; the way rotten leaves will mat down in a hole—and their smell when turned over—every patch among those trees had its character, moist or dry. I got to know the box turtle and the salamander and their spots and how the former hisses when annoyed.

It is a pleasure for me now to think of these things, but especially of the flowers I got to know in those precincts. It was a half-ashamed pleasure, I think. Jim Hyslop would be there to share those interests with me. The slender neck of the anemone particularly haunts me for some reason and the various sorts of violets—the tall blue ones, those with furry stems and the large, scarce, branching yellow ones, stars of Bethlehem, spring beauties, wild geranium, hepaticas with three-lobed leaves. My curiosity in these things was unbounded—secret, certainly. There is a long history in each of us that comes as not only a reawakening but a repossession when confronted by this world. To look up and see on a tree blooms, yellow and green, as large and heavy as the tulip, was something astonishing to me. The tassels of the chestnut—young and old trees, beggar's lice, spiders, shining in-sects—all these things were as much part of my expanding exist-ence as breathing. I was comforted by them.

It was an unconscious triumph all day long to just be able to get out of doors and into my personal wild world. Jim, the "bugologist," was interested in insects and butterflies. I'd go with him on his forays. None of the others was interested. We never interfered with each other. I'd help him collect, but flowers and trees were my peculiar interest. To touch a tree, to climb it especially, but just to know the flowers was all I wanted.

Once I heard Mother calling me. I looked from the top branches of the beech tree at the back of our lot where I was rocking, swaying with a slow delightful motion back and forth. I couldn't imagine what was the matter with her.

"Willie, come down, come down," in a half-frightened voice. I climbed down thinking she wanted me to do some errand. No. It was just that I might fall.

Fall? Why Harry Howard used to go up into a cluster of oaks I knew, and still know, on Union Avenue, where his father had a carpenter shop, and from the top of one of them jump like a squirrel into the branches of the tree adjacent and not fall. One day I jumped from the top of our outhouse, but when I landed my knees hit me on the chin with such force I was knocked sprawling.

Of course we were brats: lied, stole fruit and bits of lumber from new constructions, like any children. Always something new. Peter Kipp was our enemy and we his. One particularly per-nicious thing we did was to run through his rye fields just when the grain was about to be harvested.

One day four or five of us were well into the field, the grain higher than our heads, when old man Kipp and his colored hand crept up on us. Jim, who wore glasses, had placed himself on the top rail of the nearby fence to keep watch for us, but he was too nearsighted to be of much help. I was farthest out into the field, with a building lath in my hands to push the grain down ahead of me. Jim yelled and fell off the fence backward before Kipp's brindled bull. We all made for the edge of the field nearest the woods. The others got away, but I ran right into Kipp's arms. He grabbed me by the throat and, lifting me, half-threw, half-kicked me over the fence. I landed on my feet, lit out for cover and never looked back.

But we were not vicious. We didn't wish purposely to destroy, like those of a later generation, who finally drove the old man out of business by burning and uprooting his crops. For, as it was all part of the legend, we acknowledged our guilt but went back for more at the next opportunity.

One day we were playing ball on Elliot Place—at just about the spot where at midnight one day an owl struck me with a wing on the head as I was passing, the same place where at another time, I saw a small flock of cross-bills feeding (how old must I have been, between twelve and thirteen, I imagine, in the sixth grade?) when who should appear in the street but Lizzie Nevins and another girl in whom I was particularly, passionately interested. The other kids started to laugh and josh me, as Lizzie, grinning and loitering along the sidewalk, called to me to come over where they were standing. I was embarrassed, but finally went.

"Come on in the woods with us," she said, "I want to tell you something you want to know."

Well, in spite of my humiliation before the others and their disgust at my leaving the game, the three of us wandered off among the trees. Once there Lizzie said to me, "Wait here, a minute, her drawers are falling down."

So I waited while the two girls went behind a tree and refastened the garment. Then Lizzie began her game.

"Go ahead, you two. Go over there in the rye field if you want to and I'll watch. Go on. She wants you to. She told me she did. Go on!"

So we left her there, kids that we were, and groped our way out of sight into the green rye stalks, where we, who were under the same spell, sat down facing each other—too embarrassed even to open our mouths to ask a question.

Chapter 6

Sunday School

Meanwhile we were singing in the choir at the Unitarian Church where Mother played the piano sometimes for the Sunday School of which Pop was superintendent for eighteen years. Sometimes at formal occasions little Ed or I would carry the fanon of white satin which read in gold letters: *A little child shall lead them.*

Mr. Luce was our teacher after the kindergarten phase. He sometimes read to us passages from Kant or *The Dialogues of Plato.* One day, in a mixed class, Louise Corey asked him, "Mr. Luce, what does it mean when they talk about Jesus being circumcised? What is circumcision?"

"Circumcision is a formal rite of mutilation practiced by the Jews," was the reply.

In my delighted but disturbed world of immediate contacts with the boys about me, this world of Sunday School and church did heaven knows what to me. We were a small sect in a small church so that the need to cling together was always apparent. I always listened to everything said. It appealed to me that Christ was divine by the spirit that was in him and not by miraculous birth. This seemed democratic and to the point. I believed it. I was impressed too by the slogan: "Onward and upward forever," which the Unitarians promulgated. Also I felt early the calm which came over me when the minister said, "And may the peace of God which passeth all understanding be and abide

with you now and forever more. Amen." That was at the end of
the service. We left the church, walking upon a cloud.

A few men and women of the town, my father, Mr. Luce, Mr.
Beaumont and Messrs. Danheim, Hands and some others were
the organizers, though the pioneer in the movement had been
George Bell, a leader also in the Rutherford Heights Association
and one of its principal financial backers.

One day at one of the annual fairs, I saw a heap of rock, about
two or three wheelbarrowsful, strewn on a canvas in the center
of the church floor. It was rich-looking material, obviously ore
of some sort. We were told it was copper ore that had come from
the reopened mine of old Peter Stuyvesant, dating back to Colonial days. We all knew about the old mine on the Bayless property in Arlington where the Sunday School sometimes had its
summer picnics, but we had thought it to have been exhausted
long since.

Copper! in quantities! a rich find had turned up there after
all these years! Mr. Bell was a heavy investor. Stock in the company was for sale at par. The church itself stood to profit hand-
somely in the deal. One of its chief members, George Bayless
himself, was owner of the property where the mine stood. What
luck for us.

The dénouement, which was not long delayed, was that the
mine was as sterile as it had been for a hundred and fifty years,
that it had been "salted" with ore from Arizona, perhaps. George
Bell was cleaned out. The church, which had at once to sell the
Parish House next door, has never recovered. It killed poor Bell.

We couldn't pay a minister as Mr. Badger had been paid, so
that at times Pop would put on his striped trousers and frock
coat and read a sermon for us from George Minot Savage or some
other illustrious divine.

It was in those years that the monster insanity appeared
among us. Godwin, my father's half-brother, bearing the secret
name whose significance Grandma never would divulge, one day
came up to a group of us playing in our cellar and with a furious
face began to attack Jim Hyslop. This was the first time I had
become aware of what was going on in that quarter. I stood by

Jim, determined to murder the man if I could rather than have him injure my friend. But it was touch and go for a few minutes. I knew my own danger too because Godwin was a powerful figure twice as big as either of us.

He started by saying that Jim's mother and Jim, too, were talking about him, that he had heard her whispering, and that he had a mind to kill both of them and would if they didn't quit it. We were down in our cellar, under the beams, completely surprised by this attack, and couldn't at first imagine what had come over the man. There he stood glaring threateningly at us, his fists clenched, white in the face. Poor Jim was anchored to the ground. I talked. Godwin pushed me aside, but I kept talking and told Jim to go out the cellar door.

At first, Godwin in his paranoiac rage refused to let him go. But when I told Godwin that I'd tell Pop what he was doing and that he'd suffer for it plenty if he kept it up, he turned away sullenly and let us both pass.

Later Ed got the brunt of it and almost had to shoot the poor fellow. That even had its funny side when the cops came to arrest him after he had tried to break in our front door to attack Mrs. Dodd, a visitor. I was away at college at the time, but Ed stood behind the door with a pistol in his hand thinking any minute he'd have to use it; when the cops came, they found Godwin unarmed. But that's another story. He told them, "Don't touch me. I'm a gentleman!"

I've always had to smile over it; something of Grandma's teaching.

Those were the days when the destruction of the world was frequently headlined in the papers, and a man was building an ark somewhere on Long Island. I believed it all, or half-believed it, awaiting only confirmation by the event.

It was toward evening. I was somewhere in the house, perhaps getting ready to go to bed. There was a heavy fog coming up around sundown, when I heard the wild wailing of a new siren which they were trying out for the fire department, but it was too much of a screech, and they abandoned it later. But that night, hearing the unholy racket, I rushed to a back window and saw it, the red fog. Crimson flames were already destroying the world. I too shrieked and ran about the house in a frenzy looking at my parents for the last time before I went to lie on my bed waiting to be consumed. Mother came to me, more terrified than I, thinking that I had finally gone out of my mind. But by her assurance and gentle arguments, I gradually began to listen to her. Nothing more happened in the outer world. The sirens stopped and the blaze in the next block was brought under control. I stood up, quieted and very much ashamed of myself.

Chapter 7

To Run

One of my most triumphant days as a child was when on the Episcopal Church lawn I began to run and the pack came behind me across the side street at the bottom of a short slope. There was the usual board fence protecting an orchard there occupying a field a block long. I had a start of a hundred feet on the gang, running with no other reason than just to try to elude them.

Over the fence I went, hiding myself for a moment from their view. At that moment I made my decision. I dropped to the ground, throwing myself with the same motion into the long grass close against the lower fence-boards where I froze, hardly breathing.

When they had passed, I rose and followed them at a walk to laugh at them. But they were nowhere to be found. I heard later that they were completely befuddled at the disappearance. I strolled about the area after that for an hour or more looking for them, then sat on a square-topped post at the fence corner. They had disappeared completely. Finally someone saw me. I lit out again, they close behind me this time. As I rounded a house from the rear intending to duck into the front entryway and hide as I did the first time, I was caught. Run, run, run, that's all I wanted to do, and win, always—but it was no go. I wasn't the fastest.

It is impossible to recall whether it was in late childhood or early adolescence that I determined to be perfect; in any case it was about that time. The fascination of it still affects me: Never to commit evil in any form, never especially to lie, to falsify, to deceive, but to tell the truth always, come what might of it. The elevation of spirit that accompanies that resolve is a blissful one.

It didn't last long, for my perceptions soon convinced me that such resolves would lead, sooner than I wished, to death, definitely and without equivocation. I could see the alternative, sainthood, but had no wish to be a dead saint. But the longing I had to be truthful never quite died. I had to retreat to a more tenable position, as far forward as possible, but I knew it was a retreat. I was a liar and would always be one, *sauve qui peut!* I lay low and raid the enemy when possible, but the heroic gesture of perfection itself was not for me, though I had glimpsed the peaks and should never forget them.

I had found out during those years that though I could run faster than most, yet Deck Cormack could outsprint me; that though I thrilled at wrestling, there were many who could roll me over; that Arthur Kaufman could run his finger up a triple column (like Pop) and give you the correct sum. Not I. I looked at my face in the glass and cursed my "beauty," my eyes, my hair curling brown as it did. At the same time I "died" over my crooked ankles and skinny shanks and admired what strength I could pretend to in my pitching arm. Many boys could play hockey and skate on the ice far better than I. If I dreamed it was not about physical triumphs. What I saw was that in many fields I was outclassed. But at the same time I thought to myself that there were other areas where I might be successful. It wasn't music. The violin taught me that. Education—if I ever thought of it that way—was to find where I (for the I was foremost with me) could survive and perform with some hope of success. There must be a place for me. I would survive somehow. I should have to retreat at almost all points so far detected, but I wasn't licked and should never be. No saint but plenty of self-esteem.

Chapter 8

Switzerland

But to go back for a moment to our first European sally. In 1897 Ed and I were in the eighth grade at the old Park School in Rutherford when Pop came home one night near Christmas to say that within a month he would be going to Buenos Aires to set up a factory there for the manufacture of Florida Water and that he would not return to us for more than a year. That at least is what he must have told Mother. The first we knew of it was that we were taken out of school and told that we were not to return there for at least a year. As I remember it Pop asked us, in his usual way, if we wouldn't like to go to Europe for a year. Ed had just turned thirteen and I fourteen. We were all for it.

The thing was, Mother wanted to return to Paris for one last look before saying good-bye to her romantic youth. By renting the house at 131 to a tenant, a good part of the European costs could be neutralized, and since it made no difference to Pop where we should be living during his absence, so long as we were contented, we might as well be there as here. Furthermore it would be a good thing culturally for "the boys."

We left New York January 13, 1897 on *S. S. La Bretagne* of the French Line sailing from a pier in the North River. There was a boy on board slightly younger than I—Alfred Knopf from Linden, N. J. I've often wondered, without ever attempting to

find out, if it could have been the present-day publisher of the
same name.

On our arrival at the docks in Le Havre, the first words we
heard sounded like:

> Tarara boom de aye!
> *Voilà d'jolies violettes!*
> *Voilà d'jolies violettes!*

repeated over and over by a girl holding a basket of them on
her arm and a bunch in one hand, offering them for sale!

Ed and I were sent to school at the Château de Lancy, near
Geneva, Switzerland; we were mere infants, hundreds of years
younger than most of the sixty-two other boys there.

Those were the days! Scrambling up the Salève that April or
the next—the weather unusually warm for that time of year. At
the top we walked knee-deep in rotten snow, the ground covered
with blue gentians between the maplike snow patches. The bird-
nesting with Leon Pont, of Rajputana, India—a wild guy if
there ever was one. The day I was caned across the bare bottom
by the British contingent, the older boys of the school, for
dropping a paper water-bomb on the head of a boy named Potter.
What a beautiful shot that was from the third floor window!
It paid me for the caning. And the joke of the thing was, I really
didn't know it was Potter, I liked Potter. They had no reason to
hold me down on the bed hands and feet: I would not have
moved—and didn't. Do you think an American would have
turned a hair for an Englishman? Not likely. I thanked them,
smiled and pulled up my pants. I hadn't meant to hit Potter.

But my greatest joy was still the *ruisseau,* the icy-clear mountain brook running beside the soccer field, and the flowers growing about it, that spring, before the fields had been mowed.
There I first became acquainted with the native yellow primrose,
so delightfully sweet-scented. The green-flowered asphodel made
a tremendous impression on me. I collected all such flowers, as
many as I found, and pressed them between the leaves of a copy-
book. I grew tall and strong for my age.

Later it was soccer—I finally got into one game with the first squad. Swimming in Lake Geneva at 10° centigrade! Collecting postage stamps. General deviltry of all sorts.

There was a dark-skinned Frenchman among the students named Joncelin, one of the few boys of the school who owned a bicycle. He had little to do with either the English or the Americans, who were generally a younger group, but went about with a scowl on his face, ready to fight at the drop of a hat—and did once get into a fierce fight with Tum Devis, a Siamese prince, at the dinner table. Table-knives were raised. We smaller boys were at another table; there were violent words, but Priura, Tum's brother, grabbed him about the shoulders and M. Brunel spoke sharply to the Frenchman, so that it all quieted down as quickly as it arose. But that was the temper of the man and the temper he aroused in those about him.

There were paths through the little garden before the Château de Lancy (now the city hall of the village) bordered by thickly grown box hedges about a foot high, protected on either side by strong metal wickets, one overlapping the other. These paths were tortuous and narrow. But just at sunset it was Joncelin's solitary delight to mount his bike and pedal it at breakneck speed through those narrow ways. Perhaps he did it for effect, just to have the others see him go, but while it lasted it was a sight worth watching; for the whole thing, a sort of double figure eight, in and out among the trees, could not have covered more than two hundred feet in all.

It would be just after supper. The rest of us would be lolling around when suddenly he'd be at it, slowly at first, then faster and faster until he'd be rounding those turns in the semi-dark, reversing himself, coming out and driving in again round after round like a madman. Then he'd come out, slow down, put his bike away and disappear. He never had anything to do with the rest of us.

Joncelin, on rainy days, would ride inside the school, around the entrance hallway over its black and white tiles, as wildly as he rode outdoors. I'm surprised that they permitted him to do it.

Then one day he came up with a new-fangled acetylene bicycle lamp, the first—it always had to be the first with Joncelin—that any one thereabouts had ever seen. Fastening it to the steering post of his bike, thereafter he tore in and out through the paths among the shrubbery at night just as he had done during the daylight hours. No one interfered with him.

But occasionally something would go wrong with the bike. He'd sit patiently working at it until suddenly, thwarted for whatever reason, he'd pick up a detached wheel and swing it at arms' length, smash it on the ground at his feet in a wild fury and again and again while we watched, until it was unrecognizable—then spend a week repairing it.

We had pupils at the school from twelve nations: Russian, German, English, French, Swiss, Romanian, Spanish, Italian, Argentinian, Siamese, an Arab and Americans. You had to speak at least a little English if you wanted to play soccer. My particular pal was a little guy, but slightly older than myself, Leon Pont from Rajputana, India, whom they had dubbed "Harpagon" from Molière's comedy *L'Avare*, because he was thought to be so stingy. I never found him so. But if there ever was a monkey better at getting up a plane tree to a magpie's nest in the topmost twigs, I'd like to see him.

Pont and I lived the life in those days.

But back of l'Horloge, a building across the road from the main building that had a big clock in the low front gable, was the barn where swallows nested and back of that a small orchard with an English walnut tree in it.

Beyond that, down a little slope, was a brook with a small stone bridge over it and big trout there in the shadow. It was my particular secret place. When Mother was out to visit me one day, I had her take my picture there sitting on a tree root—it is still somewhere about the house. This is my first memory of the odor of violets. I went there when I could, which was seldom, since it was out of bounds for the younger boys who were not permitted beyond the high wall of the school grounds proper except on rare occasions.

Here at a certain time of day used to pass a bare-legged and barefoot girl to whom I never spoke, a girl of ten or twelve maybe, child of one of the poorer families of Lancy. She was always filthy, her legs grimed, her hair bedraggled, her face anything but clean, yet she was fascinating to me. I planned, though not successfully, to get hold of her somehow, strip her, wash her in the brook and carry her off.

Pont and I in the earliest spring, against the rules, went bathing in that particular stream. It fairly took our breaths away so much as to get our legs into the water, much less to submerge ourselves in it—it was a fire to us, driving us out upon the bank again to rush into our clothes wet as we were and crawl back over the wall into the school grounds.

We did share one secret, however, aside from the bird-nesting, he and I. The long, shambling gymnasium, a low, wooden shed, stood at the corner of the school lot nearest the village and just inside the wall. So that between it and that wall was a space not more than three feet wide—a waste area where leaves and rubbish were sometimes dumped—shut off from the grounds proper by an old wooden gate. Investigating every inch of the grounds for birds' nests or whatnot, Pont and I discovered this no man's land. We were out of sight there from the rest of the school grounds. The gym was locked. The upright boards of its side nearest the wall were nailed to a sill resting on the ground itself. It was no trouble at all to us to burrow, as a dog might, into the dirt, hollow it out until, eels that we were, we could crawl through, and come up inside the gym, under the stage! This was a great success, for there no one could ever discover us.

But one day, unable to control ourselves, we ran on the neatly raked sawdust of the exercise area itself, and so were undone.

While we were still in Geneva there was a great to-do when the Empress of Austria came there for a short holiday in 1898. She stayed on the lakefront at the Hôtel de la Paix, just across from the Place Brunswick with its tall, ornate Gothic spires among grass plots and slender trees. Mother was living at the Pension De Wolff, one block from the water and on the other side of the little park. From the balcony of her room you could look past the monument and through the branches of the park trees to the hotel where the Empress was staying.

This Saturday afternoon the royal visitor was to go for a sail on one of the lake steamers. Many of the visitors at the various hotels of the city were out to see her on the short walk along the wall overlooking the water to the boat landing. She, an old lady, was on the arm of an attendant: a beautiful day with crowds gathered patiently at the various vantage points, the men with hats or caps in their hands, the ladies curtseying as the Empress went graciously by at a slow walk.

Then suddenly it happened. A shabbily dressed fellow in a workman's cap came half-running toward her, jostled her rudely, seemed to throw something into the lake and escaped, running, with several men behind him. The Queen staggered, clutched her breast and would have fallen had not her attendant held her up. But as quick as it had happened, so quickly it passed. The old lady, for she was really old, rallied quickly, smiled at those about her, and motioned that the party should proceed to the boats. The boat, bedecked with flags, was cast loose, its paddle wheels began to turn as it headed out beyond the jetty for its trip to Lausanne. The ruffian who had jostled the Queen was all but forgotten.

But there was a halt, the boat's paddle wheels stopped, then started again. The boat was turning, heading back to shore. The Queen had fainted. Before anything further could be done, she was dead, stabbed through the heart with a steel file ground to needle sharpness. This was later discovered on the lake's bottom, where many remembered having seen the man fling it following the attack.

The royal funeral was a terrifying affair to Mother watching from the pension roof as the crowds surged about the park and the cavalry drove them back upon the iron fence.

One day Mother took us for the *tour du Lac*. I have never seen bluer water, nor whiter swans. The Alps were to our right— the Mole, especially familiar to me, in the middle ground, with its anthill-like summit that I climbed with the other kids, racing up the last hundred feet to try to beat them. I think I came in second at the top. The clear day, the breeze made me especially happy as, in my usual way on a trip of this sort, I jammed my body into the very foremost angle of the ship's prow to get the effect of which I was so fond—of being alone, no ship, no person, no sound but the wind in my ears as I flew with a slow lifting and falling over the crystal-clear lake. It was a thrill beyond anything I could imagine and I was enjoying it to the full.

Then I became aware that I wasn't alone in my narrow heaven. Some one else was there trying to crowd in beside me. I was angry at the intrusion and determined to fight it out for my place. Turning a little to the side I saw it was a little old man with a beard, a man strikingly well-dressed and wearing a modish hat. I could have knocked his block off if I had to. He had a walking stick and using it as a fulcrum, he had somehow shoved his right hand into my crotch, from the front, putting on considerable pressure.

Neither of us said a word. I merely backed away and left him, disgusted. Poor Mother didn't know what to make of my story and told me in fact that I had imagined it. I avoided the shrunken-up little creature for the rest of the trip, but the incident impressed me.

And when two weeks later in front of a store window, intent on examining an exhibition of postage stamps, I felt that hand coming at me again in the same position, I turned and ran. That was carrying it too far.

Chapter 9

Paris

In Paris, after we had left Geneva, we lived with our cousins, M. Trufly and his wife, Alice, at Forty-two rue la Bruyère, in Montmartre, not far from Place Pigalle, rue Blanche and Notre Dame de Lorette.

Ed and I were fourteen and fifteen respectively, wore knee pants and attended the Lycée Condorcet, one of the good high schools of Paris. In the house was also our cousin Marguerite and her cat Minnu, poor beast, which we tormented nearly to death.

Another, more distant cousin, Salvador Mestre, later to become a cuirassier during the First World War, was also at the Lycée—a tall, soft kid who wanted to use me especially to beat down his enemies with a *coup de poing Américain,* a good punch in the nose! But I had no desire for that sort of thing. How could I walk up to a guy and slug him for no reason at all?

But I could jump higher than any but one of the boys in the school, though I will say my form was not up to that of some of the others. One in particular, the very one Salvador wanted me to pick a fight with, went over straight up, feet below him together, side by side. He was pretty good.

But in class we couldn't possibly keep up with those kids, Ed and I had the language difficulty to face. We had just come from the old Château de Lancy at Geneva, where, if you couldn't talk English, you were out of everything; so we learned mighty little of the French we had gone there to study.

The result was that we didn't stay in the Lycée very long. Mother, through the intercession of M. Trufly, a down-and-out lawyer, got her money back and we studied French with Tante Alice, Alice Monsanto, who lived across from us on the same street a block to the east. She was a kindly person, a born teacher, who had been one of Mother's best friends during those blissful days in the late seventies when Mother had lived three years in her beloved Paris as an art student.

There had been there also with Mother in those days Alice's brother Ludovic, also a painter, whose full-size portrait of Mother in a black velvet dress, her hair high on her head in the Spanish style and holding a fan, hangs now above my brother's mantelpiece.

Alice, who had never in her life even raised her voice in protest against an injury, would see us every day for an hour and make us learn by heart the poems of La Fontaine and some others. Simple pieces, some of which I can still repeat. If we had remained in Paris longer under her tutelage, we should have become thoroughly accomplished in the language, but it was not to last.

Marguerite, my cousin, Alice Trufly's sister, was really hard up for a man. I was a likely kid, and Ed was of a pretty good size himself. She loved to tease us; she pressed against me from the rear as I leaned out the window looking down at perhaps the *pompiers* passing, or a boy going by shouting *Paris Sports Couplet*, or a woman yelling *A la moule! La moule est bonne, la moule est fraiche!* or again a man, *Vitrines!*—or whatever it might be.

One day Marguerite and I conceived the idea that I should go and visit Tante Alice on her birthday, but in my mother's clothes.

The rest of the family must have either been out or thought the idea sufficiently amusing to have me go on with it. So Marguerite dressed me in Mother's dress (I could still wear her things) put gloves on me, but not her gloves, I imagine, and a hat, her particular bonnet, which, unfortunately for me, I could not pin to my hair as it was done then. It was a simple street dress with leg-of-mutton sleeves and a long skirt trailing the ground.

I hadn't got ten feet from our street doorway—Alice lived in the next block—when my hat began to give me trouble. I leaned my head to this side then to that, but people began to look at me and I became jittery. But I kept on, got to the proper entry, climbed the three flights of stairs and had the satisfaction of having Alice take me in her arms crying, "Ma chère Hélène!"

When I couldn't hold out any longer and began to laugh, poor Alice was speechless. But she laughed too after a moment, until she suddenly recalled that it was strictly against the law to impersonate the opposite sex on the city streets. She scared hell out of me as well as herself, telling me to go quick, to go home and never to try such a thing again. I could have taken off the dress, I suppose, but probably didn't have much on under it. I got back, all right, but it gave me a good scare.

Mme. Trufly, in whose apartment we were all living, must have been pretty, with her round head and Mona Lisa smile, when her husband met her in Panama in the eighteen-eighties. Carlos didn't want her to marry the man who was much older than herself. But she would have him, lame and devil-may-care as he was, so Trufly carried her off to Paris in the end, and Marguerite with her—a hard worker who by her labors as a seamstress was helping very materially to keep them all going now. The couple, luckily, never had any children.

Of the two girls, Marguerite was by far the brighter. In fact, although Alice looked to be a person of considerable intelligence, she came pretty close to being stupid, poor girl. Maybe it was her early lack of education that induced it or maybe it was due to the uncertain upbringing she had. It all went back to Carlos' years in Paris as a student of medicine, rumors of which reached me through Mother all during my own childhood; back to Napoleon III, the War of 1870, a story in itself. Carlos was married to a Frenchwoman and had three children at that time. But on his return to Puerto Rico, the gal took one look, abandoned the whole outfit on the islands and fled back to Paris, where she disappeared.

Taken along when Carlos left Port au Prince for Panama, Alice met Trufly, a lawyer for the de Lesseps Company then working at the projected Panama Canal—a curious history. When the company went into bankruptcy, it took Trufly along.

Trufly had told Alice that his mother owned an estate in Normandy, which would be his later on. I seem to remember that, married though they must have been in Panama, there was some later ceremony at that place, in the country, to please his family, perhaps. For Alice told us of them all eating out of doors at a long table, *en champêtre*, with much drinking and gaiety, hour after hour when, in the middle of the feast, she felt something! a hand up under her clothes, at her knee, and screamed. Too late. The miscreant, a local wag, had seized her garter and had it off at one stroke. A great prize! I can hear Trufly, a wonderfully good-natured man, saying with a mild shake of his head, "*Voyons! Voyons!*" as the fellow came out from under the table brandishing his trophy to everyone's delight.

But these were different days. After Trufly lost all he had, bonds, château and lands, in the crash of the Canal Company, he had been stripped also of his last cash deposits in the failure of a private bank. They were living at Forty-two rue la Bruyère from day to day, week to week, largely by Marguerite's industry and the rent Mother was paying them, expecting every day to be thrown into the streets.

Many times we heard Alice, in a fury, yelling at Trufly for his failure to seize even the few opportunities he got to earn a miserable sou as a lawyer (and he had been a good one) merely by not being on hand when he was wanted, or even if he was in his little *bureau*, being too sodden with absinthe to be able to do the work. The man would take his call-down mildly enough, promise anything to have his wife lay off him, and go out and do the same thing again. She couldn't stop him. He couldn't stop himself.

In between he was a superb companion, especially for Ed and me. It was he who taught us to drink wine and water at table, the Parisian water being so *mauvais*. It was he also who taught us to crack a walnut on the edge of the table by holding it under the thumb, vise-wise, and sharply banging the thumb holding

it with the right fist. It took a bit of doing, for unless the nut
cracked, the under thumb was bruised. We finally mastered our
timidity and hit hard enough to do the trick.

Everyone was gay—except Alice, who always sensed what the
true situation was—when Trufly was in a good mood.

Trufly had been a soldier as a kid in the Franco-Prussian War.
Half-frozen one night, lying on the ground, his feet to the open
fire, his legs had been badly burned before he woke to save
himself. The result was that he was lame. But when he got
into his good suit and took us all out to a Café, to Montmartre,
or once to the theatre, his very gimpy walk was turned into a
carnival.

He knew his Paris and, being a lawyer, got around better
than most. I have a picture of him in mind the day we went
to some show near the Boulevard des Italiens. Alice, Marguerite,
Mother, Ed and I and Trufly. He was very gay and comical herd-
ing us about before him as we moved through the crowd. But
when we came out after the show, it was pouring. What to do?
We hadn't expected it, we had no umbrellas, not even one among
the crowd of us. We couldn't get a cab. So off he started, taking
Mother by the arm, his cane jauntily held over their heads,
the rest of us trooping after him, gimping along to the bus
station.

By luck it was holiday season in Paris when we were there,
Mardi Gras. We had a table in the front row, right on the sidewalk in the very center of it all—he always knew how to manage
that. We were there at the beginning of it early enough in the
morning for the pavement to be nearly bare, and still we were
there when the confetti, blue, white and red, was ankle deep from
gutter to gutter.

It was a fine day with the crowds drifting back and forth,
everyone getting handfuls of the paper bits in their faces, screaming, laughing, the girls being goosed front and back, screaming
and swinging at their attackers, everyone hilarious back and
forth, passing and repassing our fortunate tables.

There were merchants selling this and that. I recall one toy
theatre in a box carried about and placed before us. Small

figures would be performing certain acts while the proprietor both sang and operated the figures with his hands. A scene would be presented at the end of which, still in the swing of the performance, he would lilt a *Tirez la ficelle!* and down would come the curtain.

There was the *Petoman!* who lets farts! at command! Very French and hilariously funny, ending as always with the grand release of all the residual air that had been pumped into his rectum with a bicycle pump—*"Ma Belle-Mére!"* My mother-in-law. Wham! and he'd let it go.

Another man, with an enormous red papier-mâché nose fastened over his own proboscis with a rubber band around the back of his head, was selling big cardboard shears. *"Rrrrr! Sécateur!"* he would call out. *"Pour couper le petit bout—du nez. Pour la santé."*

It was the time of the Dreyfus trial, Zola, and the violent anti-Semitic feeling which even here showed itself, in the midst of the Carnival, though in a good-natured vein, it must be said.

And I can remember standing in the Folies Bergère and seeing the whole auditorium stand singing, while they waved their hands in the air, *"Vive l'Armée - é! Vive l'Armée - é! Vive l'Armée!"* after which they'd break out into wild shouts. It was very stirring and sad.

Ed and I were sent, by Trufly's advice and with his assistance, to take fencing lessons at the Salle d'armes Bernard, somewhere not far from the Boulevard des Italiens. We went two or three times a week and saw men being primed for duels. We were the only ones of our age being instructed. It was great fun. There were two or more college-age Americans there at the time, one of whom was a Roosevelt, I don't know of which branch of the family, but a good guy, as I could see. He invited us to come up to his apartment to show us his stamps and swords. We asked Mother but Trufly vetoed the proposal; we couldn't see why.

Trufly, when he had nothing else to do, which was almost every day, sometimes organized short promenades for us to show us some of the sights of Paris. Or he'd take us along when he'd be pretending to Alice that he had to meet some client in the neighborhood. We'd set out, but before we'd gone more than a few blocks, he'd steer for a café where the three of us would sit in the sun while his stiff leg thawed out a bit, he said, so he might continue.

It limbered up soon enough under the influence of the tall, pale-green drink, smelling of licorice, which he invariably ordered while we had our red drinks of *sirop de framboise* or *groseille* with water at the same round table beside him. This was the regular thing. Then off we'd go again, as we did one day to visit the catacombs.

Catacombs in Paris, of all places, seem hard to comprehend, but there they were. Did we enter them near the Panthéon? I can't remember, long tunnels underground lined with the bones of martyrs, or if not martyrs, at least those who came here to practice religious rites. Ed and I saw skulls, thigh bones and ribs piled neatly about along the passageways and were much impressed.

We climbed the Eiffel Tower, all of us under Trufly's guidance; went to various churches, particularly St. Germain des Prés, where a priest in a stone niche at the entrance held out a small contrivance, a little rod with a terminal of tiny rubber fingers in a cluster, to us as we went by. I did not notice what the others had done but, thinking some sort of souvenir was being handed me, took hold of the thing. The priest held on to the other end, refusing to release it. I pulled against him for a minute but then, feeling my hands wet, let go. I was confused. The others hearing my story, especially Marguerite, were convulsed with laughter, and Mother became nearly hysterical, walking about the holy edifice—no one else there—until Trufly with his, *"Mais, voyons, ma tante, voyons, voyons,"* quieted them at last.

When Mother had been in Geneva, toward the end of our school days there, she had met and become acquainted with two Russian sisters named Proharoff, two serious and charming girls who were studying French and seeing Europe generally, as well as they could, being two lone girls of about the age of our college girls of today. They took to Mother and her gentle ways at once, and she to them. So that when, on their travels, they came to Paris, they looked her up, intent on seeing more of the wicked city than they knew how to gain access to alone. Mother approached Trufly who thereupon offered to take the girls out of an evening himself, they being the children of "wealthy aristocratic parents," all at their own expense. In fact, we all were to go, since Trufly could see at once that anything he could show them would be sufficient to make them believe they had really witnessed the dregs.

Montmartre was only a step from where we were living, so one night out we went, a regular Sunday School picnic, to see the sights there. We drank a bottle of wine and in dark rooms heard the naughty songs with which the usual tourist is greeted. As we were leaving one place I recall several exchanges of *argot* between Trufly and the entertainers, the general drift of which was: how did he get away with that kind of stuff? Then when we actually moved toward the exit door they sang their refrain:

> *Tous les clients sont des cochons*
> *La folie don del, la folie dindon,*
> *Principalement ceux qui s'en vont*
> *La folie don del, dindon!*

We went in among the coffins of Le Néant, drank those wines and that was all.

Poor Minnu, the cat, had a hard time of it. Why do little boys always want to torment cats? I remember that sometimes when there would be meat loaf the string with which it had been bound would get into the garbage can. From there Minnu would drag it, chew it and swallow it whole. Next day, when it began to appear behind, we'd step on the projecting end of it to the poor cat's great distress. Mother would have put an end to that very quickly if she had ever caught us.

Chapter 10
Back to School

In the spring of 1899, when we returned to America, we re-entered our classes in the Rutherford Public School. It was the first year that they had had high-school classes in Rutherford; the teaching was not distinguished. Ed did all right, I think, but I, being a year older than he, although we were always in the same grade, was a lot wilder. My work suffered accordingly. I re-encountered some of the same girls that I had known in the eighth grade. The results weren't promising.

Perhaps our parents sensed the situation, or it may be that the marks I got were nothing to encourage them. In any case when the fall term came around, though I don't know how Pop could keep on sinking money into our education as he did, we were enrolled in a New York City high school. It was the best high school, so they said, in the East, Horace Mann, close to Columbia University on Morningside Heights at 120th Street. So that fall we began our daily trek from Rutherford to that distant location. Our train left our station in Rutherford at seven-sixteen. That meant that for five days a week we'd be up at six, dress, have our breakfast and leave the house in time for the ten-minute walk to the station.

At Jersey City, we took the ferry; in winter it was sometimes, because of ice in the river, a thrilling ride. Up Warren or Chambers Street to either the Ninth or Sixth Avenue el was the next step. I knew every smell of the way. Then would come the long ride when, as it often happened, we'd meet some of our class-mates, Aegeltinger, Fischer or whoever it might be, to 116th or 125th Street. Down those high steps we'd run, then light out up again through or past the park to get to school by nine o'clock. It was quite a chore, which was repeated in reverse the same afternoon. It took a lot out of us, but it was worth it. The associations and the teaching were superb.

Right at the beginning a decision was made which I have felt for the remainder of my life: it shows how little writing entered into any of my calculations. They offered three classes of courses: a classical course including Latin and Greek, an intermediate course of some sort and a course directed to scientific objectives. After a preliminary review of my predilections, on the advice of Mr. Prettyman, the principal, I was enrolled in the latter course. It included a modicum of Latin, French (which I could speak), German and no Greek. Instead I took mathematics, chemistry, physics and the elements of joinery. The classes were large and serious. I entered into the work with great enthusiasm.

Our classrooms were no less stimulating than the teachers themselves, who were the pick of the city. For the first time I realized what it meant to work, to be pushed, to be in competition with the best. But at the very start we ran into a difficulty: one of the teachers, a gaunt young man with a deep voice, was entrusted with the teaching of Latin by a new method which either was his own or which was in the nature of an experiment. We were to use nothing but Latin in the classroom. When the roll was called we were to answer *adsum,* if someone were absent the answer would be *abest. Hoc est saggita,* the estimable young man would tell us, or he would say, *Illud est saggita,* pointing far off beyond the room that we might get the idea of distance. It was a splendid idea, but it took up too much time, the class fell behind schedule and had to be abandoned. That was the extent of my Latin!

In English, however, I was more fortunate. There as the years went by I came under the tutelage of a man, Uncle Billy Abbott, who for the first time in my life made me feel the excitement of great books. It was only a beginning. I had no full realization of what was taking place but I was crazy about those classes, though I wouldn't have acknowledged it to anyone. For the first time I had actually looked at a poem. And it had interested me. I read *The Ancient Mariner, Lycidas, Comus* and studied out a process that was unfamiliar to me. I read *L'Allegro* and *Il Penseroso.* Uncle Billy once gave me a top mark for a paper retelling a story after Robert Louis Stevenson. It was a canoe trip somewhere in the Low Countries; at one point the canoe had upset, the man was spilled into the water, but in spite of everything he had not lost his paddle; that was the point, he had not lost his paddle. I stuck to that, driving the point home: he had not lost his paddle! Uncle Billy gave me an A. It was my first literary success.

I enjoyed also Greek, Roman and especially English history, with Miss Butler and, of course, French with "Mamselle," a sweet old girl who, knowing that we already knew some French, was especially partial to us. But mathematics was not one of my fortes. To this day I still wonder at the astuteness of that Mr. Bickford, who gave me my final examination in Higher Algebra. The theory of quadratics was the particular subject which was hardest for me. Aegeltinger, the mathematical prodigy, was through with the test and out of the room, probably already home, by the time I had answered no more than the first two questions. I kept plugging away. One by one the others in the class finished their work and left until I alone remained; the hour was up and I still hadn't completed more than eight of the ten questions. But the time was up and I had done what I could. My heart was pretty sad realizing, as I did, that I had failed.

Mr. Bickford was older than some of the others and had the reputation of being the best man in his department. As I stood there watching him chewing his moustache—he wore a little black moustache—as he studied the paper I had turned in, the last one left in the room, I tried to brace myself as best I could for the verdict.

He looked up at me after a while with no expression on his face whatsoever.

"You'll never be a mathematician, Williams," he told me.

I agreed.

"But you show an understanding of the process." He paused. "And I'm going to pass you!"

I couldn't move for joy. It was the most intelligent verdict, and from a teacher, that I have ever encountered. It is hard to realize how important such a moment can be in a man's life. That single piece of intelligence had more to do in straightening my difficulties, in putting me on a correct course than any single thing that I can remember. He saw my mind, and realized what it was not intended to perform. And he acted accordingly. That's what it means, at best, to be a teacher.

At Horace Mann I went out heavily for athletics. I was not big enough for football, though I tried; but in track and baseball, though Ed was outstripping me by that time, I wasn't too bad. At least I could run and had done pretty well at the games on class day at the end of my freshman year.

But that was my undoing. For when my sophomore year opened I was officially enrolled on the track squad and began to train by running around inside the fence on the grass beside the Columbia Gym preparatory to being entered in one of the armory events scheduled that year. We trained and trained. I had been entered in a novice 300-yard dash. As it was a handicap run and I had, being a novice, been given a generous yardage, they considered me a dark horse and built me up as a possible winner. Each afternoon we'd go to the 22nd Regiment armory and run, after which, as usual, I'd dress, take the el and beat it for home. I suppose it was too much for me. At any rate, one afternoon just before the race, we had just done our final quarter-mile. I had put on my sprint and was getting ready to quit when someone yelled, "You've got one more lap to go!"

I knew whoever had given us the order was wrong, I knew I shouldn't have done it, but there was the order and I had to go on. I was all in but, tired as I was, I went at it. I went around the track once more, put on another sprint and—collapsed. After a while I picked myself up, got home finally and was put to bed for a week. The local doctor was called and that ended my running. "Adolescent heart strain" was the verdict. From that time on, I was told, I would never be able to take part in athletics again; the most that I could do would be to take long walks in the country. I had to quit all my hopes, all thoughts of an athletic career vanished, I was, at a moment's notice, considered to be little better than an invalid. That, too, played a major part in determining my career. Mentally I was crushed.

How I ever got through school across the lust that burned me to a cinder in those days is more than I can say. But it passed and curiously enough left me as innocent as ever. I suppose I was more interested finally in other things. I don't know, though, for it revived later!

I went through a stage of asceticism about that time. That may have saved me, for it came between the years of my passion for athletics and the passion for art which succeeded it.

It was about then that I began to be interested in the poem. Up to eighteen or even later I had not the slightest intention of writing or of doing anything in the arts. Mother painted a little, and both Ed and I consequently painted, using her old tubes and palette which we found in the attic. I know there are several oils still lying around which I perpetrated in those days.

My first poem was born like a bolt out of the blue. It came unsolicited and broke a spell of disillusion and suicidal despondency. Here it is:

> A black, black cloud
> flew over the sun
> driven by fierce flying
> rain.

The joy I felt, the mysterious, soul-satisfying joy that swept over me at that moment was only mitigated by the critical comment which immediately followed it: How could the clouds be driven by the rain? Stupid.

But the joy remained. From that moment I was a poet.

Once at a small lake near Esopus, New York, I was deeply in love with a girl's legs I met underwater there. Their father was suspicious of me. I was a well-intended enough young man, but he damned well kept his eye on us as we played around that week in the barnyard and closely adjacent parts of the old place where the family lived. Ah, those summers at the age of fifteen and seventeen! And perhaps a bit later!

One rainy day those white legs and I found the barn, with a full hayloft, and under that rattling roof lay quietly together listening. But tiring of that, we began to burrow deeper into the hay. Our bodies were thrown close together there. It was very exciting as we must soon have acknowledged, but they began looking for us and we were chased out with loud calls and told never to go there again. How can a pair of legs defy their father under such circumstances?

One day we all went fishing together. The old man was portly and wore a straw hat. He fished from the end of the pier while we held our poles out over the water not far off—or perhaps he was in a boat or on a point under a protecting tree. It was a beautiful hot day, the water crystal clear, the bottom weedy, with small fish swimming over it. Those lovely white legs were hanging in the water side by side with mine, good enough legs for a guy about my shape, moving a little back and forth in the cool lake.

But, by accident perhaps, after a moment one of my legs touched those others in the water. They were not withdrawn—not withdrawn! and the sun and the clouds meeting over our heads did a seraphic *pas de deux*, so that I thought the world a paradise. It didn't take me long to rub my legs underwater with those others, to twine them about the others as best I could. If I should see that lake or pond today, I'd think it a mud-hole. I burned her letters to me during my first year at Penn—the final act before the next phase.

The big fight came at the beginning when I was making up my mind what to do with my incipient life.

The preliminary skirmish concerned itself with which art I was to practice. Music was out: I had tried it and didn't qualify. Besides, I wanted something more articulate. Painting—fine, but messy, cumbersome. Sculpture? I once looked at a stone and preferred it the way it was. I couldn't see myself cutting stone, too much spring in my legs to stand still that long. To dance? Nothing doing, legs too crooked.

Words offered themselves and I jumped at them. To write, like Shakespeare! and besides I wanted to tell people, to tell 'em off, plenty. There would be a bitter pleasure in that, bitter because

I instinctively knew no one much would listen. So what? I wanted to write and writing required no paraphernalia. That was the early skirmish, ending with the spontaneous poem—a black, black cloud, etc.

That having been decided, forever, what to do about my present objective, medicine? Should I give it up? Why?

Would it add anything to give it up? I never for a moment thought of the work involved in maintaining that. Oh, a hundred alternatives were discussed:

First, no one was ever going to be in a position to tell me what to write, and you can say that again. No one, and I meant no one (for money) was ever (never) going to tell me how or what I was going to write. That was number one.

Therefore I wasn't going to make any money by writing. Therefore I had to have a means to support myself while I was learning. For I didn't intend to die for art nor to be bedbug food for it, nor to ask anyone for help, not my blessed father, who didn't have it, nor anyone else. And to hell with them all.

I was going to work for it, with my hands, which I had been told (I knew it anyhow) were stone-mason's hands. I also looked at my more or less stumpy fingers and smiled. An esthete, huh? Some esthete.

Chapter 11

Medicine

I never went to college. I didn't have to, for at the University of Pennsylvania they admitted selected men to medical school in those days from certain high schools and I had been to Horace Mann in New York, one of the best; we had been to Europe for a year, besides. Of course you had to satisfy the college entrance requirements. That I did to everyone's satisfaction. In medical school I was next to the youngest member of my class of 120 men and did all right with my work.

And here let me voice a long overdue tribute to my father and mother for the way they backed Ed and me in whatever we wanted to do. Pop never in his life made more than the barest possible income on which to support at least two families, his own and his mother's. Yet we did have an occasional case of Château Lafite in the cellar.

At the University of Pennsylvania in 1902 I enjoyed the study of medicine, but found it impossible to confine myself to it. No sooner did I begin my studies than I wanted to quit them and devote myself to writing.

I shall never forget with what fascination I read *Les Misérables*, which I had just discovered, in the original, when I should have been hard upon normal anatomy. I am a slow reader. It had me groggy for a while. And just recently I have found a letter I wrote to Mother at the time telling her I had made up my mind to be "good" from then forward and not waste my time.

On the other hand, I knew that the kind of writing I would do would not be for sale. Why, I refused even to smoke a cigarette so that I might not dull the sharpness of my mind! I'd drink a glass of sherry now and then but that was all—though at the same time I coursed the streets of Philadelphia: no luck.

The struggle was on. I had been accepted by the Mask and Wig Club at Penn and began to act in their plays. The theatre perhaps offered me my chance? I thought I'd quit medical school and get a job as a scene shifter! Such was my humility. I remember seeing Kyrle Bellew playing to Janet Beecher in *Romeo and Juliet*. I wrote Miss Beecher a letter which she never answered. I always answer letters, but others seldom have answered those I sent out in my desperation. D. H. Lawrence never answered me, either, when once later I wrote to him.

It cost only twenty-five cents to sit in the top balcony and see a good play in those days. I wanted to write, to write plays— plays in verse! I saw the great Ben Greet Players outdoors in the Botanical Gardens with Edith Wynne Matthison as Rosalind in *As You Like It*. I climbed a ten-foot spike fence around the nearby cemetery to get in to that one. I had no money.

But it was money that finally decided me. I would continue medicine, for I was determined to be a poet; only medicine, a job I enjoyed, would make it possible for me to live and write as I wanted to. I would live: that first, and write, by God, as *I* wanted to if it took me all eternity to accomplish my design. My furious wish was to be normal, undrunk, balanced in everything. I would marry (but not yet!) have children and still write, in fact, therefore to write. I would not court disease, live in the slums for the sake of art, give lice a holiday. I would not "die for art," but live for it, grimly! and work, work, work (like Pop), beat the game and be free (like Mom, poor soul!) to write, write as I alone should write, for the sheer drunkenness of it, I might have added. And complete defiance of the world or what might come after it, if anything. I knew all about Chatterton.

During these days I met Ezra Pound in my room in the dormitories. I met Hilda Doolittle and must have brushed against

Marianne Moore also, without meeting her, at Bryn Mawr. I met Charles Demuth over a dish of prunes at Mrs. Chain's boarding house on Locust Street and formed a lifelong friendship on the spot with dear Charlie, now long since dead.

For I was still undecided whether or not I should become a painter. I coldly recalculated all the chances.

Words it would be and their intervals: Bam! Bam! I now began to read Keats—and did I read him! That's where I differed from Pound. He was always far more precocious than I and had gone madly on, even to Yeats—who passed through Philadelphia and read to the Penn students in 1903. I did not hear him.

It was in my second year that I went out for and "made" the Mask and Wig Club by singing "Tit Willow" from *The Mikado* for them. I had a round, smooth face, as shown by the half-tone in the Philadelphia *Bulletin*. Had my legs been equal to it, I should have got the part of a handsome girl in the varsity production which followed. As it was, they cast me finally as Polonius in *Mr. Hamlet of Denmark,* which ran at Atlantic City, Philadelphia (for a week), Wilmington, Baltimore and Washington. There, for the first time, I had the sensation of feeling an audience all my own for one delicious moment: I had interpolated a line kidding President Theodore Roosevelt for his absence just then on a bear hunt in the Ozarks. I brought the house down. Even the cast broke into a roar. I was a hero.

In medical school proper, apart from the wonders of embryology, histology and anatomy, my one enthusiasm was for Professor Spiller in neurology. I loved the man with his big round head and the prominent temporal arteries like twin snakes upon his temples. Had I felt myself stable enough, nothing would have pleased me more than to have gone in then and there for neurology. Treatment at that time was almost nil. Diagnosis was Spiller's forte. Perhaps I was just looking. In medical school also I acquired that sixth sense, the sense of surgical asepsis.

Together with Hilda Doolittle ("H.D.") I discovered, in those days, the wonders of *Aucassin and Nicolette,* the prose and the verse alternating. And so to Villon, as much as I could make of the old French; Rabelais, in the familiar translation by Urquhart, snatches of the old language, only tasted. But the sign over the gate to Paradise, *Faîtes ce que voudrais!* has never been forgotten.

In spring among the back streets, when supper would be over and we felt disinclined to return to our rooms, Charlie Demuth used to take long walks with me in West Philadelphia (where Grandma Wellcome, my father's mother, had just come to live). There was a high brick wall along the south side of Locust Street, just west of Thirty-sixth, inside of which there must have been an old garden, long neglected. The thought of it fascinated me. Charlie laughed when I spoke of it. "Not many could enjoy such a thing as that," he said, "by merely looking at the outside of the wall."

This was the time, apart from other things, when Ezra Pound was writing a daily sonnet. He destroyed them all at the end of the year; I never saw any of them. I too was writing, a monumental work, a four-book romantic poem. I have even forgotten the name of it.

Keats, during the years at medical school, was my God. *Endymion* really woke me up. I copied Keats's style religiously, starting my magnum opus of those days on the pattern of *Endymion*.

For my notebooks, however (which I don't think anyone ever saw), I reserved my Whitmanesque "thoughts," a sort of purgation and confessional, to clear my head and my heart from turgid obsessions. Ezra, even then, used to assault me (as he still does) for my lack of education and reading. He would say that I should become more acquainted with the differential calculus—like himself, of course. I'd reply that a course in comparative anatomy wouldn't at all harm him, if it came to that.

My thoughts were preserved in the series of ten-cent copybooks of which I have spoken. They had stiff board covers of a black and tawny water-wave design and a slightly off-gray cloth binding. They accumulated to twenty-three before finally disappearing I don't know where. I don't think I burned them. They were for me for many years a precious comfort.

Ed, to whom I wrote steadily during my college years, long letters, nebulous but high-minded (he kept them all), was at

Massachusetts Institute of Technology studying architecture.
There he had an English prof named Arlo Bates. Ed spoke to
Bates about his literary brother and finally arranged an appoint-
ment for me with the distinguished man. Ed liked him, that was
enough for me. So, one week-end, the week-end of one of the
Penn-Harvard football games, I believe, I hied me to Boston.
This was the same Bates of whom when he first came to the
United States Robert Louis Stevenson had asked, "Who the
hell is Arlo Bates?"

My *Endymion* manuscript rolled into a great wad, just like
that of the poet in the funny papers, had a broad elastic
stretched about it. Going to see Bates, I carried the thing un-
wrapped in my hand.

His rooms were in the old Back Bay section of Boston facing
the Charles Basin. I rang the bell. The door opened level with
the street, if I am not mistaken. His man admitted me: Mr.
Bates would see me at once. The first door to the right, please.
But as I was about to enter the library I stumbled at the sill
and my three-pound poem rolled miserably into the room. What
could I do but pick it up again?

Mr. Bates was sitting at a small desk near the window, a tall,
middle-aged man with white hair. He was very kind. My purpose
in going to him had been to ask him whether or not, to his
mind, I should quit medicine and write or go on with medicine.
Bates took his time, looked through the poem with some care
and deliberation while I sat and sweated it out. Finally he
looked up.

"I can see that you have a sensitive appreciation of the work
of John Keats's line and form," he said. "You have done some
creditable imitations of his work. Not bad. Perhaps in twenty
years, yes, in perhaps twenty years (this was approximately
November, 1905) you may succeed in attracting some attention
to yourself. Perhaps! Meanwhile, go on with your medical studies."

Then, a little pathetically, he pulled out the middle drawer
of his desk and continued, "I, too, write poems. And when I
have written them I place them here—and—then I close the

drawer." I thanked him and left. I remember how sweet the air seemed as I stood for a moment on the sidewalk looking over the Charles Basin.

Ed and I frequently "went with" sisters after we grew a little older. Finally, he became engaged to one and I to the other, whom I married, though his engagement was broken off.

That was the end of my youth. For it was the end of my passionate identification with my brother.

I have never been able to make out quite what happened at that time, for something profound did happen, something moving and final.

I have had several but not many intimate friendships with men during my life, patterned, I suppose, on my youthful experience with my brother. There have been Ezra Pound, Charles Demuth, Bob McAlmon and a few others. You could count them surely on the fingers of one hand. All artists. On the other hand there is Flossie, my wife, who is the rock on which I have built. But as far as my wish is concerned, I could not be satisfied by five hundred women. As I said at the beginning, I was always an innocent child.

Why, I remember once as a medical student falling in love with the corpse of a young negress, a "high yaller," lying stripped on the dissecting table before me.

Men have given the direction to my life and women have always supplied the energy.

Chapter 12
Ezra Pound

Ezra Pound would come to my room to read me his poems, the very early ones, some of those in *A Lume Spento*. It was a painful experience. For it was often impossible to hear the lines the way he read them, and of all things in the world the last I should have wanted to do would have been to hurt him—no matter how empty I myself might have felt, and worthless, as a critic. But I listened; that's all he wanted, I imagine, from anyone. His voice would trail off in the final lines of many of the lyrics until they were inaudible—from his intensity. I seldom let on except, occasionally, to explode with the comment that unless I could *hear* the lines how could he expect me to have an opinion of them. What did he think I was, an apteryx?

Ezra was then learning to fence with Signor Terrone, the Penn coach. I had learned to fence in Paris in 1898, French style, which is somewhat different from the Italian. I went out for the team. Ez meanwhile had quit fencing and had joined the lacrosse squad. That didn't last long either.

He could never learn to play the piano, though his mother tried to teach him. But he "played" for all that. At home, I remember my mother's astonishment when he sat down at the keyboard and let fly for us—seriously. Everything, you might say, resulted except music. He took mastership at one leap; played Liszt, Chopin—or anyone else you could name—up and down the

56

scales, coherently to his own mind, any old sequence. It was part of his confidence in himself. My sister-in-law was a concert pianist. Ez never liked her.

Those were strange spring evenings when men would sit in groups on the grass in the Triangle and sing of Lydia Pinkham's Vegetable Compound, reputed to cure all the ills of the female race!

Once Ez asked me to go on a secret mission with him—to pick up one girl, yes, *one* girl, though why he wanted *me* along was more than I could figure. He had noted that a particularly lovely thing in her early teens, surely, would pass up Chestnut Street daily, at a certain hour, on her way home from school toward evening. I say school because her arms, when I saw her, were full of books. I acknowledged it, she was exceptional.

As she came along we drew beside her, one to the left, one to the right. I was not interested and found the goings on ridiculous. Ezra was Ronsard. The poor child was all but paralyzed with fear, panting to the point of speechlessness as she just managed to say in a husky voice, "Go away! Please go away! Please! Please!" I dropped back. Ezra continued for another twenty paces and then quit also—to bawl me out for not persisting. I told him what I thought of him. After all, what was there in it for me?

I remember, also, one moonlight adventure to meet two girls outside the grounds near some school at Chestnut Hill. Equally futile.

When the senior class at Penn, under Professor Clark, presented Euripides' *Iphigenia in Aulis,* in Greek, at the Philadelphia Academy of Music, Ezra was one of the women of the chorus. I was in the top balcony. The fellow who played the Messenger was superb that night and got an ovation for the impassioned delivery of his lines. But Ez was as much the focus of attention, at least for me. He was dressed in a Grecian robe, as I remember it, a togalike ensemble topped by a great blond wig at which he tore as he waved his arms about and heaved his massive breasts in ecstasies of extreme emotion.

Ezra never explained or joked about his writing as I might

have done, but was always cryptic, unwavering and serious in his attitude toward it. He joked, crudely, about anything but that. I was fascinated by the man. He was the livest, most intelligent and unexplainable thing I'd ever seen, and the most fun —except for his often painful self-consciousness and his coughing laugh. As an occasional companion over the years he was delightful, but one did not want to see him often or for any length of time. Usually I got fed to the gills with him after a few days. He, too, with me, I have no doubt.

I could never take him as a steady diet. Never. He was often brilliant but an ass. But I never (so long as I kept away) got tired of him, or, for a fact, ceased to love him. He had to be loved, even if he kicked you in the teeth for it (but that he never did); he looked as if he might, but he was, at heart, much too gentle, much too good a friend for that. And he had, at bottom, an inexhaustible patience, an infinite depth of human imagination and sympathy. Vicious, catty at times, neglectful, if he trusted you not to mind, but warm and devoted—funny too, as I have said. We hunted, to some extent at least, together, and not each other.

What I could never tolerate in Pound or seek for myself was the "side" that went with all his posturings as the poet. To me that was the emptiest sort of old hat. Any simpleton, I believed, should see at once what that came from; the conflict between an aristocracy of birth and that of mind and spirit—a silly and unnecessary thing. The poet scorning the other made himself ridiculous by imitating that which he despised. My upbringing assumed rather the humility and caution of the scientist. One was or one was not *there*. And if one was there, it behooved one to be at one's superlative best, and, apart from the achievement, a thing in itself, to live inconspicuously, as best it might be possible, and to work single-mindedly for the task. Not so sweet Ezra.

I cannot remember the title of the poem over which I spent so much time in the Penn dormitory (while reading Keats) and over week-ends when home from my internship at the French and the Nursery and Child's Hospitals in 1908-9. I finally burned it some time around then. But if the title is gone, if it had a title (it was the poem I showed to Arlo Bates), there are some things about it that might at least be worth a line here—since here I am, still.

Like *Endymion,* it was a narrative in that vague area of thought that associated itself with a romantic past. The costumes were medieval, there were castles, kings and princes. It opened with a Keatsian sonnet for prologue, followed by an "Induction" that recounted in blank verse a tragic story.

The prince was to be married to a chaste and lovely lady of his choice. It began with the feast following the ceremony but before the marriage had been consummated; in fact they were still at the festive board. All the royal family was there.

From what motive I do not know, but from some one of the romantic (and real) motives that were always the agents in such cases, poison had been added to the cup which was to be the high moment of the celebration. It killed them all—that is, they all lay for dead, the prince also among the rest. Had not his "ancient" nurse rushed to the scene, dragged him from that slaughterhouse, found him the antidote and laid him on a bed still breathing, no poem could have resulted.

The poem itself began at that point, the young prince had been abducted in his dream state and taken to a "foreign country" at some distance from the kingdom which was now his. Here he had roused from his slumber. I'll never forget that passage of awakening! It occurred in a forest (Wagnerian?) over which a storm had just passed; it was possibly a thunderclap that had done the trick.

As he opened his eyes, he found himself alone, lying in a comfortable place among the trees, quite in the open, with torn branches on all sides of him and leaves, ripped from their hold, plastered in fragments upon the rocks about him. Unfortunately, though, he didn't recognize the place. No one was there to inform him of his whereabouts and when he did begin to encounter passers-by, they didn't even understand, let alone speak his language. He could recall nothing of the past.

There occurred here a secondary dream the scene of which was, deliberately, Boecklin's *"Insel des Todes,"* which I knew from a cheap print I had seen somewhere or other.

The prince saw himself transported to that dire place in a boat—but at this point the poem bogged down. I had elected to write this section, resembling the part taken by the players in *Hamlet*, in heroic couplets. I worked at the thing under great difficulties but couldn't wait, so left it to be completed later as I rushed on to complete the main story.

This was no more and no less than the aimless wandering, for the most part, of the young prince in his effort to get home again as well as to discover what had happened to him—he had not been able to recall the details, merely "sensed" them: That there had been a beautiful bride, a father, a mother; that a disastrous event of some sort had occurred of which he was the victim. So he went on, homeward or seeking a home that was his own, all this through a "foreign" country whose language was barbarous.

So book followed book, poetically descriptive of nature, trees, for the most part, "forests," strange forests—wandering at random, without guide, alone.

Each time I'd return to the writing, I'd invent a new scene, new troubles. (I had read a little of Edmund Spenser, Keats's favorite poet, but not more than a few scenes.) It was enthralling to have the poem burning in my head while I'd be at whatever might be on, in the operating room giving ether or the roof behind the water tank with a girl or hearing Krumwiede at the piano giving his rendition of the slow opening bars of the overture to *Parsifal*, its "unsensual" music following the orgasm of the *Tristan*.

I'd find somewhere in that "primeval forest" my theme for the week-end, go back to Rutherford, listen to Charlotte (Flossie's older sister) play Chopin and retreat to my room at home to compose.

Then, in disgust, one day, perhaps through my impatience with my "heroics," I took the voluminous script, and running downstairs before I should begin to "think," opened the furnace door and in with it!

The Wanderer, featuring my grandmother, the river, the Passaic River, took its place—my first "long" poem, which in turn led to *Paterson*. It was the "line" that was the key—a study in the line itself, which challenged me.

I quit Keats just at the moment he himself did—with Hyperion's scream. I never got far with *Lamia,* though his "Eve of St. Agnes" and the odes were as familiar to me at one time as breath itself. When recently I heard John Crowe Ransom talk on the odes (including "Autumn") it was like meeting the long deceased members of my own mother's, and especially my father's families (since he has been longer dead) in a sad but nostalgic dream. I felt as though I had written those poems myself and indeed it is true. I had written them over and over and over again, as Arlo Bates saw, and for which he gently admonished me.

At Penn, aside from Ezra and Charlie Demuth, I had few close friends among my classmates, but there was one, not connected with anything at the university, John Wilson, a painter, a man in his early fifties, I imagine, whom I dearly loved. He was a grubby little figure who lived in one of the typical small houses with low white marble steps before it which are to be found almost anywhere toward the middle of the city either north or south of the main intersection. Wilson, a failure of an artist who used to paint, right out of his head, landscapes with cows, pictures 24 × 36 inches or so, that sold as "art" for from ten to twenty dollars, had nevertheless not lost the spark that made him love his vocation. He painted because that's all that he could do, all he wanted to do. As long as he had any sort of market, he was happy. He had a wife, able enough, and though no doubt she could have used a little dough to pep up her house, she wasn't a bad sort by any means.

But the old man was my friend and I let it be known pretty plainly where I stood. For he had a daughter, Dorothy, of marriageable age, who would be around on Sundays when I'd call there and I suppose nobody would have been mad if I'd married her. Though one day when I agreed to take her to a dance and showed up in a tux the night *following* the event, they gave that idea up rather thoroughly.

My delight was in going down to the old boy's second floor, north-light studio and sitting there all Sunday afternoon while he'd work putting in his trees and cows with a low-toned sky in the background, over and over the same thing. At first I used to sit and hear him talk until one day he said, "How about trying it yourself? Here, I'll set you up a canvas," which he did. "Here are some clean brushes, here are the colors"—at which he jammed a handful of other brushes, hairs in the air, into a small jar and placed it before me—"There, paint that!"

And he turned away to get on with his own work. That was fun.

My other Sunday occupation was church. I was still lonely and poor to the point of counting pennies to see if I had money enough to ride down Chestnut Street to the First Unitarian Church where Reverend Ecob held forth, or should have to walk.

They also had a good mixed quartet at the church that used to stand in a small balcony in the left wall, facing the pulpit. But old man Ecob himself, a mysterious figure, was the one I was interested in. He was a small gray-haired fellow, an ex-Presbyterian who, more than a little to his family's discomfiture, had taken to Unitarianism, that most unpopular, almost non-Christian faith. Certainly un-Christian to popular belief. His three daughters, especially, seemed eternally ill at ease, apparently over this falling-off from orthodoxy, and they showed it in nearly all they did. The older daughter, a woman well beyond my years, played the piano—with gestures. There was a boy too, who resembled his father, a silent, introspective sort of chap, studying architecture at Penn.

The Ecob girls, especially the youngest, were a possible solution to my secret misery but, as I say, I was poor, poor. I invited this youngest girl out once for a walk in Fairmont Park. I felt that she didn't like me, if she didn't, possibly, hate the very sight of me. But she was the minister's daughter and it was a fine Sunday, so off we went, she probably at her mother's insistence.

We at least talked to each other; it was that sort of kid party. But when, at one point, we were walking up a small grassy slope, and I put my hand out to help her, she pulled her arm away and said, "Don't touch me!" I stopped and looked at her.

Whatever I said next I do not recall, but it wasn't much. I felt low enough without having to stand that sort of treatment. So let's say she went her way and I mine—on the spot.

Once before or after that I had another humiliating experience which with others of the sort finally finished me with the Ecobs.

Church was over and I, having listened, much moved, to the preacher's talk, lingered after the service to say a word of appreciation to him, for I had a genuine affection for the man. He, in kindly fashion, invited me home to lunch with the family.

"I'll be a little delayed," he said, "but you go on with the girls."

Fine. We all stood at the corner in front of the church on Chestnut Street and, when the trolley came, piled in. But when I put my hand into my pocket, I hadn't a cent, not a cent to my name. The girls had to pay my way. I never quite got over that.

Old man Ecob, I always thought, looked like an ancient Briton and I believe his name did come from the period in England before the Roman Conquest. He finally went nearly mad over Blake's revolving spheres, after which his fashionable congregation gave him the heave-ho, and I suppose his family along with him, in favor of some more practical instructor.

It became known about the campus one spring that the Ben Greet Players were going to do Shakespeare's *As You Like It* on the Botanical Garden lawn. Nothing could have excited me more. I wouldn't have missed it for anything I owned—which, unfortunately, didn't include the dollar's admittance fee.

That Saturday morning, a perfect May day, I sneaked off to wander about the grounds back of the dormitories where the play was to be held, thinking perhaps to conceal myself in the bushes somewhere against the starting time of two P.M. The players had been rehearsing. I saw where the stage was to be, near the greenhouses on an embankment surrounded by shrubbery, and going along the path by the frog pond, backstage, I saw two of the actresses in costume lying at ease on the brilliant grass, talking together. Goddesses! If that is not agony, to see, to desire and not to know how to begin, then I have never known it.

I passed them by—there was no place to hide—but I knew that, happen what might, I'd be at the play.

After lunch I began my maneuvers. The gate through the quad to the garden was guarded, so was the passageway along the front of the medical school. I might have dropped out of a first-floor dormitory window back of the trees, but I knew no one with a room there. Besides being broke, I should have had to make myself foolish in his eyes.

So I went out along Woodland Avenue to the far gate to the gardens and found them locked also. That settled it. There would be no way to get in but over the cemetery fence. Inside the cemetery enclosure there was at that time a patch of wild second-growth abutting on a ten-foot picket fence, separating that from the Botanical Gardens. I climbed that, straightened myself and jumped inside. I was in—but not yet at the play. I remember I had on a derby hat.

After reconnoitering a moment, I saw that the entrance to the seated area was down two steps into one of the greenhouses which gave at the far end onto the stage itself. I walked up to the open greenhouse door and started to pass through but was stopped.

They threw me out.

Waiting a short distance off, I decided on another try. So when I saw a little cluster of men and women approaching the wicket, I got behind them, close up, and while their tickets were being taken, pulling my hat down on my face, I pushed through the gate. Someone yelled at me, but this time I kept going.

All the seats were taken, so I lay on the grass, quite close to the actors, as the play began—you might say that from that time on I never took a complete breath all afternoon until it was over.

Pound's Wyncotte (Pa.) days were marked by an occasional party when we'd stand around the piano, an upright piano, and sing. In the group would be Mrs. Pound, a remote, even bewildered woman, erect and rather beautiful in an indifferent middle-aged way, who would play for us occasionally. I'd bring my violin. The others, Hilda Doolittle, the older Snivelys,

Bob Lamberton and two or three whom I have forgotten would be in the background. No one had a voice. We'd do our best to please Mrs. Pound. Ezra himself couldn't even carry a tune as far as I ever heard.

One day I went out to this typical Philadelphia suburb where the proprietor of the Curtis Publishing Company held a dominating position, an impressive house with lawns and the usual show of wealth. Ezra gleefully told me how the great man condescendingly, in a Christian sort of way, a good neighbor and all that, smiled at his mother one Sunday morning, looked perhaps as though he might speak to her. She snubbed him dead.

Once Mrs. Pound had asked her son, thinking he ought to get more exercise, to go out and weed the lily-of-the-valley bed. He dutifully sallied forth and pulled up the lilies. She laughed.

But this day, late in the afternoon—I had been fencing regularly with the Penn squad long after Ez had resigned—as I entered the front door he greeted me with an offer for a friendly bout with two of his father's walking sticks. I took one, made a few formal flourishes and placed myself *en garde*. But he, before I could do more than laughingly provoke him, came plunging wildly in without restraint, and hit me with the point of the cane above my right eye to fairly lay me out. I imagine I told him what I thought of him and threw down my stick. He felt triumphant that he had put the whole team of the University of Pennsylvania behind him with that single stroke. You can't trust a guy like that!

Several have asked me about Mary Moore, to whom one of Pound's earlier books was dedicated—and by the way, I recently came on a book by Stirling Ford with Ezra's name on the flyleaf. My wife's mother gave it to me; I don't know how else I could have got it.

I never remember hearing him speak of Mary Moore unless she was the girl we saw that moonless night outside the school at Chestnut Hill: Mary Moore of Trenton, N. J. But in comparatively recent times, someone, again I've forgotten who, told me that Ezra did visit at the Moores', wherever it was. It was in summer. Inside the screened porch, the French windows reached to the floor. They were open and Ezra entered through one of them. Ever after he insisted on entering the house in that way. That's all I know of Mary Moore, a queen of the man's youth.

Here's another of his books, signed on the flyleaf E. Pound. *Literary Criticisms* by Thomas De Quincey. Maybe they were school books. I see no sign in them that he ever read them. At least he put his name at the front. Maybe he once gave them to me and told *me* to read them. It would be like him. The one book he did not give me, but which I did read at his behest, was *Longinus on the Sublime.* I read also the *Vita Nuova* and *Convivio*—in translation, of course. It comes to me now as strange, speaking of books in general, that the *Apologia pro Vita Sua* should be valued now principally for its hair-splitting style and the fact that it was provoked by Charles Kingsley. Odd change of fashion. All that that period teaches now of Savonarola is that Botticelli, out of despair over his death destroyed all his sketches (how many no one knows) of young nudes at a single stroke! All gone out of an excess of passion!

The starved man treasures minor rewards that are not minor in that they are all he has. It is the imagination again just as too much flesh sates us. One woman will set us sailing the skies, another, inevitably, crushes us with too much that is too well known. The revulsions of the young are completely unaccountable, perishable as the case may be, enthralled on Tuesday, ready to vomit of a Friday over it, showing that it is all immaterial, all in the mind. And yet, the flesh is like art itself, unaltered in its appeal; it is only the manner of it that leaves us flat. Divorce takes place far oftener out of a court of law than in it. It is a principle of actions: at breakfast it has occurred, and it may run a week when by the mere passage of a few hours, another face is turned to us and—we have escaped.

Chapter 13

The Observatory

The location of the observatory in Upper Darby was ideal for country walks. The ground was rolling, lightly wooded and without serious restrictions for miles around. Open fields, small patches of woods and narrow roads everywhere.

From the Penn campus we took the cross-country trolleys of those days and were there in no time. Hilda, Professor Doolittle's youngest daughter by his second wife, was the attraction: at least she was what Pound led me there to see. It certainly wasn't to look through a telescope. There were plenty of stories about that too, and Dr. Doolittle's studious, careful measurements of the earth's oscillation on its axis in turning. A tall gaunt man who seldom even at table focused upon anything nearer, literally, than the moon. Mrs. Doolittle, considerably younger than he, would silence everyone with a look when she found her husband prepared to talk. He, looking above the heads of those sitting opposite him, would state what he had to say, after which the children and we others having waited decorously to find out if that were the end, would go on chattering again.

Hilda, tall, blond and with a long jaw but gay blue eyes was, I think, much like her father, though I never saw her pay him any particular deference.

There was about her that which is found in wild animals at times, a breathless impatience, almost a silly unwillingness to come to the point. She had a young girl's giggle and shrug which somehow in one so tall and angular seemed a little absurd. She fascinated me, not for her beauty, which was unquestioned if bizarre to my sense, but for a provocative indifference to rule and order which I liked. She dressed indifferently, almost sloppily and looked to a young man, not inviting—she had nothing of that—but irritating, with a smile.

Ezra was wonderfully in love with her and I thought exaggerated her beauty ridiculously. To me she was just a good guy and I enjoyed, uncomfortably, being with her. For sometimes I called at the observatory alone and even stayed the night there—to my embarrassment on one occasion. I took Hilda to a Mask and Wig tryout and dance one night and even got some dirty looks from Ezra over it.

"For God's sake," I told him, "I'm not in love with Hilda nor she with me. She's your girl and I know it. Don't be an ass."

Once I went alone for a walk with Hilda, one April I suppose, in that really lyrical Upper Darby country of those days. I particularly remember the grape hyacinths in a gully beside the road, deep blue, a flower with which I was completely unfamiliar. Hilda told me she was studying Greek and that she had heard that I too was writing poetry. That hurt. It wasn't something I wanted to talk about, for as a matter of fact I had in my own opinion produced nothing. Ezra, of course, was the hero.

Oh, well, she added, to help me along I suppose, I've been writing too. Some translations, she added—to escape blame. We wandered along. She with the back of her skirt dragging, no hips, no nothing, just Hilda, through the deep grass, over fences, barbed wire (I remember how Edmonson once told me, after a group walk one day, a fellow can't help but look sometimes! she was that careless).

As we went along—talking of what?—I could see that we were in for a storm and suggested that we turn back.

Ha!

She asked me if when I started to write I had to have my

desk neat and everything in its place, if I had to prepare the paraphernalia, or if I just sat down and wrote.

I said I liked to have things neat.

Ha, ha!

She said that when she wrote it was a great help, she thought and practiced it, if taking some ink on her pen, she'd splash it on her clothes to give her a feeling of freedom and indifference toward the mere means of the writing.

Well—if you like it.

There were some thunderclaps to the west and I could see that it really was going to rain damned soon and hard. We were at the brink of a grassy pasture facing west, quite in the open, and the wind preceding the storm was in our faces. Of course it was her party and I went along with her.

Instead of running or even walking toward a tree Hilda sat down in the grass at the edge of the hill and let it come.

"Come, beautiful rain," she said, holding out her arms. "Beautiful rain, welcome." And I behind her feeling not inclined to join in her mood. And let me tell you it rained, plenty. It didn't improve her beauty or my opinion of her— but I had to admire her if that's what she wanted.

Several years or maybe only a year later, Bob Lamberton, who had been a tough tackle on the varsity and a regular member of the gang, threw a final party for us all at Point Pleasant, New Jersey, where his family owned a summer cottage. It was in June, 1906. Everyone was invited and I think all came including the Snivelys, Hilda, Ezra and myself.

I had a hard time getting off. I was just about to start my internship in the French Hospital and turned up late, just past high tide at the beach where, toward noon, all had gone for a swim.

"Where's Hilda?"

So they told me.

Hilda had come down just before my arrival and, getting into her bathing clothes, had gone to the shore after the others. They all saw it. There had been a storm and the breakers were heavy, pounding in with overpowering force. But Hilda was entranced.

I suppose she wasn't used to the ocean anyhow and didn't realize what she was about. For without thought or caution she went to meet the waves, walked right into them. I suppose she could swim, I don't know, but in she went and the first wave knocked her flat, the second rolled her into the undertow, and if Bob Lamberton hadn't been powerful and there, it might have been worse. They dragged her out unconscious, resuscitated her, and had just taken her up to the house.

An hour or two later that same day another storm broke on us clustered helter skelter in the pavilion with various miscellaneous bathers. There were hailstones as big as fifty-cent pieces and of almost the same general shape. I went out and picked up a specimen or two from the sand to show the others. Then it turned to rain.

A short time later, as I stood holding a billiard cue, the butt-end on the floor, twenty or thirty people sweating in the enclosed space, a bolt of lightning splintered the flag pole right over our heads. I saw the flash go by me and out the door and felt the slap at the back of my neck, in the wrist of the hand holding the cue and in one ankle. A stout lady standing just before me fell flat on her back. But my own reaction, it was so fast, was laughter at the sense of a catastrophe averted. It was over before it occurred, one might say, and my first realization of it was that it was past and that we had come out of it.

Later that day, after the sun had set, we all went canoeing on the river and sang our farewell songs to each other. We never met as a group thereafter.

Chapter 14

Dr. Henna

The eruption of Mount Pelée in 1902 wiped out the last of my mother's family, the Hurrards.

By 1906 I had graduated from medical school, received my degree and was chosen an intern at the old French Hospital on Thirty-fourth Street, between Ninth and Tenth Avenues, in New York. I was working at my great poem week-ends, coming home stinking of ether and going back Sunday evening to resume the hospital grind.

It was then, just before Christmas 1906, that J. Julio Henna, one of the elder chiefs of the medical staff, came to me with a proposition. Henna was an old friend of my father's from the West Indian days, and had been the first to propose that I try for an internship at the French Hospital when I was in my last year at Penn. He was one of three revolutionists whom the Spanish had made it hot for. Three young physicians, he, Betanzes and one other, had had to leave Puerto Rico in a hurry in the early 1880's. He was a big red-headed man, with long, graying moustaches, who certainly had been very kind to my family. Earlier, when I first started as an intern, Henna had come to me one day and said, "Willie, do you want a million dollars?"

"Sure," I said. "How do I get it?"

"Come up to my office tomorrow afternoon. This is your week-end off. I want to introduce you to a South American widow who is up here to pick a young doctor to take over her late husband's practice of medicine."

"What!" I said.

"Yes. She'll like you."

"How old is she?"

"Oh, about ten years your senior. But she's not bad-looking. She wants to marry and I think you'll do."

I burst out laughing. He was offended. "A million dollars is nothing to laugh at," he said. "Do you know what that means? A million dollars?"

"But how do I know she'll let *me* get my hands on it? No. Nothing doing!"

"But I tell you, it's really so. She has more than a million and she is not at all bad-looking."

I merely shook my head. Later he told Pop, "That's a funny boy you have, Williams. I offered him a million dollars and he merely laughed at me."

A little later Henna came up with another one.

"I tell you what I want you to do," he said—I admired the man in spite of some of his ways and would always listen to him —"I have a patient, an old Mexican, very rich, who has had pneumonia and wants me to take him home before he dies. I can't go. Will you do it for me?"

"But how can I leave my work at the hospital?"

"I'll fix that."

He took me at once to the Belmont Hotel, at that time across the street from the Grand Central Station, and within twenty-four hours I had packed my bag and was on a special car attached to the tail of a New York Central express, bound, in a snow-storm, for San Luis Potosi, Mexico.

My patient was a really old man, a Señor Gonzales, a sheep owner and railroad executive, tremendously wealthy. He had been taken ill on a trip to France, had had pneumonia there, as Henna said, and had partially recovered, knew he was going to die and wanted to get home first. His circulatory system had broken down, he was dyspneic, edematous—his legs swollen to twice their natural size—but for all that, I found him alert and above all patient. He took one look at me when I was presented,

I one at him, he said a few words in Spanish, and the deal was on.

In the party was his son, his son's wife—in their early thirties, dark-skinned and bitter at all Gringos—and another woman. I've forgotten who. My job was to keep the old boy alive till we made his home town. It didn't look as though I'd do it. More than once I had visions of being lynched if I arrived at the border in a couple of days with a corpse.

So at six P.M. that winter's day, at the end of a through train, we started, strangely enough, northward by way of Albany.

We had him on a salt-free, high-protein diet—he didn't eat anything anyway—and there I was.

All day long for three days I sat opposite him and tried to keep his heart ticking by talking to him and shooting him, from time to time, with caffeine and sodium benzoate, which was then and still is my favorite recourse in such cases. As I say, he was a wonderful man, a tough, grizzled old primitive, always good-natured, gently trying to help me, trying not to let me down, and saying *gracias* whenever I had to do anything for him. We carried him to bed at night and put him in a chair by the window in the morning. I gave his legs gentle massage, kept them elevated always, and there we sat hour after hour, facing each other, sailing through the upstate New York landscape, down into Indiana and on across the Mississippi to St. Louis.

Everywhere the train we were to meet waited for us, we were hitched on the tail of the next express and shot out on the next lap. That's how much they must have paid. My Spanish wasn't so hot, but we all had a few words of French, the others kept to themselves, the son or son-in-law giving me dirty looks from time to time—but never the old man.

Only down through Texas did I begin to pay much attention to the landscape, which was entirely unfamiliar to me. The tracks seemed to run, in those days, right on the ground, unbanked, between the mesquite and palmettos with chollas and barrel cactus scattered here and there between them in the sand. Once I remember an Indian going along on the road patrolling the right of way, beyond the barbed wire, in the same direction the train was heading, his blanket around his shoulders, head bowed, completely absorbed. Occasionally I'd go to the back of the car and watch the tracks recede up and down, like the gentle waves of the sea, straight back with the distance.

The third day, the morning when we were approaching Laredo and the Mexican border, was like all the others before it, though everyone was excited: the old man at the prospect of soon being home, and I wondering still if we were going to make it because he had begun to turn cyanotic. I think it was only his determination to get there that permitted us to win out.

Was I happy when on the Mexican side I saw the young Mexican medico climb into the car ready to take over! Of course I was only an intern, not yet licensed to practice, and found myself treated accordingly by everyone except the old boy himself, who insisted that I go all the way with him to San Luis Potosi.

At last I could relax and did. I spent the entire day at the car window as we rolled southward over the Mexican plateau watching the natives wrapped to the ears in their serapes, the dogs, the chickens, the burros and the kids in the cold of dawn relaxing gradually, as they seemed to do, toward noon. And at noon itself we were there.

The whole town was out, the peons kneeling in the street, twenty deep, as their Señor was gently placed in his car and taken, thank God, alive to his home.

I followed, led by a young boy, one of the servants, on foot. We visited the market, kidding back and forth. I was forbidden to buy or eat any fruit, and an hour later was taken back at the old man's special request for him to say good-bye to me.

There he was, propped up in his big bed, absolutely triumphant. He took my hand and thanked me again for my care, smiled and I departed before the eyes of all those clustered about him, men and women. He was dead twenty-four hours later.

Downstairs the son counted out ten twenty-dollar gold pieces which he put into my hand, one on top of the other saying, bitterly, as he always did, and motioning about him that I might observe the well-paneled room, "You see, we live a little better— *un poco mejor que los negros*," and I realized something of what he had been through.

At three I boarded the express for New York and was greeted by the porter with a broad grin. Did he look good to me! It had taken me four days down and it took four days to get back, eight days in all, and I had only one week's leave. I had had three hours in San Luis Potosi. The authorities at the hospital all but fired me. But at that I had ten gold twenty-dollar pieces in the bank. I wonder what ever became of them.

Chapter 15

French Hospital

But innocence is hard to beat. Even the building of the old French Hospital itself is gone now—it stood opposite what is now the exit of the Lincoln Tunnel on West Thirty-fourth Street —completely vanished. It seems impossible that it was there I met the big Greek on the medical ward, stark naked as he was, and wrestled with him.

The big Greek had pneumonia and lay in the far bed to the left coming from the corridor. Miss McGrath, by no means *"petite,"* was giving him a bath behind the usual screen when, as I learned later, the man hit her suddenly between the eyes with his clenched fist. She fell backward carrying the screen, covered with a sheet, over with her. As she scrambled up he was after her, naked, a big guy muscled like a wrestler. When I got there he was standing in the middle of the floor struggling to possess the clay water pitcher we always had on a table in the center of the ward, which a little guy, convalescent from typhoid, was hanging onto with all his might. The Sister in charge with McGrath was standing barring his exit and the other girls, back of her, fascinated, were watching the show.

As I came in, the man let go of the pitcher and came for me. All I could do was grab him. Luckily for me, he'd been ill, had a high fever at the moment, perhaps 106° or more. I got him around the neck and tried to throw him, but he sank his teeth into my shoulder. I got one foot back of him and down we went to the floor together, I, fortunately, on top. All the fight suddenly went out of him. I let him stand, then, and led him back to his bed. But at that moment it became startlingly apparent that he was naked! The girls scattered, Gaskins, one of the interns, grinning like a fool, a sheet held between his hands, came behind us sashaying like a dancer from side to side. What a clown.

I remember Eugene Pool accosted me when my time in the French was finally up and asked me what I was going to do. It was he who had given me the name "the boy surgeon" when he had come upon me one day while I was trying to dissect out a Bartholin cyst abscess.

"One thing I'm not going to do," I told him, "and that's surgery."

"Why not?"

"I don't fancy a life spent dabbling in people's guts."

He laughed. "I think you're wise at that," he said. "There are plenty of young men, your age, with three times the surgery you've had, who are having a hard time getting on here in the city."

"I'm going to the suburbs," I said, "but not yet. I think I'll take another internship in obstetrics and diseases of children, then go in for general practice."

"Good boy," he said. "If you stay in the city it will take you twenty years (it's always twenty years that has to elapse between desire and achievement) then, just as you're on your feet, making a name for yourself, you're an old fogey." I knew at the time that Pool himself had married the daughter of one of the directors of the New York Hospital—crazy like a fox, I thought, and thanked him. Of course, he had money; I had no money and had no idea of ever getting any.

Once they brought in a French fisherman who had been lost for two weeks on the Grand Banks in an open boat, with only a sip of fresh water a day and a few biscuits to stead him. He had been a powerful man, but starvation had reduced him to skin and bones. And once we took care of a big Frenchman, with a thick brown beard, from Valencia, Spain, exiled from France because of his Royalist inclinations, and performances too, I can well imagine. We had case after case of malaria and typhoid among the sailors. Once a drunk swallowed a basinful of a 1/10,000 corrosive sublimate solution. He clamped his teeth, refusing to let us use a stomach tube on him. Sure, he'd let me give him a shot in the arm. Why not? But he didn't know it was apomorphine. The change in the expression of his face when the uncontrollable vomiting started was belly-shaking to behold. I once took a knife from under a sailor's pillow. The nurses were kind—but wanted marriage.

At the French Hospital, I was lying on my back naked one summer's day, resting before returning to my duties in the operating room. It was a brute of a day and I was tired. How old was I? Twenty-three or -four before I became fully aware of what had been a mystery theretofore called "love." No wonder I thought to myself when I remembered Doc Martin's lecture on the subject, "Everyone in this class has committed masturbation including your present instructor—don't let's be overimpressed by its importance." I hadn't known what he meant.

The French Sisters who did most of the ordinary work about the premises were always friendly to me, largely because I spoke French. They were of all ages and conditions, from the fat Sister Pelagia—who could hardly get out of her own way and whom the patients hated because of her indifferent clumsiness—to little wide-eyed Elizabeth, a pure peasant who was shocked when she found I, who could be so nice, was not a Catholic. Bless her sweet heart—a baby robin or a kitten was what she represented to me.

But Sister Julianna, the Sister Superior, an older black-eyed woman with a whiplike intelligence, was something else again. She was boss and no prude. We respected her. One day an old gal, one of our "chronics," hopped a window from the fifth floor going clean down into the concrete areaway in front of the building. The alarm was sounded. I jumped bare-legged into white pants and lit out for the elevator. Sister J. made the same car I did. We were laughing, merely doing our duty, no one was very excited.

"Look what I've got on," I said to her.

"Well, look what I've got on," said she, pulling her nun's habit above her naked knee. I loved her, a marvelous woman. I needed to love her and she me, for more than once it was her intercession alone that kept me in the place.

There were five of us interns if you count Krumwiede—what a name for the French hospital! We called him "The Wrath of God" from the way he looked at breakfast every morning. Smith, who fell on his back beside a recently operated-on and beautiful girl patient—he had been trying to do a handstand on the bar at the foot of her bed—his feet hit her pillow! Maloney, who was unjustly dismissed over a complaint he made to the newspapers about the way we were fed, and Gaskins, my immediate pal—one of the most hilarious, comical men I've ever met and the best pal in the world. Eberhard came after Maloney had been fired. He was a fat guy from Brooklyn.

Charles Krumwiede, the pathologist, would get up late mornings after reading until two or three A.M. at his 20-volume *System of Abnormal Anatomy*. We all respected him, but we'd be sore because we'd have to make a seven or eight o'clock schedule and it didn't go so well with us to have him lazing in to a leisurely breakfast just as we were swallowing our last sip of weak coffee preparatory to going on duty. Krumwiede particularly liked me because of his piano. Playing the scores of various of the operas, I'd dub in the voice with my fiddle as he'd play the orchestra parts. We'd have grand times together.

Once we four interns had a maid, if you could call her that, a rough-and-ready dish smasher who at least did bring our food in to us and inhabited a skin as tightly packed with goodies as a young intern could desire to pinch. She was Irish and she was quick, strong and ready. Eberhard caught her off balance one day and took her in his arms, but she came back swinging and broke away. He followed. As she ran through the glass-paneled pantry door, he no more than a whisker behind her, she swung the door back so that his powerful right paw went through the glass—without really hurting him. I never saw four men disappear so suddenly. I never did discover how they did it.

I was Senior at the time. With the crash of the glass, or so it seemed, Sister Superior was in the room. I hadn't moved.

"What's going on in here?" she shouted.

"Nothing very serious, Sister," I told her. "We'll pay for the glass."

She stood there looking at me a moment and then smiled.

"Tell me what happened."

I told her.

"Well," she said, "as long as it's you, we'll say nothing more about it."

"Thank you, Sister."

"But don't let it happen again."

"No, Sister."

One night I came in with a bad cold. I was hardly able to talk. Sister Julianna happened to meet me in the lobby and took me by the shoulder.

"Come with me," she said. "You young men!"

We went into the Sisters' dining room, it was late, the room was empty. There she made me sit at one of the little tables. She brought out a saucer and placed a teacup on it. She got the sugar bowl filled with lump sugar, then she dug out a bottle of brandy and began her operations.

First she put three lumps, square lumps of sugar, in the bottom of the cup. On top of them she placed two lumps and finally one lump to complete the pyramid. I watched her intently. Next she filled the cup with brandy, and I mean filled it.

"Hey, wait a minute," I said.

"You wait a minute," she said. "*I'm* doing this."

At that she struck a match and lit the top lump of brandied sugar. Together we watched the blue flame while she lectured me on my behavior and gave many such admonishments. The brandy burned and burned—it took several minutes finally to flicker and die out. At that moment, the sugar dissolved, the solution heated from the burning, much of the alcohol gone, she pointed to the cup and said to me, "Drink it!"

I drank it down in one sweep.

"Now go to bed and behave yourself."

Perhaps it was the next evening I was passing Saks's window at the corner of Thirty-fourth Street and Sixth Avenue. I came on an incident that really startled me.

It was cold, wet and gusty with hardly anyone out. There was a cab at the gutter and standing, her back against the shop window, was a young woman. It was a spot much frequented by the prostitutes of the quarter. In front of her was a priest facing her and arguing with her intently. I could see from her looks what was going on. I'd seen it for half a block before I actually came up to them: he was talking to her earnestly, trying to get her to go straight. She was looking down, turned slightly away from him, refusing to listen—when just as I passed, I saw the cab driver come up behind him. The priest didn't see the man until he tapped him on the shoulder from behind. The priest turned. The man smiled inviting him and the girl to take advantage of his cab and go off together. I had just time to witness the outraged fury of the holy man and the girl's guilty smile.

This was the French quarter where Mouquin had his celebrated restaurant of iron grilles and outdoor stairs leading up to the ornate second floor.

Poor priests, I heard enough of priests, for the most part Paulist Fathers, and their unhappiness, in that hospital to last me a lifetime. I washed out their stomachs, comforted them as best I could and saw them die too, more than once. I pitied them. One told me that he blamed his bad stomach on the life he led somewhere in one of the far western parishes where he would have to go fifteen to twenty miles horseback between churches, sometimes, to say Mass, but could not eat a bite until the last was over. They found me patient. The one I am thinking of would let no one else pass the stomach tube. God rest his soul.

But we had all sorts. A poor whore came in one morning in an awful state. I hardly knew women and felt tender to them all, especially, like any man, if they retained some vestige of beauty. This woman was young and full-breasted. She had been cruelly beaten. Her eyes were closed, her lips bloody where her teeth had cut them and her arms bruised and bleeding. But the thing that knocked me over was that her breasts were especially lacerated and on one could be seen the deeply imbedded marks of teeth, as if some animal had attempted to tear the tissues away.

The old hospital, on Thirty-fourth between Ninth and Tenth Avenues, was one short block away from the excavation then

being made for the new Pennsylvania Station. We had sand-
blast victims in the clinic every day. But one day they brought
in, unconscious, a big lump of a man in dirty overalls. He'd been
dumping broken stone from a wheelbarrow off the end of a
trestle to the pile below when for some reason he'd fallen,
barrow and all, onto the heap twenty feet down. When we saw
him he was messed up generally, bleeding from the mouth and
nose and, as I say, unconscious. I looked at him, smelled whisky
and told the girls to undress him. I wasn't sure whether he had a
fracture of the skull or was malingering. It isn't always easy to
make a snap diagnosis in such a case.

I went back to sit in the chair at the chart desk but almost
at once heard the girls cry out and come piling from behind the
screen.

"What's up?"

"Come see."

I went and was not a little astonished at what they had discovered. The man was a big guy, a plump specimen in bloody
clothes, but when they had begun to remove the outer clothing,
they found he had on a woman's silk chemise with little ribbons
at his nipples; that his chest and finally his legs were shaved;
that he wore women's panties and long silk stockings.

The girls wouldn't have anything more to do with him. I
called the orderly, and that was that! He was still unconscious
and obviously in bad shape. His wife was notified of the accident
and when told of her man's unusual dress, said merely that he
liked that sort of thing, that he was a good husband and that
she had no complaint of him. She was genuinely broken up by
his critical condition and went away weeping.

The next morning—the man still being unconscious with an
obvious skull fracture—a magnificent open car of the 1907
breed, something of unusual luxuriousness, pulled up in front
of the hospital and out of it stepped a figure which cannot be
forgotten. He was over six feet tall, erect and so dressed that
everyone about him looked like a lackey. He inquired for his
friend, the injured workman. I saw and spoke to him in the lobby.
His hair, pure white, was worn in tight curls covering his really

fine head. He was quiet but insistent. I reported the condition of his friend and told him how the cards lay.

"Have him moved to a private room. Give him the best there is." No, he didn't want to see him. "Send all the bills to me." He gave me his name—which was one of the most prominent in the state—and came every day thereafter to inquire about the man's condition. When the man died, the body was returned to the wife for a decent funeral.

It was sometime after this that Maloney left. He was forced out. We'd had an emergency case one night. I took care of it, though I didn't see the first part of the show. A cab had driven in to the ambulance entrance. Before we could identify anyone, a young guy was pushed out and his friends had gone. So we looked him over and found a stab wound in the chest, not too bad. But in those days, any wound of the chest was bad, and we admitted him—just a kid in his teens.

But next day, the reporters were on our necks getting past the Sister at the window, coming up the elevators unannounced, trying to pick up a story. There was no story to amount to anything, just a stabbing. So one of the brighties of the press began snooping around for something to send to the city desk. I don't know how he hit on it, but he got hold of Maloney and perhaps by chance asked how the food was in the place. As it happened, the grub was rotten at that moment, as it often is in certain hospitals, and we had more than once kicked about it. For instance, they had served us for dinner a brain of some animal, perhaps a sheep or calf or pig for all we knew; there it lay ungarnished on the platter looking as if it had come from some autopsy table. We damned near threw it out the window.

So poor Maloney let go on all our gripes, and the reporter made a hit story of it. If I recall the time correctly, there had been similar incidents in other hospitals of the city, so that we merely confirmed such findings. Maloney was hauled before the Board of Governors and out he went. I was moved up six months and so instead of serving two years in the hospital, served only eighteenth months before going over to the Nursery and Child's. It certainly altered my life.

Gaskins was the other intern, six months ahead of me. He was a book in himself: a born comedian, rotund, not more than five and a half feet tall with his little blond butterfly moustache and big round head—you laughed just to look at him. When he finished his internship, he said, he was going to Jacksonville, Florida, where his father was agent for the Standard Oil Company. He planned to buy the biggest automobile he could get hold of. He'd have it painted red and fill the trunk at the back with surgical instruments, drive up and down the streets, and that's just what he did, and became one of the best known gynecologists in the state. Gaskins would always look for the graft angle in any setup. When he saw me for the first time, having from my name expected a rough, sandy-haired Welshman, he let out a wild howl.

"There it is, there it is. Didn't I tell you?" He blamed Henna and family connections and whatnot for my success in getting on the staff. But the truth was that when, at the examinations, they gave me my surgical case to go over, I asked for a rubber glove, did a rectal on the poor guy and diagnosed an inoperable cancer—or at least an obstruction that I told them was undoubtedly malignant. Krumwiede said I had missed malaria, which I should have recognized in a blood slide he had set up for me, but he let that pass. Sister Julianna told me later that I had made a high mark. One of my rivals from Johns Hopkins had been furious over the results. Gaskins never believed anything but that Henna had put the deal over.

I have never enjoyed a brief friendship more. Between us, hard workers both, we managed to make that year at the hospital a gay festival, summer and winter. One night in summer, at the risk of everything we had to hope for, we went at midnight to dance with the nurses in their dormitory on the sixth floor above us, they in their nightgowns and we in pajamas. You may well believe that we didn't stay long.

The poor guy died after a few days' illness in 1918 at the time of the great flu epidemic that decimated the world's population.

Sister Eleanor, one of the other Sisters, was of a different sort from poor little peasant Elizabeth. She was specially excused from the strict rule imposed upon the Sisters requiring them to wear their robes at all times and on all occasions. In the operating room, since that was her field, she was permitted to take off the outer black habit and bare her beautiful arms to the shoulders for scrubbing. At such times, she would be in spotless white, a voluminous skirt, naturally, but her torso from the waist up was tightly held in a starched bodice which fitted her to perfection. Big dark eyes, full lips, and she said to me one day in excellent English, "Doctor Williams, if I were not a Sister, I would marry you."

Then she laughed.

"Well," I said, "if you were not a Sister . . ." And I laughed too.

It was in the old French hospital I saw my first patient die—in the room between the wards where they'd put the patients we knew were *in extremis*. It is a hard thing for a young man to look at. But there, after the man is gone, you are left, with a young nurse beside you, watching you, and suddenly you are alone with her.

There was a nursing school at the old French, girls trained by the Sisters to work along beside them. That was something else again. We'd sneak out on the roof and hide together behind the water tank at night and look at the stars. But my life was too fixed for much gaiety of that sort. I remember old Eberhard, who was always trying to incite me to bitchery, saying he had two girls over in a room in Brooklyn for us that night. He was disgusted with me for not stepping out and later told me he'd had a time taking care of both of them.

Chapter 16

"The Wrath of God"

Krumwiede, "The Wrath of God," as we called him, was an out-standing pathologist in the making in those days. He read inter-minably; his laboratory was maintained on a scrupulously exact basis as far as his equipment would permit. I had a good deal of sympathy as well as respect for him, and he for me, on most counts. I admired that German devotion to detail, that thorough-ness, that relentless determination to come at the evasive core of a problem until it had been laid bare. But I couldn't keep at it the way he could. When one time he had to leave for his two weeks' vacation, which we all took each summer, he put me in charge.

Well, we had a lot of malaria to treat at the old French. I had been pretty well coached in recognizing the plasmodium on the slides, so Krumwiede figured he'd be pretty safe in letting me take care of that particular detail.

The slides were collected downstairs, or I'd do the work myself, stain them and give the reading. I spotted a number of cases of malaria that summer and put them under treatment. But to make assurance doubly sure Krumwiede cautioned me to save each slide, properly identified, so that when he returned he could check up on me. And when he did return he found and proved to me that I had overlooked several positives. His face was a study, that I, a man whom he had trusted, had so deceived him—I could see myself then and there go down in his esteem and forever.

I still remained his friend, though from that time on I would find myself pigeonholed in a far lower bracket than theretofore. He loved his slides. Anyone who profaned his blood slides was little better than a criminal.

The old French was not a particularly modern hospital even for those days. As at all hospitals the battle against vermin went on endlessly. And this was an old building.

Blood for the Wiedal tests, a drop or two on each glass slide, would be collected, dried, and sent up to the lab. Krumwiede would sometimes have a dozen sent up for study. They'd be placed on the laboratory table with the identification slips under them for the pathologist to test them in the morning. And in the morning not a drop of the dry blood would be found on them. The cockroaches would have eaten it, eaten it clean. "The Wrath of God" would stamp up and down, tear his straggly hair and curse anyone who had been involved in any way in the misfortune.

"Why don't you cover them? Why, if you haven't the brains to do it yourself, don't you ask someone who knows?"

One day he approached me, dubiously, asking me to assist him. No one else would even listen. He had an idea. It was planned for that night. No one else was to know about it—they would have laughed at him—but he was absolutely serious, even in a frenzy of seriousness, as he bade me follow him to the dark laboratory.

As we approached and stood before the closed door he told me what he had in mind, at the same time handing me a can of ether and a pin with which to puncture the soft metal cap. In complete darkness now the laboratory door was pushed back and we tiptoed in. I picked one section of the tables while he posted himself at his own chosen spot. I punctured my ether can. He armed likewise did the same.

"Now! When I flash on the light," he whispered, "let them have it. Ready? Go!"

A hundred cockroaches, some as long as my little finger, made a break for the feed pipes along the wall and in the corners about the sink—the tables were covered with them! But as they streaked for the escapes I directed the stream of ether, fine as a needle, at the exit point for which they were headed, knocking them over as they came up. He did the same. In a moment we had slaughtered two dozen or more and he was wildly aiming at the stragglers. His delight was savage, though he could see as easily as I that far more had escaped than we had killed. I don't know how long we kept it up. As far as I could see, the job was hopeless.

Poor Krumwiede, he later became chief of the Board of Health Laboratories of New York City. A man I respected.

The man seemed old to me, though I knew he was no more than in his twenties. He was also, to me, typically the German, a thinker, a man devoted to the literal truth, the born scientist. He was intent on fact, a commodity to be found often in books —at least in books lay often the key to the meaning following an intelligent interpretation of nature.

Call such a man a skeptic if you like, an agnostic, but that is merely the surface view of him. He is a believer, has a faith that will bear the hardest knocks and for which he will go cheerfully through whatever the opposition may be to get at what he is convinced is the root of the matter in hand. He keeps his senses open and detests only the obscurity which would occlude his detailed perceptions. Thus Krumwiede was an unbeliever, as the facile patter goes—one who looks at the captured man, the man who has stopped thinking, as something pitiful, more or less an idiot. He was intolerant of such men and believed that I was not one of them. When he admired such another or had an affection for him he would as a consequence try to give him what he, Krumwiede, considered the best he had, his own very skepticism toward formal religion. He wanted to free the man, to make a better human being of him.

He had no work to do with me for I already understood and respected him. But one day he told me of a college friend, a Catholic, on whom he had worked diligently for a year trying to demonstrate to him the value of a scientific awareness, a pre-Whitehead belief, shall we say, in science as the only possible faith of a truly intelligent man. And he was successful in his attack. After patient and painstaking work he convinced his friend that his former beliefs were untenable, that science was indeed queen. But to his horror, Krummie had to confess to me, he soon discovered that he had succeded only in making his friend supremely unhappy. He thought at first that this might pass, but when, after a year, the man remained miserably depressed, Krumwiede resolved, he told me, never again to tamper with a man's hereditary convictions.

"Let them believe anything they want to. What difference can it possibly make?"

I smiled, since I was not affected either way; we found great systems on the imagination and never trust to the hierarchies of the imagination itself.

Chapter 17

Hell's Kitchen

At the Nursery and Child's Hospital, Sixty-first Street and Tenth Avenue, where I interned next for almost a year, the setup was entirely different from what I had known at the French. Its situation, in the first place, was different. It was still on the west side of the city, but somewhat further uptown in a notorious neighborhood called San Juan Hill, from the site in Cuba made famous by a colored regiment which had assaulted and captured the place during the Spanish-American War. The old name had been just plain Hell's Kitchen.

Pound had gone to London. Thence almost at once his books began to arrive: *Personae* (his first success) and then *Exultations*. "Come on over," he had written me, "and help me chew off a chunk." But how could I leave? Then one day Hilda Doolittle wrote saying that she also was off for London. That was a surprise. I went down to the dock to bid her good-bye and found her sitting on a trunk, her father, the old astronomer, beside her, uncommunicative as always. I doubt that he even saw me. It was a disconsolate picture.

Sometime before Hilda's decision to go abroad, Ezra had come back to this country because of an attack of jaundice and stayed for a week at our house in Rutherford. One day we went for a stroll around the old Kipp farm which then occupied the center of Rutherford. Ezra was always afraid of catching pneumonia and had borrowed a heavy white sweater of Ed's, a regular football sweater, to protect him from the cold wind. As we went along Union avenue, Ez walking with his usual swagger, I said to him, "Look, Ez, there's the winter wheat (it was three or four inches high) coming up to greet you."

"It's the first intelligent wheat I've ever seen," was his reply. That's the way he felt. Such thoughts were always near the surface of his mind. It seemed to become him.

Ezra's insistence has always been that I never laid proper stress in my life upon the part played in it by my father rather than my mother. Oh, the woman of it is important, he would acknowledge, but the form of it, if not the drive, came unacknowledged by me from the old man, the Englishman. I'd question that sometimes, about his being English, in that Pop grew up in a Caribbean island surrounded by a semitropical sea rather than near the Baltic. Yet he was, one had to acknowledge, at heart a northerner. He was a stickler for fundamentals, I'll say that, and when he took hold of a thing insisted on going through with it to the bitter end to find out what it amounted to. If he couldn't understand a thing at last, he'd reject it, which was not Mother's saving way of facing the world.

When Ezra was staying with us once for a short time Pop looked at him with considerable doubt. He acknowledged that Ezra knew a good deal, though what he knew Pop was not by any means sure. He knew also that Ezra, being my friend, was welcome in our house. He was curious about Ezra: he wanted to hear this young man expound theories which, generally speaking, the older man rejected on general principle but, being both intelligent and generous-minded, he wanted to give my friend an opportunity to express himself. He wanted, in other words, to hear Ezra read his poems, to have him interpret them as he wished to, after which my father would make up his mind and that would be his judgment of their value.

So one evening Ezra read several poems. Pop listened. I listened also and so did Mother, who said nothing. The selection was from the early work, naturally, and I knew that it wasn't going across. But one poem especially Pop stuck on.

Ezra had composed a short piece on the backs of certain books
standing on the shelves of our bookcase or, if not our bookcase, though I think he composed it while he was with us, at
least some bookcase. He spoke in the poem of certain jewels,
red and blue and green. It wasn't a bad conceit and Ezra
resolved it with considerable passion and ability. Pop couldn't
get it.

"What are all the jewels you speak of?" he said. I must say
I don't think I myself was entirely clear on the subject. "You
make a good story of it," went on Pop, "but I don't know what
you're talking about."

I don't remember precisely what went on after that nor
Ezra's exact reply or how he approached it. But Pop and Ezra
were on good terms, Ezra respected the older man, so that
it must have ended in the direct and simple statement, "The
jewels I speak of are the backs of the books in a bookcase."

"Oh," said Pop. "Of course," he went on, "being books
and being precious to you as a student and a poet you treasure
them, therefore you call them jewels. That I understand. But
if that's what you wish the reader to understand, to make
an intelligent impression on him, if it's books you're talking
about, why don't you say so then?" Ezra appears never to
have forgotten the lesson.

It was at this time that Ezra made the proposal, which,
when I asked my father about it, caused him only to shake his
head. It was as follows: That we get a big supply of "606,"
the new anti-syphilitic arsenical which Ehrlich had just announced to the world, and go at once with it to the north
coast of Africa and there set up shop. Between us, I with my
medical certificate and experience, he with his social proclivi-
ties, we might, he thought, clean up a million treating all the
wealthy old nabobs there—presumably rotten with the disease—
and retire to our literary enjoyments within, at most, a year.
Maybe there was something in it, I don't know. But if I had
ever spoken to Ez of a Herxheimer reaction he would have
thought I was talking like a Pennsylvania Dutch farmer.
Risks? The practical details meant nothing to Ezra. It reminded
me too much of a job I had been offered—to take a wealthy

but insane young man with homicidal tendencies on a European tour. But Ezra couldn't see my side of the argument. We didn't go.

How I ever got into the Nursery and Child's Hospital is more than I know. I think I applied and they grabbed me, that's all. I had hardly a week between quitting at the French and beginning there. Doc Richardson was my Senior; there were only two of us. The man I wanted most to work under there was Charles Gilmore Kerlcy, one of the leading pediatricians of the day. I was extremely happy at my good luck.

This was a very different setup from what I had been experiencing at the French, as different as night and day, a very much looser organization—and no Sisters of Charity. The main building, just completed, was on the corner of Sixty-first Street and Tenth Avenue, a six-story brick structure just across Tenth from the most notorious block in the New York criminal West Side, San Juan Hill or Hell's Kitchen, as you preferred to call it. We didn't go out much after dark unaccompanied, man or woman. There were shootings and near riots and worse practically every week-end. That block, the most heavily populated in the city, was said to be honeycombed with interconnecting tunnels from flat to flat so that a man who had taken it on the lam, once he got inside an entry, was gone from the police forever.

Our children's ward was back of the main building, the maternity section. It was a two-floor brick cube consisting of two small wards, holding eight beds each, right and left, with a similar second floor.

The management of the place, aside from the nursing, was riddled with corruption. There were a few nurses from various outlying hospitals who had been sent there for their pediatric and obstetric training, but there was no school. Miss Cuthbertson, a large, straightforward Canadian woman, was in charge of the nursing program. Miss Malzacher, a dark, sweaty-looking creature with furtive, bulging eyes, was in charge of the office, and another mild plump little woman, whose name I have forgotten, was the over-all director in residence, a decorative fiftyish little figure, who kept a wonderful table for Richardson and me, but that was all. She had said, in fact, that that was the only way she could hold any resident physicians in the place: by feeding them well. Our sleeping quarters were nothing, worse than nothing, in fact on more than one occasion full of bedbugs. But the food was marvelous and we were interfered with in our work almost not at all. I can still remember those meals with the lady boss herself and Miss Cuthbertson—the four of us. The madam insisted that the Senior in charge carve the roasts, chickens and other meat she served. She felt it was part of her duty to teach us manners. We literally ate it up. Miss Cuthbertson was our pal. It worked out beautifully in that small intimate dining room on the back corridor of the old part of the original building.

There was plenty of work. That's what saved the place, medically speaking. During my time there I delivered three hundred babies and faced every complication that could be thought of. I learned to know and to admire women, of a sort, in that place. They led a tough life and still kept a sort of gentleness and kindness about them that could, I think, beat anything a man might offer under the same circumstances. I never saw one yet, white or black, that didn't give me a break if I treated her half-decently.

Miss Diamond, who wore a gold tooth in the front, was a first-rate Supervisor and head of the delivery room. Miss Becksted, Chief of Pediatric Service, a tough little Englishwoman, was another of my pals. At the beginning it seemed just what I wanted. Miss Diamond was the right woman for her situation. As she once said, "I'm going to run a three-foot streamer around this place below the sixth-floor windows and it's going to read: 'BABIES FRESH EVERY HOUR, ANY COLOR DESIRED, 100% ILLEGITIMATE!' "

She wasn't fooling, either. The women at the Nursery and Child's were the dregs of the city, a fine crew. Once I was called by Miss Diamond to help her separate five of them in a fight. They were lying, all approaching full term, on the stone floor of one of the upper hallways, snarling and spitting like cats. She told me that two or more were pregnant from the same man, and the others had joined in on one side or the other.

She'd grab one by the foot and try to pull her out of the pile, but the floor was polished and Diamond was so strong she'd pull the whole sputtering mass in one direction or other. I stood looking at her, somewhat reluctant to join in.

"Grab a leg and pull against me," she yelled. So I did what she wanted but I couldn't hurt the things.

"Pull!" she said. But the women had their hands locked in each other's hair and we got no results.

"All *right*, you bitches," she told them, "I'll get the ether can!" And that she did. She got a towel, soaked it with ether, and waded in among them. They all let go all right and scrambled up without a word. It was the first time I had seen such a thing and told her so.

"Oh, that's nothing. We have it every once in a while around here. All we need is a ringleader and they're at it. I know who it is now, I got my eye on her. It won't happen again."

Miss Diamond—I don't think I ever knew her first name—was a big, sharp-chinned peroxide blond, the gold tooth right in front of her face, young and not at all bad-looking, somewhat of a Mae West type. When she set her jaw and her blue eyes began to snap, the women usually cowered; but she was a good nurse and a fast worker. In the end, the women knew she was for them. They respected her. So did I. She taught me a lot about obstetrics.

When I had come on duty during the first summer with the pediatric work—there had been nothing of that at the French—I was fascinated by it and knew at once that that was my field. We had 'em of all sorts, as you may imagine. We got most of the foundlings from all over the city when Bellevue didn't want them.

I'll never forget that summer. Some charitable-minded woman from the Riverside Drive section, fashionable at that time, offered us her apartment for a convalescent home on one condition, that we were not to put any sick children there, that is, very sick infants who might die on the premises.

It was agreed. She had removed the furniture from her parlor and dining room, covered the mirrors and carpets with proper drapes and runners. On each side we installed cribs and assigned certain nurses and attendants to care for a dozen or more infants who were to be kept there. It was a fine gesture on her part and we lived up to the agreement to the letter.

But something happened, as it usually does under such circumstances, to ruin all our plans. One of the children developed a severe case of infectious gastro-enteritis and before anyone knew it, had died, in three days! Something we were absolutely unprepared for. We couldn't let the lady find it out, but obviously we had to do something with the body. So that I, being on Pediatrics at the hospital, was assigned the job of covering up. I was dispatched by streetcar to the apartment with instructions to bring the dead infant to our morgue in a suitcase, which was provided for me. And I did it, by public conveyance, the suitcase under my knees as I sat there looking about me. I was not happy over it, all sorts of notions going through my head as I thought of what would happen if the rickety container should fly open and the body of the child fall out just at the wrong moment. I tell you I sweated over that job, plenty. When I got back I told them: No more!

In a day or two, the whole group at the residence was affected, we lost 90 per cent of them, but I never went back for another body. They had to close the place up.

It was when I was on duty with the infants and older children in the little building at the back of the Nursery and Child's that I was visited by Viola Baxter, one of Ezra's friends of the Utica days when he was at Hamilton College. She was beautiful and sympathetic, but when she saw what we had under our care, the very scum of the city streets, she was shocked—at our cruelty!

"Cruelty!" I said. "What do you mean? We can't dress them in pretty garments to make a show of them."

"But look at the poor miserable brats! Hear them cry. You're brutal, you're heartless—you're impossible."

"You don't know what you're talking about," I told her. "You ought to have seen this brat when we got him. He was the most bedraggled, neglected, dirty, emaciated piece of garbage —you couldn't possibly imagine what he looked like—sores, rickets, his legs out of shape, and look at him now—he's beautiful!"

"Beautiful? He needs his diaper changed this minute! Where are the nurses? You don't understand these things as a woman does. He smells."

"What do you want me to do?" I asked her. I could have kicked her out of the place. As a matter of fact, that particular infant was our special pride and joy, the most patient little beast I have ever witnessed—and one of the most understanding.

They weren't all like him. Some were enough to drive me half-insane with their screaming. I was, I must confess, to lose my temper one day, at a brat I had broken my heart over trying to recondition him. He'd yell at night, every night and only at night, right under my bedroom window across the alley-way, until one night I went to his crib—I could find nothing the matter with him to make him yell—and slapped a piece of three-inch adhesive over his mouth. He could still breathe through his nose, but I thought better of it after a few minutes and took it off again.

That gave me an idea. One night I got hold of my nurse on duty—she used to wear long drawers—and told her I needed her assistance. We had a somewhat older boy than usual in one of the downstairs isolation rooms who had become particularly troublesome. Nothing we did seemed to make him comfortable. So that evening I primed her. We switched off all the lights, darkened the windows and went into the boy's room.

"Here's a flashlight," I said. "Stand there, right where I put you, and when I say go, you flash that light on the youngster where he lies." Oh, shades of old Krumwiede!

"O.K."

"Ready," I said.

"O.K."

"Go!" and I threw back the covers with one stroke leaving the child naked on the sheet!

About twenty enormous bedbugs darted in all directions from his carcass and disappeared into the corners of the bed. I had solved my problem!

Next day I got permission to buy half a barrel of bar-sulphur, big pieces round as my wrist. I got myself six old enameled basins, put them on bricks in the center of the wards and other rooms of the building, poured half a pint of alcohol into them and, having had the engineer seal up the cracks around the doors and windows, except those about the exit-door—leaving all used sheets, blankets, and clothing in the building—the weather being fine, I had the nurses deliver each child to me, naked, at the one door that remained accessible. There I wrapped each child in a fresh sterile blanket and carried it to a spot outside the building, in the sun, where I laid it on a board along the south wall. It was very amusing to see them lying there. We took pictures.

When this was finished and I had inspected the building to see that everything alive except the bugs was out of it in the fresh air, I set matches to the alcohol in the pans one by one, beginning at the far end of the second floor. The stuff went up like a flash. I had to run for it. Outside I sealed the final door. We all for a while stood outside looking in as the sulphur clouds in the room became denser and denser. I could see the damned stuff in the nearest pan bubbling as it burned.

When we opened the place up later in the day, you never saw such heaps of insects on the floors and in the corners of each bed! We swept them up dead into veritable pyramids.

I had turned out to be such a famous exterminator that I got the nurses' dormitory as my next job—but the heavy fumes trickled out under the main door there, cascaded down the stair and damn near suffocated the private patients in the rooms below.

Once later I did a job on the main business office where an infant, critically ill with diphtheria, had been sitting for two hours while we tried to find a place for it. There I burned a formalin candle. Hours later when I opened the door, one of our famous cats flew out from under Malzacher's desk coughing and spitting. I hope its fleas were impressed.

Then one evening there was a terrific to-do on the avenue: screams and finally a pistol shot followed by the ringing of the out-patient bell. Hell's Kitchen or San Juan Hill was merely living up to its reputation. I thought nothing more of the affair but went about my business as usual until the gossip as to what had happened reached through to me.

The police had brought in a young girl who had been plenty roughed up. We didn't usually care for that sort of case, but under the circumstances the nurses had to straighten her out at least a little. They discovered that it was not a girl at all, but a boy. He had apparently been soliciting trade in doorways and the street entries to the various houses on the block, the usual two-bit stand-up, when one of his customers got wise to him. For the boy or young man had an inflated rubber replica of the female genitalia pulled up and strapped between his legs to make him marketable. It must have gone fine for a while until this guy found himself cheated, got his hands on the thing and then hauled off and clipped the vendor on the jaw. And so the riot began!

A colored gal from the Bahamas at full term went in one of the back wards one day, sat on the toilet and had the child there, keeping the water running until it came out under the toilet door onto the tiles until the whole room was flooded. When we broke in, took her off the seat and cut the child's cord, it turned out to be as good as ever. We discharged them both a week later. It was midwinter, and the infant was found next morning wrapped in newspaper under a bench in Prospect Park. Automatically it was sent in to us. One of the girls looked at it and immediately recognized it.

"Why, that's Joe we sent out of here yesterday! Look at him, isn't that Joe?"

Everyone clustered around. Sure enough, it was Joe.

One day I was examining a fifteen-year-old white girl—a cute kid who had been brought into the clinic for diagnosis by her mother who wanted to know what made her belly so big. The kid was not dumb and fought us every step of the way. Finally after threats by the mother and persuasion on my part, we got her dress off, but at that point she flew at us all and in her underwear dashed out the door and up the street like a young doe. That's the last I saw of her.

Another time I was delivering a case when they wheeled in a second. It was neck and neck. I stood between the tables, a glove on both hands and two nurses in attendance, when Miss Diamond brought in a third, dragged in a mattress, covered it with a sterile sheet and told the gal to go to it—on the floor. That was her style.

These were the ward cases. They'd come in around the sixth to the eighth month and work around the floors or just do nothing until they fell into labor, all sorts of women. One I remember was a morphine addict who begged me for a shot of the dope, three grams she wanted. I told her I'd give her a quarter of morphine but that was all. She begged and pleaded for more, but I had no instructions and didn't want to kill her. How did I know what she was up to? I guess I looked easy and they all tried to break me down. I got up to a half with her, then three-quarters of a grain every six to eight hours and kept her there until her time, she saying we were killing her.

We also had a few private rooms. Those women were of a different type. I remember my first twins were on that floor. Then one day I found myself taking the history of a young woman who quietly told me this story!

It was late in June, she had recently finished her year at a local college. The year before she had been seduced by her father's overseer at their farm in the Middle West. Finding herself pregnant, she induced her father to let her go east to college. She visited friends during the Christmas vacation, then at the end of the term, came here with us. It was a simple case. She gave the baby out for adoption and went home for the summer. I grew very fond of the woman.

The hospital backed up on some colored apartments. We would look into them idly sometimes going about our work. There were stray cats everywhere. At night, looking for food, I suppose, they'd climb the dumbwaiters making an awful racket so that someone offered a quarter a tail for any we could do away with. Occasionally we'd corner one in the pharmacy, catch it and give it to the big Swede, and I mean big, who took care of the furnaces. We did it at least until we learned that with his enormous hands he'd avulse the poor beasts' tails, to claim the bounty, then throw the carcass in at the open furnace door—scratch him as the things might.

We often put up our own drugs at night in the pharmacy. One day the new night superintendent of nurses came there for something and before many minutes, I had her in my arms. She wasn't as young as I, and had a sad story—the place was full of sad stories. Some one of the attending surgeons, a Dr. Tuttle, wanted her to take charge of his convalescent home somewhere in the mountains of Virginia. I never did find out where the girl came from—extremely pretty, unusually well-made, but hardly an intellectual—a futile, dispirited, lonely sort of woman, just the sort that would take the job of night superintendent in such an institution. Miss Cuthbertson seemed to think she was all right, but there certainly was a mystery about her. She seldom smiled. I suppose she had been married, or double-crossed in some way, or maybe her professional credits weren't up to the mark.

It became a bit serious in the pharmacy evenings after that. One day she asked me if I—or perhaps I asked her—if I might visit her in her room, on Twenty-third Street, that old row of houses that used to stand there between Eighth and Ninth Avenues.

"Yes," she said. She had full lips and big baby-doll eyes.

So I went. The room was on the fourth floor, right under the eaves, room for little more than the bed, the dresser and one chair. The poor child seemed really poor and humiliated in such surroundings. She had decorated the place with red candles and a fancy bedspread with roses. I wanted to lie on the bed with her. She shook her head.

"But you asked me to come and here we are."

She demurred. "Just say one word," she told me, "and you can have anything I've got."

So it hung, now, on one word. What word? I wondered, since I'd heard that before. Marriage, obviously. I still remember that little room under the eaves on West Twenty-third Street. It was so neat and futile.

By this time, Richardson had finished his term, the first half-year was ended and I was put in charge. I'd never had anything to do with Malzacher in the office, but we got along all right, so I was wholly unprepared for what was to follow. For at the end of the first month of the year 1909, I was handed the official forms from Albany to report the business of the hospital for that month: patients received, deaths, recoveries, patients discharged and so forth. It was an extensive and explicit sheet which I, as Resident Surgeon, had now to clear and sign.

The hospital, I thus discovered, was in part state-supported, though it had its separate Board of Governors, headed by one of the most distinguished figures in Wall Street banking circles. Each month we received funds from Albany commensurate with the admissions and discharges for that month. Miss Malzacher handed me a slip of paper giving the essential facts, which I was to fill in, in my own handwriting, sign and return the sheets to her to put with the other matters to be sent to the state capital.

"Fine," I said. "But how do you get these figures?"

"From the blue cards, you know," she said.

"Fine again," said I. "Show me the blue cards." The thing was we had blue and salmon cards, one for the out-patient department, which was large, and the others for the kids in the little back ward.

"I can't do that," she said. "This is a business matter, not a medical matter, and we can't release them."

"Is that so?" I said. "Then I can't sign the report."

"Why, no one has ever made such a fuss over so small a matter before. You'll have to sign them."

"Sure, after I see the cards." You see that's what I had been taught by my parents and I had no choice in the matter.

So the report went to Albany without my signature. Then all hell broke out.

They fired the report back at us and Malzacher began all over again on me.

But my back was up and there it was to stay.

After Malzacher, the doctors took their turn. They were some of the leading men in the East, though this was not one of their major appointments: Kerley, Davis, Mabbott and several others—

"Maggoty" Mabbott the girls had nicknamed him, because of the way he lingered over a vaginal examination. Kerley was one of the worst, all this at a bad time for me because Kerley had asked me what I intended to do after I had finished at Nursery and Child's. When I told him that I had no plans, he asked me if I would not come into his office for the first year. What an opportunity! A New York specialist. I was practically made, I thought.

Kerley came to me and said, "Look, Williams, why don't you sign that report? This is just a routine matter. It's been going on for years. There's no reason to suspect dishonesty. You know who's at the head of the Board. Sign the damned thing and forget it."

"I'm sorry, Dr. Kerley," I said, "but unless I can verify what I'm signing, I can't put my name to it." He walked off disgusted.

Davis tried to laugh it off without success, and then Mabbott, dear old Maggoty Mabbott, tried his hand at it. Meanwhile our operating funds were being withheld.

"Williams, we all like you in this place. Your work has been excellent, outstanding. You have a brilliant future before you either in pediatrics or obstetrics. I know you're young and a stickler for your principles. But look, we doctors can't go against the business of an institution like this. Our business is to cure patients, not to worry over where the money comes from. You're actually doing everyone an injury by this eccentric conduct. Look, sign those papers and get the silly business over with." He stopped and smiled benignly at me.

I looked at him and said, "Dr. Mabbott, if someone handed you some scribbled figures on a piece of paper and told you to copy them into an official report, figures which you had no way of verifying, could you as a self-respecting person put your name to those figures, and would you do it?" I spoke straight to his face.

He looked hard at me and I could see the color rising. He remained silent only a moment, then he said, "No, I'll be damned if I would," and turned and walked out.

Good old Maggoty Mabbott. But the Board would not release me. They said that they had arranged for the treasurer of the institution to sign the report and that I was suspended for two weeks for insubordination.

My head seethed, but before I left, Miss Cuthbertson, who had followed the proceedings with mounting excitement, begged me not to quit but to keep on, that she had some information that would be brought forward at the right time and place, please not to quit under attack, not to go back on her. I spent my two weeks at home. Pop had no suggestions other than to say that I was right in doing what I did. At the end of the two weeks, I returned to duty. Everything seemed fine.

But at the end of February, it began again. The previous month's report signed by the treasurer was not satisfactory to Albany. It had to have my signature and the office still refused to let me see and count the cards. Then Miss Cuthbertson played her card—but not officially, only to me where it did no good. She didn't come out publicly with the facts.

One day she had gone, not quite by chance, but knowing someone was in the Board Room, to see why they were so quiet there. Opening the door she discovered Miss M. on the end of the table, the President of the Board facing her, in a position that she, Miss Cuthbertson, would not describe to me. There it was, plain as daylight, the whole reason why the woman was being allowed to get away with her petty graft—that wealthy man.

If I could spill this in the papers, I thought. But Pop advised me against it.

A lawyer?

No. How can we afford to fight it? and with some of the leading specialists of New York too cowardly to back me, afraid of big money and what their stinking little hides might have to take for it. Sick, I had a horrible sore throat, in fact I could hardly talk above a whisper, I resigned. I didn't tell anyone about it, but I wrote a letter to the Board giving them a piece of my mind and started to close up shop.

The girls were marvelous to me. They were coming into my room with hot drinks, putting cold compresses on my throat, all but getting in bed with me to warm me when I had a chill, kissing me good night—but still I wrote the letter, went down and mailed it in the inside box at the door of the office.

Miss Cuthbertson had seen me go and, knowing my mood, rushed up to ask me what I had been up to.

"I've resigned," I said. "I wrote a letter to the Board of Governors telling them what I thought of them and mailed it."

"You fool. Where?"

"In the box at the office."

She ran out my door for it was not a U.S. Mailbox and could be opened with a key. But in a few moments she was back, licked.

"You've done it. That woman was too quick for me. She must have guessed what you were up to. She has taken your letter and has gone out and mailed it at the corner. I asked the officer at the door. He saw her do it. You fool—just when we could have beat them."

I didn't give a damn. I felt better in fact than I had felt in two months, unhappy as I must have been internally. I couldn't work with that gang any longer. My resignation was officially accepted. I packed and said good-bye and went home. My days of internship were over. Not a single doctor of the attending staff had stood by me. To hell with them all, I thought.

Chapter 18

The First Book

It was during the next few months of spring weather that I first observed Flossie, the kid, on Park Avenue in Rutherford, and my whole life came to a head. Without a job, I had finished and we began to rehearse my play, *Betty Putnam*, the first play of my proposed plays for outdoor performance, which we gave on the embankment at the Rutherford Town Tennis Club.

Ed was competing for the scholarship in architecture at the American Academy in Rome. Pound was for the moment in this country. My big opus, the *Endymion*-like romantic poem, was finished (perhaps already burned) and I was idle, if restless, for a few divine weeks! I went into the fields along the river at times to do some painting as Mr. Wilson had taught me. I had no idea where I was headed—an altogether idyllic moment.

At about that time, 1909, appeared my first book of poems. I was still raw from the wear and tear I had suffered at the hands of John Keats; I had been interminably occupied with my romantic poem; my hospital affairs were coming to a smash finish, when knocking about, not knowing where I was heading, I decided to have a book of poems published at my own expense. They had to be got out of my system some way. This was to be the answer.

Who would do it? Maybe that's where some of my Mexican gold went. There was Mr. Howell, one of my father's friends,

106

who, quitting his job as a printer in New York, had bought a small place in Rutherford and decided to open a shop there of his own.

The man was a good reader and enjoyed books, in fact, all literary matters. I told him my story, showed him my script. He was very indulgent and told me the deal was on—the price could not have been more than fifty dollars. In the same deal was included a small book also for Jim Hyslop on some of his observations of insects about the neighborhood. They were to be really no more than paper-covered pamphlets. The local journeymen must have had a tough time of it, never having set up anything of the sort in their lives, because when I saw the first finished volume I nearly passed out. I've still got the thing in my trunk in the attic: about half errors—like the Passaic River in its relationship to the sewage of that time. I notice, by looking over that disastrous first issue (which never appeared), that it bears the marks of Pop's corrections and suggestions all over it—changes most of which I adopted. Poor Pop, how he must have suffered.

The poems were bad Keats, nothing else—oh well, bad Whitman too. But I sure loved them. Where does a young man get the courage for such abortions? I can tell you my need must have been great. There is not one thing of the slightest value in the whole thin booklet—except the intent.

Well, there it was. Now corrected, the best that I knew how to perform, full of inversions of phrase, the rhymes inaccurate, the forms stereotype. Ed made me a design for the title page; I picked short quotations from both Shakespeare and Keats as legends and took a dozen or so of the books to Garrison's Stationery Store in town to offer them for sale.

Ezra was silent, if indeed he ever saw the thing, which I hope he never did.

There at Garrison's they lay for a month or so; there had been four purchasers: one dollar. The rest I brought home, giving them about the family. The stock, a hundred or so copies, Mr. Howell wrapped in a neat bundle (I may have been in Germany by that time) and put away for safekeeping. They were inadvertently burned after they had reposed ten years or more on a rafter under the eaves of his old chicken coop.

I had a great time making up my mind what my literary signature should be—something of profound importance, obviously. An advertising friend of my father's spoke up strongly for plain W. Williams. "It's a common name," he said, "but think of the advantage of being *the* W. Williams." To me the full name seemed most revealing and therefore better.

As I was still rather young to start practice, and my chance of becoming a New York specialist had by my recent experience been pretty well blasted, I remained, for a short time, at loose ends.

Pop had said, "If Ed wins the *Prix de Rome* I'll send you to Germany for a year." Ed co-operated as usual, and won the prize.

I proposed to Floss and was conditionally accepted, penniless as I was. So with half a kiss from my bride to be, I left New York in mid-July on a second-class vessel for Germany.

Chapter 19

Leipzig

I chose Leipzig—to Pound's disgust. I didn't want to go to London. What was there for me to do in London? I was a physician; that was to be my life, especially as I had no ability at all for literary intrigue. I knew I could not live as Pound lived, and had, besides, no inclination to experiment.

My German was not much, but by going over in August I believed I could pick up all I needed for a start before the September term. I had taken a ticket across Germany to include a Rhine cruise, from Köln to wherever the devil it went, but got so homesick that I gave it up after reaching Bonn and returned to Köln where I took the sleeper for Leipzig the same night and let it go at that. The last thing I remember noticing after Aachen was the *Westphalischer Schinken* running about in the fields as the train passed through. Perhaps going to Leipzig was a mistake, but I had been in love with the concert pianist who had spent three years there at the Conservatory, so there I went.

Arriving, desolate, at the old Saxon city, the first thing I did after the first night was to look up the "Rooms for Rent" ads in the local paper. I consulted my purse and landed somewhere or other, I have forgotten where, in the apartment of a woman who seemed all right until I came upon her one evening entertaining her "cousin" in the dining room. I guess it wasn't easy to scratch a living in Leipzig in those days.

The first Sunday I almost passed out for loneliness. Walking on the Ring, a little girl came up to me and said, *"Wie viel uhr ist es?"* I couldn't answer her so I just took out my watch. She smiled and thanked me. I'll never forget that happiness; someone had spoken to me and I had replied.

On a second try for a room I found Frau Jeneke on Münz Gasse, poor soul. She once gave me an egg for supper that to this day has me puzzled. It tasted of vinegar and must have been hard-boiled and pickled. It wasn't too bad. She it was who introduced me to smoked salmon, *lachs* was the name.

Later I'd hire a bike and ride on the paths of Die Nonne, a wooded park, beautifully kept, that afforded me about as much fun as I found in those days. Karl, Frau Jeneke's son, was a frequent companion: we drank *brüderschaft* one Sunday at the Obstschencke, south of the city, where I nearly had my head spun off by a husky peasant girl with whom I was dancing the *drehe*. The details are too trivial: the old woman sweeping the cut grass in front of the Rathaus every fine morning; the neat flower beds, stiff and formal. No use.

I wrote nothing, or very little. I was looking for a short form which would not be a sonnet. Even then I detested sonnets. I had devised a thing with an *abba bccb caac* scheme in iambic pentameters. One day I decided to take a solitary trip out to Grimma, near Leipzig, to see the remains of the nunnery where Katherina von Bora, Luther's bride, once lived. It was a romantic holiday, horribly sentimental in its implications—but I shall never forget it. I wrote something about that but that was all. The one practical incident was a delicious *hasenpfeffer*, full of buckshot, at the local tavern. Those things have vanished from my world.

In Leipzig I saw Ibsen's *Ein Puppenheim* for 15 cents at the Altes Theater and *Die Wilde Ente* on the Ring. I can still see the tree-enclosed building, low among its shrubbery. Also I attended the whole of Schiller's dramatic works from *Die Räuber* on. I heard there, too, Sohmer singing Wotan in *Götterdämmerung* and Strauss's *Elektra*. On Thursday afternoons I often attended the practice sessions of the motets of Bach at the Thomaskirche. And at Christmas I saw the tall tree illuminated only with slender white tapers at the altar of the Nikolaikirche.

Strange, unrelated memories. But I am glad for all that that I have them. I read Heine avidly and Sudermann's *Frau Sorge*; also his *Johannesfeuer*.

To offset the monotony of my medical work (I was getting along pretty well with the German by that time) I took a course in modern British drama at the university, but I didn't realize it would be in English until I went to the first class. I was looking for German. I found instead a young instructor with a distinctly southern drawl! I sat right in the front row of a small class and looked at him. He looked at me. But I didn't let on, not for three lectures, while he talked of Bulwer-Lytton and a lot of other stuff that didn't interest me. "I wondered about you," he said later, "but couldn't make you out. I put you down for a young Russian."

At the Allgemeine Credit Anstalt, when I said, "Doctor Williams," the old boy at the window shook his head. *"Nein,"* he said, thinking I was mixed up in my talk, *"nicht Doktor, aber Student von Medizin."* He wouldn't believe I was a graduate. I was still too young looking.

I didn't have much fun in Leipzig. I might have got along better, though, had I stayed longer. My American teacher finally, toward the end of the year, introduced me to some of the members of the Philosophische Verein; I think they even made me a member. I know I attended one of their *Kater Bummels*—a boisterous beer party at which I drank marvelously to some lusty *mädchen* who seemed more than willing to be saluted. I never really got to know a girl all that year except one British music student, named Ivy Peabody. Oh yes, I did take one American gal to the opera one night, to the *Elektra*, but I got so overwrought at the neurotic music, forgetting her, that she never would go out with me again. Besides we both had chilblains.

But one night I picked up a young streetwalker with my halting, *"Gehen Sie ganz allein?"* I thought I was out for a big time at last. Sure she was alone. When we went into the big restaurant, though, all lighted up, the whole assembly nearly screwed their necks off looking at us. I think she was known to the entire city. She wanted champagne, but when I insisted on no more than beer—another occasion when poverty was a distinct aid to virtue—she left me at the table for a gang of South Americans. I'll never forget how she did it. She asked me for *zehn Pfennig* to go to the ladies' room, adding, *"Aber Sie sind wie ein Professor."* Maybe she was scared—I don't know—in any case she never came back. I was glad to get rid of her. I decided that I had had enough of Leipzig. Ed was at the Villa Mirafiore, in Rome, and asked me to spend some time with him before returning home to work. Ezra said to come to visit him first. That's where I went, passing through Holland on the way.

Chapter 20

Ezra in London

In those days the "Great Man" was living in a small room on Church Walk, Kensington, which he generously offered to share with me. But I had met Ivy Peabody, and she had asked me if I wouldn't first go to visit her parents in Olney, Bucks. It was in April; I was eager to take at least a look at the English countryside. Ezra was furious—as usual. "Did you come to see me or the sheep in Hyde Park?" he asked. But I enjoyed Olney for that one day and a night, and was duly impressed with the violets growing thick on the railway embankment.

The Peabodys were a charming and large family. Peabody *père*, who owned a small tannery, was a medium-sized, lightly built man in his middle forties, I imagine. He insisted on singing, that evening, "When the Swallows Homeward Fly," to his wife's accompaniment. It took all her persistence and guile (she complained that her glasses were poor and that she could not see the notes) to contain him. The whole family was terribly self-conscious in the presence of an American. All except the small girls. They were fairly busting with amusement at me.

Just at dusk, after supper, Mr. and Mrs. Peabody, the son of the family and I went for a short walk. The son was heading toward South Africa in his dreams. God help him, with the First World War just five years away. That walk has been England to me ever since: past the church wall, thick with ivy, over a lawn of earth-hugging daisies and primroses, which the family thought only to extirpate in order to improve the grass. Some large bird got up at our feet as we approached a small field, a pheasant perhaps.

Next morning at breakfast (I wish I could remember what sort of bed I slept in), with the entire family present, I was passed a sort of circular and revolving cruet-stand containing ten or more soft-boiled eggs. I took one, then looked around for a cup, holding the hot egg meanwhile in one hand. I had left the cup in the circular cruet in which egg and cup, as a unit, had been offered me. A horrible moment ensued. I was puzzled and the family was tongue-tied until one of the little girls exploded. Mrs. Peabody's face was crimson; Mr. Peabody was all bluster as he turned angrily upon the child. "Oh, I see," I said, as I reached for the empty cup. I thought it all marvelous.

In London that week I met Ezra's friends the Shakespeares. That is to say, Mrs. Shakespeare and Dorothy, who was later to become Ezra's wife. One evening I was taken along with them to see William Butler Yeats.

It was a studio atmosphere, very hushed. We tiptoed in. Yeats, in a darkened room, was reading by candlelight to a small, a very small gathering of his protégés, maybe five or six young men and women, members of the Abbey Theatre group. He paid no attention whatever to us as we entered and seated ourselves, but went on reading; reading, of all things, Ernest Dowson's "Cynara"—in a beautiful voice, I must say, but it was not my dish.

After a while, never even having been greeted, we got up to leave. Nobody had noticed our presence up to that point, as I remember, but as we were practically at the door Yeats called out, "Was that Ezra Pound who was here?"

We had already rounded a corner of the corridor. "Yes," someone told him, "that was Ezra Pound."

"Tell him to wait a moment, I'd like to speak to him." The rest of us went out, Ezra returned and remained a few additional moments with the great man while we waited. That was in 1910. I don't know whether or not that was Ezra Pound's first acquaintance with Yeats.

Once during that week, Ezra and I were going along a street near Church Walk, past the very church itself, perhaps, which gave the place its name. Ez was in his heavy, all-purpose fur-lined overcoat and broad-brimmed hat; as we passed a bunch of faded violets lying on the pavement he looked down. We both noticed the flowers. He stopped, hesitated a moment, then lifted them from their low position and—at a loss for a moment what to do with them—looked up and, noting the high, wrought-iron church-yard fence, placed the flowers on the bar connecting the pickets near the top—all with a swagger not to be overlooked.

Another night we had been given tickets for a benefit lecture by W. B. Yeats, at the Adelphi Club, on the work of some of the younger Irish poets. It was a very fashionable affair, to be presided over by Sir Edmund Gosse, who, it appears, hated the Irishman's guts. The tickets were a guinea each.

I sat alone, Ezra and his crowd being at some other section of the hall. I was fascinated by the proceedings, listening closely to what was being said. The hour was drawing to a close when Yeats began to speak of those young men, Lionel Johnson among them, who had been consistently denied an audience in England though in his opinion they well merited it and more.

What was there left for them to do, then, but to live the decadent lives they did? What else, neglected as they found themselves to be, but drunkenness, lechery or immorality of whatever other sort?

He got no further, for Sir Edmund, to everyone's consternation, at that point banged the palm of his right hand down on a "teacher's bell" on the table beside him. Yeats was taken aback, but after a moment's hesitation went on or tried to go on with what he was saying. Again Sir Edmund rudely whammed his bell —and again Yeats tried to continue. But when it happened the third time, Gosse, red in the face and Yeats equally so, the poet was forced to sit down and the lecture came to an end. My own face was crimson and my temples near to bursting but I had not been able to get to my feet and protest.

"Why didn't *you*?" some of the ladies were saying to Ezra. "Why didn't you say something for your friend? None of you was up to it. You let him browbeat you—without a protest."

What a chance it had been for me—but I wasn't up to it. I must have shown by my face, however, how near I was to an explosion, for a woman back of me, an extraordinary-looking woman, almost spoke—but didn't, and so I sank back once more into anonymity.

Another evening Ez and I went alone to a local restaurant, as fine a one as he, Ezra, could afford. He ordered a *risotto,* a cheap and filling meal in itself, and a bottle of cheap wine. It was good and we were hungry. That was all. We sat together while he looked boldly about him, wriggling in his chair, turning to examine the faces about him in his bold way, while I sat indifferently across the table eating. Then, we having finished, he pushed back his chair and stood up. I immediately took his heavy coat from the rack near us preparatory to holding it for him that he might slip his arms comfortably into the sleeves.

With that he turned on me, laying me out in no uncertain way for my presumption, jerked the coat out of my hands and, presenting it to the waiter, made him hold it, as he continued scolding me, saying that one didn't do things that way in London. Angry now, I waited, gave my coat to the waiter to hold for me and as the whole restaurant smiled, we made our way to the street.

One evening we went to hear some young men read Ibsen's *Ghosts* aloud to a small group for an hour—for a fee, I suppose. Not a bad idea.

Ezra kept a candle on his mantel continually burning before the photograph of some girl whose identity he never revealed to me. His coffee-making was an important ritual. It was the finest Dutch coffee that could be bought, powdered and carefully guarded in a closed jar. This coffee Ezra would open every morning and prepare by placing a teaspoonful of it on a piece of cheesecloth or fine linen perhaps, stretched somehow over his cup, through which boiling water was poured, a drop or two at a time. This alone, according to the poet, made coffee fit to drink. We shared it between us, strong and good.

And then, the grand finale to my memories of that fabulous

week: he and I went together to the National Gallery to see the Elgin marbles and certain of the pictures upstairs, work of Bellini and the early Renaissance.

They were doing some repair work on the sooted rococo panels of the high ceiling. A light scaffold had been built in the middle of the floor to hold a platform on which two laborers were busily at work.

But there was in this room also a young woman of a certain exceptional attractiveness, a tall, rather wan creature, a curious, detached figure, who, walking about looking from picture to picture, immediately attracted Ezra's notice. Everything else in the room—which but for her, the workmen and myself, was empty of people—disappeared for Ezra. He postured, leaning back on his cane (did he have a cane? perhaps not), his legs apart, his pointed beard atilt, and stared steadily toward her. She, on her part, conscious of his position, began to move her thighs and pelvis in such a way that it became very apparent that she was thoroughly conscious of what was going on. She turned her head away, but it was plain that she was greatly moved and excited.

At this point a snigger sounded from the ceiling. I, from the background, wondered what would happen next. Now Ezra stepped a few paces back and changed the direction of his stare from the young woman to the workmen on their platform and there he remained, staring at them, until they quit their amusement. But by that time the woman was gone—a figure that might well have served as model for the one who, in *Mauberley*, had been likened to a skein of silk blown against the railing.

It was an instructive week for me. We shared a small second-floor room. It was an intense literary atmosphere, which though it was thrilling, every minute of it, was fatiguing in the extreme. I don't know how Ezra stood it, it would have killed me in a month. It seemed completely foreign to anything I desired. I was glad to get away.

Chapter 21
Paris and Italy

In Paris I stopped for a few days with Eliza Anduze, an English-woman living in Paris and well acquainted in government circles. She was a relative or acquaintance of my father's, though in what way I never quite made out, and seemed happy to make the acquaintance of Williams' son, now a physician. She lived simply, even poorly, alone in her apartment, but seemed to have independent means.

The morning after I arrived, waking early, I began to read to myself aloud, though softly, as I lay in bed, from Heine's *Buch der Lieder.* I had only recently got to know Heine well after finding a second-hand copy of his lyrics somewhere in a Leipzig bookstore just before quitting Germany. So there I lay intoning the poems one after another to myself. Beautiful things. I was learning several of them by heart.

"What in the world are you reading?" said Eliza, standing at my open door.

"Reading to myself," I said.

"But what are you reading?"

"Heine's poems."

"Heine? In German?" She was really upset, I know. Realizing that I had been to Leipzig for the past year, she believed me to be partisan of the belligerent Kaiser. That pained her. I put the book down and having dressed, went in to breakfast.

She took me with her the next evening to the Comédie Française, to hear *Le Monde où l'on s'ennuie,* which had a chilling effect on me: remote, stilted, completely artificial.

In the foyer where everyone went to promenade between acts to see and be seen, all I could seem to do was to step on the tail of her gown—in misery. I imagine Eliza found little to be enthusiastic about in her remote young cousin. It was no atmosphere for me. I couldn't wait to be released.

And yet, thinking it over, my awkwardness, reading German poems aloud in *her* house, offensive to her, La Comédie Française, the standardization of the official language—so French! To them the meaning of art is skill, to manipulate the parts to produce an effect diametrically opposed to my own values, my lack of skills forced to proceed without them. Poor Eliza Anduze.

On the train passing Lausanne, a priest in my compartment began to talk to me, a man in his middle thirties, who, spotting me for an American, could not contain his curiosity but must ask me about that miraculous country to the west. What was it like? Was it really as rich as they say? Was it true that anyone could go from the bottom to the top in one lifetime?

I told him that that really was the case. A half-dozen lemons, according to a then popular account, had resulted in a fortune.

He shook his head incredulously. "So it's true after all. Here we are poor, nothing will change that." And you could see that he, poor guy, was really poor indeed. "But America is the country of the future for the Catholic Church." Was I a Catholic? No. "That's too bad"—but that was to be understood. But in America he felt that his church had a great future.

I asked him how far he was going. He said only a few more miles, that he was returning to his parish after a short rest. "You see that little valley going in there among the mountains?" It was just back of the Dent du Midi. "Well, in there they make a very good wine and strong!" he said. "You sit down to the table at a meal and drink that wine. It seems light and innocuous —but when you come to stand up afterward *ça vous coupe les jambes*—it cuts off your legs"—with a violent gesture and a big toothless laugh.

"Wonderful!" I said. "You will find nothing like that in America."

So much has to be left untold; the zeppelin during the last days of my stay in Germany coming down out of the fog over Leipzig while army cars rushed through the streets following it; the Dutch picture galleries; the boat from The Hook to England, as well as the greater part of my trip to join Ed in Italy; coming out of the wintry tunnel under the Alps at Domodossola and seeing the waterfalls leaping from the rocks on all sides above me in a full glory of the Italian sun. I'll never forget that! I must have been a very impressionable young man.

Certainly coming out of the winter of the Swiss tunnel into the brilliance of the Italian sun at Domodossola is beyond adequate description—no art could have equaled it for me. It was a bewilderment, it was incredible!

In Italy Ed took me under his wing, introducing me to the wonders of medieval and renaissance architecture and painting: Siena, in one sudden burst; Bramante's dome of the Duomo; the frescos of Pinturicchio. There was the trip to Fiesole; the golden Greek temples at Paestum; Amalfi, of course; Sorrento; Capri, and the call we made on Elihu Vedder there. Wild Anacapri out on its point of rocks meeting the sea—pre-Christian surely, if anything in Europe is that. The girls carrying baskets of new-picked lemons down the cliff stairs. Pompeii. Naples, where small boys in the street threw stones at us where we stood on the cathedral steps because we insisted on carrying our own luggage.

Ed had a letter of introduction to Vedder from Mr. Crowninshield of the American Academy at Rome. The old boy was glad to see a couple of American kids bent on opening their minds to the beauties of Italy. He lived on a bare height somewhere in the fields of central Capri above the sea, and showed us his device for ridding his studio of flies. The screen door at the entrance was arranged in the usual two panels, one above, one below, a crosspiece at the center. But this crosspiece was set an inch back from the wire mesh, above and below, these edges thus remaining free.

"Flies always want to get out," he explained to us, "and will fly to the screen and the light of day. But we prevent them from escaping by barring the exits. I leave a space for them. Thus I don't have flies." And he didn't, not many.

Ed and I climbed down the cliff from which Tiberius used to throw his women when he tired of them to a small, sloping ledge of bright grass twenty feet below the summit, and lay there stretched out side by side in the sun, isolated and happy, high above the sea, marvelously content. But above us appeared a uniform filled by wildly gesticulating arms and maledictions. The bastard. We had to climb up again.

The forum is too gone for a moving impression of the past, but there were the great baths of Diocletian and the Venus Andromeda which I would stand before until I was ashamed to be seen in its presence.

Once in the hotel restaurant at Siena after bedbugs bedeviled our first night, Ed and I had been served honey for breakfast. As I helped myself, the honey stuck to the serving spoon as usual, and I, as usual, took my own teaspoon in the other hand to gouge it off. Ed, who used to affect white vests when we were younger, looked at me. "What's the matter?" I asked. "Why, if you want more honey," he answered, "take another ladleful." I could see that he was right.

Then good-bye, Ed. From Naples my ship stopped at Palermo with its blinding sunlight for which I had to wear dark glasses. At Palermo I saw the Monreale with its sheet-of-gold mosaics. But as the ship headed for Gibraltar on its way back to the New World, with which my mind was teeming in those days, I began not to feel so well. It was an old German ship. I have forgotten the name. As it went on I developed a severe pain in my right side. Being a physician, I didn't have to ask anyone about it. I stopped smoking, stopped eating, and lay on my deck chair for those two or three days, determined, after having looked at him, I wasn't going to let *that* ship's doctor open *me* up. Not on your life. I'd try to hold out until the next stop and there look up some British army surgeon. At least I'd be on dry land where there was a hospital.

After a night in the hotel at Gibraltar, the ship having gone on, I found myself to be perfectly well. I'd have to wait two weeks for the next boat of the line. With sixty dollars still in my pocket, I decided to see Spain. Never did a mild attack of appendicitis pay off so well. If only I had had a little more experience with the world, what a time I might have had—on sixty dollars!

But at that I didn't do so badly. I especially wanted to see Palos or Huelva, rather, from which Columbus had set sail on his first trip to America; a bare, sandy place among the low dunes, small summer shacks, fronting on the water, and a strong wind blowing seaward. It looked perfect to my purpose—if I should ever have a chance to write of it.

Then Seville, *"El que no a vista Sevilla,"* as Mother would say, *"no a vista maravilla!"* The cathedral there—that mountain—in front of which I caught a beggar changing from his rags into a decent business suit. He smiled at me with a shrug.

In Seville they were having carnival, the streets were crowded. I saw one marvelous kid, she couldn't have been more than fifteen, doing the fandango on the stage of a little booth, with an enthusiastic crowd in front of her, that never to this day have I seen even approached on any more sophisticated stage for brilliance. Had I had the nerve or the insanity to follow the little whore who waved her buttocks at me near the plaza that evening, I don't know where I might not have landed in this world or out of it. But I didn't, and so I am a writer.

Granada—that's the end of the world. But no one, least of all I, had heard of Lorca in those days. I saw spring water running continuously in a narrow runnel down the center of the stone rails beside the slow garden steps—to cool the air under the pomegranate trees. But, as usual, I broke away from the charm of it; from watching the beggars, who to this day wash the sands of the little stream below the Alhambra walls for gold. You may imagine how much of it they find.

I broke away to the bare yellow hills back of the town, to be alone, to shake my shoulders from such impossibilities of past glory. There, or on the way down, rather, I was picked up by a gypsy girl, twelve or fourteen years old, with whom I talked innocently while she guided me out of the village paths where I had been lost. I told her how beautiful she was—though pretty grimy. She told me how beautiful I was. With that we bowed and said good-bye. Just a kid.

At Toledo I spent an evening in a tiny bar among a few drinkers, shepherds, I think, listening to a guy playing a guitar. That's another place in which I might have stayed forever without loss. They might have robbed me, stuck me with a knife and thrown the body over a cliff and no one the wiser for it. As a matter of fact we all drank a few rounds of cheap wine and I went home to my hotel to bed, as usual.

At Toledo—caught, as it were, in the coils of the narrow river deep in the gorge at its feet—lonely as I was, I had the one impression of primitive Spain that is most engraved upon my remembrance. I had gone out to look around when I came to the narrow bridge that connects the citadel, which the place really is, with the outside world.

It is an extremely narrow, old stone bridge that might easily have been constructed by the Romans. No sooner did I get out on it and begin to cross when a big, ragged man, accompanied by two lean-bellied dogs that reached nearly to my shoulders, slouched by followed by a few sheep. Then before I knew it, the old bridge was packed solid with sheep baaing and shoving one another past me, hundreds of them from parapet to parapet. It could have been any moment in the past two thousand years as I stood smelling and feeling the animals flood past me among the rocks on all sides. Then they passed, followed by another ragged shepherd and his hang-headed dog, as large as the others, pacing along behind them.

Another day I saw an oxcart drawn by a yoke of big beasts stalled at the bottom of the steep hill. The load was a heavy one of rock or rubble of some sort, but it didn't look too heavy for the animals who, nevertheless, refused to go on with it.

The carter with a long, pointed stick was standing before them trying to lead them on. No result. He stood at the head of the off beast; then, dancing backward toward the cart, to give them the idea of forward motion, I thought, prodded the ox with his sharp stick, yelled some wild oath first at one of his animals, then the other. No result. The animals refused to budge. At that he stood at one side, lit a cigarette and rested. I thought he had given up.

This turned out to be not so. For I saw at that moment another teamster like the first who was unhitching his yoke from another cart loaded like the one at the bottom, at the top of the hill which he had already succeeded in negotiating.

Now, I thought, they'll hitch the whiffle-tree of that yoke to the end of the pole between the others and together they'll take the second load forward.

The animals from up the hill were wheeled around, placed in front of their brothers. I was waiting to see the harness adjusted, when instead I heard the second fellow cry out to the first, *"Quando usted quiere!"*

Brandishing their sticks, the two men simultaneously let out their shouts, the four oxen started as one and up the hill they went—except that the head pair were *not* fastened to the others in any way. They just walked ahead, unattached; the second pair followed dragging the load.

Then Madrid and the Goyas. El Escorial, nothing like it for bare Spain—though I do remember the odors of a factory for the manufacture of chocolate near the railroad station. There I was conscious of being tracked by a young man, perhaps a government agent. I had seen him also in Granada. We got to talking later. He seemed all right.

Finally I got down from the train across the river from Cordova's low-lying mosque, one of the great Moorish remains—with a Christian chapel disfiguring its superb symmetry at the very center of the perspective. And there I beheld a priest, who, during the service, hawked and spat over the rail while a little altar boy, in a white surplice, looked down from above at me, as I stared at him, and smiled.

Part Two

Chapter 22

First Years of Practice

Home and the practice of medicine to be begun. There was little money. I, of course, hadn't any. I used our front hall as a waiting room and the old kitchen pantry for an office. I walked to my calls or rode a bicycle. Then I hired a little mare, Astrid, for a few months. I made seven hundred fifty dollars my first year. Then late in 1911, I got my first Ford! A beauty with brass rods in front holding up the windshield, acetylene lamps, but no starter! Sometimes of a winter's day I'd go out, crank the car for twenty minutes, until I got it going, then, in a dripping sweat, leave the engine running, go in, take a quick bath, change my clothes then sally forth on my calls. Once the thing kicked back and the handle of the crank hit me above the left eye. It might have been worse. The trick was to use the left hand in cranking, so that when the kickback came the handle would jerk out of the fingers instead of striking the wrist and breaking it. I had used the left hand, got it over the eye instead.

My first case was one of dandruff which I treated with some simple remedy and cured much to everybody's delight. But my office was not in a prominent part of town, and I'm afraid that I didn't inspire much confidence in my potential customers. How could I? I didn't have much confidence in myself and my mind was wild—as anyone, I thought, must have seen.

Floss and I were not yet married but saw each other every day or night: three years is too long to wait to be married. I could see it get a little on Pop's nerves as I wore the streets out between the two houses. Happy days and nights—if lovers are ever happy!

Floss was little more than a kid still and God only knows what I was.

It must have been around the spring of 1912 when it couldn't be borne much longer. I talked with Pop, asking if he didn't think we could fix up the house at 131 West Passaic Avenue for two families, he and Mother to live upstairs and Floss and I below, near the office. He talked with Mother and consented to the change. I was delighted and immediately began to turn things around in my mind, planning enthusiastically and out loud before him just what I'd do and how I'd do it. His expression became icy.

"No," he said, "not while I live in the house. No. I will not permit you to do it. It's still my house as long as I live here."

I was stopped cold. In a fury I told him that *either* I had my way with what was to be mine, or I'd find some other place to live in. He gave me no encouragement, so I turned my back on him, put on my hat—it was about ten in the evening—and left the house.

I couldn't go to Floss at that hour, and besides I wouldn't distress her with such things. It was hard enough for her anyway to put up with my indecisions. So I started walking north along the highway to Hackensack. It was a fine night and I kept walking not knowing what the end might be.

Quit the damned town? Go to upstate New York? I had my license to practice medicine in both New York and New Jersey; Floss would go with me some place where I could afford to live and begin all over again.

I walked until about two in the morning and got almost to Oradel, ten or fifteen miles up the road. Then, having cooled off, I turned around and walked home again.

Poor Mother! She said neither she nor Pop could rest until they heard my latchkey in the door toward dawn. I remember, by the way, what a thrill it was when I got my first latchkey.

The idea of two families in one house was out. I don't think either Pop or I ever so much as mentioned it again. I kept my office where it was, arranged with the Ackers next door for an apartment. Floss and I planned to be married in December. Pa Herman took us to parties at the Liederkranz in New York, and at least once during this engagement period, both Ezra Pound and Hilda Doolittle visited me in Rutherford. Floss was not at ease with either of them, but we all got along together more or less. The Hermans had us to supper one night with wine, Rüdesheimer 1905, I think. Ezra, in an excess of enthusiasm, knowing New Jersey's reputation, stood on his chair at table to kill a mosquito on the ceiling. Pa Herman was patient as usual.

Another evening they had a party for us at which Millard Ashton, one of our friends, much to dear Ezra's annoyance, was acting the clown. At dessert and the passing around of ice cream and cake, said Ezra to the young man, "A special portion with arsenic is being prepared for you in the kitchen."

That summer the Hermans spent at Cook's Falls on the upper Delaware, where I visited them, walking into the fields with Floss, a book always in my pocket—I had to do a lot of readjusting to come out softened down for marriage. Floss and I wandered about fumbling with our emotions. I think that long period of breaking in was all that made our later marriage bearable. I have a snapshot of her standing erect and defiant in a black-berry patch, a picture of a slim-waisted girl that I still look at with amazement. The bride-to-be of the pale young poet and physician, whom surely, at one point or another, she must have thought more than a little weak in the head. She told me later how her family periodically warned her against me and my ways—not her father, however. Paul Herman was himself some-what of the artist. Anyhow at Cook's Falls he loved to fish and would frequently bring in a good string of trout to the hotel kitchen. We sometimes went with him on his rambles.

One day, following him carefully as he approached his favor-ite pool, I saw him unfurl a bit of leaf from the butt of his cigar and flip it into the water. There was a swirl and a flash as the face of the pool was broken and a good-sized trout took the bait. He had boasted that he could catch a trout with the help of no more than a cigar stub and had thus made good on his word.

It was at this time I wrote the poem "A Coronal." Floss

and I would lie among the trees as I read to her. My mind was always rebellious and uneasy. This was my wife-to-be, excluding all the rest. How could one stand or understand it? And yet, there was Flossie, no Venus de Milo, surely—Flossie, in some ways hard as nails, thank heaven. She had to be.

And so to our marriage. After three years of close companionship we had got to know each other pretty well. What had either of us to do with this mummery? To me it more resembled a performance of the Mask and Wig Club than anything serious. I must confess, though, that I was touched, as I stood there waiting, at the sight of the pale girl coming up the aisle toward me on her father's arm. I wanted to go forward to protect her.

After the ceremony the champagne flowed like brook-water; Pa Herman knew how to throw a good party when he wanted to. They roped the front door against us when we wanted to leave. The ride to the city in an open car in December; the holding of another in one's arms, the explorations, the interpenetrations, the grim seriousness of the thing among the confetti and artificial rose petals! We had timed the celebrations so as to be able to take the ship for Bermuda the next day. When Floss had taken the ring to be engraved with the date selected for our nuptials the jeweler said, "Hum, that was clever!"

"What was clever?" said she.

"12-12-12," he showed her. So our marriage was fated to be successful. But they postponed the sailing for five days, and we went instead to Boston to visit Ed there (he was teaching at Boston Tech). He got rooms for us at the Hotel Victoria. Looking for a little diversion the next day, I took Floss out to Concord where, poor child, she was sick on somebody's grave.

Bermuda, after the rough trip down, was tropically beautiful, a relief to us; the small, brightly colored fish in the clear water near the ferry dock, the prolific poinsettias in full flower. Oh, well . . .

After our return from Bermuda, we went to live "at the Ackers'," the former Norsworthy residence, next door to my father's house at 131. There we had two rooms, at least our own, a large front room where I did a little painting now and then, another with twin beds jammed into it, almost filling it, and, luxury of luxuries, such as it was, a private bath. We ate at Mother's table: not much greens, which Floss loved, but plenty of beans, rice, potatoes and meat, thoroughly cooked, the way Pop liked them. It was to be a rough breaking in for both of us.

We were as raw at our pleasure as any other young couple. It astonishes me sometimes to think of it. We enjoyed ourselves, though, in a strange way, knocking down the barriers one by one in our efforts to get to know each other as we went along. I must have done a good deal of painting in those days. I really amused Floss once, I remember, with one of my works. It was painted on a narow wooden panel knocked out of an old door: A narrow stream coursed down the length of it from right to left about which in grotesque positions nude figures of various qualities of sex and age were strewn. To this day Floss laughs to think of it.

We were both puzzled when the young wife began to feel nauseated sometimes in the morning before breakfast. I couldn't believe it was the small amount of arsenic in the pill I was giving her as a tonic after the hard winter. But before we could dwell further on that something occurred to take our minds entirely off the subject.

Dr. Wood, our dentist and a fellow Penn alumnus, told me one day casually, as though in passing, that he wanted me to buy his house at Nine Ridge Road. In my wildest imagination I hadn't even thought of such a thing, so that it caught me quite off my guard. I objected that I couldn't afford such a house, one of the most prominent in town.

"What am I going to do for cash?" I asked him.

He only laughed at me. I confess I was flattered and impressed by his insistence that it would be no trouble at all for me to carry the loan. His wife wanted to move away from the business section, he wouldn't ask me for much down, it was an ideal site for a young physician, which it was . . . And so forth and so forth. I told Floss about it. We realized now that she was pregnant. We couldn't go on living where we were. Why not chance it? I needed a loan. It was impossible for Pop to do anything more for me, so with Flossie's consent I went to her father.

Dr. Wood had named his price. "Offer him five hundred less," said the old man. I carried the news to the doctor. He smiled, but wouldn't come down in his price, so after a few more preliminaries, the deal was closed and we began to get ready to take possession of our magnificent new property.

Neither Floss nor I shall ever forget the day we moved in. You might think it had been the palace of one of the Medici. She was by then heavy with child, at the seventh month in fact.

The big front room, irregularly oblong in shape, had a spot where the floor, due to a failure of the underlying beam, had sunk a good two inches. If you'd jump up and down on the spot the whole house would rattle. The men had put the hogshead of majolica ware just at that spot; Ed had sent it to us from Rome as a wedding present. It was just about all we owned. We looked at each other and shook our heads.

I remember Pop's reaction when I first told him what we had done. I knew he wished he could have helped. He envied Pa Herman his generosity, as if he, my father, Mother too, hadn't carried me long enough. I told him so and reassured him that I had not forgotten. We paid off the interest on the loan regularly but just as regularly Pa Herman gave it back to Floss as a birthday or Christmas present.

We were thrilled with the new house, though the terrace before it was in horrid shape. Single-handed I regraded it, giving it a gentle slope, and filled all the holes, asking the kids next door to keep off. They did and we got to be good friends. Two incidents that arrested me occurred while I was working out there exposed to public view. The first was something said by a colored woman whom I had already got to know pretty well. She stopped and watched me for a moment sweating there with spade and shovel and said, "Doctor, you're taking work away from someone who could use it."

"Looking for a job?" I said. That ended that. But the second incident was different. I had begun to dig a three-foot trench following the foundation along the front of the house. I planned to fill it with leaves and throw back the dirt against the time I'd be ready to plant rhododendrons there. As I sweated at the job a young woman of my acquaintance, passing up the street, paused and said to me, "Happy?"

It stopped me cold.

"Sure, why not?" I said. She laughed and went on.

"What's biting her, I wonder," I said to myself. "But am I," I wondered, "happy? Who can tell?"

The next ten years, from 1912 to 1922, were crowded to the full for me. I was going to pediatric clinics in New York three days a week. First it was the Babies' Hospital for a year and a half, and later the Post Graduate for the same period of time.

Plays seemed to attract me, for about that time I wrote three of them. One, called *Frances for Freedom*, pretty closely followed the pattern of Shaw's *Fanny's First Play* but another was more original. It was about a tough guy breaking up from under into local society. I have always remembered this play because of its theme, for it was one that was later developed with considerable success by Clifford Odets in *Golden Boy*, even to a fight, though with gloves, in a private kitchen. Both these plays I burned later, after having them typed at considerable expense by a New York professional. Too bad.

Chapter 23

Painters and Parties

There was at that time a great surge of interest in the arts generally before the First World War. New York was seething with it. Painting took the lead. It came to a head for us in the famous "Armory Show" of 1913. I went to it and gaped along with the rest at a "picture" in which an electric bulb kept going on and off; at Duchamp's sculpture (by "Mott and Co."), a magnificent cast-iron urinal, glistening of its white enamel. The story then current of this extraordinary and popular young man was that he walked daily into whatever store struck his fancy and purchased whatever pleased him—something new—something American. Whatever it might be, that was his "construction" for the day. The silly committee threw out the urinal, asses that they were. The "Nude Descending a Staircase" is too hackneyed for me to remember anything clearly about it now. But I do remember how I laughed out loud when first I saw it, happily, with relief.

It was then, 1913, that Ezra, in London, got my small book, *The Tempers*, published by Elkin Matthews. It had in it one poem, at least, that he liked: "The Coroner's Merry Little Children." It had in it too, "The Lady of Dusk Wood Fastnesses" to Flossie.

—this house is mad with bells: telephone, back door, front door, office bell. Today I woke up at dawn, it seemed, with the

134

*sharp sound of the office bell in my ears. I half-dressed, went
down and no one was there. No one had been there. It was in
my head. Now the house bell has been ringing. Floss was upstairs. It rang again and again. Floss went down. Someone to
recover the book,* Make Light of It, *which I had just autographed
for the daughter of an old schoolmate.*

Walter Arensberg and Alfred Kreymborg had, together, inaugurated a small poetry magazine called *Others.* Walter retired from his leadership almost at once and thenceforward
devoted his time and resources to pictures.

Grantwood was the focus of all these events. I was hugely excited by what was taking place there. For some unapparent reason, someone, years before, had built several wooden shacks there
in the woods, perhaps a summer colony, why, I cannot say—at
least they were there and were rented for next to nothing. Several
writers were involved, but the focus of my own enthusiasm was
the house occupied by Alfred and Gertrude Kreymborg to which,
on every possible occasion, I went madly in my flivver to help
with the magazine which had saved my life as a writer. Twenty-
five dollars a month kept it going, and the scripts began to come
in. Kreymborg got the money somehow. I never knew how,
though I helped as I could.

Orrick Johns, who had, jointly with Edna St. Vincent Millay,
just won the first *Lyric Year* award, was famed anew at that time
for his "blue undershirts on a line." Orrick and his wooden leg,
sometimes lost or stolen after a drunken spree; Peggy Johns, Malcolm Cowley lived there for a while and Man Ray, looking
suspiciously about, getting ready to quit for Paris. I'll not forget
my rather awed delight at meeting Duchamp, the great Marcel,
who would be there now and again. I could rarely get away
other than on Sunday afternoons.

At Grantwood, the one "big house" was that of Bob Brown.
Elsewhere among those sticks, you'd find Orrick Johns, Alanson
Hartpence and his wife Slade, Man Ray, perhaps Malcolm
Cowley, Peggy Johns, and, as visitors on such occasions, Helen

Hoyt, occasionally Arensberg, Mina Loy, once in a while Marcel Duchamp, Sanborn, myself and several others including, later on, Maxwell Bodenheim. It doesn't sound exciting, but it was. Our parties were cheap—a few drinks, a sandwich or so, coffee— but the yeast of new work in the realm of the poem was tremendously stirring.

I had instinctively avoided a New York City practice just as my son has done. I simply didn't want it. I wanted to live a while, to be myself, and find out what was what. My objectives were long range.

I'd sneak away mostly on Sundays to join the gang, show what I had written and sometimes help Kreymborg with the make-up. We'd have arguments over cubism which would fill an afternoon. There was a comparable whipping up of interest in the structure of the poem. It seemed daring to omit capitals at the head of each poetic line. Rhyme went by the board. We were, in short, "rebels," and were so treated.

That winter began the evening meetings at various hide-outs around Fourteenth Street, either at Kreymborg's place or the rooms of Lola Ridge. She made a religion of it.

Somewhere in there—was it at the first Armory Show or another similar show?—they had poetry readings at which both Mina Loy and I appeared. It was a big place, I remember, blocked off by screens.

That afternoon I read two poems, "Overture to a Dance of Locomotives" and "Portrait of a Woman in Bed." As I started to read this latter a tall, well-dressed woman got up, turned her back on me and walked out. Mina, to my surprise, pronounced me the best of those on the program.

There were parties, mostly of painters, at Arensberg's studio. These were of a different sort from the usual "broke" goings on. Arensberg could afford to spread a really ample feed with drinks to match. You always saw Marcel Duchamp there. His painting on glass, half-finished, stood at one side and several of his earlier works were on the wall, along with one of Cézanne's "Woman Bathers," the work of Gleizes and several others. It disturbed and fascinated me. I confess I was slow to come up with any answers.

One incident at Arensberg's remained well indented on my skull, something that filled me with humiliation so that I can never forget it. After all, most of us were beginners in matters of art, no matter how we might struggle to conceal the fact; bunglers, surely, unable to compete in knowledge with the sophisticates of Montmartre. There was to a great extent a language barrier also. No wonder some wanted to fly off. Anyhow, we were not, or I wasn't, up to carrying on a witty conversation in French with the latest Parisian arrivals.

Seeing on Arensberg's studio wall a recent picture by Duchamp showing five heads, in pastel shades, the heads of five young women in various poses and called, I think, "The Sisters" (I think it was a picture of his own sisters), I wanted to say something to him about it. He had been drinking. I was sober. I finally came face to face with him as we walked about the room and I said, "I like your picture," pointing to the one I have mentioned.

He looked at me and said, "Do you?"

That was all.

He had me beat all right, if that was the objective. I could have sunk through the floor, ground my teeth, turned my back on him and spat. I don't think I ever gave him that chance again. I realized then and there that there wasn't a possibility of my ever saying anything to anyone in that gang from that moment to eternity—but that one of them, by God, would come to me and give me the same chance one day and that I should not fail then to lay him cold—if I could. Watch and wait. Meanwhile, work.

Duchamp was working then on his glass screen. It was in the studio as yet unfinished and was said to be a miracle of leaded-glass workmanship. I bumped through these periods like a yokel, narrow-eyed, feeling my own inadequacies, but burning with the lust to write.

Once I attended a *soirée* given at Grantwood by the plutocrat of the colony, Bob Brown. But I was not a drinker, and so found myself disinclined to take part in the wilder, later parties Bob gave. For that reason I didn't get to know him then, to my regret, as well as I did some of the other *habitués*.

As he said he'd do, Bob had made his hundred thousand somehow or other, and quit work for life. He'd just returned from a trip around the world and here he was—one of us. It was a fabulous moment. He had, I heard it said (I only saw it when it was empty), a garden urn, on the concrete railing of his front porch, full of old Roman coins to which anyone who wished could help himself as he pleased. Many did. The coins soon disappeared.

Everything was not by any means reflected upon that surface. Here was my chance, that was all I knew. There had been a break somewhere, we were streaming through, each thinking his own thoughts, driving his own designs toward his self's objectives. Whether the Armory Show in painting did it or whether that also was no more than a facet—the poetic line, the way the image was to lie on the page was our immediate concern. For myself all that implied, in the materials, respecting the place I knew best, was finding a local assertion—to my everlasting relief. I had never in my life before felt that way. I was tremendously stirred.

Kreymborg was writing his verse plays for Poet Mimes. The Provincetown Players had opened in MacDougal Street with some of the earlier O'Neill works and, shortly after, Kreymborg told us that they had offered to put on his *Lima Beans*. It had three parts: the soubrette, to be played by Mina Loy; the huckster, to be undertaken by the promising young sculptor, Bill Zorach; and I was to play the lover.

Mina was very English, very skittish, an evasive, long-limbed woman too smart to involve herself, after a first disastrous marriage, with any of us—though she was friendly and had written some attractive verse. I remember her comment on one of Kreymborg's books, *Mushrooms*—something to the effect that you couldn't expect a woman to take a couch full merely of pink and blue cushions too seriously. But when the Provincetown Players had accepted Kreymborg's play, Mina had consented to take the lead. I was to play opposite her.

It was tough, but I somehow got in to rehearsals from Rutherford three nights a week after office hours. It fascinated me. I had had some minor experience on the stage at college and, who could tell? there, perhaps, lay the future.

Anyhow we set to work. Often we had to wait in that narrow, cold hall while one of O'Neill's plays was being drilled. I can remember the one playlet *Fog*. I've never forgotten it—a small boat offshore, half seen before a fog improvised with a voile curtain of some sort, and men calling to each other in a dangerous situation. Out in the hall stood old man O'Neill, he of Monte Cristo fame, yelling out directions and suggestions to his son and the actors. Very moving.

Then would come our turn to run through our lines. Bill Zorach, looking like Harpo Marx, would call out his wares and I'd do my best—but it was a fragile bit. I had to take Mina in my arms at one point and kiss her. I couldn't see it as a passionate gesture but rather as a glancing sort of china-doll kiss. I went through it but someone in the dark of the hall yelled up at me, "For God's sake, kiss her!"

It wasn't my idea of the part. As a result no one was satisfied. We played it three nights. A qualified success.

One night, the night, I think, of the opening or more likely the dress rehearsal, after I had called for Mina at her Fifty-seventh Street apartment, I left my brief case with all my recent work in it in a taxi. Completely forgot it. The loss seemed irreparable. It was that evening she asked me what my annual income was from my practice of medicine. The question struck me as odd. I told her three thousand dollars.

A few days later I received a letter from Burgess Williams or perhaps some other Williams who lived in the same building next to Carnegie Hall where Mina had her room. The taxi man had opened my case, seen the name Williams and when the Williams to whom he delivered it saw the name, he was quick-witted enough to claim it and return it to me.

I too wanted to have a play on that stage and wrote one calling for an improvised curtain made of newspaper with a flagpole sticking through the center of it over the first seats of the audience. At the start of the play the paper screen was ripped down by the actors and the play was on. A lascivious sort of action of some sort with players designated as Bright Young Men, etc., which Mattie Josephson said reminded him of Dekker or whoever it might be. The whole piece disappeared.

Then, and this was important, I wrote my first small playlet in verse called *The Old Apple Tree*. Floss was fascinated by it. The blossoms were her daughters called upon by the bees, their suitors. I remember at one time the old tree-mother offered one of the callers a cup of tea, that is, the sap of the tree itself.

"It's bitter," said the man.

"Have some more," said she.

Kreymborg lost the manuscript. I was sick over it. He said he just didn't know what had happened to it. Then I had another small play and he and I were to present a bill at the Bramhall Theatre. A wonderful chance. But nothing happened. I was busy with my work and thought there'd been a delay of one sort or another until one day in the city I asked Kreymborg what had happened.

He was embarrassed and said he was broke and a man had to try to make a dollar here and there as he could and that in fact he was putting on a bill with Edna St. Vincent Millay, a play called *Da Capo* and did I mind?

Did I mind? Well, it knocked me cold. I saw the bill and really enjoyed it, but from that time on Kreymborg and I didn't get on so well.

I remember one day I dropped in on him at one of his small diggings and found Gertrude's mother there with her. I didn't know until after how matters stood. The apartment was on two levels, the room where Kreymborg and the ladies were sitting was a foot or two higher than where I had entered. My entrance, completely unexpected, had apparently broken up an embittered, at least serious and insistent conversation, between mother, daughter and Kreymborg, for on seeing me he made a dash and a leap to greet me. But as he dove through the low connecting doorway his head struck the top of the frame full force. It's a wonder it didn't kill him. The tension was relieved all right!

Once Mina invited me to meet John Craven. I was a bit late and the small room was already crowded—by Frenchmen mostly. I remember, of course, Marcel Duchamp. At the end of the room was a French girl, of say eighteen or less, attended by some older woman. She lay reclining upon a divan, her legs straight out before her, surrounded by young men who had each a portion of her body in his possession which he caressed attentively, apparently unconscious of any rival. Two or three addressed themselves to her shoulders on either side, to her elbows, her wrists, hands, to each finger perhaps, I cannot recall—the same for her legs. She was in a black lace gown fully at ease. It was something I had not seen before. Her feet were being kissed, her shins, her knees, and even above the knees, though as far as I could tell there was a gentleman's agreement that she was not to be undressed there.

I looked and turned to Mina. But she was engrossed with Craven. I was introduced to the man after a drink or two and in the end wandered wearily home as was my wont.

Later Mina married Craven and went to Central America with him where he bought and rebuilt a seagoing craft of some sort. One evening, having triumphantly finished his job, he got into it to try it out in the bay before supper. He never returned. Pregnant on the shore, she watched the small ship move steadily away into the distance. For years she thought to see him again—that was, how long ago? What? Thirty-five years. He was reputed to be a son of Oscar Wilde and had been a capable boxer and boxed in fact with Jack Johnson once in Spain.

I remember Skip Cannell telling me once of big boy Johnson's actions during a near riot in a café in Paris. They began tearing the chairs apart for clubs. When it was all over and the lights went on again they found the World's Champion under a table scared stiff.

"That's not the kind of fight I'm interested in," he said frankly.

I know Kreymborg, who retired from the editorship of *Others* after the first ten or twelve issues or so, thought I had sabotaged it at the end. But it was finished. It had published enough to put a few young men and women on their feet—Kreymborg himself, Maxwell Bodenheim, myself—but had really no critical standards and offered only the scantiest rallying point for a new movement. It was individually useful to many of us; it gave a hearing to us in the face of the universal refusal to publish and pay for available new work by young poets. It helped break the ice for further experimentation with the line, but that was all. The places at Grantwood were being abandoned: the First World War was on.

The parties around the Fourteenth Street, however, went on, with new figures constantly being added. John Reed, Kay Boyle, Louise Bogan, Louise Bryant. I particularly remember one night when Reed showed up. A plump, good-natured guy who had taken the bit in his teeth and was heading out. He played with the poem but was not primarily interested in writing. The story went around that he was a sick man, had already had one kidney resected, but it didn't seem to put much of a crimp in his style. He looked at us as if he couldn't quite make out what we were up to, half-amused, half-puzzled. Louise Bryant, his wife, who was with him that night, had on a heavy, very heavy, white silk skirt so woven that it hung over the curve of her buttocks like the strands of a glistening waterfall. There could have been nothing under it, for it followed the very crease between the buttocks in its fall. No fault there. She too looked to be outward bound along with John of Portland, Oregon. Wise man he to get started early.

Chapter 24

Our Fishman

One of the outstanding examples of instruction in the virtues was that held before us unflaggingly by a young Italian named Joe who came to our back door selling fish in 1913. I once asked him his last name. He told me but I have forgotten it. That was Joe. I wanted to dedicate one of my books to him. The name is recorded somewhere in my files.

He'd been coming next door with fish for sale before we moved into Nine Ridge Road. We often saw him but he made no move to approach us until one day we asked if his fish was good and were told, "The best."

From that day, when we first made our bid, Joe stopped at our house with his wares for thirty years, twice a week, winter and summer. Never in that time did he sell us an inferior morsel of seafood. Never did I hear him open his mouth except to answer a question as to the sort or price of the produce he sold.

He would appear in a workman's coat and cap, pushing his small three-wheeled cart uphill, where we lived, back it in toward the curb and, coming to the back door, in a soft voice, his face quiet, hardly smiling, go over his list. Sea bass, haddock, bluefish, fresh cod, porgies. Then Floss would give her order, he'd go out to his cart, clean and cut his fish, weigh it and bring it in on a tin plate. Then Floss would hand him the china plate on which the fish would be deposited—absolutely impersonally —he'd take his money and off he'd go. If you said, "Not today," unless there was some good reason, he would not stop the next time. He liked regular customers and served them as such; what he had was for them.

For thirty years he'd pick up his fish at the Fulton Market in New York, arrive with his basket on his shoulder here on the 7:45 train, go from the station to the empty lot back of a machine shop on Erie Avenue, where he kept his cart leaning against a wall, stow his fish in ice there and start out on his route.

He'd come to us two days a week, that is, to the east side of town. On other days he had similar routes about the west side. One day he'd go across the tracks to East Rutherford and on Saturdays, if he got enough orders, he'd come out with lobsters, crabs, oysters and clams as it might be. Always the best and though the prices were high, the fish were always your money's worth, exceptional in being fresh from the sea, fish of superior quality. For thirty years he never failed to appear.

It was he who introduced us to whiting, "frost fish" he called them. They'd be picked up frozen at the beach where they had been driven by larger fish. He would occasionally come up with Atlantic Coast salmon, a red snapper at certain seasons, smelt or if the market was favorable, some other novelty or superior buy.

On very bad days when he couldn't push his cart because of the icy streets or deep snow, he'd go it with his basket on his shoulder, but that was not often—a compact, well-proportioned young man with mild, intelligent eyes, a soft voice, never raised above a quiet statement of the best of what he had for sale.

We heard, possibly from him, that he had several children. Floss always assumed that he lived in New York City. She thinks she still remembers, in the later years, a boy who once or twice made the rounds with him.

Early in the afternoon, if by that time he had not entirely emptied his barrow, he'd turn off to one of the streets at the bottom of the hill near the meadows, in the poorer section of town where he'd sell what he had left at half price.

What can he have made in the day's turnover of one hundred pounds of fish! I don't know. Certainly not more than ten dollars or fifteen dollars at the most, I imagine. Fish was pretty cheap in those days. Floss says she seldom paid him more than a dollar.

His wife may have worked also. Maybe in the end the children took over, as often happened in such cases. He may still be alive.

But early in the 1940's he began to slow up. Said he had rheumatism, though Floss was pretty sure it was his heart. He looked thin and pale. Then he stopped coming. He had told Kitty Hoagland he thought he had cancer of the stomach, as plain as that. No one took his place. Like our old cat, who after twelve years went down to the cellar one night, lay under an old chair and died, he must have gone home and given up the ghost.

Chapter 25

The Waste Land

These were the years just before the great catastrophe to our letters—the appearance of T. S. Eliot's *The Waste Land*. There was heat in us, a core and a drive that was gathering headway upon the theme of a rediscovery of a primary impetus, the elementary principle of all art, in the local conditions. Our work staggered to a halt for a moment under the blast of Eliot's genius which gave the poem back to the academics. We did not know how to answer him.

Marianne Moore, like a rafter holding up the superstructure of our uncompleted building, a caryatid, her red hair plaited and wound twice about the fine skull, though she was surely one of the main supports of the new order, was no luckier than the rest of us. One night (Mina Loy was there also) we all met at some Dutch-treat party in a cheap restaurant on West Fifteenth Street or thereabouts. There must have been twenty of us. Marianne, with her sidelong laugh and shake of the head, quite child-like and overt, was in awed admiration of Mina's long-legged charms. Such things were in our best tradition. Marianne was our saint—if we had one—in whom we all instinctively felt our purpose come together to form a stream. Everyone loved her.

The Dial, with Scofield Thayer's money back of it, was at the gate. *Others*, the now aging pioneer of these arts was (after fifteen issues or so) yielding in interest to Kreymborg's preoccupation with the drama, his verse plays.

Mencken's *The American Language* stood in the background as a sort of formal liturgy. Men like Marsden Hartley, the painter, would occasionally join our parties. No one had any money, but there was excitement and a sense of the conjunction of all the arts (*The Seven Arts* was an important publication of the moment, as was *The Soil*—three issues—of R. J. Coady, which came later). Each was an unconscious collaborator in fostering the new spirit.

Some of the issues of *Others* were landmarks. Never shall I forget our fascination with Mina's "Pig Cupid, his rosy snout rooting erotic garbage."

Amy Lowell had written to Bodenheim saying she wished she had "seen" his image of a brown cloud. I saw her once, at a party in her apartment at the Belmont Hotel, pontifical, but rather self-conscious, protecting her privileges as a wealthy woman, of which she was none too sure, and smoking, though not self-consciously, her fat cigar. I had nothing much to say to her.

Once she invited Bogey to visit her at Brookline. She must have sent him carfare. When he arrived he found a large house embowered in trees and surrounded by a high iron fence. Entering the grounds, almost at once he was set upon by several large dogs. Perhaps their intention was to be no more than playful but he had a time with them; they knocked him about, tore his clothes. Only on Miss Lowell's hearing the uproar and discovering his plight was Bogey able to escape to the house. There his hostess took care of him, refreshed him and, in the end, bought him a new suit.

Bodenheim stuttered badly, but not when the cadences of verse carried his voice forward. He told me that at one point in his career he had been a U. S. Marine. The training at Parris Island being severe, Bodenheim soon found he had had enough of it. I remember he spoke of the pace: in a broiling sun, full equipment and carrying a heavy pack, bayonets set, you drilled sometimes by the hour; advanced, at a run, so many paces, then, at command, dropped on your face in the dirt. You got tired of it. It was before the First World War, no great pressure on him to stick, so he decided to quit.

Whatever the procedure is I don't know, perhaps he was insubordinate or tanked himself up or did something otherwise improper. He was court-martialed. At the end, the officer in charge asked him if he had anything to say in his own defense. He stood up straight, his flat face and forget-me-not-blue eyes straight before him and said, stuttering as only he could stutter, "You are uh uh uh no more uh than the sh sh sh sh shadow of a mu mu mu man."

That finished him. His poems were always colorful and their images sensitive and well-observed.

What were we seeking? No one knew consistently enough to formulate a "movement." We were restless and constrained, closely allied with the painters. Impressionism, dadaism, surrealism applied to both painting and the poem. What a battle we made of it merely getting rid of capitals at the beginning of every line! The immediate image, which was impressionistic, sure enough, fascinated us all. We had followed Pound's instructions, his famous "Don'ts," eschewing inversions of the phrase, the putting down of what to our senses was tautological and so, uncalled for, merely to fill out a standard form. Literary allusions, save in very attenuated form, were unknown to us. Few had the necessary reading.

We were looked at askance by scholars and those who turned to scholarship for their norm. To my mind the thing that gave us most a semblance of a cause was not imagism, as some thought, but the line: the poetic line and our hopes for its recovery from stodginess. I say recovery in the sense that one recovers a salt from solution by chemical action. We were destroyers, vulgarians, obscurantists to most who read; though occasionally a witty line, an unusual reference, or a wrench of the simile to force it into approximation with experience rather than reading—bringing a whole proximate "material" into view—found some response from the alert.

Practice was going well. My wonderful friends, the Wops of Guinea Hill, were calling me regularly now that their old friend Doctor Calhoun, who had first introduced me to them, was getting tired. At one time during those years I "gave birth," as one woman phrased it, to nearly every baby born on those streets above the old copper mines.

The Monacos, the Albinos, the Coggianos, the Petrillos, all of them had me. I'll never forget some of my predicaments. Such as the day when I had an oldish woman with a retarded placenta. Some still older neighbor came with an empty bottle when I had the undelivered placenta in my fingers but could not effectively withdraw it. The old gal presented the empty bottle to the patient and jabbered to her in Italian. I looked up. The woman in the bed, surrounded by at least eight friends and neighbors, her husband and several kids among them, pulled in her breath and, putting the neck of the empty bottle to her mouth, gave an awful heave. That did the trick: my hand holding the placenta was expelled forthwith! I shook my head and began to clean up.

Another time, on a cold winter's night, in a tiny house of two rooms, one above the other, I had a good woman down across the bed, her husband holding her in the armpits across from me, and I with forceps on the infant's head doing my best for her.

I had been at this for an hour or more, not even a pot of sterile water in the place or any heat or any way to get it. I was pulling with all my strength when the hydrocephalic head burst and the delivery went on without further incident. She was up the next day doing the washing.

You always had to have a drink with the uncles and grandfather at the successful completion of the birth operation. I had plenty, mostly anisette or maybe it was authentic rye. But one time I got a mouthful that really knocked me. Politeness or no politeness, I spit it into the sink. It was distilled from an ordinary kettleful of mash of some sort, the essences rising in a rubber tube tied to the ceiling at one point and descending gradually from there to a bottle in the sink where the distillate was collected. Wow!

Once at Coggiano's, Joe, at three in the morning after the job was done said to me, "Doc, I'm going to ride back with you to Rutherford Avenue. How're you going?"

Through the cemetery.

"O. K." I noticed he had a gun in his coat pocket.

I drove along the road, not being sure where exactly I stood, when at the cemetery exit he told me to stop. I stopped and he got down.

"What's it all about?" I said.

"Oh," he replied, "I saw a couple of my wife's cousins from Newark looking at your car. They're no good. But if they knew I was in with you they wouldn't bother you."

"Well, thanks," I said. "What are you going to do now?"

"Walk back. Go ahead. See you tomorrow."

This was the man who later, during Prohibition, made wine for us, a barrelful, out of grapes we bought for him. It was good, too. He wanted the lees, which we gave him. He said the second working was the best. The whole house was full of the odor all during the weeks and the cellar full of fruit flies; but it really was worth it.

They did their very best for me. I never knew better people. One night, while I was sleeping across three chairs (I didn't trust the beds) they put clean sheets down for me and gave me a fresh pillowcase. But when I awakened during one of the woman's noisier moments, the bedbugs were all over that whiteness.

When I'd go home, at three A.M. let's say, I'd get into the dry bathtub, overcoat, shoes and all and undress by stages, dropping each garment on the floor outside the tub after I had inspected it. I'd find three or four riders each time I'd do it. One day in summer after I'd followed the ritual, the day after a delivery, I suddenly bethought myself of my straw hat. Pulling down the leather band inside, there she was! big as a lentil and as plump. I got out of the car, found some roadside dust an inch thick and put her to sleep in it.

Chapter 26

Charles Demuth

Poor old Charley Demuth, this was before the days of insulin, and he was dying of diabetes. His studio then was the third floor front in one of the buildings of Washington Square South. He called me there one day to see him. He wanted me to inspect his back, which looked as though a young tiger had clawed it from top to bottom. They were deep, long digs, recently scabbed over. Charley was worried about infection.

"What in God's name happened to you?" I asked him.

"Do you think it is dangerous?" said he.

"No. But how did you get such digs?"

"A friend."

"Charming gal," said I thoughtlessly.

Demuth also was interested in writing. He had a style reminiscent of Whistler's, whom I have reason to believe he sedulously copied, and did some creditable work in it. I wonder what has become of his play.

Upon his return to this country Demuth was in bad shape. That, I think, was when I first saw his mother. She was a horse of a woman, a strange mother for such a wisp of a man: he was lame, tuberculous, with the same sort of chin as Robert Louis Stevenson and long, slender fingers. He had an evasive way of looking aslant at the ground or up at the ceiling when addressing you, followed by short, intense looks of inquiry.

His mother had taken him home to Lancaster, Pa., to care for him. Her small city back yard, not more than twenty-five by thirty feet, surrounded by a high board fence with a rectangular path around it bordering the narrow beds, was where he did most of his flower paintings.

Dr. Allen opened a sanatorium for the dietary treatment of diabetes at Morristown that year. Demuth was one of his first patients. His intake was reduced to the caloric minimum. The result was frightening. Charley faded to mere bones, but he was able to live. They occasionally permitted him to be taken home to us for a short visit but I had to return him the same evening. He brought with him a pair of scales and weighed his food carefully. I never saw a thinner active person (this, as I say, was before the discovery of insulin), who could stand on his feet and move about.

I visited Demuth several times while he was at Dr. Allen's sanatorium and once, I think, I took Marianne Moore with me. At least she went to see him there and he was grateful to her for it. We had great talks. He always called me Carlos and once painted a "literary" picture around my name and a poem I had written to "The Great Figure" (the figure 5 on the side of a fire truck in wild transit through the New York streets). Insulin came in just in the nick of time to save Charley from dissolution, but he was careless and died later anyway while on his way home to Lancaster, either from lack of insulin or an overdose; I was never able to get the answer. During those days he once decorated the side of a barn near his home with original designs on the theme of the hex insignia common in that country. I don't know which barn it was, but the innovation was successful with the local people.

In the spring of 1916, before our entry into the war, we threw one big party in Rutherford. Floss was six months pregnant with our second son. She wonders today how she did it. It began of a Sunday morning, before noon, I think. The Walter Arensbergs stayed only a short time, but most of the other guests had to be thrown out early Monday morning. We wondered what the town

would think, but the town, as on many other occasions in the
past, behaved beautifully.

We fed 'em and wined 'em all day long. They were under the
cherry tree when the snapshot was made of the Arensbergs, M.
Gleizes, Marcel Duchamp, Kreymborg, Sanborn, Man Ray, Hartpence and Bodenheim. In another picture were their wives and
sweethearts, Gertrude Kreymborg among them. There were besides Ferdinand Rhyer, and Skip Cannell leaping upon the trunk
of a car which was on its way to my brother's to fetch ice that
Sunday. I was afraid he would be thrown off and injured. Duchamp was much amused at Bodenheim's tragic posturing. We
were in and out all day over the lawn. If anything was said I've
forgotten it. Yet it was a good party.

After digging up and removing the stump of a chestnut oak in
the back yard, taking out the grape vines and the grape arbor,
and building a trellis for roses along the top of the bank facing
the street, I began to make myself an outdoor stage for the plays
I was writing. First I had Tom Hairston, a big colored man in
the neighborhood, haul with his team Doc Woods's single garage
down from the extreme southeast corner of the yard to a place
nearer the street. My son Bill was big enough by that time to sit
astraddle one of Tom's horses and have his picture taken there.

The whole back lawn, thus cleared and screened from public
view, sloped, however, from the rear of the yard toward the house.
I reversed that, built the back higher, leveled it, then gave it a
sharp drop in front and the rest of the yard a tilt from the house
outward toward what might be called the orchestra pit—where
we first had planted roses but later grew cabbages.

We gave one performance, not a play, in that theatre. Four
acts. Bill was about five years old and wore a bunny costume, pale
blue with long ears. He danced with Jane Grafe, who wore a
similar costume. He has yet to live it down when his younger
brother is in the mood. Peggy Orr, a plump fairy, did a moon
dance, and we had a professional, Charles Henri, for an adult
interpretive dance, Debussy's "Sunken Cathedral," and several
other numbers. But the audience of uninvited kids and some
grown ruffians egging them on from the driveway next door,

whistling in the shrubbery at the rear, made the effects a little precarious.

We used the newly placed garage as a dressing room and entrance on the left and had a piano behind a screen on the path from the house. There were bushes, right, and Ed worked the spotlight from our bathroom window. Thus my theatre in the back yard blossomed and died. We learned at least that much from experience, that without greater privacy, impossible to achieve in that spot, the attempt to give a play there would be impossible.

In the house, "Dudu," Julia Burrell, had come to help Flossie with the work. Kathleen, a young girl, helped also, especially with the children, and "Wee Wee," our friend, who took charge when Paul was born, stood always in the background. There was also Mother Kitty, the black Persian cat, which Kathleen had picked up in the street as a kitten. Three weeks later we all had ringworm on our arms, chests and necks. Soon cured. I took the cat, wrapped it in a towel, and dunked it, head and all, into a pail of weak Creolin solution. It survived and lived twelve years after.

The war was on and Pa Herman, being by birth an East Prussian from near Breslau, was emotionally deeply involved. This marked a basic phase in our lives. I was all for the man whom I profoundly admired. It was a tough spot. We were officially neutral before 1917, but individually most of us were pro-French if not pro-British. But Pa Herman was outspokenly pro-German. He was also president of *the* social club of the town, which met fortnightly, a semi-dress affair, and when the club as a group wanted to write to the President advocating assistance to Britain, he voted no.

A move was made to make the motion unanimous. He again voted no. As a result, when we finally declared war on Germany in 1917, he was put down as a disloyal citizen, and his house was under surveillance by the local vigilance committee, among whom were some of his best friends. This cut him to the quick, since no one in the town could have been a more loyal citizen than he. Never in his life could he have taken part in an underhand action of any sort. In fact, once we were at war, he did everything he was asked to do to assist the government—except one thing. He refused to give up the floor occupied by his printing plant to accommodate Lord Northcliffe whose propaganda against Germany he knew to be mainly lies. He was offered a handsome bribe to get out. He refused. But his three-thousand-dollar Liberty Loan contribution was given in N. Y. City and not Rutherford much to the chagrin of the local committee.

As a result of this and other things, the Hermans left Rutherford permanently, moving forty miles up the Erie to Monroe, New York, just over the Jersey line where they had been spending their summers for many years.

It is incredible how much can happen in a few years—from happiness to disaster. But before the Hermans left Rutherford, since I defended Pa Herman in everything, even my own little mother turned on me. With fury in her eyes she accused me of being pro-German. "You," she said, "who are half-French (which wasn't true by half) and half-English! I can't understand you!" (She never could, unfortunately.) "Now you support the Germans."

That wasn't true. It was true, however, that she was violently anti-Prussian, a childhood inheritance from the Paris just after the War of 1870.

The asinine stories being circulated in the town of a German regiment being recruited in Carlstadt, the next town but one to the north of us, infuriated me. Our dear Wee Wee, Louise, came from Carlstadt, as did several other of my friends. I immediately joined the Carlstadt Turnverein where the mythical company was training and had a marvelous time of it.

One of the local physicians in Rutherford even wrote a letter to the papers calling me a pro-German and telling people not to consult me. Later the same mouths were calling me a Communist, saying that Flossie had gone abroad to divorce me because of my lascivious life. I just kept writing my protests into poems, essays, plays and reviews.

His change of residence because of the way the town had treated him was disastrous for Pa Herman. First he bought a run-down farm on the Harriman side of the town. He plunged too heavily, at a bad time, in building a stone house and barns, and in cows, fruit trees, horses, pigs and chickens. Flossie's elder sister, after breaking up with my brother, Ed, walked out with a married man. This really ended Rutherford for Pa Herman, and sent him permanently to live in Harriman. Then Paul, his only son, Flossie's fourteen-year-old brother, tripped over a strand of barbed wire hidden in the grass at the top of a steep cut, fell, and was accidentally shot and killed by his own gun which slid after him down the bank.

Nevertheless, Floss and I had many happy hours on the farm over those ten or twelve years with the boys as they grew up. Sometimes we'd go to Connecticut where, in a little shack near Grandma Wellcome's place close to the rocky shore, we'd camp out. There were abundant clams to be dug, bathing, walks to take, but Floss was never happy there.

After that we began the summers at Wilmington, Vermont, where Flossie's aunt and uncle lived on an old farm near what they called Mount Olga. Hilda, Flossie's aunt, had puchased it many years before for a few hundred dollars. We really enjoyed that, every one of us. There I got to know Flossie's Norwegian forebears and their kindness.

"My beautiful mountain!" Flossie's aunt always called it for it reminded her of her native Norway. She finally had to sell Mount Olga when she was too old and blind to care any more about it. It is still to be found on the map of the geodetic survey, south of Hogback.

There we went summer after summer for a month at a time: once in April to a sugaring off in old man Aldrich's woods, helping to collect the sap buckets for him, watching the steaming pan and all the rest of it. But I never had any real desire to live the year through in Vermont.

Chapter 27

Sour Grapes

Sometimes Floss would go with me to the literary meetings in New York, but for the most part she didn't bother. I went my own way. I imagine it couldn't have been easy for her.

I had up to that time produced three books, *Al que quiere*, which means, unless I am much mistaken, *To Him Who Wants It*. Alfred Kreymborg noticed that the cacophony was a re-echoing of his name and felt complimented. We were very close friends then and I think his surmise was a proper one. The second book followed closely. It was called *Sour Grapes*. This brought the psychiatrists about my head, if not the Freudian analysts.

"*Sour Grapes*! Do you know what that means?" they said.

"No. What does it mean?"

"It means you are frustrated. That you are bitter and disappointed. You are too . . . too . . . You don't really let yourself go. You think you are like the beautiful god, Pan. Ha, ha, ha, ha! The young Frenchmen, yes, they really let go. But you, you are an American. You are afraid" (this from the women and the men also) "you are afraid. You live in the suburbs, you even *like* it. What are you anyway? And you pretend to be a poet, a POET! Ha, ha, ha, ha! A poet! You!"

I got it from all quarters: "*Sour Grapes*, yes, that's regret. *Sour Grapes*—that's what you are and that's what you amount to."

But all I meant was that sour grapes are just the same shape as sweet ones:

Ha, ha, ha, ha!

The third book was *Kora in Hell*. Damn it, the freshness, the newness of a springtime which I had sensed among the others, a reawakening of letters, all that delight which in making a world to match the supremacies of the past could mean was being blotted out by the war. The stupidity, the calculated viciousness of a money-grubbing society such as I knew and violently wrote against; everything I wanted to see live and thrive was being deliberately murdered in the name of church and state.

It was Persephone gone into Hades, into hell. Kora was the springtime of the year; my year, my self was being slaughtered. What was the use of denying it? For relief, to keep myself from planning and thinking at all, I began to write in earnest.

I decided that I would write something every day, without missing one day, for a year. I'd write nothing planned but take up a pencil, put the paper before me, and write anything that came into my head. Be it nine in the evening or three in the morning, returning from some delivery on Guinea Hill, I'd write it down.

I did just that, day after day, without missing one day for a year. Not a word was to be changed. I didn't change any, but I did tear up some of the stuff. Later, having picked up an old book which gave certain brief paragraphs upon a theme and then, with a line under them, gave a brief moralistic statement explaining the text, I did somewhat the same. I read over the improvised bit and, without thought, or too much of it, I interpreted, with what grew below the line, all that was above. It made an attractive novelty. With a preface which I then wrote, it was printed. The cover, with an ovum surrounded by a horde of spermatozoa about it, a dark one being accepted, completed the design.

For each of these three books I paid the Four Seas Company of Boston something in the neighborhood of two hundred and

fifty dollars. They paid the remainder of the publication costs. I
never received a penny, so far as I remember, on sales.

To get a book published! What a marvelous thing it was to
me. My own spillings. What else did I have? Nothing but a wife,
two sons, a father dying of cancer, a mother who was, unquestion-
ably, a foreigner to me.

One evening when Pop was still on his feet but knew he was
doomed, he turned to me at the door of my office and said, "The
one thing I regret in going is that I have to leave her to you.
You'll find her difficult."

The war was in full swing; it was only Pop's illness and the
responsibilities involved that kept me from following my brother
overseas. I was thirty-two and at that time I knew I would not be
drafted. I hesitated several times on the brink of enlisting but
finally didn't go.

There was enough to do at this end. For in the early months
of 1918 what doctors remained here were driven off their feet by
the work.

Pop had finally had to quit going to his office, and, losing
weight and strength rapidly, had resigned himself to his room,
arranging his papers and getting ready to die. That thirty-five-
year trek to the city every day to business in New York was over.
I can clearly remember the last months seeing that figure,
slightly stooped, wearing a sort of dark combination mackintosh
and overcoat, the squarish derby, going down Park Avenue before
my own house every morning for the 8:18. I would still be dressing, perhaps, in the front room. All I could do was shake my
head and feel my heart drop to my very shoes at the sight of him.
What could I do? But finally he was going downhill so fast that
he had to be confined to the house where I visited him every day,
sometimes oftener.

Then the flu hit us. We doctors were making up to sixty calls
a day. Several of us were knocked out, one of the younger of us
died, others caught the thing, and we hadn't a thing that was
effective in checking that potent poison that was sweeping the
world. I lost two young women in their early twenties, the finest

physical specimens you could imagine. Those seemed to be hit hardest. They'd be sick one day and gone the next, just like that, fill up and die.

One day I thought I would be the next. I figured I'd work until noon then quit and hit the pallet. I took some aspirin, worked like mad to finish my list, and at noon it was over. I felt tiptop and kept on working. Everybody in our family was laid low but Pop and myself. Floss and the kids had it and Floss came up with pneumonia; Ed's family had it and one of them also got pneumonia; Mother and her Mexican Indian maid, Marguerita, had it; Kathleen had it. That made twelve people in our immediate family group, among whom I was the only active male, who had it. Fortunately no deaths occurred.

At one point, Grandma, having turned Christian Scientist, and seeing her eldest son so desperately ill of his malignancy, tried to force one of her readers into the case. As far as I was concerned I didn't give a damn if it would please Pop.

"Go ahead," I told him.

He, of course, wanted to please his mother. I think the woman did appear once. But it was only once, believe me! Mother took care of that. I had been, in fact, called the Christian Scientist doctor of Rutherford. When they were ill, seriously ill, or dying they always wanted me: for "diagnosis only," it was made clear, or to sign the death certificate. I paid no attention to them, but always did what I could.

I've seen some terrible cases: a woman with six children living over a tobacco shop who died following a criminal abortion; a case of placenta previa with every joint in her body infected (I drained them one after the other over a period of at least three months while she lay there) and she got well; an untreated case of diphtheria strangling on the floor because of an excess of religious fervor on the part of the parents; a woman shrieking in a room over a candy store from an inoperable cancer of the uterus while her bemused husband, overwhelmed by doctrinaire convictions, looked at her with stony eyes.

Mother didn't figure things my way. Where I could smile, she went into a frenzy of outraged dignity of understanding.

"What! You a doctor, letting a stupid woman like that come

in and put herself above you to take care of your own father when he is dying! I don't understand you."

"But, Mother, she can't do any harm, and if it makes Pop happier, what harm can it do?"

I suppose her rage was partly induced by the way she had fought with the old woman in the past. Be that as it may, the poor reader never got in the house again—nor Grandma, either, as far as I know. Pop was marvelous, as he was always, anyway, when it came to silent resignation to events.

Poor, darling mother, she had her way, little as it got her. I could only chuckle at it and applaud her. I guess I was a strange son in her eyes.

The epidemic over, April 1918 was as lovely as ever. The war was on its way out; German ambitions would be beaten, and I had an invitation to go to Chicago to read my poems in the studio of a certain Ann Morgan. I was to go alone. Kreymborg had preceded me by a month or so, and it was a great occasion.

I had never been to Chicago. I was to stay at the house of Mitchell Dawson, whose old mother was a daughter of pioneers in the state. She was then in her seventies. She told me she had decided for herself to take an interest in what the young people were doing to keep from dying of ennui. Mitch met me at the station and drove me to his home through a wild April storm. Later in the day I went out for a walk along the lake front and was amazed at the height and power of the waves which pounded in over the barriers.

I talked that night before some press club, read some poems and recited, improvising as I went, the story I later wrote for *The Knife of the Times,* "The Buffalos." I never performed better. You could hear them breathe; it nearly frightened me out of my purpose. Ben Hecht, Carl Sandburg, Mitch Dawson and Marion Strobel were there. I later wrote the poem, "A Goodnight," for Marion Strobel. Harriet Monroe particularly admired it.

It was April, the air next day was delicious. It was a romantic interlude. So much so that on the return to Newark and home the mood continued with a girl bound for the East to meet and marry a student about to graduate from West Point. We sat up until late that night, together, after she found out that I was a writer, a poet. Women are strangely impressionable before such apparitions. She seemed *not* to want to go on with her journey.

When I arrived home I was dazed to realize that I in fact *was* married, and when I greeted my kids I couldn't imagine what had happened to me.

Chapter 28

The Baroness

Along with everything else I was still going in to the city Mondays, Wednesdays and Fridays, to pediatric clinics, first to the Babies', then the Post Graduate Hospitals, for advanced training. It was tiresome, hot work in summer, and in winter the commuting was hard, but I enjoyed it. On Fridays, which was my day off, I'd stop over sometimes for a party during the evening. The group often met on the second floor of a small Fourteenth Street apartment, most often at Lola Ridge's, that Vestal of the Arts, a devout believer in the humanity of letters; narrow quarters where anyone might on occasion show up.

I can't remember all the names, but once, Mayakofsky, the Russian poet, appeared with his friend and manager who was wearing a particolored vest, half green and half white. Mayakofsky read aloud for us his "Willie the Havana Street Cleaner." A big man, he rested one foot on top of the studio table as he read. It was the perfect gesture. He had a good voice, and though no one understood a word he said, we were all impressed by the tumbling sounds and his intense seriousness. I remember there were two giggling poets of the smarter and younger generation who, while thinking him wonderful, were more, as far as I could tell, impressed by his size than by anything else. Two nice little "girls." For myself it sounded as might *The Odyssey* from the mouth of some impassioned Greek.

Scofield Thayer, so the rumor ran, had proposed to Marianne

Moore who had begged off, though continuing to work at the *Dial* office. Kenneth Burke later took over Marianne's *Dial* job.

Plenty was happening to me those days. *The Little Review* had been using some poems by a huge mountain of a man from Maine, weighing three hundred pounds, according to Marsden Hartley, and named Wallace Gould. Marsden introduced him to me. Marsden in those years was a kind of grandpapa to us all, male and female alike. But he had a face that doomed him, the nose of a Wellington projecting from the edge of his cheeks like a medieval pike's point. But to get back to Wallace Gould. I was fascinated by the poems' romantic tenor, I suppose, but there was more than that to them. Gould used the local material in a broad way with loose, undulant lines that I greatly admired. In fact, it was not the nostalgic glamour of these Victorian passages at all, but the firmness of the images and a smoothness of diction that I praised to Margaret Anderson and Jane Heap.

Visiting Margaret Anderson's and Jane Heap's apartment— with its great bed hanging from four chains from the ceiling— was an experience: Jane Heap looked like a heavy-set Eskimo, but Margaret, always more than a little upstage, was an avowed beauty in the grand style. In later years she was a friend of Mary Garden and Georgette Le Blanc.

At their apartment I also saw for the first time, under a glass bell, a piece of sculpture that appeared to be chicken guts, possibly imitated in wax. It caught my eye. I was told it was the work of a titled German woman, Elsa von Freytag Loringhoven, a fabulous creature, well past fifty, whom *The Little Review* was protecting. Would I care to meet her, for she was crazy, it was said, about my work.

I wrote, fatally, to Margaret or Jane, saying I wanted to meet the woman. They agreed I was precisely the one who should meet her and defend her. But unfortunately she was at that moment in the Tombs under arrest for stealing an umbrella.

Briefly: I went to the Tombs on the day of her release, met her, took her to breakfast somewhere on Sixth Avenue near Eighth Street, and promised to see her again soon. She was about fifty at the time, a woman who had been perhaps beautiful. She spoke with a strong German accent and at the moment was earning a pittance in the city posing in the nude as an artists' model. She was quite in demand—a lean, masculine figure.

Yes. I met her, all right! Once later she had an intimate talk with me and advised me that what I needed to make me great was to contract syphilis from her and so free my mind for serious art.

She was a protégé of Marcel Duchamp. She sent me a photo of herself, 8 × 10, nude, a fine portrait, said to have been taken by him—a picture I kept in my trunk for years, finally handing it on to Berenice Abbott. I was sick of seeing it lying around. A first-rate piece of photography, though.

The Baroness pursued me for several years, twice coming to Rutherford, of which more later.

At about this time Wallace Gould arrived in New York from his Maine hide-out and almost immediately found that it would be impossible to support himself here. Some woman who admired his work had loaned Wally an apartment. When I found him he had on a black stock, a black suit with great white cuffs, and if he wasn't trembling with fright, he wasn't far from it.

That day, in fact within the hour, he had been standing at the bottom of the stairs, his hand on the newel post, when his hostess had come downstairs had pressed her breast upon the back of his hand, pinning it there, so to speak. He had been too frightened to withdraw the hand, and there she had him.

The pupils of his eyes must have been half an inch across. "I'm up shit creek!" were his exact words. He had almost dropped dead of annoyance, or so he told me, and begged me to get him out of there as fast as I could. "I'm broke," he said in terror. "What am I to do?"

It was around Christmas. "Look," I said, "get your stuff and come out to Rutherford with me. I've got the car at the door."

He stayed with us all winter, giving little Bill piano lessons for his board, though I hadn't asked it. But when March arrived the Indian blood in his veins—he was quarter Abnaki Indian on his mother's side—asserted itself and he packed his kit. I gave him twenty dollars or so to start him off. He went by train to Washington, D. C., thence to start walking, which he did, to end up after a few days at Farmville, Virginia, where he spent the remainder of his life.

The Baroness, though, didn't leave me so easily. She reminded me of my "gypsy" grandmother, old Emily, and I was foolish enough to say I loved her. That all but finished me!

November 11, 1918: The war was now really over. Pop had lived it through. England had once more come through on top. But on Christmas Day, 1918, he died. He never at any time complained of any pain or made the slightest difficulty for anyone during his illness. But when he went he carried the secret of his birth with him. I should have liked to have known something from him of my grandfather.

Certainly that is one thing I shall never know. For, after Irving's death the next year, the old lady who remained, the sole survivor of her clan, having buried all her children, my father, his two half-brothers as well as my Aunt Rosita, the epileptic, also remained as silent as he to her death.

I'll never forget Pop's death. Only after the hardest trying did I manage, the day before, finally, to get the tube into his emaciated body for the enema. I knew I had forced it through only by unjustifiable pushing—a stiff tube with a loose wire core to give it added rigidity, and I knew I could never do it again. He had not so much as parted his lips in complaint at the maneuver.

Christmas morning, 1918, he had all his gifts for the family laid out, each in its place, and labeled. The one for me was a small cubical bronze bell, as a handle for which he had had fitted, the support welded in, the ivory figure of an old Chinese philosopher. Himself? Mother woke and they spoke to each other. She fell asleep again. At seven she arose. He remained apparently sleeping. He was almost finished.

She called me, and I went up from Nine Ridge Road as fast as I could. It must have been a cerebral accident, perhaps from my efforts to relieve him the day before.

"He's gone," I said. But he shook his head slowly from side to side. It was the last thing I could ever say in my father's presence and it was disastrous.

At that moment the telephone rang. It was a maternity case at the hospital. (I met the woman last week and we spoke of it.) There was no one to take my place, and I had to leave Pop forthwith. When I returned he was gone.

That night, Marguerita, from fear or loyalty, brought her mattress and bedclothes in a roll, clasped in her short, thick arms, down from the attic. She spread them on the floor by Mother's bedside and remained there like a dog.

Our first born had come four years earlier. We'd waited for him through Christmas and New Year's Day. "It'll come when the first snow flies," said Floss. January 7th, by early morning, the snow had begun. Dr. Ogden arrived at five A.M. He had forgot to bring any chloroform. I didn't have more than ten drops in a bottle in my own obstetrical bag. No drug store would be open until nine. At the last drop the baby emerged. I rushed to the phone to tell my dad. I couldn't get him. "Hey," said Central, "you're calling your own number."

In 1920, it was my grandmother's turn. She had become, as I say, a Christian Scientist. Her sight was nearly gone from some change in the eye itself which she never permitted me to treat. She had, besides, a large skin cancer on her face, just off the nose, which I knew must, in the end, destroy her.

She had been invited to have a turkey dinner with one of her staunch friends at the shore. My young cousin, Bill Wellcome, accompanied her. Next morning Bill wired me that she had had a stroke. I went up and did all I could for her, but within a few days she was dead at Grace Hospital, New Haven. There was a life for you!

It was the passion, the independence and the determination of this woman, born Emily Dickenson of Chichester, England, and orphaned as a small child somewhere in the 1830's, that had begun our whole history in America. Her son, my father, William George Williams, was conceived in London, though he was born, so he told me, in Birmingham, the son of an Episcopal minister, or an iron worker—exactly whoever it might have been I was never properly informed.

The young woman must have been dropped by the Godwins—
she always said she had never received her just rights—and after
an apparent delay of five years came to America in a sailing
vessel loaded with car rails. The ship was driven by a storm
to the Azores and later ran adrift on Fire Island shoal. Pop
once told me that as a child of five he recalled being on deck,
in his mother's arms perhaps, and seeing the bowsprit and prow
of another vessel loom above him out of the fog and strike the
side of the ship he was on.

The woman and infant disembarked at Castle Garden, moved
to a Brooklyn boarding house and there met a Mr. Wellcome,
up from Saint Thomas to buy photographic supplies. He saw
the young woman, married her and took her, with her son,
back to the West Indies. There, the boy who was to be my father
grew up. Grandma had wanted to be an actress; that was her
objective in coming here. She had plenty of sand. All she wanted
of it, finally.

We brought Grandma's body from the shore—her fabulous
shore where she bathed daily in summer until she couldn't get
up from the pebbles for the weight of her wet old-fashioned
bathing dress. She lay in state in my front room where I did
a pencil drawing of her really impressive features. The old cat
slept under her coffin.

But back to the Baroness. All the old gals of Greenwich Village
were backing her: coal scuttle on head on Fifth Avenue, black
Mother Hubbard with moons cut out front and back for ready
reference. Her attacks were persistent to a point where it concerned me seriously. But I never have been particularly concerned with others' ideas or opinions when they controverted
mine. I couldn't be moved.

I called on the woman one day, gave her small amounts of
money. Ashes were deep on her miserable hearth. In the slum
room where she lived with her two small dogs, I saw them at
it on her dirty bed. But she herself at that moment was courtesy
itself. We talked and that was all. We talked well and I was
moved. But when later she went into her act, I put up a fight.

Wallace Stevens at one time was afraid to come below Fourteenth Street when he was in the city because of her. And there was a Russian painter who on turning in one night in his small room had her crawl out naked from under his bed. He ran, ducked in at a neighbor's across the hall. She refused to leave the premises until he agreed to follow her to her own apartment.

Bob McAlmon was here at supper one night when I received a call to see a sick baby at Union Avenue. I took my bag and went out to my car which was standing at the curb. But as I went to get into it a hand grabbed my left wrist. It was she.

"You must come with me," she said in her strong German accent. I was taken aback, as may easily be imagined, and non-plused besides, because—well, she was a woman.

It ended as she hauled off and hit me alongside the neck with all her strength. She had had some little squirt of a male accomplice call me from supper for this. I just stood there thinking. But at that moment a cop happened to walk by.

"What's the matter, Doc, this woman annoying you?"

"No," I said, and she lit out down the street. "Let her go."

I bought a small punching bag after that to take it out on in the cellar, and the next time she attacked me, about six o'clock one evening on Park Avenue a few months later, I flattened her with a stiff punch to the mouth. I thought she was going to stick a knife in me. I had her arrested, she shouting, "What are you in this town? Napoleon?"

But she promised from the local jail, sticking her hand out between the bars, never to do it again.

It was funny to see her walking down the street trying to take hold of Officer Campbell's arm and he pushing her away. I was really crazy about the woman.

Later I gave her two hundred dollars to get out of the country. It was stolen by the go-between. I gave her more and finally she went, only to be playfully killed by some French jokester, it is said, who turned the gas jet on in her room while she was sleeping. That's the story.

Chapter 29

New Faces

A new series of parties, new faces, new objectives opened up for me after the First World War was won. I suppose the vile bathroom gin we put away was an incentive to art. It didn't bother me much aside from brief moments of asinine behavior, for I was never a drinker.

It was then that Marsden Hartley's genius was beginning to be recognized. He had returned from Berlin, some time in 1914, where his canvases of bursting shells, or what later seemed so many colored stars and flaming globes scattered over violent skies, had caused a furor. This was shortly before the war had broken out and in a sense Marsden's work predicted it. But his pictures didn't sell. (Steiglitz finally asked him to look elsewhere for a patron.) His pictures were too bold in conception, too raw in color. No one ever felt comfortable near them, though at times a pair of pink lady's gloves would surprise an observant person. He was one of the best men of the group; his small Dresden china blue eyes under savage brows made him look as if he were about to eat you. Which he would have liked, I suppose, to have done. None of us took him seriously—except in his work. He was too kind. He told me how once he had made rather direct love to Djuna Barnes—offering his excellent physical equipment for her favors. It was he also who told me of her first husband playing with their parrot and having his nose almost bitten off. I can see old Marsden now, with his practical approach,

explaining to Djuna what he could offer her. Djuna and her
evasive ways. Marsden was very fond of her. He was one of the
most frustrated men I knew. Marsden was happiest toward the
end of his life among the Down East fishermen of the Maine
coast. A tragic figure. I really loved the man, but we didn't always get along together, except at a distance.

The Dial had set up shop, and as usual the intellectuals began
to intrude upon the terrain opened by the lunatic fringe of three
years before. Kenneth Burke, Matthew Josephson, Louis Zukofsky, Hart Crane and Malcolm Cowley appeared, with Marianne
Moore. Amy Lowell came down from Boston for an occasional
fling, and Carl Sandburg, after his Chicago success, sometimes
showed up. Harriet Monroe would on occasion offer a staid
party, but, in general, it was the local gang that kept up the
fireworks.

The Others crowd was still there, but I was more taken up by
the newer talents and faces. Djuna Barnes, Margaret Anderson
and Jane Heap; on the other side Charles Henri Ford and
Parker Tyler, Wallace Gould, the Baroness Elsa von Freytag
Loringhoven, Cyril and Evelyn Scott. All were there at one
time or another.

One night I particularly remember, at Mat Josephson's place,
I met Charles and Katherine Sheeler. Blaise Cendrars, I think
it was, sat among the legs of a piano stool turned upside down.
We drank some beer or wine—and perhaps Hart Crane was
there also after Floss and I had gone. I never met Hart Crane,
though I once bought a picture from him by a man named
Sohmer, whom he was befriending, and once I accepted a short
poem by him for Contact the second series. I don't remember
which poem it was, but it was an early one.

It's hard to summarize those days. The Little Review was
putting up a fight for Joyce's Ulysses; Gertrude Stein was having
everyone by the ears. Then one night at Lola Ridge's, Hartley,
whose pictures, along with those of Demuth and Charles Sheeler,
I always went to see, brought a young man with him named
Robert McAlmon.

Marianne was there and read her "Those Various Scalpels";

Marsden read his "On the Hills of Caledonia"; I read something, I don't remember what, and something clicked for me. Before long McAlmon, who was drifting after having done a bit in one of the Canadian regiments, had set up plans with me for the magazine *Contact*. Djuna's comment was that "the one thing about it you could be sure of was that there wouldn't be any contact!" That's the sort of thing that went around.

Once on a hot July day coming back exhausted from the Post Graduate Clinic, I dropped in as I sometimes did at Marsden's studio on Fifteenth Street for a talk, a little drink maybe and to see what he was doing. As I approached his number I heard a great clatter of bells and the roar of a fire engine passing the end of the street down Ninth Avenue. I turned just in time to see a golden figure 5 on a red background flash by. The impression was so sudden and forceful that I took a piece of paper out of my pocket and wrote a short poem about it.

I remember once, returning to New York from a visit to us in Rutherford, Marsden and I were waiting on the Erie platform when an express train roared by right before our faces—crashing through making up time in a cloud of dust and sand so that we had to put up our hands to protect our faces.

As it passed Marsden turned and said to me, "That's what we all want to be, isn't it, Bill?"

I said, "Yes, I suppose so."

That particular clinic day I was admitted by Marsden, his blue elephant's eyes looking out beside his big nose as usual with great caution.

"Well," he would say, "Bill!" Then, relaxing and drawing me in, "Isn't this nice of you. Come in."

I went down the narrow corridor to his room at the back and sat down to a cup of tea with him. I was exhausted and stretched out on his couch as he sat opposite me looking at me as he always did, with that odd air he always assumed, half-quizzical, half-amused.

At that moment I heard signs of life quite near me on the other side of the partition. It had been a one-story setup, two rooms on the first floor of an old Village house connected by a folding door or an archway or whatnot, anyhow a wide opening. This opening had been boarded up to make two small apartments. On one side was the couch in which Marsden slept, a few inches away was the bed of two young lovers.

"Yes, they often entertain me at night," he said.

I felt sorry for him, growing old. That was the moment he took for his approaches. I, too, had to reject him. Everyone rejected him. I was no better than the others. One of our finest painters. He told me I *would* have made one of the most charming whores of the city. We were close friends until his death. I bought several of his pictures at the auctions at the Anderson Galleries; but I couldn't afford the big prices all these men had to have to live from their sales. And when Marsden showed me some, a half-dozen of those he could let go for fifty dollars or so, I threw them out as worthless. That didn't bother either of us except that I had at least my practice, and he didn't have anything much as far as I could tell.

Chapter 30

Pagany

Richard Johns, who, when he read my novel, *A Voyage to Pagany*, a little later, established the magazine *Pagany*, was another.

Then out of the blue *The Dial* brought out *The Waste Land* and all our hilarity ended. It wiped out our world as if an atom bomb had been dropped upon it and our brave sallies into the unknown were turned to dust.

To me especially it struck like a sardonic bullet. I felt at once that it had set me back twenty years, and I'm sure it did. Critically Eliot returned us to the classroom just at the moment when I felt that we were on the point of an escape to matters much closer to the essence of a new art form itself—rooted in the locality which should give it fruit. I knew at once that in certain ways I was most defeated.

Eliot had turned his back on the possibility of reviving my world. And being an accomplished craftsman, better skilled in some ways than I could ever hope to be, I had to watch him carry my world off with him, the fool, to the enemy.

If with his skill he could have been kept here to be employed by our slowly shaping drive, what strides might we not have taken! We needed him in the scheme I was half-consciously forming. I needed him: he might have become our adviser, even our hero. By his walking out on us we were stopped, for the moment, cold. It was a bad moment. Only now, as I predicted, have we begun to catch hold again and restarted to make the line over. This is not to say that Eliot has not, indirectly, contributed much to the emergence of the next step in metrical construction, but if he had not turned away from the direct attack here, in the western dialect, we might have gone ahead much faster.

It was fair enough, I had to admit. But to have the man run out that way drove me mad. I have never quite got over it in spite of Pound's advocacy and the rest of it. *The Criterion* had no place for me or anything I stood for. I had to go on without it.

Our poems constantly, continuously and stupidly were rejected by all the pay magazines except *Poetry* and *The Dial*. *The Little Review* didn't pay. We had no recourse but to establish publications of our own. For after all, the outlets being so meager, we had otherwise far too long a time to wait between drinks. It was the springtime of the little magazines and there was plenty for them to do.

Bob McAlmon was the instigator in the *Contact* idea which, ten years later on, after a weak start, did so magnificently. But when we began it, it didn't promise much. There was some good stuff lying around that should not be lost. We'd printed it; direct, uncompromised writing.

Pa Herman cut up some paper for us and sent us a ton of it— *I'm still using it and shall be for the rest of my life I imagine, I'm writing on it now*. That's the way he did things, though he didn't approve of the contents of the magazine; in fact, didn't understand what we were after; didn't, I imagine, even read us.

There were the first two issues, mimeographed and clipped together, then one printed on the same paper, with a printed cover; then a final issue, printed and bound, on white paper. That was the last. Nobody bought—and there was much else in the wind.

We printed some fine poems by Marianne Moore, Hartley and a few others. But the talking and the plans that went on constantly, between McAlmon and myself especially, were not lost. Bob was a coldly intense young man, with hard blue eyes, who at that time found a living posing in the nude for mixed classes at Cooper Union. He had an ideal youth's figure—such a build

as might have served for the original of Donatello's youthful
Medici in armor in the niche of the Palazzo Vecchio. He got a
dollar an hour, and was tough enough to take it for nine con-
secutive hours sometimes in various poses; he lived for a time
on a scow in New York harbor to be able to make a go of it.
Most of his cash, I imagine, he gave for a time to the magazine.
I helped, but I wasn't supporting it and he didn't ask me to. I
suppose I never really knew how hard he was pressed. That was
his racket, not mine.

About then I got word from H. D. that she and a friend were
coming to New York en route to Los Angeles where they were
thinking of making their home; and wouldn't I like to drop in on
them at the Belmont Hotel (the same old Belmont) some afternoon for tea?

"Wanna see the old gal?" I asked Bob.

"Sure. Why not?"

So one afternoon we decided to take in the show. Same old
Hilda, all over the place looking as tall and as skinny as usual.
But she had with her a small, dark English girl with piercing,
intense eyes, whom I noticed and that was about all.

"Well, how did you like her?" I asked Bob when we came
away.

"Oh, she's all right, I guess," said Bob. "But that other one,
Bryher, as she was introduced to us—she's something." The
women were leaving next day for the coast.

Bob was at that moment about to ship on a freighter for China
and had made the preliminary arrangements. But a card from
Bryher changed his plans. After a week they had been fed up
in California and were bound back to England and Bob must
not do anything, especially not leave New York until Bryher had
seen him once more.

She arrived in the city shortly after, saw Bob and proposed
marriage to him. She turned out to be the daughter of Sir John
Ellerman, the heaviest taxpayer in England. Bob fell for it.
When he told me, I literally felt the tears come to my eyes,
whether from the anticipated loss of the man's companionship
and the assistance of his talents, or joy for his good fortune, I
couldn't decide.

Everything had to be done in the greatest haste to coincide

with the sailing of the White Star liner *Celtic* on which Sir
John had reserved the bridal suite for them. First to the tailors,
then haberdashers, etc., etc. Then, the night before sailing, an
intimate supper in a small private dining room at the Hotel
Brevoort.

Bryher was there, H. D. was there, not joining too excitedly
in the ceremonies; there was Bob and Grace, his sister, who had
rushed east for the occasion, Flossie, Marianne Moore, myself and
good old Marsden, the most wonderful of party men.

What we ate is of no importance unless Floss can remember.
But I'll never forget the orchids; neither will Floss. I could
not imagine what to give the wealthy young couple as an adequate present on such short notice until Floss fell on the ideal
gift: a box of the rarest orchids we could gather.

The key to the situation was Edward Roehrs, the corn-mellowed
grower of what had been and still was the finest orchidry, or
at least, one of the first great commercial collections in America.
Roehrs's Nursery was in East Rutherford just across the track,
right next to the old Bagellon house (then still standing) where
I had lived as a child.

"Sure," said Edward, "anything you like. When do you want
them?"

"Today."

So round that greenhouse he went clipping every rarest blossom
he could find, things I for one never had so much as dreamed
of. He laid them loose, and carefully, in a cardboard box.

Now here we were opening it at the table to our united amazement. They were rare ("Roehrs's Beautiful Orchids"), they were as
fresh as they were lavish in their variety.

As we oh'd and ah'd over them, it was Marsden who spoke the
perfect comment—for imagine what some smart reporter, English or American, would not have given for the chance to exploit
the secret wedding of the daughter of Sir John Ellerman to an
impecunious young American, no matter how talented. We had
been passing the box around the table in the small room when
Marsden sat back laughing as only he could at such a time,
"Imagine," he said, "what it would look like in the papers tomorrow, the headline: POETS PAWING ORCHIDS!"

Two days later Floss and I received a postcard representing a scene from some hit then playing showing several actors, men and women with their hands in a pot of money, and signed, obscurely, D. H., in bold capitals. I accused H. D. later of being the sender, but she violently denied it. I never believed her.

Bob left and took his disastrous story with him—but that's for him to tell, not me.

I had begun to think of writing *In the American Grain*, a study to try to find out for myself what the land of my more or less accidental birth might signify. I had made a few preliminary studies. The plan was to try to get inside the heads of some of the American founders or "heroes," if you will, by examining their original records. I wanted nothing to get between me and what they themselves had recorded: a translation of a Norse saga, *The Long Island Book*, the case of Eric the Red, would be the beginning; Columbus' Journal; the letters of Hernando Cortez to Philip of Spain; Daniel Boone's autobiography; and so forth, to a letter, entire, written by John Paul Jones on board the *Bonhomme Richard*, after his battle with the *Serapis*. So it would go.

But it was getting to 1922, ten years after our marriage, when Floss and I had planned, come hell or high water, to take a year off and go abroad.

Chapter 31

A Sabbatical Year

We had the two kids, Bill, aged nine, and Paul, six. It would be hard, but we felt it had to be done, as long as no harm should come to them. Nana and Pa Herman were in Monroe, Mother was here, Ed wasn't too far off, Lucy—our faithful Lucy of whom I have not as yet spoken—would live right in the house with them, and in direct charge would be "Watty," Mr. Watkins, the physical training director and football coach at Rutherford High. He had been "Razor" Watkins, formerly of Colgate.

For the care of my practice Albert Hoheb, my cousin, and his wife Katherine, both physicians, having completed their joint internship at the Passaic General Hospital, would have a room in the house and take over my office. It was a foolhardy thing for us to do on some counts, but we had to rely on many contingencies to live, anyway you look at it, and we thought we owed it to ourselves, so we went through with it.

For the first six months of the year we decided we'd live in New York and have the boys with us week-ends. If we found it worked we'd sneak abroad for the next six months. The town was tolerant, as I found out later, though no doubt many thought me completely batty. We didn't have the money! What a way to treat their children! To abandon them that way to strangers! etc., etc.

As a start we sent the boys to Watty's camp at Lake Mattawamkeag, Maine, and little Paul, the first crack out of the box, got a beaut of a shiner from standing too close behind a batter. Later, however, he showed his nerve by jumping off the end of the rowboat, without knowing how to swim, into Watty's arms. Bill was the fisherman, always has been and always will be.

In New York Floss and I shared an apartment with our old pal Louise Bloecher, Wee Wee, as the kids still called her. I joined the New York Fencing Club and we were off.

That summer, we visited the kids at camp. How old was I then? Nearly forty. I was still playing a little ball. I still remember those Maine evenings just at dusk for the way we played some game that required a good deal of endurance. The older boys and counselors divided into sides, one side went north beyond the ball field and the other deployed to keep them from filtering through and reaching "home." I ran my guts out after those twelve- and fourteen-year-old kids, down along the lake front, everywhere, and caught them too. Quite a party.

Then in the early fall we paid a visit to Wally Gould in his Virginia hide-out. We drove down in the old Dodge. The persimmons were just ripening on the roadside bushes as we crossed Appomattox Creek on an improvised bridge.

When Wally had left us a year or two before, getting off the train at Washington, he had fished in the Potomac, cooked his catch at an open fire, and started south, resolved, Indian that he was at heart, that he had had all the snow he wanted to see for the rest of his life. He was going south, south through old Indian country—and that's all he knew.

He panhandled it through the farms doing a few chores here and there. He told one woman he was an ex-cavalry man and knew horses. Maybe he did. She brought out her old nag, which was sick, and asked Wally what to do for it. He looked at its mouth, told her it was too old to spend any money on, and let it go at that.

Finally (and it was final for him) he arrived one evening at Farmville, close to the North Carolina line, and still having a nickel, decided to stop in at the movies. Things began, at that moment, to break for him. The mechanical piano had quit. Wally went back to the projection room and found the proprietor, who was the local veterinarian. Wally offered to play—

it had been his job back in Madison, Maine, where he came from
—and was taken on. He could play anything and was forthwith
hired at fifteen dollars a week. That night he slept at Doc
Staley's house and that's how it went.

Farmville is the site of a big woman's normal school, the home
of Peggy Hopkins Joyce, whose father was the local barber, and
the place where General Grant had his headquarters just before
Appomattox and the surrender of General Lee. The place was
saturated with Civil War tradition. They showed the spot, un-
touched, where, when Grant was standing on the second-floor
balcony of the hotel, the round shot landed which had been
aimed at him from the near distance.

It must have been the vet, who, when Wally was looking for
a convenient and cheap place to bunk outside the town, mentioned the small cabin owned by Miss Mary Jackson. I suppose he
had no intention of staying there permanently; it was way out
in the sticks, but there, in fact, a year or so later, we still found
him. He had had a rare piece of luck. He'd made wonderful
friends and, being a huge man, impressive in appearance and a
writer of distinction, he was making a great go of it.

There was Mrs. Parks, the Rabelaisian wife of an Englishman
who was making a good thing of a model pig farm in the region,
and who kept an old bathtub in the yard behind the house
where he stripped and took a plunge every morning, winter and
summer. She was New England like Wally and grasped the situation at a glance; she was thrilled to escape the boredom which
surrounded her, and she knew everybody. A sharp-tongued, intelligent woman, and sharp-faced too, who couldn't wait I imagine
to tell her pal, Miss Mary, what had hit the town.

Miss Mary was something else again. Of Knickerbocker stock
on her mother's side, she was the descendant of Judge White
at whose gatepost Lee had stopped on his way to the last moments of his military career: You can imagine the situation, Lee
sitting astride his horse, his loyal partisans, broken-hearted, trying
to do all they could to comfort him. One of the ladies offered
him a cup of tea. Tea! a thing all but unheard of in the impoverished Confederacy. Lee accepted and a cup of it was brought
to him which he drank without dismounting. From such a family

had sprung Miss Mary, middle-aged, about Wally's age, perhaps a little older, the local high school principal, about to retire now that her father had just died. She still lived in the old brick house where the servants came up barefoot behind your chair to startle you sometimes.

Wally took us in. We stayed there for a week quite comfortably. He was maintaining himself by baking, packaging and selling three kinds of pound cake by mail. He was a superb cook, and, as he lived two miles from town, had a little nine-year-old colored boy to assist him and do his errands. Otie. We discovered Otie, a moment after we arrived, halfway up the pine tree observing all we did.

I wandered those old fields, gulched and overgrown with yellow gorse, heard the story of how some campaigner had carried a pocket full of the gorse seed wherever he went during the Civil War so that the various camp grounds of the Confederacy would be marked forever after. I picked up Indian arrowheads and big lead bullets showing that many a skirmish had been fought on those grounds in the old days.

Once Lee, passing along these roads, had seen one of his seasoned troopers eating an unripe persimmon. "You know better than to eat that," said Lee to the fellow. "What's got into you?"

"Shrinking up my stomach to fit my rations, General," said the one thus addressed. Lee bowed his head and went quietly on.

It's a long story about Wally and Mary Jackson. She married him finally and made a home for him there until his death a few years later. She found him one morning in his old brown wrapper lying on his face at the wood pile. She followed a few months later—still a virgin, by all accounts.

At the time of our visit Wally had become interested in Tennyson and wrote his last book, *To Aphrodite,* following Tennyson's style. I violently objected. That ended our friendship, but I cannot forget Farmville, the drives and the companionship; the Brunswick stew made of squirrel meat in a heavy mix of beans and whatnot; the chocolate soil of that part of Virginia, which Parks thought the finest in the world. He, an Englishman, had traveled the world over and farmed in many countries, but, now past middle life, had married and settled down there in what in his mature judgment was the finest climate in the world. I remember seeing at Farmville the biggest boar I could ever have imagined, and the finest conical holly tree in full berry. The vet told us of coon hunts—one night we heard one going on—of catching a wild turkey snared in a barbed-wire fence, and of the myriad turkey traces everywhere to be found after a light snowfall.

During this time when Floss and I were still at our base in New York I had actually started to write *In the American Grain* and gave practically every free moment to the preliminary reading. I went almost every day to the American History Room of the New York Public Library.

One day the De Soto chapter was burning in my head. So I took out my paper, sat down at a table and, not waiting to take out a book, began to write furiously. I'd been going for five or ten minutes, I guess, when the attendant, a stupid ass with a British accent, came up behind me and, tapping me on the shoulder, said I couldn't write in that room. I was furious.

"I'm writing a thesis," I said.

"You have no book," he said.

"I'll get one in a minute," I said.

"You can't write here without one," he said.

So I had to get up, go to the desk, get out a book, put it on the table before I could go on. My day was ruined.

Floss did *all* the reading on the Aaron Burr, Alexander Hamilton theme and what with her notes and what she told me, I was so stirred that I completed the chapter at one sitting. The Columbus chapter gave me a good deal of trouble, since at first I couldn't bring the thing to a dramatic end. I wanted to end with the discovery, terminating the first voyage, but I wanted also to get in the other three voyages and all they entailed. I wrote and wrote and wrote, but it wouldn't come out. Then almost a year later, on the Riviera at Villefranche, I finished it. Waldo Frank discovered and admired this ending. I was quite touched.

The Tenochtitlan chapter was written in big, square paragraphs like Inca masonry. Raleigh was written in what I conceived to be Elizabethan style; the Eric the Red chapter in the style of the Icelandic saga; Boone in the style of Daniel's autobiography; Franklin was in Franklin's words; and John Paul Jones I gave verbatim. Thus I tried to make each chapter not only in content but in the style itself a close study of the theme.

Chapter 32

Our Trip Abroad

At length the day of our departure for Europe was approaching—Wednesday, January 9, 1924—as my diary reads. A lovely sunshiny day, and we were off on the old *Rochambeau,* surrounded in our cabin by flowers and baskets of fruit from our relations and "the gang." My diary says that the *Laconia,* coming in, delayed our departure fifteen minutes and that later on we encountered the *Majestic* entering the harbor.

From here out, for the sake of what accuracy may be gained thereby, I shall follow the diary for a while. Some entries may prove worth quoting verbatim.

The night before our departure two of my immediate friends, Earl and Doug, tried to put me under the table at the Columbia University Club in New York. It was my introduction to many subsequent experiences.

I remember at the bar I overheard someone saying, *"J'étais un homme très vulgaire, j'étais un voleur."*

From Wednesday, January 9, 1924, New York, to Wednesday, January 30th, we traveled through Paris to Carcassonne and Marseilles, a matter of three weeks (nine days of them on shipboard). It doesn't seem possible that all the memories of Paris from that time could possibly have been crowded into those few days.

It was Bob McAlmon who introduced us at the start, everywhere. His position in Paris was important, though far from
happy. *Contact,* the venture he and I had started in New York
before his marriage, had, as a consequence of that marriage, become an influential one with many of the leading writers of the
day. Due to Sir John's fortune, he was an extremely important
factor in bringing out many books—such as Gertrude Stein's
The Making of Americans, and Hemingway's beginnings. The
list is noteworthy.

It had been a pleasant trip, after we made the break, for both
of us. The sea, as always, fascinated me. It was not the sea that
our son Bill knew many years later at the Aleutian Islands in
winter, nor the "tin can" sea Paul knew in the Atlantic. We were
on a passenger boat bound for Europe for pleasure, but for all
that, it was still the sea.

After the first few days (a slow ship) I devoted myself to seeing
a whale and the many gulls and other birds, that "come up from
under the very beam, it seems, and flop, flop, flop away awkwardly or dive and disappear," porpoises, a freighter in the distance. We ran into fog at the southern tip of the Grand Banks.
Next day, a storm. It was staggering. But it passed and once more
we heard the little violinist, Barbara Lull, in the next cabin
begin her arpeggios. Floss was invited to her bath by a charming
French steward and had to confess afterward, "This is living!"

Then it began again, worse than before, January 13th, storm
all day. Cold wind from the northwest. The ship rolls far over
to starboard. I saw sailors go down in the hold to inspect cargo.
Portholes tightly closed and bolted. Ropes up along the deck
and in the smoking room. Huge waves from behind the ship, lifting up the stern. The wind howls and drives the spray ripping
the foam to lace.

Watched the sea for hours. Saw a freighter. At bedtime, a wave
drenched the deck.

It is, in fact, the opening chapter of my first (limping) novel,
A Voyage to Pagany, following the complete itinerary of the
same trip Floss and I were now on, though the chief characters
were not ourselves.

Kay Boyle had come down to the train at Le Havre urging us to stay over at least a day for a visit among those stone-roofed houses where she was so lonely, knowing only her grocer, as she said. But we couldn't do it. We had to get to Paris where she, poor girl, would gladly have followed us.

The yellow gorse, much to my surprise, was in flower along the way. The willows were in the catkin stage, far in advance of anything at home. We passed through Rouen. Bob had radioed that he had engaged a room for us at the Lutetia (40 fr.). So there we were at last, astonished to be present, but eager to meet all those we had come to see.

Floss admired the electric clock we found in our room, no tick! We had supper that night at the Vieux Colombier. I, an American, naturally, would have beef, a Chateaubriand, and got my well-deserved first fleecing. The waiter cut the order in half, serving the first half to me and placing the second on a little shelf near us in full view, be it said. When I had eaten my portion, he removed my plate and brought my vegetables! I, feeling my French a little rusty, made no move to claim the rest of my meat! Very good. I hope he enjoyed it. Back to the hotel to our comfortable beds, and so the first day passed.

It is strange to me to realize now that I had taken so many half-finished manuscripts with me to complete in Europe: the first chapters of *In the American Grain* to do over and many poems. But on Saturday, January the 20th, the whirl started that was to continue during our entire stay.

That morning at eleven o'clock, a beautiful day, we called Bob and met him on the Boulevard Raspail. Thence walked with him to the Luxembourg Garden past the gloomy Senate to Twelve rue de l'Odéon to see Sylvia Beach, but found her out. In her window we thought we saw my books looking somewhat dusty. It was like a spring day. Bob had grown stouter; his mind also had become far less youthful, more discerning, as we talked, and we did talk, walking; I could see that though Paris had become indeed his home, he was on easy terms with it, and as far as I could see, everyone in it, including the best and the worst; he was not melted by it in any way but kept his own western manners and counsels. He had, for instance, shared a room for a time with Louis Aragon, the young French surrealist, until he couldn't stand him any longer. "The sort of person," said Bob, "who would get out of bed early, shave and leave the only towel in the place wet and full of bloodstains from his decapitated pimples."

That afternoon we went to see Brancusi in his studio on a side street nearby, a short compact peasant of a man, with his long gray hair, like a sheep dog, and well known to me because of his polished bronze "Bird in Flight" and the "Madam Pogany," the phallic head and neck of a woman that I had seen exhibited in New York.

There were that day the four of us, Floss, Bob, Brancusi and myself. not to mention Polaire, a white collie. The man had not been expecting us, but he put aside his work and bade us sit down wherever we could in his cluttered studio. It was a barnlike place filled with blocks of stone, formless wooden hunks and stumps for the most part, work finished and unfinished. I remember especially his "Socrates": a big hole through the center of the block showing Socrates the talker, his mouth (and mind) wide open expounding his theses. There was the head of Isaac also. Brancusi served us cognac, poked up the fire and then began talking of Ezra Pound's recent "opera," *Villon,* which he must have heard at the performance at the Théâtre des Champs Elysées a day or two before. He pronounced it a scandal.

"Pound writing an opera?" I said. "Why, he doesn't know one note from another."

Brancusi was furious, resented it, actually resented it as a personal affront. Bob was astonished to hear him speak so positively, as Brancusi was a very mild-mannered man, a true peasant.

It was a pleasant meeting. We were invited to come again and he would prepare for us a beefsteak according to his own famous cuisine. We arose to go. There was a columnar carving of wood that reached nearly to the high beams of the ceiling, a pillar made of interlocking blocks, chainlike in construction, one following the other to and beyond the sky, you might say, to represent eternity.

From there we went to a small place nearby where we waited for Bill Bird and drank whisky and soda. Bill Bird was the editor of the Three Mountain Press (*Mons Veneris* to the fore, as some would have had it, coupled with what two other mountains it mattered little). Bill was a tall, sharp-bearded American business-man who looked as though he had been mellowed in Chambertin, gentle, kindly and informal. I fell for him instantly. We heard besides that he had a fine cellar which we should sample some-day not too long distant. His interest in books was the real bond.

And so for the event of the evening, supper with James and Nora Joyce, at the only place at which Joyce would eat, the Trianon.

Joyce was not a tall man. He had a small, compressed head, straight nose and no lips, and spoke with a distinct, if interna-tionalized, Irish accent. He would take no hard liquor, only white wine, a mild white wine, because of his eyes. He was almost blind from glaucoma. It was a wonderful evening. Nora, a sturdy one, hardly said a word.

Joyce, who was working at that time on the early Dublin parts of *Finnegans Wake*, was particularly anxious to talk with Floss, because she was Norse-speaking on her mother's side and the Norsemen had played a great part in Irish history.

We were all drinking white wine out of courtesy to Joyce, who, as he talked, went to fill Flossie's glass; but his aim was poor, the wine going beyond onto the table until she moved her glass into a position to catch it and so saved the day.

As we started to drink another round, Bob McAlmon, who may have been a little tight, proposed, "Here's to sin!"

Joyce looked up suddenly. "I won't drink to that," he said.

So Bob took it back with a laugh and we all sipped our wine again silently.

Nora, who had been Nora Barnacle, Joyce married on the plea that she'd stick to him. She was having her hands full, in a cold flat with her two children, the man himself near blind, and little enough money to do with except what came in out of the air you might say. But the worst of it was, what to do with a huge painting of Joyce's father, with no wall space at all to hang it where they were living. Joyce wanted it there. One can imagine such a painting, symbol of a rigorous Irishman's devotion, in the city of Paris, dominated as it was by painters: *"Spectateurs de la lumière."*

Joyce invited Floss to come up to his flat someday to help him struggle, as he did with great pains, over words of the ancient language. She never followed it up.

Later we adjourned for Portuguese oysters, coffee, drinks to the Dingo where we re-encountered a red-haired woman who had come over from Plymouth on the ship with us; a gay, drunken evening, with Joyce and Nora along *"beati innocenti,"* as he put it.

The Paris of the expatriate artist was our only world—day and night—and if bread is the staff of life, whisky, as Bob was fond of saying, is the staff of night life, both products of the same grain. *Everyone* was in Paris—if you wanted to see them. But there were grades too of that cream. We were not concerned with the moving-picture colony or the swanks, though money was admitted, but on the artist's terms, and it was astonishing to see what came to the top in those days and what sank to the bottom. This was what we had come, also, to enjoy.

We were living as cheaply as with reasonable comfort we could. But for those ten days the Hôtel Lutetia was still within our price range, at 390 fr. the first week, whatever that amounted to, less than the cost of Man Ray's six photographic prints, as we found out later to our alarm.

We had begun to talk the moment we had met McAlmon on the Boulevard Raspail and gone on with it interminably thereafter with few pauses. It was our first meeting with him since the well remembered wedding supper at the Brevoort in New York. He told us for the first time in full of the disastrous outcome of that experience, his wedding and of H.D.'s part in the affair. The drinking seemed a natural consequence. We talked and talked, at our hotel rooms, in taxis, at bars—and it went on for a month to come. He was in Paris now alone, Bryher and H.D. being off somewhere together in Switzerland.

If I said McAlmon "served" Joyce, that would of course have to be seriously qualified. Bob had been useful to Joyce, whom he respected (though he had as much sympathy for Nora and their children), absorbed his gripes and did what he could. But the

Joyces were only a hundredth part of his occupations. Paris was his very twin. He was at home here as only an American expatriate could be. Especially at his best. When he had sometimes insulted the wrong persons, with his blinkless and cold-eyed remarks, taking them down as liars to their faces (he weighed not more than one hundred and fifty pounds), a barkeep might have to reach over, grab him by the collar, yank him over the bar and hide him until he could sober up and escape. The next day he was handing out money to some unknown—Antheil at one point, at the rate of one hundred dollars a month—feeding Joyce, giving me a big party and whatnot. He told me of being picked up by dozens of females in distress—implying, though he never mentioned them, generous deeds of all kinds. It was Sir John's money, but if Bob hadn't earned it, nobody ever earned a nickel. He spent it like a prince, the niggardliness, if there was any, being at the source. *Contact* had really come to life, this time as a publishing venture. If it could go on this way, in no time at all it was bound to become the most powerful influence in the publishing field that we had ever known. Contact Editions, together with Bill Bird's Three Mountains Press had created a front we could all profit by, if the money continued. But the mark was on Bob's face. No man could go on at that pace forever; he knew no limits, physical or for intellectual honesty. Nothing pleased him. He didn't know much French, for instance, but everyone understood him very well.

Floss and I were not always with Bob, but went about Paris on our own whenever the opportunity offered. The first time we went to the Louvre it was closed. We saw the rue de l'Opéra, walked in the rue de la Paix and admired the jewelry in the show windows there, visited the Place Vendôme. From there we taxied to the Théâtre des Champs Elysées, where we had difficulty obtaining tickets for *Dr. Knock,* Jules Romains' hit, the following Sunday: the success story of a young physician in a small French village where, through his zeal for cures, he all but ruined the health of the entire community.

Thence to the Trocadéro, across the Alexandre III bridge to the Eiffel Tower (closed) which Floss saw for the first time. To the Gare Montparnasse by streetcar, lunching at a cheap but excellently simple place nearby. One could live in Paris then, by virtue of the exchange, on almost nothing. Floss went back to the hotel, but I continued to the Magasins du Bon Marché, where to my amazement I saw a "white sale," the sheets in heaps on the floor, often trampled by the crowds. I met a young salesman with a little English with whom I discussed our own sales methods, the way change is made, the speed, the simplicity of it.

"Yes," he said, "I have heard of all that. I wish I could see it." From him I bought a hairbrush and white collar. But the complexity of the sales slip, the entry on a tall ledger of some sort, really had me shaking my head.

"Yes, our methods are not as quick or efficient as yours," he said, "but we are used to them."

Sometimes we'd sit either in Bob's room at the Unic or in ours at the Lutetia and read or talk, talk, talk. Floss might sleep, or she might go shopping with a friend, Kitty Cannell, whom we had known in New York. One day I read his *Portrait of a Generation*; another time I finished my poem, "The Gulls."

The first Sunday, another perfect spring day, after our *chicoré* (for coffee) and brioche, Floss and I walked down the boulevard where we saw the gutter market—oranges, bananas, leeks, the various "greens"—all the stalls were open till noon. As we crossed to the Champs Elysées, we saw them fishing in the Seine with long poles, their gut-lines fastened to wooden bobbers painted red at one end. They catch little sardinelike "shiners," though seldom by the mouth but as often by the tail, accidentally.

The grass was green in the Tuileries Gardens. Thence, after lunch, to the Birds' where we met Sally, Bill's wife, for the first time—at Eight Place du Palais Bourbon. Sally, whose superb voice had conditioned all their lives. The quiet Bill, married to that dynamo, was something to observe. Once, the story went, he had come home, the tired businessman! to find her rehearsing (for her try at the Opéra Comique) the role of Mimi. Without waiting for her to finish, he had been so moved that he forthwith and on the spot seduced her. Good old Bill.

His two children, Francie and the boy, were there, he closely observed by his nurse, Miss Nelson, who was strangely disturbed by our presence. When the boy was born he came under her care. He did not thrive. In fact, he went so rapidly downhill that, thinking he would die, the Birds were glad to have her carry the infant off to Denmark in great haste where under her expert care and with the aid of the Danish doctors, he recovered. But from then on, he was *her* child. She may have resented Sally—who knows? The situation was strained.

Another time Floss and I "did" Notre Dame and from the top of one of its towers, where we came upon three Japanese tourists, saw the Sacré Coeur in the distance upon the hill of Montmartre, reminding one, through the mist, of pictures of the Taj Mahal. We had dinner, Place Clichy, thence walked to Twelve rue de l'Odéon where this time Sylvia Beach was at home and extremely cordial. Adrienne Monnier, a woman completely unlike Sylvia, very French, very solid, whose earthy appetites, from what she told us, made her seem to stand up to her very knees in heavy loam, came in from across the street to make our acquaintance. Somehow we got to talking of Brueghel, whose grotesque work she loved—the fish swallowing a fish that itself was swallowing another. She enjoyed the thought, she said, of pigs screaming as they were being slaughtered, a contempt for the animal—a woman toward whom it was strange to see the mannishly dressed Sylvia so violently drawn. Adrienne gave no quarter to any man. Once, when Bob in a taxi had taken her in his arms and kissed her, she sunk her teeth into his lips so that he expected to have a piece torn out before she released him. A woman, however, of unflinching kindness. At the slightest invitation from Sylvia she would close her shop door, on the opposite side of the rue de l'Odéon, to see a writer from abroad. To conserve and to enrich the literary life of her time was her unfailing drive. They conspired to make that region of Paris back of the old theatre a sanctuary for all sorts of writers: Joyce, of course, and many of the younger Americans found it a veritable home.

That evening we went with Bob to meet the excitingly young and provocative American composer George Antheil and his wife Bjerska. George was wearing his hair in a bang over the forehead; Bjerska, a small, foreign-looking "child," hardly opened her mouth the whole evening. The talk, at a modest restaurant on the rue Blanche, was of music—the jazz opera, especially the forthcoming jazz opera which George was to write, was in fact writing while young French composers would be leaning over his shoulders to steal what they could from his score. Stravinsky, a cousin, had sponsored him. Ezra Pound had written prominently of him.

Bob McAlmon became impatient, but it was exciting, leading as it did after a year to the concert with fourteen grand pianos, foghorn, an electric alarm bell and whatnot in Carnegie Hall after our return to America. As we drank—and whisky was to the imagination of the Paris of that time like milk to a baby—we imagined ourselves the first fingers of a sea that coming up to a shore would one day inundate the whole region. Unsteadily we walked home to our hotels.

To jump from the diary to memory is an exercise resulting in curious complications. Sometimes there is no meeting of the two elements, a name remains blank to the mind. But sometimes the match of the written word scrapes upon the sandpaper and a light flares.

After the first few days, Bob came for us one evening with Kitty Cannell in her squirrel coat and yellow skullcap, which made the French, man and woman, turn in the street and stare seeing a woman, approaching six feet, so accoutred. Bob was giving us a big party.

It may have been somewhat after the usual supper hour but we had, that evening, practically the whole left wall of the Trianon, with its red plush benches, to ourselves. The tables were pushed together for a banquet, ten or fifteen of us to a side. I was in the middle facing the wall, Floss next to me on the right with Joyce and Ford Madox Ford opposite, their wives and the others close about us; Harold Loeb with Kitty Cannell, Antheil, Marcel Duchamp, Bill Bird, Man Ray, Mina Loy and her daughter, Sylvia Beach, Louis Aragon; some were invited and some merely showed up (at Bob's expense). It was a good meal with all the wine that properly accompanies each course. It was my first view of Ford Madox Ford, the lumbering Britisher, opening his mouth to talk, his napkin in one hand, half-stammering but enjoying the fun, a mind wonderfully attractive to me, I could see that.

I had, naturally, to make a speech. What had I to say with all eyes, especially those of the Frenchmen, gimleted upon me to see what this American could possibly signify, if anything? I had nothing in common with them.

I said thank you, naturally, to Bob, thanked them all for their kindness and then told them that in Paris I had observed that when a corpse, in its hearse, plain or ornate, was passing in the streets, the women stopped, bowed their heads and that men generally stood at attention with their hats in their hands. What I meant was my own business, I did not explain, but sat down feeling like a fool.

To relieve the bad moment, someone asked Bob to sing "Bollicky Bill" (did they mean me?), which he did from beginning to end. After that it was "She Was Poor But She Was Honest." We all joined in; then the Frenchmen having eaten and gone off with Man Ray, we deployed to the Dingo. To bed at three, Joyce and everybody drunk.

The next day, after a restless night and six glasses of warm water swallowed, I managed to get out for a long walk alone, bought a pear and, eating it, stumbled on the medieval Place François Ier, as French in its way as anything I have ever known, of that French austerity of design, gray stone cleanly cut and put together in complementary masses, like the Alexandrines of Racine. I don't know that the spot even exists today or if it has the classic appearance which I saw that morning, a half-eaten pear in my hand like any countryman or visiting colonial, but it made a deep impression on me. Perhaps it was humiliation after my stupid speech of the night before, contempt for my drunkenness, or just a bad stomach which hit me so hard, but I saw a France that day which had wholly escaped me theretofore.

On the way home, feeling chastened by the vision I had had, I saw a poor woman selling sprays of mimosa just outside the Hôtel Lutetia. She selected one spray from her bunch and held it out to me, but when I heard the price, and knowing how Floss loved mimosa (as my mother also loved its color and fragrance) I took the whole bunch from the woman's hand and paid her, to her astonishment, far too much for it. A couple who were passing looked at me with distaste, griping half under their breath at the idiocy of these Americans, how they were spoiling Paris. Quite true.

After a tour of the Louvre with Bob, my eyes still blurred from the night before, Floss, Bob and I went to Brancusi's again, this time for supper, that is for beefsteak cooked by Brancusi himself, the Romanian shepherd, something for which he was famous. We talked, everyone in Paris talked, talked, talked, surrounded by his creations in wood and stone, like the sheep, one might say, cropping out of the chaos of unorganized masses (later to be worked upon), the rocks and trees of a shepherd's world in the flickering half-light about us.

We talked of the French. I was in a somewhat ecstatic mood about the French, their tolerance, their courtesy. Where else in the world could one feel the reticence, the freedom for the individual, the willingness to permit such creatures as we Americans, drunken, loud, often obscene, to exist in their city?—and so on and so on.

Brancusi said, "Yes, they are tolerant. They do not object to anything, but that is in only a certain class. Among the aristocracy in France, you will find a rigidity of manners greater than anywhere in the world. And just try to open a butcher or a grocery shop in the block, anywhere in Paris—you, a foreigner. They'd cut your throat. Literally. It can't be done, they will never permit it."

Bob had told us that Brancusi had made several attempts to attract American women he saw in his studio. He wanted to have an affair with one of them. There was in fact one in the offing at that very moment whom he thought he might get off with. But nothing would happen. He was too much a peasant, too gentle, too gauche.

All sorts of stories flew about Paris in those days. There was the young man captive in the apartment of a muscular homosexual. He had been heard screaming his refusals all night long at the top of his voice, only to be found the next morning taking his place at the particular café where their kind congregated; of the American girl who, wishing an affair, had gone to a room in a hotel with a young French officer she had been picked up by. Stripped and lying on the bed, she had watched the man standing before the mirror combing his hair, waxing his moustaches until, beginning to laugh, she got up, dressed and, saying good-bye to him, went home.

Brancusi saw the beauty and spirit of many of the American women he encountered but, generally, no more than observed them; they *"déraillent"* too easily, he said, jump the track, go into the ditch too easily for the most part, want to play but do not "take the pin," as Bob paraphrased it.

Leading Polaire, Brancusi walked part way home with us in sabots. Bob left us a few moments later as we continued along the rue du Cherche Midi feeling lonesome, Bob also I guess. And to bed.

Chapter 33

Cousins

One day I went alone, by train, to visit my two cousins, Alice and Marguerite. I could not neglect them. They were now two aging women, poor and surprised by their poverty, widowed, having nothing but each other to cling to in such a world. And I, the young American doctor, here, in Paris, for no purpose certainly than pleasure, with time for no more than this glance that took in their cheated existences. Coming out from that famous world of *le quartier Latin,* gay, drunken, young, not wanting even to eat at their poor table, coming by train past the crumbling city fortifications, long down, where goats eat for the practical purpose of giving milk. I felt half-annoyed, half-ashamed.

Trufly, the absinthe-drinking lawyer husband of Alice, had died ten years since; but Weber, the gentle engraver who, in his old age, had married Marguerite to have someone to cook for him and warm him in bed, had only recently gone under. Never was there anyone so gentle. She, however, enraged at his slowness and inability to make even half a living, used to scream at him in anger and tears.

Yet, even these two old gals, once they got themselves dolled up in their patched-up hats and a few rags, could forget the whole business and step out happily. That is Paris. Marguerite, who used to come behind me at the rue de la Bruyère leaning upon my young buttocks as I looked down into the street, was a clever seamstress, and Alice, who had been rather beautiful though never bright, had a steady job in a first-rate millinery shop. They lived! And were delighted to see me. So "handsome and successful." Ah, America, that rich country. They had prepared supper for me, regretted Florence's absence. I invited them to come the following week to the hotel to have dinner with us and fled back to Montparnasse.

A day or two before, Man Ray had said that he would like to take my photo. It seemed a good idea. So Bob led me to his studio. Moving curiously across the back of the shop was the figure of a young woman whom I have always regretted never having got to know better. She merely appeared for a moment and disappeared. She was said to be learning her trade there— Berenice Abbott, Man Ray's assistant. She gave only one look, but it was a fine head, an impressive face, and the look was penetrating.

Man Ray posed me. I kept my eyes wide open. He asked me particularly then to close them a little and I, not knowing, did as he told me to do, not realizing the sentimental effect that would be created. (I opened them, though, later when I got his bill.) I was infuriated when I saw the finished pictures, but it was too late. I did not want that look on my face. I felt already sufficiently humiliated not to be the hard, "take it" sort of person all these other characters about me seemed to represent. I felt soft enough, messy enough with my eyes well open, but this was too much and too late also when I found it to be a *fait accompli*, with the beautiful, courageous girl a thousand years off, experienced, unobtainable—in the background, laughing at me.

The Sunday night after my visit to my cousins we had been invited, Floss and I, to dine at the apartment of Eliza Andruz, my father's old friend or relative. This was something else again. Quite a climb to the sixth floor, with little triangular cane-bottomed chairs at each landing to ease the fatigue of mounting. This was old Paris, fifth- and sixth-floor apartments always being those of choice, inasmuch as they lay farthest removed from the street and no one living above. But to live there, as with all that is elevated, the physical cost would be high. It was just that, just the sort of domicile that Eliza, a woman already aging, must have chosen.

Her life, her active life, was past. She closed herself in here apart from the world of today, impoverished by the inflation, her *rentes* bringing her in only a much restricted revenue. She had known not so much the literary as the political figures of twenty to forty years ago—but still had the desire to entertain—in an all but forgotten style.

This was another France. We talked of the West Indies, the Simmonses of St. Thomas—whoever they were—the Prussians in Paris in 1870, of Poincaré, the mathematician as premier, of the Ruhr, how France did not want it but only wanted reparations. That she, Eliza, had not drunk wine for three years and ate little meat or none; the exchange and how it had affected her. Paris is one-quarter foreigners, she told us; for them it must keep gay.

The night before our departure southward, after dinner with Mina and her really lovely children, we went to a party to which we had been invited at Ford Madox Ford's, a sort of garden apartment somewhere neither in the city nor far out of it. Everyone was there, and high and dancing. Almost before we had got our coats off a woman had been knocked flat on her back on the floor by the man with whom she was dancing. No one seemed to pay much attention, least of all the host.

"Who is it?" I asked.

"Berenice Abbott and some English fairy. Forget it."

And sure enough, he helped the woman to her feet and they went on with the music. There were too many people in the place. Floss and I made our excuses and went home early. Ford seemed not to be amused.

During the next month we visited Carcassonne, like a picture from the *Nouveau Petit Larousse Illustré,* standing there by virtue of stone, to remain still, dominating the plains, looking to the Pyrenees, empty and sad, a cold wind seeking out the crevices in the masonry and the ramparts of its loneliness—only the washerwoman with red arms at the stream below its walls giving it life again.

We did not, as we had at first thought to, stop at Arles. It was cold. At Marseilles we put up at the Hôtel Splendide and had the only possible bouillabaisse to be eaten anywhere at a restaurant on one of the quays, the fish heads confronting us from our plates balefully.

Next day Toulouse.

At Villefranche we stayed for a month at a pension with a garden on a sort of miniature cliff above the sea. It had a balcony with an iron railing running around the house on the second floor upon which our rooms faced, with as fine a view of the harbor of Villefranche as one could desire. Back of the Pension Donat the street was crowded with mimosa trees in massive bloom.

To the left, facing the sea, the pink stucco building where we lived was flanked by the old fortifications where in the past the people could retire before raids by the Barbary pirates from the coast of Africa. To the right was the casern of a troop of Chasseurs Alpins. We were waked each morning by their trumpeted reveille.

At the moment of our arrival they were practicing various salvos by squads, loud blasts, remotely resembling, though livelier, Verdi's music, the triumphant entry of Radames into Thebes, from the opera Aïda, with many twirls and flourishes of the polished instruments themselves. All this was in preparation for the Mardi Gras parade and the coming *bataille des fleurs*.

The proprietor of the place was a seriously wounded but well set-up veteran of the last war who had come there hoping for the best, his tall, rangy wife with him, surely not from the South she. Wonderful Gaïte, their little Breton cook and maid of all work, whose childish mind, though not her cooking, delighted us, and a big German police dog named Loving, who had the run of the garden inside a high, woven-wire fence, made up the rest of the family. The cooking was advertised as Parisian. It wasn't. We were the only guests.

Just at the left, at the very entrance to the garden gate, began a narrow cliff-walk, cut from the rock, six feet above the water around the face of the abandoned fortress. On bad days it was impassable because of the waves; it had an odor of its own, very

French, of seaweed and the *pissotière* to be found at its mid-point
on the way to town. But on fine days nothing could be more wist-
fully redolent of the sea, the tideless sea, and a savage past beyond conception.

Nice was only a step westward, and Beaulieu only a slightly
longer step eastward approaching Monaco, Mentone and the
Italian Riviera.

Behind the little town rose the first range of the Alpes Mari-
times with their famous roads above the Mediterranean, the
lower and upper Corniche, which we got to know thoroughly.
The air was full of rumors of the various visitors who frequent
this coast: the writers and artists, that is; not the tennis players.
It was unmatchable for a February vacation.

And we did walk and we did enjoy the cuisine of Nice and the
cold weather when we burned oak roots, mined on the mountains,
in our grates. But we appreciated more the full sun, with carnations in the small gardens and violets among the rocks on the
hillsides. We went everywhere, saw everything from the gaming
tables at the Sports Club at Monte Carlo to the submarine fauna
at the Nice museum. I even saw, once, one of the obstetricians
from my old Nursery and Child's, standing humbly, hat in hand,
before a creature of the *haut monde* about to enter an expensive
limousine near the portal of the Hôtel de l'Europe. Very funny.
I happened to be leaving there, waiting for Floss to try on a dress
when I heard that voice! I could have put out my hand and
touched him. He would have been surprised. Such things happen
in France.

One day we entertained Nancy Cunard, surely one of the major
phenomena of that world, and her cousin Victor. They came to
look us over, Victor to sniff at the municipal gas tank beyond the
mimosa to the rear of the pension, Nancy to invite us for a
walk to Sospel back of Mentone and to talk, of writing, of anything that was in her mind; and if there was anything that was
not in that courteous, cultured and fearless mind, I have yet to
discover it. Nancy was to me as constant as the heavens in her
complete and passionate inconstancy. Out of passion, to defeat
its domination, that tall, blond spike of a woman whose mind

never, that I knew, was clouded by drink, kept herself burned to the bone. What else have the martyrs done?

Bob and she had much in common, in their tastes and in their lives and were intimate, in that remote way that deracinates of the world can be intimate, man and woman. Nancy had come down out of admiration and friendship for all of us and to look the situation over. She also was very fond of Floss and later protected her on more than one wild occasion. A tall wraith of a woman looking as though any wind might blow her away but without restraints.

We did walk there about Villefranche; we talked, we ate, drank and played otherwise as we saw fit and did considerable writing besides during those weeks. I finished the De Soto piece from *In the American Grain* and one or two others. It can't all be told.

Gaïte, the maid, said she would one day marry a sailor if he came from a *grande ville*, and promised to put on her Breton headgear for us but never did. A sweet child if there ever was one.

On my way back one evening from a trip to town, M. Barte stopped me at the door.

"May I have a word with you, Doctor?" I followed him into his small *bureau* where he placed a chair for me before sitting at his desk.

Before he started he gave me a quick glance, then proceeded at once to the business.

"It has been a great pleasure for Madame Barte and me to have you young Americans as our guests."

I replied that as far as Mrs. Williams and I were concerned, the feeling was mutual and that we never had more enjoyed a vacation than this one by the edge of the sea at Villefranche.

"You see," he went on, "I am here in reality for my health. I was a *grand blessé* of the last war."

"I'm sorry to hear that"—thinking a chest wound, since there was no palpable deformity, not even a limp, perhaps tuberculosis on top of that and . . .

"We do not have to earn a living like this. We have a small

income. Our tragedy is that we are married for five years now and have no children. In fact, we can have none. I am impotent —as a consequence of my wound."

I looked at him, making no comment.

"You see Madame Barte; she is exceptionally strong."

It was true, the woman, while not beautiful of face—a still, brooding face, she seldom smiled or even spoke more than a word or two—was erect and well-built; a fine if somewhat masculine figure.

"I wouldn't talk this way if you were not a doctor, a physician. But a doctor at his best is a confessor to us other poor people. And you have been especially kind, so that I have the courage to speak to you man to man."

"Have you thought of adopting a child," I began, "because there must be so very many French orphans?"

"Yes, and we may come to that as a last resort. . . . You mustn't take offense at what I am going to say."

He paused and looked at me hard once more.

"Madame, my wife, has been so pleased with you, who have come like this out of the skies to us. We had a talk together last night. You would make us extremely happy if one of you, you are the doctor, so I can say this to you, would give us a baby.

"You mean . . ." I began.

"Yes, precisely that."

"But you would shoot a man who would so presume."

"On the contrary. I would embrace him. You are not offended?"

"Not at all." Hmm!

"We are so pleased with you. You are young and especially you are from America, a people so much admired by the French."

"But I'm sure you couldn't permit it. . . . And your wife . . ."

"It was she who . . ."

"No, I'm sure."

"Yes, it was she who suggested it."

"And you agreed?"

"I accepted the thought with enthusiasm. You are not offended?"

"No," said I, thinking to myself of the woman, in her late thirties, perhaps, "not at all. I will speak to Mr. McAlmon."

"Either of you."

"I can't promise anything," I finished, wondering what Flossie's idea might be on the subject. So M. Barte and I parted.

I asked Bob how he felt about it, but all he would concede with a surly grunt was, "I'll leave my door open."

But nothing ever came of it. As far as I was concerned, I felt rather cheap over it.

Nancy, who was living at Monte Carlo that winter, near her mother, Lady Cunard, visited us several times to sit on our narrow balcony above the lemon trees, chrysanthemums and the carnations of our small garden.

It was often extremely cold, sometimes rainy; we'd keep indoors then, hugging our oak-root fire and read or write. We discussed plans for the future of *Contact*, whether or not to take in an African visit, a trip to Greece, to go to Naples by boat (too expensive), to stop off at Rapallo to see Pound, but finally gave up all these ideas.

One beautiful day, it was in fact St. Valentine's Day, the mistral having blown itself out, we decided to take the long-postponed hike on the upper Corniche. Gaïte had told us at breakfast of waves breaking in over the walk past the old fortress. "*La mer est méchante*," she said. At 9:30 we started. Floss found her first violets, pale but sweet. I remember just at the peak of the swift rise an almond tree in full bloom. Bob had been singing surprisingly well on the way up. I asked him why he didn't go into it professionally; he had an excellent high baritone voice. He only laughed.

That morning we followed the upper Corniche circling back of a mountain. It was especially cold as the cliff rose to our right between us and the early morning sun, while to the left was a sharp drop to the valley with snow peaks to the north. This was a bypass we were glad not to have missed.

At upper Eze we came out into the Corniche road proper again, then down to the middle road at Eze where, by luck, our tongues sticking to our teeth, we had the luck to strike an attractive *auberge*, with a few tables outdoors, though it was still cold, where we had an excellent lunch. It consisted of an omelette

aux fines herbes, bread and some salad greens, together with the
finest bottle of wine I have ever in my life enjoyed. It was a Vieux
Pommard, served ice cold, against every imaginable injunction
for the proper serving of such a wine! But we were so fatigued,
sweaty, and, above all, dying of thirst after the morning that it
was nectar to us just as it came to our glasses. We guzzled it as
we ate and watched some women and boys clubbing olives from
a large tree into a sheet on the ground under it, there to be
picked up in small baskets.

Stiff as we were, we went on from here another eight kilometers
to Monaco which we reached at four P.M. and home at dusk by
train. Floss took a bath. It was always something of an event in
that country.

Floss in bed in red kimono reading *Orley Farm,* the diary says,
about the unhappiness of success. I wrote on the "Boone." Paid
weekly bill: Floss and me 483.25 fr.

Another time Nancy invited us to meet her in Monte Carlo.
Thence we drove to Mentone, then by taxi to Sospel back of
a wild taxi driver who took those dizzy turns at top speed.
Dinner at the Hôtel Étranger. Thence we hiked back to Castillon
(7 k.) and by taxi again to Monte Carlo. Had supper with Nancy
and Victor Cunard, who invited us to see him in Rome and to
meet Norman Douglas, which I was happy to promise I would
do. Read E. E. Cummings' *Tulips and Chimneys,* discussed it at
length. Nancy described a zeppelin raid.

Another day Nancy had us again to Monte Carlo for the
gaming at the swanky Sports Club, where, having lost my ten
bucks, my limit, but Floss having won five hundred francs on the
number seven. I persuaded her to let me put it on black and
won again. That did it. We drove back the entire distance to
Villefranche, by taxi at four A.M. by moonlight, feeling like
millionaires on fifty bucks!

Later we saw Djuna Barnes and Thelma Wood, who had lost
all the cash Djuna had given her at Boule then borrowed from
Floss and lost that also. Djuna wanted me to go with her to
interview Maeterlinck, but it didn't come off.

Another day Bob and I swam, walking gingerly over the hard

pebbles in the icy water while the little Chasseurs on the embankment watched us, shaking their heads as though we were cracked. Met a chunky Swede in the water, one day, who made us look silly. At ten degrees centigrade, according to him, the water was little less than tepid.

Bill Bird came down for a day and stayed the night with us. Both he and Bob were all for our going to Marseilles with them for bouillabaisse and a big time before Floss and I headed for Italy and Vienna. But I couldn't see it though Floss would have gone.

The next month, the month of March, Floss and I spent traveling about Italy. In Rome, Norman Douglas had us to tea in his sixth-floor rooms overlooking the Roman forum to the north. We talked for two hours—of contemporary writers, their lives, his own life, of his son whom he had not seen virtually since birth. When, the boy having grown to be a man, they met again, each was strongly attracted by the other's qualities, each a man of whom the other thoroughly approved. It was a satisfying experience for them both. It was at that time that Douglas gave me his opinion that the best thing a father can do for his son after he conceives him is to die when he is born. I suppose I had been expressing some doubts as to our wisdom in going off and leaving our own children behind. That was his answer.

As we talked, moving about the apartment, we could look out over the wrecks of antiquity, the forum as it had been unearthed in later years. Douglas doubted that anywhere other than at the windows of his rooms would one find so impressive a view. But, as with all human affairs, this too promised to come out badly; the new authorities were thinking of tearing the place down where he lived so happily.

There was, however, an ancient wisteria vine, or tree, one might almost say, whose trunk even at this height was as thick around as a man's arm, growing from the ground below and continuing as high as the roof above. Each year this magnificent growth covered the entire side of the building up to the eaves with abundant purple flowers. Douglas had a nefarious scheme in mind which through his friend, the local Guardian of Public

Works, he thought he might be able to put into effect. It was no less than to have this vine officially declared a public monument. This was the plan by which not only the vine itself but the building and the whole situation might be saved.

It would be idle to attempt to describe our experiences in Italy, rich as they were to us, scenes and events spoken of at length sometimes, under the pretext of an imagined story in my *Voyage to Pagany*. The same for the trip through the Austrian Tyrol to Vienna, where I spent a valuable month studying at the famous university there. It would take a book in itself.

Chapter 34

Paris Again

On our return by train to Paris our first stop was at Salzburg. It was May first, and the Communists were parading with a red flag before the hotel. That night we were served baked carp, a famous recipe. Two old aristocrats, man and wife, sat formally at dinner, he half-asleep, she bejeweled about the hair, neck and breast, heavy rings on her fingers, trying by her coy remarks to keep him from falling over. It had rained all day long, the paraders marched, without music, stolidly up the street, the square red flag before them.

After Salzburg and the visit to Lancy, where I saw again my old school, the primrose-grown soccer field, and George Brunel, son of the old director, we went direct to Dijon. We had been invited to meet Bill and Sally Bird there for a wine-tasting spree under Bill's guidance. It was an opportunity not to be missed.

Arrived at Dijon six P.M. We met Bill and Sally Bird at the Hôtel de la Cloche, the original perhaps, at least in spirit, of all the great old candle and crystal chandelier days of a hundred American hotels of the last century. After we washed up, Bill took us at once to Ernest's, a famous restaurant, where we tasted his favorite, Richebourg and Chambertin, and heard Ernest himself (he knew Bill as an authority on wines) tell us of *les Américains* stationed in Dijon during the war. Whisky was all they wanted, or a shot of brandy on occasion. If they could be persuaded to broach a bottle of burgundy they slugged that in too, just as they took the other stuff, cultured or raw. It had broken Ernest's heart. He had finally given up hope and had poured them what they asked for, disclaiming any possibility of there being any rare vintages left any longer in his *cave*. They wouldn't know the difference. But for Bird, Ernest really dug down and brought up the best. Floss and I were, of course, not quite up to it, but we had to admit that it tasted like nothing we had had before —except perhaps one bottle of Swiss, grown near Sierre on the slopes toward Italy, which we remembered. We didn't enter into that with Bill and Ernest.

In the evening we wandered with Bill and Sally about the worn and empty streets of the old ducal city. Stone of the most antique feudal cut, stone, stone, stone—underfoot, between silent stone walls, even the roofs are stone—asleep perhaps forever, perhaps not: made one think of Beauty and the Beast. If there will ever come a prince to wake us from our modern utilitarian sleep, he may be from under a gray stone roof of Dijon, smelling of the grapes of the Côte d'Or where lived Vercingetorix, the last of the Gauls to hold out against Caesar. He was betrayed by his own tribesmates, as we all are in the end.

Maybe the vineyards we saw next day on our way to Beaune got their flavor from the very blood of these men still in the soil. Some of the most famous bouquets in those sunbaked hills, the Nuits-Saint-Georges and their kin, come from no more than half an acre of the precious soil. It has been cultivated for generation after generation in the same spot, another spot, not a thousand feet off, giving a grape of a slightly different flavor. And yet there would not be a grape left in France were it not grafted on pest-resistant American stock.

The day after, at midday, we arrived at Beaune in the heart of the Burgundy country, Bill pointing out to us as we went the location of one famous vineyard after the other. We had dinner at the Hôtel de la Poste, white and red wines of Bill's selection with cognac at the end. We saw the amazing Hôtel-Dieu (God's Hospice), fifteenth-century work, the kitchen and, fascinating to me, the chapel ward: Beds for the poor and sick embayed into the wall where, in a saintly atmosphere, the unfortunate and old were served by the nuns, still walking about in their black

gowns and immaculate white starched head-covers, like flying
swans, going about their charitable duties as in Gothic paintings
and sculpture. It gave me the most lively sense of the reality of
the poor that I have ever had. Bill and I saw the gargoyles while
the ladies rested.

That night, between Bill and Ernest, we were almost ruined.
We had spent the day at Beaune, I had done my best *"goûter"*
the finest wines in the world, to appreciate and differentiate, to
suck air in over the tongue with a mouthful of those beautiful
vintages!

Next day, we bought small pots of the famous mustard of the
country, entrained and listened to Bill's long lecture on the wines
of France, north and south, dozed our way to Paris seeing
Tonerre, the Cathedral at Sens, fields of fleur-de-lis. At Paris,
at the Gare de l'Est, we had to show our little pots of mustard to
the officer of the *douane* (le douanier Rousseau's job). Bob
had procured good quarters for us at the Hôtel Unic and here
we were again for our last stand before returning to America and
home.

That very night we landed full in the thick of Parisian life at
a pace much quickened over that we had known in January.
After meeting Joyce on the street it began at once when we
taxied that evening to hear Clotilde Vail sing a program of
Brahms lieder and other songs, which she did well, at a narrow
hall somewhere in the quarter—a young woman in white silk on
a small stage. Aragon and some other young Frenchman of the
period sat prominently in a box to our left, much more intent
on being seen, I thought, than on hearing the young American.
The place was packed with friends.

We went thence, our own small party, for drinks—Harold
Loeb, the Birds, Bob, Mina and daughter, Mary Butts and
myself. As we were sitting speaking of the concert, in the usual
belittling manner, Clotilde entered with her brother Lawrence.
He was already high. She, the strain of the concert no longer
upon her, was parched for a drink. Regardless of restraints she
went over the back of the settee where I had been an attraction,
the young poet just arrived, and jammed herself between me and

Sally. We were packed like sardines into the small place. The
ladies generally were not pleased. It was at least a way to get
acquainted.

The next day it was raining but cleared, and the sun came
out brightly. Rode a bus to the Louvre and walked thence,
buying a few stamps at the outdoor market on the Champs
Elysées for Bill. At the hotel neither trunk nor baggage had
arrived; ate at Trianon, then to Dôme. Met Hemingway on the
street, a young man with a boil on his seat, just back from a
bicycle ride in Spain. The three of us back to the hotel where
I swiped Bob's best socks; he gave me several neckties.

Bob told me of an incident which happened during a train ride
he had had with Hem on his way back from Spain a year before.
They had stopped and the passengers had alighted for a breath
of fresh air. Beside the track was a dead dog, his belly swollen,
the skin of it iridescent with decay. Bob had wanted to get away
from the stink as fast as he could, but Hem would not. On the
contrary, he got out his notebook and began, to Bob's disgust,
to take minute notes describing the carcass in all its beauty.

"I thoroughly approve," I said.

That evening Bill Bird took us to the top of Monmartre where
we had supper near the Sacré Coeur. Down from the top we drank
at a famous small place run by a character in a Russian peasant's
blouse, beret and a gray beard, a contemporary surely of Ver-
laine, who sang for us, alone in that small, evil-smelling place,
to his own guitar music. A place full of "atmosphere." But
there was in fact another person there whom Sally recognized
at once as the reigning tenor at the Opéra Comique, a famous
name. She was all a dither.

How it began, I don't know but somehow or other—we perhaps
egged her on—she began to sing the soprano part of the duet
from *La Bohème*. He at once joined it with his magnificent
voice. Together they completed the episode, an unrivaled performance under the circumstances, to the strumming of the old
guy in the beret. Sally was almost fainting at the tragic close.
They had been sitting hip to hip at the crude table about which

we had all gathered, good reason for her ecstasy. We had all we
could do to get her up and out of the place.

Wednesday, the 16th, a brilliant and cool May morning. Hope
my trunk and baggage get here soon. Bill Bird has planned a trip
for us over the week-end starting Saturday at 8:30 A.M. Floss
shops today and I shall see pictures. Visited Louvre with Floss
in morning—the space usually occupied by the Mona Lisa,
blank, the canvas having been cut out of the frame and stolen
only a week ago. Harold Loeb went with me to the *Salon*. A
few sculptured pieces (about four) were interesting, but in general the exhibit was terrible. I was surprised. The pictures the
same or even worse and in Paris! The amazing thing about it
was the sheer number of works and the size of the hall—that was
the best thing about it.

Had supper with Philippe and Mme. Soupault and George
Antheil at Restaurant l'Avenue, where I admired as always the
unique hors d'oeuvre, plates of cubes of carrots, beets, all sorts
of simple and amusing dishes. It was a good evening. I myself
felt very happy talking to Soupault about Picasso, his poor beginnings, his profusion, one of the greatest reasons for his success, the women who had walked into and out of his life, his
single-mindedness. We talked of America, of which all Frenchmen are secretly jealous, especially of our money. Later we went
to the Dingo. Clotilde came, Nancy came in and left abruptly,
to everybody's irritation: Paris is like that. Ford just thumbed
his nose.

Thursday, Floss and I taxied to the Vails' for lunch, being
passed by Joyce in a taxi near the Arc de Triomphe. I shall never
forget his face on recognizing us, from his taxi, we in the other
vehicle of the same sort, passing. It was a guilty sort of face,
half-surprised, half-embarrassed, like a fellow caught at the site
of a recent crime. I never could quite make it out. I once in conversation with him offered that if it could be decently arranged
and there were enough intelligent people in the priesthood, he
wouldn't mind being elected Pope. He gave me then the same

look I saw from the taxi. I even wrote an "improvisation" about it later.

At the Vails' we had a suburban sort of party that was really amusing. At table, Peggy Vail (née Guggenheim) and her pink ice cream about which Mrs. Vail Senior was very insistent. At each place the *petit pains* had been hidden in the napkin to keep them warm. Floss and I and Mrs. Vail spilled ours on the floor! After lunch a photographer arrived to take pictures, Mrs. Vail very much upset by his incompetence. She tried several times to remove lamps from the background. These pictures were published in the *Herald Tribune* Paris edition. Bryher and H.D. appeared later in the evening. We all, Bob, they and we, supped together. It was the first time we had seen them since the Brevoort party. Floss and I to Stravinsky concert at Opéra in the evening and *walked* home.

The next day I woke to find Floss ill, sore throat and fever, really down and out. I looked in and got a scare: white spot back of right tonsil. Aspirin and cold compresses. I beat it over to Bill's office to call off trip for that week-end. He was out. Tried to get gargle I was familiar with and failed. Bought "sterilized" milk and beat it home. Lunched with Bob and his family, that is Bryher and H.D. Not good: he showed signs of irritability. Sat after with Floss. At six Bill Bird called on phone and Harold Loeb brought his ms. which I took upstairs and started to read. No luck. Floss insisted I go out. Went to Soirée de Paris but shied at the crowd. Came back and fell asleep on bed, woke and out at eleven o'clock. A *poule* stopped me with the usual proposal—reminded me of my cousin Alice. I told her no, that I was married and quite happy. She shrugged and proposed the usual alternative, a cigarette, which I gave her. Sat late at Dôme with Clotilde Vail.

Saturday, May 24. Floss was real sick. It is *not,* however, diphtheria. Now I worry as to whether or not it will turn into a quinsy. Spots have gone over to left side also, more extensive than at first. In evening I went with Bob, Bryher and H.D., to

Soirée de Paris, evening clothes. My old tux looked like two cents in all that extremity of mode. I felt particularly awkward, out of place, unhappy.

A first-rate show, for some charity or other, many distinguished people of all nationalities, the *haut monde* on all sides. The orchestra had struck! But after a long pause, things went on. The Ballet *"Salade"* I liked well, but it might have been the girl who tried to dislocate her knees and elbows assuming the angular poses assigned to her. When I told H.D. I had enjoyed that one, she merely laughed in her cryptic and irritating way as much as to say "you *would*." "Gigue" also and the "Blue Danube," were excellent.

I felt out of place, self-conscious and alone in that mob. My clothes were dull, my manners worse. The drink, as always, meant nothing, worse than nothing, to me. I was too alert to it, had no intention of going on with it. Among the whole crowd of talents about me not a face was open, not even among my own group. I saw women who seemed to want to open up, but the only one I felt anything for was that young girl taking the solo part in the ballet *"Salade."* Everyone else was closed, closed tight, with eyes like something under a submerged rock, waiting covertly to feed. From what I knew of even those in my own group, painfully in detail, the cupidity, the bitchery, the half-screaming hysteria, I wasn't attracted. It was a gelatinous mass, squatting over a treasure; a *Rheingold-musik.* Calculating bitches that they were, not only toward me, but toward each other, they were biding their time while the cash was worth their attention. By what I knew of their moves, the cheapness, the grimaces, even their manner of standing or sitting on a chair, I hated them. They revealed all too brilliantly (if one could read) how the hand was offered and food put to the mouth, foully enough among my own intimates; how then should one interpret the whole mass of dancing, laughing figures? They were completely indifferent, you might say, to the performance on the stage as to me. Their own lives and movements were (naturally) far more complex than the dancing and the music. Strain as she would, the little ballerina, break her bones even though she might in the grotesque routines, she could never equal what lay before her.

So that, in a sense, if I had known it, the indifference to both dance and music in this straining crowd of French social automatons was justified. They looked and revealed nothing of themselves: nothing that I, at least, could see, though I judged (from what I did know in detail, accurately) that it was for sale to the highest bidder, as usual. At least they were here, they had come and it was worth it to them. The show on the stage was not serious: the success of the work presented depended on its ability to put that indifferent crowd in its place—art vs. society. This evening society was in the ascendant. No score for art.

Could these works be rescued, or something of them be rescued for use against a lesser intelligence? That's what the contest between new works of art and an alert *haut monde* means: The fight that goes on between the stage and the audience. For it is certain that though the onlookers appear indifferent, talk, turn their backs, they have eyes there too.

It is the cruel battle of wits that goes on in all cities and as between city and city. I was a rustic in my own eyes, completely uninitiated, but it is certain that though I was in no way affected by the well-dressed crowd, and it was the alert best of Paris, I ground my teeth out of resentment, though I acknowledged their privilege to step on my face if they could. Anyhow I was having a rotten time and I liked the little dancer.

Sunday Floss recovering from tonsilitis, in bed—headache. Stayed in room and had meal sent in from the corner. Later ate alone at Trianon. There met Bill Bird. We arranged to go see some fights above Montmartre in a sort of courtyard there out of doors. No seats. Men standing about. Saw about eight bouts, flyweight, middleweight, etc.—some were fairly interesting, no knock-outs. One good-looking lad received a left, right in his bread-basket and sat down so suddenly that it was amusing. He got up at the count of eight and went on to win the fight a few rounds later.

It rained. Back to hotel in the most rickety taxi I ever saw, had been used in Galliéni's famous *sortie* from Paris. Kitty, Harold and Murphy called. We talked of Kay Boyle and Le Havre.

Floss reading Melville's *Mardi*, which she likes. Floss has been quite ill but seems on road to recovery now.

Monday. Floss about well. Temperature 98. Sent off voluminous laundry. Got boys' school papers sent by Lucy, much amused at Bill's "Poison." *Pneumatique* to Harold. Then took Floss out to lunch for first time, she weak in the knees but otherwise well. I urged her, against her will, to take a couple of whiskies then brought her home. Temperature 102, but after rest, normal again. Bob and I walked about, talked at Café des Deux Magots. Met Locher, Charlie Demuth's friend.

T. S. Eliot had come to Paris about then, appearing at the Dôme and other bars in top hat, cutaway, and striped trousers. It was intended as a gesture of contempt and received just that.

I was told of a dance that was being given for a little girl well-known at that time in the quarter. She had T.B. and was being sent away for treatment somewhere in the country, a cute kid everyone liked. She was coughing all over the place and showed that she had been going downhill fast. She had an American sailor in tow that evening who had been sleeping with her during his furlough in Paris. Dancing, drunk, gay, through her tears she was saying a sorrowful farewell, a hat was being passed for her, while everyone in the place was exposed to her malady.

Took Floss to supper with Bob, Bryher, Harold Loeb and H.D. at l'Avenue. Good talk. Took Floss back to hotel, then at Dôme sat with others, after Bryher and H.D. left, until late talking of everything. Bob silent.

Next day up and out at ten A.M., took photo to Sylvia Beach, got tickets, haircut, money and back to hotel by noon. Then with Floss to Trianon where Bob and Bryher were giving a little family lunch for Mina and her children. Afterward Bob and I walked toward Luxembourg, he uncommunicative, glum, souring me also. Rather than go on, I left him on the spur of the moment, saying I wanted to see the pictures in the Luxembourg as an excuse. He continued on. Enjoyed impressionists, Manet and Cézanne, a few Degas there too. Came home and rested, then to Dôme where I saw Harold and Clotilde Vail. She wanting a baby. We offered ourselves. She unconvinced. Supped at Trianon where we had long talk with Joyce and Nora, also with painter Toohey, who later committed suicide, I believe.

The 28th we lay in bed most of the morning, I reading Harold Loeb's novel. Taxied to Nancy Cunard's for lunch at 1:15. First time we had seen her rooms on quai d'Orleans, which we admired, admiring also Brzeska's "Faun" spoken of by Ezra Pound in his book on the work of the young sculptor shot through the head during the First World War.

Nancy had not yet arrived, but came in a few minutes later saying that George Moore, whom we had expected to meet, didn't want to come. Nancy tied handkerchief we had brought her around her neck. Told us of trying to climb tree at Bal Brouillier the evening before and of falling. All scratched up, black eye, etc.

Earlier the same day played tennis with Hemingway and Harold Loeb, four sets. Hem and I finally quit even, he unable to break my service and I, his: would have gone on till evening, perhaps.

"You've got nothing," he told me. "My knee gives out if I keep it up too long. Let's call it off."

There was a story current in Paris at the time of the rival partisans of Joyce and Proust, who had arranged a meeting at a reception one evening between the two great men. Two chairs were placed side by side in the middle of the room. There the heroes were seated while the partisans ranged themselves right and left, waiting for the wits to sparkle and flash.

Joyce said, "I've headaches every day. My eyes are terrible."

Proust replied, "My poor stomach. What am I going to do? It's killing me. In fact, I must leave at once."

"I'm in the same situation," replied Joyce, "if I can find someone to take me by the arm. Good-bye."

"*Charmé*," said Proust, "oh, my stomach, my stomach."

Met Bob and Bryher at Dôme, H.D. having finally been shaken. Supper with them at "Chez M" in Montmartre, then to

Nancy's again at ten to meet Clive Bell, Michael Strange, André Germain, fussy as always, and Iris Tree with her straight blond hair about her head, as though she were a young knight of the round table. She was unsmiling, but solidly made, very appealing to me. Bob skeptical of her wit. Too stolid.

Stayed late, drinking and talking, had fried eggs at a stand with taxi drivers toward morning. Home at five A.M.

Thursday stayed in bed, more or less, till noon reading Loeb's ms. Then ate at cheap restaurant near Trianon, extremely simple but good. Met Bob at Dôme, went with him to see Locher, Demuth's friend, at Hôtel Jacob. Not in. I told him what Demuth had told me of trying to get to see Proust when he, Demuth, had been in Paris, and that Proust had begged off. Dropped Bob at Dôme, probably the fact that wife and H.D. were in Paris together had him down. Had told us of long train trips about the continent with the two women quarreling in the compartment driving him nearly insane, hard to go on like that.

Floss and I to Mina's. She tried to do my portrait in pencil while Floss slept. I fell asleep. Then I slept while she did a fine, if too delicate, one of Floss. Later tried me again. No go. We supped with Loeb, then to Dingo and home. Later I went out alone at 11:30 to Dôme. Met Clotilde, who told me she is going to the country next day for a party with her brother. This is the origin of the brother-sister incident in *Voyage to Pagany*.

Up and out Friday, May 30th, to get a few supplies for Floss. Finished Loeb's ms. reading till noon. Lunched with Bob, Bryher and H.D. at Trianon, rotten service. Floss and I then to Kitty's where they talked while Harold and I went over his ms. I then to Mina's. She tried my portrait again while Joella talked and sewed curtains. Nice supper at l'Avenue, eight of us, Antheil, Adrienne Monnier, Sylvia Beach, etc. Good talk with H.D. over old times, Ezra's sudden interest in music. Sat at Dôme, saw Kiki, Mary Reynolds, etc. Sat at Dôme with Antheil, Bob who left at twelve. Floss and I home.

Next morning to Bill Bird's office with Floss. He politely took us downstairs and gave us vermouth. To bank, cashed $150 for Floss, then walked down Avenue de la Paix to Tuileries Gardens and Luxembourg Annex. Saw Whistler's "Portrait of Mother," roses in garden. Taxied home. Floss and I alone lunched at l'Avenue.

In afternoon went privately to hear Antheil play his own works, good, if startling stuff. Then to Birds' to tea. Bob leaves note. Finally decided not to go to dance with Nancy and, tired, lay in bed reading Bob's *Village* till midnight.

Eight A.M. Sunday morning the first of June. It is a day worthy of the date: brilliant, hot sun, screaming of swallows or swifts outside open triple window, the peculiar, pagodalike church bells are ringing in all their eccentricity.

Who are these two young and arresting women, or any of them all, with whom we have been thrown during our brief stay in Paris? I speak especially of Nancy Cunard and Iris Tree, though we saw less of Iris than Nancy. Surely they were riding above the storm in the Paris that we were witnessing. Nancy Cunard, straight as any stick, emaciated, holding her head erect, not particularly animated, her blue eyes completely untroubled, inviolable in her virginity of pure act. I never saw her drunk; I can imagine that she was never quite sober. If the Irish in her, through her American mother, made her daring, it was the German in Iris Tree that made her still, almost dull. She, stockier than her fellow Englishwomen, had she been mounted on a proper charger in mail, her thick blond hair brushing her shoulders, would have made an ideal picture of Sir Galahad.

There were the others but these two seemed to stand out for me—perhaps because they were absolutely remote from any desire I might have had toward them. They possessed Paris, as much of Paris as they wanted, but I couldn't make them out. I'm sure I didn't look at them as women. They were a momentary phase of a thing as fixed and permanent to me as the stones on which we walked. If I went to Paris again, I'd expect to find them just as they were at that time, young, detached from reality, without passion. That's it. They seemed to be completely devoid of passion. They, young as they were, had had bitter early experiences without emotional response. There was nothing left in either of them. They were completely empty, and yet they were young, appealing and unassailable. No one could touch them to harm them in any way or be deeply moved by them. They were as quiet in their moods and as profligate in their actions (it was said) as figures cut from chalk, or so I addressed their images in my mind. For a strange reason, I felt a strong affection for them. Either of them, but particularly the almost stupid-looking Iris, was powerfully desirable to me, from a Paris that was dead, dead, dead.

There was nothing I wanted to do about it; and I was happy to know that if there had been a possibility of raising a love from such stuff, it would be quite impossible to describe it.

It was a feeling such as one has in going about the corridors of a gallery of sculpture. The stupid believe that it is amusing to think of Galatea coming to life, but they haven't the slightest idea how far she would have to travel to regain breath. And if she should regain it, what a terrifying thing it would be: the past being something which we cannot even in our imagination resurrect. That's how I felt about those two English society girls, gross as I knew them to be. By their profligacy they were asserting a veritable chastity of mind which no one could disturb. The trouble of mind of a Clotilde, of a Mina, to me had come to some sort of resolution, but in Nancy especially, after some sort of purgation, it had reached a final end.

The story went around that Lady Asquith, meeting Lady Cunard in London, said to her in a loud English voice meant to injure, speaking of Nancy, "What is it now, Maud, whisky, opium or niggers?"

That too Nancy put behind her, shortly, by marrying Henry Crowder, who had been General March's colored chauffeur during the First World War. Nancy, the perfect bitch if ever there was one, came out above it, unlying—and Iris, like Berenice Abbott, who had the same quality, affected one with the same elevated feeling, as of a religious experience. Had it not been recognized by others? Iris, the saint in Max Reinhardt's pageant *The Miracle*. It is an experience remote, childish, like the very first feelings of love, unassociated with sex. For they had called it by a name, if you cared to say so, by their "suffering" come through with a depraved saintliness. Depravity was their prayer, their ritual, their rhythmic exercises: they denied sin by making it hackneyed in their own bodies, shucking it away to come out not dirtied but pure.

Adrienne Monnier was something else again. She was, to be sure, French, gross, heavy-legged. The English to the north might think themselves more spiritual, but she smacked her lips and enjoyed where they hardly ate at all; hardly, at least, tasted. The French would never commit self-destruction until they had first drunk up the wine in the cellar. This woman loved food, the senses were her meat. She achieved equality with Nancy and Iris on another plane. It was the women, all of them, from the commercial puffed-furniture-Soirée-de-Paris type, to Flossie herself who in Paris fascinated me. The men merely served as their counterfoils, from the piddling French surrealists of the day to myself standing in the mere outskirts of the picture. But Clotilde, failing to get a father for her "child," Kitty Cannell, employed as a fashion detective, H.D., the millionaire's daughter Bryher, they were the ones I looked at hardest.

What do I look for in a woman? Death, I suppose, since it's all I see anyhow in those various perfections. I want them all in lesser or greater degree. Most men make me laugh, especially when they most "possess" a woman. I have nothing but contempt for them. The story was told of a girl who, having come to Paris for experience, decided after a while it was time to go to bed with a man. So she picked one that was gay and seemed, from his talk, to be sufficiently expert and would not fumble and muff his performance; a good-looking southern kid who appealed to her.

After he had so far committed himself that it was impossible to hold back, the heart almost went out of him when he realized, with a shock, that she was a virgin.

He began to feel remorseful, and a little scared, realizing what he had done. All she said was, "Is *that* all it amounts to? Hardly worth the trouble. Thank you for helping me."

And a college boy, approached by a young wife and mother in Paris for the voluptuous pleasure of it, found himself completely unmanned by the older woman. He was unable and frightened almost to death. Escaping, he rushed to a French prostitute of his acquaintance who, by her kindness and skill, in no more than a moment, restored his pride completely. What asses we are to be crushed when we fail by mere lack of mental agility! We fix ourselves in orders of being and think that that is the end of us. The wise French are more labile.

That Sunday in June, we had lunch at a small restaurant, then taxied to a fight at Buffalo, the local stadium, where a ring had been set up in the center of the sports field. Saw some interesting preliminaries. Saw Townley, with hardly any opposition at all, take the count from Paolo Uzcudun, the Basque wood-cutter, just a clean right to the jaw. And Criqui licked by Frush, an American, in the eighth round: a good fight ending in a typical French way. Criqui, at one time a World's Lightweight Champion, had had a face wound during the war, necessitating the insertion of a plate in the lower jaw. But he wanted to fight, so they gave him the chance against this younger American opponent. Frush, obviously, tried his best not to hurt his man, but Criqui, sensing the situation, started to hammer away until Frush, after seven rounds, let one fly at last breaking Criqui's jaw and ending the fight. As soon as he realized what had happened, Frush in tears rushed up, threw his arms about the old champion and led him to the ropes.

Silver gin fizz, then to supper, a memorable one at Adrienne Monnier's, who with her own hands, as she had promised, prepared for us the much-praised chicken after her secret recipe. Sylvia Beach, Bryher, H.D., Bob, Floss and I made up the party. But before it had got fairly started there was a shout from the street. It was Ezra Pound, just arrived from Rapallo. Adrienne called out of the window to him, but he refused to come up, so I ran down to see him for the first time in many years. He looked thinner but otherwise just as always. We talked. He gave me his address and so for the moment I left him.

Next day: Sensing the end of our magnificent year at hand, wondering what to do, we took the #43 train to Porte Maillot and walked in the Bois. A sudden shower came up. We stood under a tree. Then took lunch (only fair) in the Bois. Floss went for a dress and a hair wave. I had a time finding a *cabinet* which I finally got to in the Gare St. Lazare after buying gum and a ticket. Floss bought stockings at Le Printemps. Home by taxi in a heavy rain.

Men are the technical morons of the tribe, women keep some proportion, remain sound even in debauchery, relate the parts to a whole, act, that is with the body, the related parts, together, not a part of it, as to be sure, they must to survive. What could I possibly do to them or for them in that complete sense? Nothing. Or they for me? I wasn't interested in the cash value. The timely postcard signed D.H., after Bob's wedding to Bryher, meant more upon that subject than met the eye, an anthropologic outcry of some carrying power.

These young women, some of them wealthy, love because they have nothing to do, they have no employment, like myself, in one sense, which explains my affection for them. The part of them that is valueless (priceless) is as Yeats said of the debauchery of the Lionel Johnson group: They are as they are because no locus is *permitted* them in the society in which they should be active members. This explains the fury of Edmund Gosse, the fury of a Stanley Baldwin facing the King: defendants of a society which refuses me, would jail me if it could, any of them, right down to my nearest friends. It is the shock of my father's face when he asked me, "What do you want to do?"

"Nothing."

It is my instinctive affection for these "lost" girls that is the best part of me—and them. I loved them all. Like Toulouse-Lautrec (who had the advantage of his deformity), I would gladly have lived in a brothel (of them) for the warmth (extra-curricular) and the comfort to be derived therefrom.

We said good-bye to Bryher and H.D., who were leaving town the next day, the first inkling of the termination of our month in Paris and the end of our memorable "debauch." Tea with Bob at André Germain's, a fussy fool. Supper at Nancy's with John Rodker, Pound, Antheil, Bob, Iris Tree. In the evening to La Cigale for Jean Cocteau's *Juliet and Romeo* of which I remember nothing at all save that it in no way resembled Shakespeare's

story. Yet I should remember *something*. Nothing. Home alone
with Floss. Poor mood.

Next morning I went to see Ezra in his room. As I was nearing
the place, I passed his wife Dorothy on the street but not being
certain, I made no move to greet her or she me. The erectness
of the British walk, the shoes, but especially the design of the
hat she had on, could never have originated in the French capital.
If it is she, I thought, I'll see her later, let her go.

Ezra has a nice, big studio with an attractive courtyard, rather
unkempt, but pleasant, on which roofers were working. We talked
of his appendix, renaissance music, theory of notation, static
"hearing," melody, *time*. I have always felt that time was Ezra's
chief asset as a music appreciator. A man with an ear such as his,
attuned to the metrical subtleties of the best in verse, must have
strong convictions upon the movements of the musical phrase.
His praise of music and his interest in it, though, were to me
always suspect. It was necessary for Ezra, in self-defense, though
it was far beyond his natural abilities or capabilities, to include
music in his omniscience concerning the modalities of the arts.
Tones, I am certain, meant nothing to him, can mean nothing.
His interest lay in the melody, the musical "sentence," the time
variants (as in Antheil, when he could be listened to), renaissance
music, the early composers, before Bach. Ezra could be listened
to with profit in that field. Let him go on. It was worth it.

Ezra in my opinion, like W. B. Yeats, does not know one tone
from another. This, if it is true, is interesting, for it is known
that a lack of one gift frequently is compensated for by an
extreme subtlety of perception in another. Pound's sense of time
is extraordinary. His engrossment with music would come from
that cause, virtually a compelling necessity with him, for the
very reason that he has no tonal ability. He had ordered copied
on microfilm, for instance, just before the last war, from the
collection at Dresden, a large number of unknown Vivaldi
sonatas. So that with the destruction of the originals by the
Allies, Vivaldi's work has not been lost to the world.

So, I say, an artist may at times turn a fault into a virtue. It
must infuriate Ezra to know that there is *something* in the world
of which he is not the supreme master.

But when I talked in Brooklyn to Yves Tinayre, who sang

the leading role in Ezra's *Villon,* he, while loyal to Ezra, could hardly stop laughing over some of the effects that turned up. He acknowledged that the music was ludicrous, the composer hadn't the slightest idea of the normal voice range, but occasionally a "figure," a musical figure, such as that indicating the approach of the crowd, *die lumpen, hoi polloi,* was extremely amusing and effective. The music went along in explicit sentences, Tinayre wondered only who put it on the paper for him. Antheil, perhaps.

When, an hour later, Dorothy, his wife came in, I saw at once that it was she whom I had passed earlier on the street. I had seen her briefly in London fourteen years before, but her mother had been the more prominent in Ezra's life then.

There was some talk of lunch at this point. But since Ezra was cook in the ménage and did much of his cuisine over an alcohol lamp on a shaky-looking table, I persuaded him to come, rather, with me. We found a place near the Odéon. Dorothy had refused to accompany us.

Back at the studio and talked with Dorothy of Paris, which she intensely disliked, as much because of its people as its winter weather, neither fish nor flesh. Italy, as with all Englishmen and Germans, she adored. We fetched Floss wearing a new hat at 4:30. Saw Dorothy's painting, like herself, linear, gray, Flossie's favorite color. She gave us one of rocks on the Dartmouth moors, cubistic in feeling, flat and cold. Had tea over the alcohol lamp at which the Maestro himself officiated.

Supper, Floss and I, with the Hemingways in a small place nearby. Saw baby and Miss Johnson. All went to prize fight after. In the row in front of us (it was an old theatre, the ring being the stage), was Ogden Nash, upon whose back, when one of the fighters got bloodiest, Floss pounded as she screamed, "Kill him! Kill him!" to my horror and astonishment. Home by taxi early.

It doesn't seem possible that we sail for America in eight days. Yet we do. Paris has gotten violently into our blood in one way or another. I wonder if I could be happy here as a child specialist.

Sally has been urging it on me. They say if you wish to practice, all you have to do is to become some French doctor's "assistant." You pay him a fee, after which you are on your own. It might go. With the promise of a quiet life, I might do it, but not in Montparnasse.

Went to Hemingways' at 10:30 to see the baby. Found him to be two pounds underweight, otherwise well. Retracted his foreskin. He naturally cried, to his parents' chagrin. Taxied to hear Sally Bird sing in her teacher's studio. She did marvelously well. *Figaro* and *Bohème*. To lunch with her after at Prunier's near the Madeleine, talking of singing and many of our mutual friends.

Sally has been perpetually on the threshold of an Opéra Comique debut, all but in. She has a much praised voice. But in France the artist must purchase her own costumes, that is to say, she must have some "angel" to support her, to pay all her expenses. For this, in the usual way, she must exchange her intimate favors. Had not Felix Faure, president of France, dropped dead in the boudoir of the première danseuse at the opera? Bill Bird wasn't rich, and for him it would have been, a mere husband, too risky a gamble, both ways. So Sally, though she sings beautifully, gets no nearer the top. She might have gone into the provinces, built up the hard way, but this wasn't Sally's idea of the thing.

Had lunch with Ezra, Dorothy and Bob McAlmon at l'Avenue. Ezra kidded Bob about mistaking him (Ezra) for his (Bob's) old man. Nice lunch. Taxied to bank with Bob, left him at Twelve rue de l'Odéon. Supper at small restaurant alone and after rest at hotel, went on to Nancy's where we had a good drinking time. It turned out to be, in fact, one of the more alcoholic evenings of our visit to Paris. Jean Cocteau presented his hands, of which Nancy showed us either a photo by someone or a sculptured piece representing them, hands nearly unique in my experience. His hands are narrow through the palm, with fingers of extreme slenderness such as I can recall seeing elsewhere only upon the wrists of a tall Negress, captain of one of our local high-school basketball teams.

It was no more than *"Charmé"* from the man whom Ezra had

praised so extravagantly to me. Then he was taken off by his
intimates. John Rodker was there and the Prince de Dahomy,
a football guard of a king's son from Equatorial Africa, ebony
black but wearing a cordon of some distinguished order across
his chest and speaking English and French with ease and refine-
ment.

The crowd was dense and heavy drinkers all. Bob grew furious
at Nancy for using him as a servant to run down into the cellar
to bring up more bottles as she needed them. He told her what
was on his mind but she merely went herself and ignored him.

We all had many *fines*. Everyone talking, flinging up his arms,
dancing in drunken hilarity. At one moment Nancy, who never
lost her head, had to speak sharply to the Prince, warning him
that this, in a certain case, was not his meat. I soured on the
scene, went off into a room alone where a Frenchwoman came
also for a breath of air, saw me and said, *"Il y a toujours un
homme sérieux qui se met à part des autres qui se jouissent,"*
and went off again not to disturb me. Typically French. Floss
was having a good time. Home by taxi at one.

Fine morning, with Floss in Bagatelle gardens where she
wanted to see the roses once more before leaving Paris. Saw a
troupe of actors from a moving-picture company getting ready
to have some pictures taken there.

That afternoon I went with Ezra, it was one of his cultural
trips for me, to Natalie Barney's. Ezra has always been thought-
fulness itself in his efforts to bridge the gap between my academic
lacks and his superior learning. It isn't that he is ever patronizing,
and so I take it as it is given. But it worries him that my knowledge of the world of letters is so inferior to his. I respect his
uneasiness and try my best to adapt myself to his well-meant
efforts.

It appears that there still existed a shred, a remnant of Rémy
de Gourmont's (badly accoutered) old *salon*, one of the wonders
of the last century, presided over by a certain hardy character
named Natalie Clifford Barney. You might think it was something preserved in amber from the time of the Renaissance. Ezra
was full of homage for Natalie Barney, *l'Amazone,* as she was
called at one time. But Ezra has always paid homage to old

distinction: it is one of his handsomest traits. So we were to have tea with Natalie, a tremendous concession on her part toward me, one of the primitives of Ezra's earlier years.

She was extremely gracious and no fool to be sure, far less so than Ezra under the circumstances. She could tell a pickle from a clam any day in the week. I admired her and her lovely garden, well kept, her laughing doves, her Japanese servants. There were officers wearing red buttons in their lapels there and women of all descriptions. Out of the corner of my eye I saw a small clique of them sneaking off together into a side room while casting surreptitious glances about them, hoping their exit had not been unnoticed. I went out and stood up to take a good piss.

The story is told of some member of the Chamber of Deputies, a big, red-faced guy who had turned up there after a routine social acceptance. To his annoyance, as he stood lonely in the center of the dance floor, he saw women about him, dancing gaily together on all sides. Thereupon he undid his pants buttons, took out his tool and, shaking it right and left, yelled out in a rage, "Have you never seen one of these?"

Saturday, June 7th, Bob, Bill Bird, Sally, Floss and I took the 8:30 train from the Gare de l'Est for Rheims, where we walked about but did not enter the famous cathedral. Bill, the newspaperman, came forward with a special permit for us to visit the famous Veuve Cliquot champagne cellars.

This was my first view of anything of the sort, a local industry if ever there was one, from the limestone character of the soil which permits the mining out of the series of underground chambers where the wines are made and aged, to the mild green flavor of the grapes themselves. Very genteel men demonstrated and explained the whole six-year process of the manufacture of champagne, and as we were about to emerge at the end into the outer air, a big fellow with a full beard was waiting, stopped us and opened several bottles of their best.

Took train then out of Rheims and saw again from a distant hill the great cathedral. Walked ten kilometers in the woods as if no battle had ever been fought there. Took beer at Café Rendezvous des Chasseurs. Train again to Épernay.

Next morning Floss and I in our little room at the hotel got

up early and walked in the garden of the Hôtel de Ville, a small
official park such as one often sees in recent painting directly
fronting the city hall of the provincial city. Saw pink roses blossoming on standard stems.

Rain! It was the *Fête des Pompiers*, the fireman's parade, very
much dampened. In spite of the downpour, we took a steam
train to a little town in the woods to which Bill was guiding us.
Rain! But later it cleared, so instead of returning to Paris, we
had lunch at a tiny drinking place, just a room or two, the Hôtel
des Trois Millstones, with a lovely small garden where thirteen
men had been killed by a shell during the First World War.
Local tradition remembers such things.

From there we set out southward along the road, the five of
us, stretched out by two's, three's or going it sometimes alone,
mile after mile. We talked of the best shoes to wear on a hike.
Sally had on heavy walking boots, which hurt her badly, while
Floss had on her ordinary footwear in which she was perfectly
comfortable.

I remember once when Bill and I were going it together, we
passed two peasant girls, arms about each other's waists, and he
kidded me about country Lesbians, laughing at my expense over
something I had grumbled at earlier: that the practice was
universal.

We saw trout in a stream and wild strawberries growing between the stones of a deep culvert beyond our reach, try as we
might to reach them. These were the famous *fraises des bois*,
sweeter than anything in America, as the violets of Europe generally are sweet and ours odorless. I never could understand
that. Anyhow I didn't get them.

We walked all afternoon through woods, the wet banks of
whose streams were often profuse with yellow iris. Train to
Château Thierry, whose broken tree trunks were enough for us
without looking further. Train again to Paris that evening.

Monday, June 9th—three more days to go. I walked alone in the
Luxembourg Gardens. Thereafter Floss and I lunched once more
at l'Avenue, which we had come to prefer to other restaurants of
the quarter. Then train to St. Cloud and enjoyed a luxurious

auto ride all about the park. Holiday crowds, very relaxed and happy. Looked for Clotilde Vail. Beat it for Mina's, saw Djuna there. Back with Joella to Dôme. Met Pound. Back to Unic. Good-bye Bob. Somewhat to my surprise, he went off in a taxi without explanation. Supper with Pounds, to Brancusi's, he out. Returned and sat late at Pounds'.

Chapter 35

Good-bye, Paris

Up late. Went to Red Star office to arrange details of departure and to know if *S.S. Zeeland* is really leaving on the 12th. All arranged. I beat it back to Manship's studio, then with Pound to visit Fernand Léger at his studio, a very businesslike person with little to say. His picture on the easel did not move me, looked wooden, too much the actual figure, blunted for some purpose of design, of course, but what design? Honest, but work so red, black, blue that I was at a loss to appraise it. I remember saying, awkwardly, that, "one thumb of one hand of one figure looked dislocated," just as a dislocated thumb looked in a surgical text-book. Was that what he intended?

He gave me a photo or two of his pictures. Why, I could never understand. Hard to sense his neat, mechanical drawings of the human figure adapted to fit a canvas—all on one surface. Why bother with the recognizable details? He talked, but I could not follow him as he spoke.

Next morning Mina came in as we were at breakfast. She sketched me in pencil, left profile as a "wild Indian." Good-bye Mina. Floss wrote note to Nancy. Taxied to Twelve rue de l'Odéon, inviting Sylvia Beach and Adrienne Monnier to lunch. Sent flowers and note to Nancy. Rain.

Lunch with Sylvia and her mother. Mrs. Beach very lovely. Thence to Bill Bird's. Sally came to his office to meet us. All teaed on Champs Elysées. Danced. Bill glum! Good-bye Birds! Back to Twelve rue de l'Odéon. Good-bye George Antheil, Bjerschke, Joyella, Adrienne Monnier! Sylvia. Flowers. Good-bye at Dôme. Met Alice and Marguerite later at supper. Mrs. Baffrey dropped in with daughter—who longed for America. Good-bye Pound at ten P.M. To bed.

Up early and off in taxi at 7:14 A.M., no letters. Stopped to see Pound. He still asleep. At station Alice and Marguerite. Latter gave me presents and three bonds with coupons to keep for her.

Six-hour train ride to Cherbourg. Three women in compartment talking of Italy, dancing, etc. Curious cathedral at Bayeux. Dairy country, poppies, foxgloves, etc. We walked about Cherbourg seeing Napoleon's statue looking toward England where, but for Nelson's victory at Trafalgar, he would have gone. A cart full of sand sharks, which they eat here. Children at Communion, kissing peasants, airdrome, gray roofs. And in a café, where we stopped for a drink, we overheard a conversation between an older Frenchwoman, a big shamefaced English sailor and a very young French girl.

"No, you can't do that," said the older woman. The man mumbled some excuses. The girl was crying.

"Yes, yes," continued the older woman. "That's true. But you can't leave a young woman like that, you must do something at once, or we will find other ways."

Off in tender at 5:45, I feeling a little fagged. Saw *Zeeland* coming in, a narrow but fair enough looking ship. On board had supper. Saw Island of Alderney and to bed early—very tired. Quiet sea.

On board the following Monday, I started in the early morning to write over the Boone chapter for *In the American Grain*.

The next day got up at three and again at six A.M. to write on Boone. Think I have it mapped now.

Tony Sarg on board.

Next day had a hot argument with a fanatical Temperance lady who later tried to smuggle some lace past the customs officer.

Beautiful clear day. Sea oily calm. Several three- and four-master schooners about us. Passed red Nantucket Lightship. Getting hot. Home at last.

Chapter 36

Home Again

On our return to America we found that the children had come through all right. It was June, Friday the 20, 1924.

These were the lush Republican years when money flourished like skunk cabbages in the swamps in April. . . .

Damn it, the phone ringing again. . . . That was Mr. Taylor who said excitedly, You never wrote a poem in your life, Doc. What you write is prose, like Shakespeare.

when Doc K. was selling week-ends at two hundred dollars a shot, complete: liquor, keep and a woman guaranteed; and when stupidity had no measure.

My first job was to resume my practice of medicine. We were broke, of course, or near it, and that was important. I wasn't sure what would happen, but enough of my former patients came back to me to form the nucleus of a new beginning. I was definitely committed to the practice of pediatrics and, being young, everything seemed rosy.

The boys went back to camp, we spent a couple of weeks with them at the end of August, and that fall I had my tonsils out. Happy Days!

During my year off I had finished my book, *In the American Grain,* but as yet had no name for it. One day during a conference with Charles Boni, casting about for an effective title, I

235

was saying to him, "I want to give the impression, an inclusive definition, of what these men of whom I am writing have come to be for us. That they have made themselves part of us and that that is what we are. I want to make it clear that they are us, the American make-up, that we are what they have made us by their deeds and so remain in the American . . ."

"Grain," said Boni.

I leaped at it. "Right you are," I said, "and that's the title."

"But what about Lincoln?" he added. "You haven't even mentioned him. Do a piece on Lincoln and we'll be ready to go to press."

It was my first book by a commercial publisher and I was dancing on air—because to that point nothing I was writing had any market: I had either paid for it myself or had it accepted, for the most part, without pay. The Bonis made a beautiful book of it, for which I shall be forever grateful, but, as far as marketing it, they did next to nothing.

As a book it fell flat. I made trip after trip to the publisher's offices until they got so sick of seeing me that all of them would give me a nod and walk by, talking together, and close themselves in before me, leaving me sitting there: a beautiful brushoff. They let me know they did not intend to put more into advertising or promotion and so, bitterly, I had to see my high hopes of success go skittering out the window. In no time at all the thing was remaindered and I began to pick up copies wherever I could.

However, I made some friends. Stieglitz found the book somewhere and wrote enthusiastically to me about it. He even said it had given him the name, An American Place, when he moved to the new site for his gallery on Madison Avenue. From that time forward for many years until Stieglitz's somewhat crotchety old age I frequented that gallery. But when he dropped Hartley I began to fall off from him. He talked me deaf, dumb and blind. I tremendously admired him, as I did Georgia O'Keeffe, his wife, but I couldn't take it anymore. Later I took a small part in Dorothy Norman's enterprise, *Twice a Year,* but it was too much for me, my direction had shifted.

Another good friend I made through my book was Martha

Graham, who wrote me saying she could not have gone on with her choreographic projects without it. This was extremely moving. I met Martha once in Bennington when she was rehearsing for the new season there, but she was so closed about by the sheer physical necessities of her position that nothing interesting came of it.

In any case, so far so good, the book had been printed and had to find its place as best it could. My first idea was to do a second volume, taking up the skein at Jefferson and coming up, this time with a big jump, to Grover Cleveland; and then, more slowly to the present day to end with Pancho Villa. But the bad reception I got put an end to all that.

I had a great amount of material in the form of memories of our trip to Europe in my head. I had to write something, so capitalizing on that, I decided on a novel. It would be dull, though, to tell of a mere husband and wife junketing through France, Italy, Austria and Switzerland. So I'd use the material, invent a story and let it go at that. I didn't know anything anyway about the novel form, which I detested as "romantic," so wrote one of the damned things for what I might get out of it. I called it *A Voyage to Pagany*, since I had found Europe to be largely pagan—but most thought it a travel book.

It was wonderful how Charles Boni's eyes brightened when the rumor reached him that I had a novel under my belt.

"Bill! don't tell me," etc., etc.

It was published by a man from Passaic, N. J., operating under the title of the Macauley Publishing Company. My brother did the jacket—"The Worm" encircling the world. It didn't sell either. Not so happy days. The Bonis were justified and soon went out of business.

At about this time McAlmon in Paris along with Bill Bird and his Three Mountains Press came to my rescue with books printed abroad: *Spring and All*, a book of poems, and *The Great American Novel*, a satire on the novel form in which a little (female) Ford car falls more or less in love with a Mack truck.

During this period my manuscripts were typed by a patient of mine, Katherine Johns: Mrs. W. Johns, a Vassar girl and former court stenographer in New Haven. Her mother had been an Ives, related to the American composer of the same name —it impressed me.

Mrs. Johns was, well, restless. She had her boy, but felt at loose ends in Rutherford. She offered to do some typing for me when she heard that I was a writer. Later we made a trade. For ten years and more Mrs. Johns did my typing and I took care of her children and self. There was a birth, pneumonia, appendectomy and mastoiditis—a frequent occurrence before the advent of sulfanilamide. I wrote longhand, by machine, the scripts often wildly corrected past my own deciphering. She knew how to straighten things out. She did the finished scripts for *In the American Grain, A Voyage to Pagany* and several other books and plays.

For I had returned to the play and was intent on doing a libretto for an opera on the theme of George Washington.

Some of my friends in Passaic, Drs. Hughes, John and Butterfield, set out to get me, at this time, on the staff of the hospital there, the Passaic General Hospital. The times were prosperous and I had a good background for my specialty, pediatrics. All I needed was to establish residence in the city of Passaic and they would get me on the staff. I joined them in renting an office in the Passaic National Bank Building there and forthwith, after a little maneuvering they did their part. So I had two offices, one in Passaic and one in Rutherford, and my hospital rounds besides. It didn't make my life easier.

It was a small office on the fifth floor of the bank. At least it gave me new acquaintances in the profession, and the work in the hospital challenged my abilities and broadened my opportunities for helping the unfortunate and the unhappy. Later some of the nurses from the hospital would drop in from time to time to tell me their troubles. I became a sort of father confessor to three or four of them especially. It had its good sides, but it was too much of a drain on me, dashing back and forth. So that later on, after eight years, I turned the place over to one of my associates.

The writing in those years went on as usual, though the life was uncertain. Prohibition was on. We had to drink, though

drink has never amused me; I always grow amorous, then remorseful, waking (as I never hope to do again) with a head split
in half with pain.

The last year the boys were at camp in Maine at Mattawamkeag was an example. We parents had rented one of
several cabins on the premises—that is, at Bill Sewell's adult
camp a little down the lake. Then one day a group of us (I
was not with them) dropped over into New Brunswick, just
across the line, and loaded up. The men stuffed bottles down
their pants legs, the women suddenly grew busty, and as soon
as they approached the customs officials poured out of the car
that it might be searched.

For some odd reason I took that night to drinking rum, raw
—possibly to escape the vile gin or other stuff. Until noon the
next day I can see myself walking the woods, afraid to lie down
lest the trees rush upon me to knock me over.

We fished. Bill Sewell, who had been Teddy Roosevelt's
guide when Teddy took to the woods in his youth to build up
his physique, told tales of his favorite friend around the fire
at night and of early days in the Maine woods. He was the first
white child born in that part of the country.

Merrill, his grown son, sometime guide and railroad man,
would never smoke a cigarette in his father's presence. Once
Flossie asked Bill, "Bill, if you met me straying in the woods,
what would you do?"

"Well," said Bill, "I wouldn't shoot you."

There I once saw a great blue heron take off from near the
shore line and disappear silently among the trees. I heard the
loon for the first time, and fished for the abundant bass which
no one wanted—and if it had taken the hook too greedily and we
had to kill it, we'd bury it under a stone. Wild rice grew at one
corner of the lake. The boys were developing rapidly. On Sundays the three or four Catholic boys would be taken off in the
canoes to Mass in the village. We observed the silence of the
woods, backwater if ever there was one—alive with a desolate
faith. When we came home after such an experience we seemed
to have arrived from history and had to adjust ourselves to
an artificial makeshift of today.

I was a great gallery-goer at that time. Saw Stieglitz often and if there was an exhibit of the French masters or any show at the Modern Museum or the Whitney Gallery I'd be there. Paul Rosenfeld was a good friend, with his half-embarrassed rotundities. He'd often ask me to meet this one or that one, Aaron Copland or Miss this, that or the other. It was a special atmosphere.

There's a good story, which I have told many times, about Hartpence, a man tough as his name—I never knew a name that better fitted a man. A good friend. He was spare and of medium height, a face sandy as his hair, and as dry looking. His coat, as I remember, was of about the same color. And he would be attached to a sleek-haired dancer named Slade, Helen Slade, though whether or not they were man and wife it didn't seem much to matter, nor he to show it.

Alanson Hartpence was employed at the Daniel Gallery. One day, the proprietor being out, Hartpence was in charge. In walked one of their most important customers, a woman in her fifties who was much interested in some picture whose identity I may at one time have known. She liked it, and seemed about to make the purchase, walked away from it, approached it and said, finally, "But Mr. Hartpence, what is all that down in this left hand lower corner?"

Hartpence came up close and carefully inspected the area mentioned. Then, after further consideration, "That, Madam," said he, "is paint."

This story marks the exact point in the transition that took place, in the world of that time, from the appreciation of a work of art as a copying of nature to the thought of it as the imitation of nature, spoken of by Aristotle in his *Poetics,* which has since governed our conceptions. It is still the failure to take this step that blocks us in seeking to gain a full conception of the modern in art.

In painting Cézanne is the first consciously to have taken that step. From him it went on, often by nothing more than the *vis a tergo,* rushing through the gap where the dyke has been broken. But with such a man as Braque it had basic significance. Braque is said to have taken his pictures outdoors, on occasion, to see if their invention ranked beside that of nature worthily enough for him to approve of it.

Almost no one seems to realize that this movement is straight from the *Poetics,* misinterpreted for over two thousand years and more. The objective is not to copy nature and never was, but to imitate nature, which involved active invention, the active work of the imagination invoked by such a person as Virginia Woolf. A man makes a picture, it is made of paint upon canvas stretched on a frame. In spite of endless talk, this has never been sufficiently brought out. One doesn't paint an "abstract painting." One makes a painting. If it is a dull painting, an unimaginative painting, if the elements of paint are emptily used, the painting would prove empty even though it represented some powerful dictator or a thesis of Sartre.

It was not only among the painters that this step up from the worn-out conceptions of the late nineteenth century, even with its Blakes and Whitmans, took place. Gertrude Stein found the key with her conception of the objective use of words.

Certain "stories" from the past held us back. We had Apelles, the Athenian, painting cherries so lifelike in appearance that the birds pecked at them when they were exhibited—in the Athenian light, let it be added. We have, above all, for our own Occidental thought, Shakespeare's, "To hold the mirror up to nature"—as vicious a piece of bad advice as the budding artist ever gazed upon. It is tricky, thoughtless, wrong. It is NOT to hold the mirror up to nature that the artist performs his work. It is to make, out of the imagination, something not at all a copy of nature, but something quite different, a new thing, unlike any thing else in nature, a thing advanced and apart from it.

To imitate nature involves the verb to do. To copy is merely to reflect something already there, inertly: Shakespeare's mirror is all that is needed for it. But by imitation we enlarge nature itself, we become nature or we discover in ourselves nature's active part. This is enticing to our minds, it enlarges the concept of art, dignifies it to a place not yet fully realized.

I had won in 1924 the Guarantor's Award offered by the magazine *Poetry* and then in 1926 *The Dial* gave me its award, two thousand dollars. Unfortunately I had just been sued for fifteen thousand dollars for a short story of mine printed in another magazine. It had been settled out of court for five thousand, so that the *Dial's* money came in handy. I ran up to Flossie's bed, having just opened the early morning mail, with tears in my eyes.

The thing is I had been told the story by a young person of my acquaintance, now long since dead, and had found it so extremely good that I rushed home, pulled up my typewriter and pounded it out, about six or eight pages. I didn't think I had remembered the names but read the thing over and shoved it in my desk drawer where it remained for several months.

Then one day the magazine wrote asking for something. I picked up the story, put it in a large manila envelope, and mailed it to them. I received no reply, and, being used to refusals and all that, I half-forgot the incident, thinking that when they sent me the galleys I'd go over it changing anything that might seem necessary.

Then one day I received the magazine, with my story in it, already printed and being distributed. I almost dropped dead for I realized at once what I was in for. A prominent member of the bar, whose name I have since detested, was supposed to look over all material accepted by the magazine for possibly libelous matter. He had not even looked at it, but did a beautiful fade away, wealthy as I knew him to be. The editorial gang had nothing, so I was left holding the bag. And the trouble was that because of the nature of the material my misdemeanor turned out to be a tort. Though everything about the tale was originally related to me as factually true, later my pal, the person who had given me the details so beautifully, signed a statement against me. Quite a party for a struggling young doctor in a small town. Floss, of course, was marvelous, but she let me have it, all right.

"I've told you, time and time again, not to use real names."

"But I've got to," I said, "if I'm going to write convincingly."

"That's ridiculous!"

"I planned to change the names later."

"All right, if that amuses you, go right on, but you have children and you have your . . . !"

I had a good, messy, old lawyer who chewed a cigar most of the time and let the juice run down on his vest, and he got me off for $5,000. I'll say this, though, that the young lawyer who would have prosecuted me, when he saw the true situation, told his client that either he'd settle for the amount stated—he wanted a lot more—or he'd give up the case. God bless him. I've forgotten his name if I ever knew it. I understood he drove up in front of my house one day and stopped the car to see how much I might be worth. I added five thousand dollars to my insurance to protect Floss and the kids, but, had I been ruined, I planned a different outcome.

Floss cashed the extra insurance in a few years later just to relieve me of what she thought an added burden.

The *Dial's* award, though it was given for general excellence in writing during the year (1926) was specifically pointed up by their publication of a four- to six-page poem of mine, *Paterson*, on which I based the later and more extended poem.

Those were the years when the little magazines were at their height. I had something in most of them.

Money was free, the market kept climbing, young men were ridiculing their parents for their conservative ways. For people to make thirty to forty thousand dollars in a week was a frequent occurrence. We invested moderately, buying outright what we could.

Marjorie Allen Seiffert would come to New York (I had met her earlier at one of Kreymborg's parties) for a sabbatical two weeks from her husband and children. She would invite all of her male friends, all for whom she cared, to join her for an evening—a supper, the theatre, or as she chose. We would go to a speakeasy, discuss our affairs and the world, rush off, as we did once, she and I, to O'Neill's *Desire Under the Elms,* then at the beginning of the second act, she'd excuse herself and leave me alone to see the play out while she kept another engagement.

Charles Henri Ford asked me to do a preface for one of his books of poems, his first perhaps. I wrote it and sent it to him.

A year or two later, perhaps sooner than that, he showed me the book. I looked at the preface, as he stood smiling a little sheepishly. I couldn't imagine where I had seen it before, and then I noticed my name at the end of it.

"I hope you don't mind," he said.

He had changed what I had written, adding whatever his fancy dictated without, of course, removing my signature at the end. I didn't mind. Why should I?

I remember of those days Alice, who followed our Kathleen. Then came Sadie. One day we had been out for the evening, to the movies I suppose, leaving her in charge of the boys fast asleep upstairs in their beds. We didn't even have the radio then and this big, full-bodied kid must have been hard put to it to keep herself amused. She was a good girl, and aside from her thirst for adventure, natural enough at her romantic age, could not have been more loyal to us in her services. We tried to keep her amused. But all such state wards, such girls as we had had experience with, are lonesome creatures craving affection, not only craving it, but actively going out to get it where and when they are able. They particularly, I suppose, seek the equivalent of a father. They got badly under my skin; it wasn't easy for me to act that part along with the other things that occupied me. So they felt cheated. I was very fond of them all.

The evening of which I speak Floss and I came through the back door at eleven expecting to find Sadie asleep on the couch in the front room where she liked to lie when we were out. The kitchen was dark. Chairs were lying on their sides. Floss, sensing something wrong, called the girl's name. No reply. There had been several burglaries in the neighborhood during the month just past. We had told Sadie to keep the place locked up and not to open either outside door without first asking who was there.

We hurried into the dining room and switched on the lights. Here also everything was in disorder, chairs thrown about but added to that the drawers of the sideboard had been pulled out and left that way. All our silver was gone! I think we heard a groan. Floss went into the front room, dark also. She switched on the lights and there on the floor in front of the upright piano we had at that time, her legs lashed to one of its legs, a gag in her mouth, her wrists tied behind her back, lay Sadie.

I was taken off my feet.

The girl was mumbling unintelligibly, trying to say something to us as I got a knife and cut the ropes, freeing her arms, her legs, and disengaging the gag which had been tied about her mouth. Sitting up she excitedly told us that the silver had been saved. She had had a suspicion that something was going to happen that night and so had taken the precaution of putting the silverware in an old suitcase of mine and hiding it in the fireplace. I ran to take off the blower from the cold hearth and there, sure enough, just as she had said, was the silver, all of it, safe.

Wonderful!

Then, rubbing her wrists, she described how she had sat terror-stricken as she heard the men coming in through the cellar. Before she could move or cry out—she did not dare leave the children!—they were upon her, clapped a hand over her mouth and . . .

"Did they harm you?" I cried excitedly.

Oh no, nothing of that sort.

Instead they had gone upstairs as she lay powerless and she could hear them going through the chiffoniers there. Floss ran up, looked in at the children who were sleeping quietly, as we had left them earlier, but in our own room found everything pulled out of the drawers in a wild jumble all over the floor. By this time Sadie had been hugged and praised alternately by me and was talking more coherently. There were two men, white; at a certain point, just before we had come in, perhaps it was our coming in that had frightened them, they rushed off through the cellar as they had entered, not ten minutes ago. I ran down to see if there were any further evidence there and found an abandoned suitcase lying open on the concrete before the open doorway. I went upstairs and called the police.

By this time Floss had come down from the second floor and finding that nothing, really, had been stolen, that the children had not even been awakened, and that the whole thing looked fishy, didn't say anything to me but sat down quietly to await Officer Rosenfelder, a big, kindly chap with a good head on his shoulders. We told him the story, Sadie correcting us here and there; then I asked him if he didn't want to go down in the cellar to see what there was there. He and I went down together. When we got there, having turned on the cellar light, he looked at me and smiled.

"She did it herself," he said.

"What do you mean?"

"Just to be a hero," he said, "and to get you to praise her."

Floss had already made up her mind to the same thing. Anyhow, I told Sadie after we had got all straightened out that she surely had put on a good show. "But how the hell did you get the gag into your mouth after you had your hands tied?"

"I didn't," she said.

Chapter 37

A Maternity Case

In February one day I received a call from the office of one of
the younger men in town. He used occasionally to take Flossie
out to parties when they were kids, but he being a Catholic and
she not, that was soon broken up. They were classmates in the
public school. It was a call to go to Lyndhurst, the next town,
to help a young doctor stuck there on a maternity case. The
man whose job it was had sent his young assistant, being himself
laid up with the grippe. What could I do but go? I've forgotten
what time it was, a holiday, Lincoln's Birthday, that's it. I was
pretty sore at being disturbed. Anyhow, I went; a small house
in the poorer part of town.

But when I got there, I had a surprise. The door opened as
I had my hand out to ring the bell and a burly looking man, in
vest and shirt sleeves, said, "Come in."

I entered a dark and narrow corridor, had started to take off
my coat when I took my first good look at the guy who had
admitted me. He was built like the driver of a beer truck, with
his shirt sleeves rolled up. He was beginning to be bald at the
temples, and he had more than half a load on, but his pants
were what stopped me. Evidently he was a policeman—to be
seen not by the pants alone, but he also wore a belt strung with
cartridges and carried a .45.

"Where's the patient?" I said. "Upstairs." And just then I

heard screams in a deep woman's voice mingled with enough curses to make your flesh creep.

"Go on up. She needs you, Doc. There's another doctor up there; I don't know how good he is but he's done nothing for her. Why didn't Doctor W. come himself?"

"You got me," I said, and taking my satchel, I walked upstairs. The young physician came to the bedroom door hollow-eyed.

"Am I glad to see *you*!"

Before I could answer him my eyes were filled with the sight before me. In the poor room was a double bed on which lay the woman—filling it, both from side to side and from the bottom up. The springs rested on the floor. She was a mountain, the rings of fat around her small head only paralleling the size of her belly.

The minute she saw me she let out a string of curses at the young man before her, at Doctor W. and everyone in general who had got her into this state and from which we seemed to have no way of getting her out, at which she dozed off and snored like a hog.

The young doctor had been there since the day before—up all night unable to sleep or eat or so much as leave the place for a moment, because of the man below who, tapping the gun on his hip, told him he'd not leave the place until the baby was born, and that if it was killed or the woman herself was hurt in the process due to his clumsiness and incompetence, by God, he'd go along with them.

"You take over," he said to me. "I'm exhausted."

"Not on your life," I said, "wouldn't that be an acknowledgment of a fault on your part? Stick it out. I'll give her some dope at her next pain and see how it's going."

Then it began. First she would grow restless, then, "Here it comes again!" she yelled, sweating and straining like an ox trying to pull a cart out of the mud where it had been stuck to the hubs. She screamed and cursed and labored.

"It's been going on like this since yesterday," he said. "It's awful."

"Let me examine her," I said.

"It's about time somebody knows what he's doing," she howled at me. "Go on, find out what the trouble is, if you're any better than the other," and she parted her heavy thighs like—there's nothing like it unless you've seen it.

I went in and found the cervix fully dilated, the membranes ruptured and a head presenting. It was fully engaged and nothing as far as I could see wrong. Probably a posterior position, but I didn't stop to find out, no need under the meager circumstances, the low bed, the lack of assistance.

"Have you given any Pit?" I said. Pituitary extract in such cases was very new then and the young man hadn't any with him.

"Have you got any?" he said.

"Yes."

"Won't you take over?"

"No. But I'll give her a shot. She's not sick otherwise, is she? How much does she weigh?"

"Three hundred pounds, they say."

So I gave her a c.c. of Pit and went back to the chloroform at the head of the bed. With the first pain after my shot, a terrific contracting occurred and before we could do anything, a male infant, all tangled in the cord and screaming as if we'd stuck *him*, lay in the muck hole in front of the mother's buttocks—there's no other way to say it.

The young doc almost fainted from relief, while the woman, raising up her head, yelled to her husband downstairs, "It's a boy."

"What does it weigh?"

"From the look of it," I said, "not an ounce less than eight pounds."

"Is it injured?"

"What would injure it? No," I said, "he's a regular cop, by the shoulders on him."

"Glory be to God. It's over."

I pulled back the covers enough to get at the woman's belly to get hold of the fundus, to express the placenta. "Wait a minute," I said, and paused. Everyone concerned looked at me.

"Is there anything wrong, Doc?" said my young assistant.

"There's another here!"

"What did you say?" yelled the woman.

"Twins, at least twins," I said. The young doctor damn near passed out.

"Get that first one out of the way over there on the other bed. Here it comes!" And there was the other, bigger than the first, a vertex also, screaming and squirming—cursing if you'd want to believe it.

"Is that all?"

"Yes, that's all," I said. "What do you want?"

"Let me go to sleep," she said.

"Well, give us another minute for the afterbirth," I said, "and you can sleep, forever, for all I care."

When the husband came to the door and I told him he had twin sons, all he said was, "Thank God. How is she?"

"Perfect."

"That's fine. You sure came in the nick of time," said he.

"No, he was doing all right. I was just lucky after the work he'd done to carry her through. And it's, by God, Lincoln's Birthday, at that."

"We'll call one of them Abraham and the other Lincoln," he said.

"And what's the last name?" I hadn't had time to find out yet.

"O'Toole," he said.

"Abraham and Lincoln O'Toole," I said, but I didn't laugh. "What's wrong with that?" he said. "Not a thing, unique to say the least. It'll bring them luck, unless I'm far wrong."

"How much do I owe you, Doc?" he said to me, reaching for the wad in his back pocket.

"I'll take it up with Dr. W. I don't know what he wants me to charge you."

"Let him try and get it out of me, after these goings on," said the man.

"He'll sue you," said I laughing.

"Sue me," said the woman waking up. "Let him sue me for the dirty drawers I got on." And that's the way we left it.

Chapter 38

Gertrude Stein

I can remember the terrible landscape one summer at Hilldale in Vermont; the half-wit Elsie, tall and white, bathing in the small stream at the bottom of the valley among the alders, and the men in the far field on the hillside stopping their haying to turn and look down at her.

There was the most clear and abundant spring in the deep woods near there at the foot of Mount Olga. I would go there with the boys and sit and watch them play, looking for a frog and popping the seed cases of the touch-me-nots that grew there so abundantly.

I wrote a little, now and then, usually poems, climbed Haystack or Stratton with Floss or a group of us. Little Bill even went up Haystack with us one day. Vermont has always quieted my nerves.

Richard Johns kept after me for the chapters of *White Mule* which I began to write and which he so generously published in *Pagany*, after reading the first chapter, which had been lying in a drawer in the attic for a year or more.

And then, the time seeming propitious, we decided to send the boys to Europe for a year to school—to make up to them in some manner for the months when we had run away from them in the earlier twenties.

251

Bill was a freshman in Rutherford High and Paul was wandering through grammar school, two years back of his brother; Paul was getting long in the leg and more and more casual about a lot of things as time went along. There was also the family tradition on both sides to urge us to the decision. All our parents were foreign-born. Floss had been taken to Germany and Norway with her little brother when she was a child and remembered picking lilies of the valley near Oslo in the woods at eleven at night under the "midnight sun"; Ed and I had gone to the Château de Lancy at about the same ages as our boys now were.

So in the summer of 1927 off we went, the four of us, for Antwerp, Paris and Geneva.

We went to Antwerp this time, as I had done on my way to Germany in 1910. The kids enjoyed it, especially the lioness and her cubs in the zoo there. Then down through Basle, Lausanne, Chillon, the Dent du Midi and so quietly along the west shore of Lac Leman, the Juras on one side, the Alps on the other, to our destination and the end of the first part of our journey. The kids seemed to be looking forward to their European trip with full anticipation of a wonderful year.

Leaving the children in school, Floss came up to Paris with me for one final spree before I left her to return to America. We went in search of a room, found a good cheap place, but after one night had to leave, it was so uncomfortable. We had taken the room for the week so that when we told the proprietor next morning we were leaving, he was furious. He, poor man, in his miserable little office, had probably not had a well-paying guest for weeks and must have been highly pleased at our appearance, so that it meant actual loss of food and drink to him now that we were leaving. He let fly a stream of abuse at us, *riches Américains* who were rolling in wealth to come to France, which was poor, to take advantage of the exchange. What did we want for the miserable pittance we paid him? a palace?

Bob once more took charge and found a room for us in his own Hôtel Istria, for this was the week of the first decentennial bivouac of the American Legion in Paris. Few rooms were to be had and the feeling against the Americans for the way they treated the Frenchwomen, in particular, was running high. We were in a fair way to being hated. I could feel it everywhere. Nor from what I could see did I blame the French for their resentment.

One afternoon in a restaurant of the quarter, Floss and I were eating a little lunch when I asked for a bottle of Meursault, a somewhat rare white burgundy which I very much admire. It was expensive, but I wanted it and it was brought out to me and opened. I can talk a little French and understand more. To our left I overheard one of two young men say to the other, "Look at them. There it is again. *Dégoutant*—disgusting."

I took it that they probably thought: Here are two barbarians drinking one of the finest wines of France at lunch! One of our most expensive wines, which we cannot afford, a wine of whose rarity and special taste they haven't the slightest idea. All that was written in their faces.

Of that meal, I remember also that being particularly fond of watercress, we ordered something, a meat order of some sort, perhaps *filet mignon,* which happened to have served with it a large amount of cress. On top of that, since we didn't know what we would get with the first order, we had asked for a cress salad besides, so that we were fairly smothered in cress, but we ate it all and drank our wine besides. It was one of our last meals together on that trip. We were served the meal on the terrace, on the street that is, Floss remembers, since a ragged woman walked up and down in front of the tables, complaining bitterly of those who could afford to eat so well while she was in misery.

But the highlight was tea at Gertrude Stein's. I had looked forward to this with great expectation. A small place to which we were admitted by someone, probably Miss Toklas, to find that two or three others had preceded us, Miss Stein herself coming forward to greet us and find chairs for us beneath that astonishing wall of Picasso's paintings, largely of the "blue period," in three tiers above us. It was a good-sized, very high room more or less cubical in shape—the lot of us sitting around, where we could, facing a small cabinet at the end wall with doors that opened right and left.

There was some little difficulty about the chairs which opened the conversation upon the mention of a visit there only a few

months earlier by Ezra Pound. One chair in particular, an antique, one which Miss Stein especially treasured, was offered
him with the warning that it was not very strong and would he
be a little careful how he used it. With which he sprawled in it
in his usual fashion and broke one of the back legs. She never
forgave him. That was a good start.

We looked at the paintings. Who could not have done so? It
was one of the sights of Paris. Tea was served, after or during
which Miss Stein went to the small cabinet, opened it and began
to take out her manuscripts, one at a time, telling us the titles
and saying that she hoped some day to see them printed. I can't
remember the exact sequence of what followed, but one way or
another she asked me what I would do were the unpublished
books mine and I were faced with the difficulty she was experiencing.

It must have been that I was in one of my more candid moods
or that the cynical opinion of Pound and others of my friends
about Miss Stein's work was uppermost in my mind, for my
reply was, "If they were mine, having so many, I should probably
select what I thought were the best and throw the rest into
the fire."

The result of my remark was instantaneous. There was a
shocked silence out of which I heard Miss Stein say, "No doubt.
But then writing is not, of course, your *métier*."

That closed the subject and we left soon after.

Later by mere chance, I discovered in Sterne's *Tristram Shandy*
a passage in which the qualities of certain words as words, like
"rough" and "smooth," were presented and discussed in a manner
similar to that used by Miss Stein in certain of her writings.
And when I wrote a short comment upon the subject, she was
very pleased. She sent me several letters after that full of kindest
regards and presented me with at least three books with her autograph and affectionate greetings inscribed in them.

Let me quote from *A Novelette and Other Prose (1921-1931)*,
which was published at Toulon by TO Publishers in 1932. In one
of the shorter pieces contained there, "The Work of Gertrude
Stein," I wrote as follows:

Would I had seen a white bear
(For how can I imagine it?)

Let it be granted that whatever is new in literature the germ of it will be found somewhere in the writings of other times; only the modern emphasis gives work a present distinction.

The necessity for this modern focus and the meaning of the changes involved are, however, another matter; the everlasting stumbling block to criticism. Here is a theme worth development in the case of Gertrude Stein—yet signally neglected.

Why in fact have we not heard more generally from American scholars upon the writings of Miss Stein? Is it lack of heart or ability or just that theirs is an enthusiasm which fades rapidly of its own nature before the risks of today?

Now I quote from Sterne:

The verbs auxiliary we are concerned in here, continued my father, are am; was; have; had; do; did; make; made; suffer; shall; should; will; would; can; could; owe; ought; used; or is wont. . . .—or with these questions added to them;—Is it? Was it? Will it be? . . . . . Or affirmatively . . . Or chronologically . . . Or hypothetically,—If it was? If it was not? What would follow?—If the French beat the English? If the Sun should go out of the Zodiac?

Now, by the right use and application of these, continued my father, in which a child's memory should be exercised, there is no one idea can enter his brain, how barren soever, but a magazine of conceptions and conclusions may be drawn forth from it.—Didst thou ever see a white bear? cried my father, turning his head round to Trim, who stood at the back of his chair.—No, an' please your honour, replied the corporal.—But thou couldst discourse about one, Trim, said my father, in case of need?—How is it possible, brother, quoth my Uncle Toby, if the corporal never saw one?—'Tis the fact I want, replied my father,—and the possibility of it as follows.

A white bear! Very well. Have I ever seen one? Might I ever have seen one? Am I ever to see one? Ought I ever to have seen one? Or can I ever see one?

Would I had seen a white bear! (for how can I imagine it?)

If I should see a white bear, what should I say? If I should never see a white bear, what then?

If I never have, can, must, or shall see a white bear alive; have I ever seen the skin of one? Did I ever see one painted?—described? Have I never dreamed of one?

Note how the words alive, skin, painted, described, dreamed come into the design of these sentences. The feeling is of words themselves, a curious immediate quality quite apart from their meaning, much as in music different notes are dropped, so to speak, into a repeated chord one at a time, one after another—for itself alone. Compare this with the same effects common in all that Stein does. See *Geography and Plays.* "They were both gay there" To continue—

Did my father, mother, uncle, aunt, brothers or sisters, ever see a white bear? What would they give? How would they behave? How would the white bear have behaved? Is he wild? Tame? Terrible? Rough? Smooth?

Note the play upon rough and smooth (though it is not certain that this was intended) rough seeming to apply to the bear's deportment, smooth to surface, presumably the bear's coat. In any case the effect is that of a comparison relating primarily not to any qualities of the bear himself but to the words rough and smooth. And so to finish—

—Is the white bear worth seeing?—
—Is there no sin in it?—
Is it better than a black one?

In this manner ends Chapter 43 of *The Life and Opinions of Tristram Shandy.* The handling of the words and to some extent the imaginative quality of the sentence is a direct forerunner of that which Gertrude Stein has woven today into a synthesis of its own. It will be plain, in fact, on close attention, that Sterne exercises not only the play (or music) of sight, sense and sound contrast among the words themselves which Stein uses, but their grammatical play also—i.e. for, how can I imagine it; did my, what would, how would, compare Stein's "to have rivers; to halve rivers," etc. It would not be too much to say that Stein's development over a lifetime is anticipated completely with regard to subject matter, sense and grammar—in Sterne.

After a week I put Floss on a train bound back for Geneva and the same day headed for Cherbourg, the *S. S. Pennland*

and America. It was hard leaving her. We were both half-unhappy over it and half-excited by the adventure. Perhaps I was over-demonstrative, but I can still see some other Americans going by the same train to Geneva talking and smiling together at our expense: These foreigners!

It was the tenth anniversary of our entrance into the First World War, the American Legion had just completed its first decennial encampment in Paris and we, on the *Pennland,* were bearing home the remains! Day and night we heard them singing through the corridors of the ship:

> We're tar-heel born,
> We're tar-heel bred;
> And when we're gone
> We'll be tar-heel dead!

The whole trip was a riot. There were protests from some of the more staid customers; that only redoubled the fury of the racket. The ship was theirs; they had paid for it, and if you didn't like it you could get out and walk. The revolution was on, but subsided as we approached New York.

One of the stories told me by a somewhat nervous subaltern about having picked up a girl somewhere over near the Eiffel Tower and living with her the whole time he was in Paris became the basis for Bob McAlmon's story, *Silk Pyjamas.*

As I heard it, the kid had been more than kind to the man and after the week was up she asked him timidly if he would grant her a little, special favor when he was about to leave her. Would he let her keep the really beautiful silk pyjamas he had used during their nuptials?

No, he told me he had told her. They were expensive garments. Why should he give them to a dirty little whore like that? It nauseated me to have to talk to the man. The French got enough of Americans that time, I think, to last them to eternity.

So, returning to my practice, I went back to work in my home office, in the hospital and to my office in Passaic. Almost at once I received a cable from Floss saying that Paul had contracted diphtheria.

She had grabbed him up one day at the school when she realized the condition he was in and what an incompetent ass was treating him, got herself a taxi, broke all the laws of Switzerland and rushed him into the Municipal Hospital in Geneva. There she contacted the best pediatrician in the city and put the kid in his care.

I cabled the man to give an initial dose of 50,000 units of the antitoxin if it was a laryngeal case.

"Yes," he replied, "I know how you give those big doses in America, but we don't do it that way here." I was hamstrung by the distance in my attempts to move the man.

Paul, however, in the end got well; the doctor stood and ate his roast chestnuts as he talked to him later on while the little guy sat and watched him.

On his release from the hospital, Flossie took him for two weeks to a resort in the southward-facing mountains above Italy. On the train, after eating some chocolate, the kid got a vicious reaction from all the horse serum they'd been pushing into him. He choked up, his body broke out into giant hives, and for a moment, Floss thought she was going to lose him.

It ended, at Sierre, with Floss playing bridge with Lord and Lady So and So at the hotel. Paul never went back to that school, but by luck got into the École Internationale at Onex under M. Lucien Brunel, whose father and mother had been my own preceptors when I went to their school at Lancy. Billy soon joined his brother there. The situation had been saved by Flossie's intelligent and courageous actions in spite of all obstacles.

During that year I wrote furiously at *White Mule*, at the poems, and at the short stories that later made up *The Knife of the Times*, as well as many prefaces and critical essays of various complexions.

Mother lived with me at Nine Ridge Road, and kept house with Lucy. I think she enjoyed it. Once during that time, while I was alone with mother, E. E. Cummings came out to see me. It was a Sunday morning, a very quiet day, no one on the streets. I had given him specific instructions how to get here, so that when it got to be nearly one o'clock, knowing his reputation for indifference to conventional order, I went out to look for him.

I shall not forget the impression I got of a lone person meandering up a deserted Park Avenue stopping at every store window to look intently in at the shoes, ladies' wear, now and then a bank window perhaps, or at an Easter card, or a brace and bit in Dow's hardware store.

Mother had fixed up a chicken. Afterward we talked, if one could talk during such a visitation. Mother was interested because his father had been a Unitarian minister—not that she wasn't alert to his general aspects. We had a batch of Persian kittens in the kitchen at that time. We played with them on the dining-room table. He thought they resembled birds in the nest. It was a nice afternoon. Mother thought him gentle but strange.

Wally Gould's anger at my refusal to accept his verse was reflected in his disapproval of our sending the kids abroad, "Why take them to Europe? Why don't you send them down here to school," he wrote, "and make white men of them?"

Floss was furious but didn't reply. We never heard from the guy again. He had already said he had been asked by Miss Mary to marry her but refused.

"Imagine the two of us in bed together!" he had told us. "Preposterous!" But he married her just the same in the end.

Chapter 39

Christmas Day: Bronx Zoo

It comes to mind how I went on Christmas Day that year to the Bronx Zoo to be alone with the animals, because the rest of my gang was abroad.

Either my brother or any one of several close friends would have taken me in for the Christmas celebrations, but I refused to make a choice among them. Rather I decided to remain alone, for the entire day, and to think uninterruptedly of Floss and the kids just as though they were there beside me. It was a sentimental notion, but I felt sentimentally inclined. To carry it through presented several practical difficulties. I could get my own breakfast, but where was I to have my dinner? It seemed stupid merely to go sit in a restaurant for a big meal I didn't want, and stopping off somewhere for a sandwich and a cup of coffee wouldn't accomplish the feeling of the lonely celebration I had in mind. Then the perfect solution presented itself: why not go eat with the animals? I'd be rid of all humans, I'd have company, the right sort of dumb company I wanted, and they do serve food. I remembered a rather good meal I'd once had at the Bronx Zoo of a Sunday. I decided I'd leave early and remain all day.

It was a cold, slightly overcast December day, one of those windless pearl-gray days that you see at that season of the year before there is any snow, the shortest days of the year. The sun never gets high enough to give any warmth, just an even cold,

gray day. Hardly anyone was about as I headed for the city along
Paterson Avenue. No trucks were out, and the whole region
seemed deserted. It was just the feeling I wanted, to be alone,
unmolested. Then as I drove quietly along crossing the meadows
I saw a figure ahead of me, also alone, going on the right side of
the road in the same direction as I.

As I approached I made it out to be a young man, wearing no
overcoat, a cap on his head, his hands in his pockets; not a boy
but a man of about thirty, looking rather frail and cold. I
expected him to turn and try to thumb a ride but he didn't turn;
he just kept plugging ahead. There wasn't a car or another
person around.

So I passed him and stopped the car waiting for him to come
up with me. As he did so I opened the car window and asked him
if he wouldn't like a ride.

"Would I?" he said. "Are you offering me one?"

"That's why I stopped. Get in."

He looked at me as he settled himself beside me. I handed him
a cigarette, showed him the lighter, then after he had got a light
and as we rolled along, I asked him where he was heading.

"The big city."

"Where'd you come from?"

"Paterson. Spent the night there in a flop house. It sure was
cold on that road. This is marvelous."

"Looking for work?"

"Just want to see the city."

"Never been there before?"

"Always wanted to see it."

"You're not from Paterson, then?"

It turned out that he was from the Middle West somewhere,
had come in on the rods, had found himself broke and had
decided to hoof it the last few miles across the flats—on Christmas
morning.

"Look at those buildings," he said, as the New York skyline
began to appear above the heights of Weehawken.

"How you gonna get across the ferry?"

"Is there a ferry?"

He hadn't thought of that, but imagined he could walk right

in among the city streets and begin to look around. He hadn't had any breakfast and had no apparent idea what he would do next. I suppose he must have known what he was up against or he wouldn't have got this far but the whole situation had come up so strangely to fit my mood that I hardly believe it.

"What a Christmas you picked for yourself," I said to him. "Look, lemme tell you what I got on my mind." So then I told him what I was up to. He grinned when I spoke of Floss and the kids in Switzerland, about the Zoo, about my wanting to get off alone with the thought of them. Then I said to him, as we pulled up to the front of the ferryboat so he could get the panorama of the New York docks and ships, the buildings behind them and the river itself across which we were ploughing, "Look." I took out my pocketbook. "I don't know what I got in here but half of it's yours." I opened my wallet and counted it out, twenty-two dollars. "You get eleven, I get eleven. Here, take it."

"No, I can't take that."

"What do you mean you can't take it? Here it is, hold out your hand," and I gave it to him.

"Say, you are Santa Claus," he said to me, as he took the money.

"Now listen," I said. "Take my advice and go down around Fourteenth Street, that's as good a place for you to start as any. And don't flash your wad or you won't have it ten minutes. Look up the Salvation Army down there somewhere, they'll probably feed you. After that it's up to you."

He gave me his name, I gave him mine, we shook hands and that's the last I ever saw of him. But it was worth it. The animals were wonderful, few people were out, it being Christmas. I wandered about thinking of Floss and the kids, had a good turkey dinner in the restaurant and drove home in the early evening feeling completely happy and refreshed. I don't know when I've enjoyed a more contented day of complete dedication.

Chapter 40

When a Man Goes Down

The night before Floss and the kids returned, my sweet friends almost ruined me: It was a big drinking party. I had taken Grace Hellwig, our neighbor and a nurse, with me both because I had always liked "little" Gracie, now a tall blonde, and because I didn't want to go alone—poor kid, she is long since miserably dead. I always loved her.

Anyhow, I drank plenty, returned Grace to her family at two or three in the morning as virginal as she was when I picked her up, and next morning, having asked Bill Quinton, a customs officer and old friend, to get a pass onto the dock for me, went to the pier more than an hour before the ship was due.

I saw it far down the bay, but I was behind the barrier and I lost track of it as it drew nearer. No Bill. I stood there, now beginning to grow more and more restless waiting for him. Of these moments a life is made up. For nearly an hour I had been waiting there, walking back and forth. I could have murdered him. The ship was in the slip. I became frantic. I pleaded with the Pier Master, with individuals who I thought might know Bill. The passengers were coming down the gangplank when Bill, dear Bill! got there. By that time I was a wreck, both because of my disappointment and what I knew would be the disappointment of Floss and the kids. (She told the kids, I found out later, that just such a thing as this might occur.) But at last,

I got to the ship's side and saw Bill, my son, on an upper deck and waved to him.

They had had a wonderful crossing with a gay crowd and Floss herself had had all she wanted and more with the guys in the bar the night preceding. The family was once more happily united and drove home, for the first time, through the newly completed Holland Tunnel.

Thinking, talking, writing constantly about the poem as a way of life, during those years, one day I met Louis Zukofsky in the city after I had been sketched for a caricature by a person named Hoffman. Louis and I became good friends. He was an admirer of Ezra's verse, and upon Ezra's recommendation had met Basil Bunting who was then in New York.

Basil had been a conscientious objector in England during the First World War and they had given him some rough treatment. It is worth noting, however, that for the Second World War he rushed across the United States from California to go to England, as fast as he could, to enlist.

With Charles Reznikoff, a New York lawyer and writer of distinction, and George Oppen, in an apartment on Columbia Heights, Brooklyn, we together inaugurated, first, the Objectivist theory of the poem, and then the Objectivist Press. Three or four books were published, including my own *Collected Poems*. Then it folded.

The Objectivist theory was this: We had had "Imagism" (*Amygism*, as Pound had called it), which ran quickly out. That, though it had been useful in ridding the field of verbiage, had no formal necessity implicit in it. It had already dribbled off into so called "free verse" which, as we saw, was a misnomer. There is no such thing as free verse! Verse is measure of some sort. "Free verse" was without measure and needed none for its projected objectifications. Thus the poem had run down and became formally non extant.

But, we argued, the poem, like every other form of art, is an object, an object that in itself formally presents its case and its meaning by the very form it assumes. Therefore, being an object, it should be so treated and controlled—but not as in the past.

For past objects have about them past necessities—like the sonnet—which have conditioned them and from which, as a form itself, they cannot be freed.

The poem being an object (like a symphony or cubist painting) it must be the purpose of the poet to make of his words a new form: to invent, that is, an object consonant with his day. This was what we wished to imply by Objectivism, an antidote, in a sense, to the bare image haphazardly presented in loose verse.

Oppen supplied the money, as much as any of us. We had some small success, but few followers. I for one believe that it was Gertrude Stein, for her formal insistence on words in their literal, structural quality of being words, who had strongly influenced us. Miss Stein was always extremely kind to me, especially after I had written that note upon her work. It all went with the newer appreciation, the matter of paint upon canvas as being of more importance than the literal appearance of the image depicted. Nothing much happened in the end.

When a man like McAlmon goes down, others go with him. In fact, to a greater or lesser degree, the whole front of good writing collapses. If it is not a McAlmon it is some other. He represented the man or woman with a certain amount of capital at his disposal, or intelligent direction, who will maintain the attack upon the dry rot which overwhelms writing at various periods—as it did approaching the advent of the little magazine in the early part of the century. The little magazines never more than barely kept going, their five and ten contributions from some semi-submerged group of five or six young men and women —who mostly want to publish their own rebellious work—serving, though the hopes are big, to get no more than a few issues out before they collapse. It is only in the aggregate that they maintained a steady trickle of excellence, mixed with the bad, that served to keep writing loose, ready to accept the early, sensitive acquisition to the art. But at that it was a precarious business.

But when, often at the very moment of success, some prominent support is cut away, nothing for years may get published. Loose ends are left dangling, men are lost, promises that needed culture, needed protection and wit and courage to back them simply die.

One book, here and there, gets a preliminary hearing and remains isolated, while the overwhelming flood of insensitive drivel floods the market.

The little magazine is something I have always fostered; for without it, I myself would have been early silenced. To me it is one magazine, not several. It is a continuous magazine, the only one I know with an absolute freedom of editorial policy and a succession of proprietorships that follows a democratic rule. There is absolutely no dominating policy permitting anyone to dictate anything. When it is in any way successful it is because it fills a need in someone's mind to keep going. When it dies, someone else takes it up in some other part of the country—quite by accident—out of a desire to get the writing down on paper. I have wanted to see established some central or sectional agency which would recognize, and where possible, support little magazines. I was wrong. It must be a person who does it, a person, a fallible person, subject to devotions and accidents.

There were two prominent one-book men about New York in those days who promised great things. Emanuel Carnevali and his wife, Emily, were living in a room, somewhere near Tenth Avenue overlooking the freight yards near Fortieth Street, when they invited Floss and me in to eat polenta: codfish and cornmeal home style. They were just two kids, she a girl who had happened to live across the corridor some place where he was staying. She was not literary. He was straight, slim, with a beautiful young man's head, keenly intelligent—an obviously lost soul. Before him she was in obvious adoration. She was a peasant from the high mountains of northwestern Italy, he from one of the cities of the northern plains: here they were in New York, headed out but not toward money. This was New York at its best, the highest potential which you saw there with a catch in your throat, knowing it was almost certainly doomed to destruction.

Floss, Emily, Emanuel and I sat there looking out over the freight yards, eating our polenta and talking of Em's life with his eccentric father in Italy, of the young Italian writers of that time, of love, while all of us, I think, watched his face.

Emily told us how the first time he read in public somewhere, he had made her sit on the platform beside him, scared, not knowing much what it was all about—but he insisted on it, that those who heard might know *who* the writer was, not just he, but the two of them.

We drank our cheap wine—those are things that only the little magazine can serve and to which it is dedicated.

McAlmon published Em's book, which no one remembers, one of the best examples of—what? a book, a book that is all of a man, a young man, superbly alive. Doomed. When I think of what gets published and what gets read and praised and rewarded regularly with prizes, when such a book as that gets shoved under the heap of corpses, I swear never to be successful, I am disgusted, the old lusts revive. What else can a book do for a man?

Em earned his living often, when he made a living, while learning English and to write in English, by serving as a dishwasher in an Italian joint. His book was to be called *A Hurried Man*. That's the way he would work. He'd pile the dishes up, tell everyone to keep away. Then when the time came he'd get his soap and hot water ready and go at the heap of soiled things, madly, furiously, with murderous ferocity—though he didn't break anything—and in one-third the time it would take another to do the work, he'd come out exhausted, the job well done. The others would laugh but follow him spellbound.

Emily had a job, of course, which made it possible for him to write and for them to go on together. She wanted it that way. She was, I think, a year or two older than he. She was governess to two little girls whom she taught French. She and Em spent several week-ends with us in Rutherford, especially one year when the cherry tree was in blossom. That night I had to go out to a meeting of the Mosquito Extermination Commission in Hackensack and asked him if he wanted to come along while she stayed home for a talk with Flossie.

It was a bit late, a rainy night, and I was in a hurry. There had been a police drive on in East Rutherford to sell tickets for an entertainment for charity of some sort and I had been stopped several times for a contribution during the day. So that night when I saw a cop at the crossroads of Paterson Avenue and Hackensack Street holding the tickets up in the semi-dark and

waving them at me, I shook my head, moved my hand *No* and
kept going. There was no traffic light there at that time and he
had not blown a whistle.

But at that he let out a yell, blew his whistle wildly.

I stopped as he came rushing up to me, furious. "Where the
hell do you think you're going?"

"To a meeting of the Bergen County Mosquito Extermination
Commission."

"Well, I got to get out of this rotten job somehow. You're
arrested. Turn around and drive up to the City Hall."

"I gotta go to a meeting."

"You do what I tell you."

Em was sitting beside me ready to explode. I told him to keep
out of it. The cop got on the running board of the car and I
drove him the two blocks to the City Hall where I was handed
a summons and allowed to proceed.

Oh well. I had to appear some time following the incident with
Em as a witness. Nothing came of it.

A year later *Poetry Magazine* held up high hopes of a career
in Chicago for him if he would come there. Whether any definite
promise was made I cannot say, but Emily told him that as long
as it was for the advancement of his career as a writer he should
go, she would remain in New York at her job. Later he would
send for her.

He didn't, but wrote enthusiastically of successes. She was
thrilled. We heard also that he was doing well. Then, one day,
she showed us a final letter. She would only be in his way, as she
could readily understand, toward his assured literary success; all
their plans for the future were now no good—in short, he was
leaving her, with deepest love. Perhaps some day she would
understand and forgive him.

Emily was heartbroken. Flossie invited her to stay with us
after which, it being summer when the children were away, she
went with us to the farm at Monroe, New York. It was like home
again to her to be out in the country, if not Alpine scenes—among
the chickens, the cows, the cats, the dogs—with berries and fruit
abounding, the vegetable garden, the flowers. She stayed perhaps
a month or six weeks. Ma Herman loved her, as did we all. But

it couldn't go on. New York meant for her the tragic end of all her highest hopes. In a short time she moved to California where she found employment, still writing to us of her new life and asking always what we had heard from Em.

In Chicago, after an initial success, he contracted a disease which finally ruined him. I have heard various stories though I never saw a proper report on the subject. Someone told me a gal that used to wander the lake dunes in summer had infected him. But to me his affliction seems more as though it had been encephalitis than syphilis, with considerable damage to the brain tissues resulting, always hard to measure. He recovered after the acute phase, but became a nuisance to his former friends.

I have been told that when invited to a party at some attractive home, he'd ask to be shown the bathroom where he'd close the door, fill the tub and take an immediate and prolonged hot bath. Even this didn't clear his distressed mind. He walked, they say, bent almost double.

In the end he was shipped back to Italy in his father's custody, where they put him in a small charitable institution near Bologna run by some nuns. I had several letters from him or from friends close to him over the course of the next few years. He tried to write. But young as he still was, the game was finished. That single book published by Contact Editions is as far as I know his sole testament.

John Herrmann was a different sort of guy. His *What Happens*, however, a truthful story of his early life as a middle western jewelry salesman, always stands in my mind beside Carnevali's *A Hurried Man*. Both were young, both were born writers, both knew the uncertainties of a truth-teller's chances in a game where the big money wasn't interested. But John, six foot three, a Michigan grad, son of a well-to-do father, had a different background. He was married, when I knew him, to Josephine Herbst who had met him one night in a New York dance parlor.

Jo and he had put down what cash they had on a small, seventeenth-century sandstone farmhouse nestling in a narrow valley near Erwinna, Pennsylvania, just over the Delaware from Frenchtown, N. J. An old covered bridge spanned the river at that point at one time, but such idyllic things can't last in our day. It is rich man's country now, not far from Doylestown. John and Jo thought they had solved there their lives together.

They'd grow their own vegetables, live cheap, do their own work (o shades of Kenneth Burke), be, in short, the new peasant. They did, the first summer, spade up or at least hoe and plant the small half-acre in front of the house. They did it barefoot—it felt so good—and gathered their first crop from that rich soil across the brook from their front door. But you can't live that way today.

They had visits from the family, his family, her family, I've forgotten which. One wealthy uncle, after sleeping and eating on the premises, gave them excellent advice. Leaving, a few days later, he left a five-dollar bill under his pillow. "The son of a bitch," as John expressed it.

The old stones of the house were a superb background for nasturtiums. John did some passable rustic furniture jobs under shelter of the wreck of the barn. He wrote when he could. She wrote industriously. But after a while they both grew restless. He disturbed her and, as for himself, he just quit writing altogether and began knocking around with the farmers of the valley who told him where the best applejack could be found, until one day he just drifted back on his own to the big city.

There he'd go into a bar, he told me, with a copy, big as a Bible, of Gertrude Stein's *The Making of Americans* (Contact Edition) under his arm, order a drink and begin to read aloud. He'd have them spellbound. It wasn't a gag. He just knew it was interesting stuff and if people could get to it they'd like it. It's the old true cry of the enthusiast, but who ever gets to listen?

At such thoughts one doubts one's own life, one's own integrity. One grows old and foul-minded, though there always remain a few whom we can look up to. John Herrmann is one of those. So is the unsuccessful novelist Josephine Herbst (Herrmann). I have never been able to praise, as I should like to, Jo's devoted work. But to Jo herself I constantly have my hat off.

We often drove out to Erwinna. Pep West went there, admired, even bought a farm in that country. Mike Gold and several of the movie people did the same thing. But it's of no interest to me any longer. I think Jo still owns the house but doesn't live in it.

John lost interest in writing, took to drinking as a serious occupation and got mixed up in the labor racket. One day during the big St. Louis streetcar strike, he saw a gal who was leading a demonstration and fell for her. She was young, violent and full of fight. The attachment was instantaneous, mutual and complete.

When they came down to Rutherford they stayed with us once over a week-end. We had to leave for some party or other. John and his new wife remained in the house—with a couple of cases of beer and what else to drink I don't know. They had a lot of dirty wash they'd thrown into the back of their car. She dumped that into the washing machine in the cellar. So we departed.

They must have had a good time together which they ended snapping the spring of the electric iron at each other until that broke. Floss insisted, Monday morning, that she at least pick up the laundry, which was still soaking, wring it out and take it away with her. We weren't mad, just inconvenienced. I understand she got mixed up with one of Edmund Wilson's wives at one time and had to be rescued from the outside ledge of a window box where she was hanging two floors above the street in Greenwich Village somewhere.

Haven't seen John since then. He was a great sailor and I believe captained a small coastwise schooner of some sort on a government mission during the Second World War. He and the girl from St. Louis were still together the last I heard of them. His *What Happens* remains the first book of a gifted novelist.

Sailors Don't Care, by Edward Lanham, was another book to remember. But once McAlmon's influence faded, the freshness of Lanham's early style faded also.

I always remember with the greatest pleasure also Paul Rosenfeld's only novel, *Boy in the Sun*. It was the best of Rosenfeld: standing in the roseate glow of an 1890 midday, one of the most lyrical novels I have ever read. In fact, it explains the man and his pervasive influence at that time when he was so generously active among the painters, writers, musicians of the day. He could not have made a more direct statement in his own defense. Cherubic, a baroque cherub in the paneling of a Washington Square salon, describes him, a true *Boy in the Sun*. I always felt pleased with Rosenfeld: there was a gentleness, a devotion to his friends, an industry for fine art about him, sometimes mistaken but never lying. He was never for sale. His death left a mark upon those who knew and loved him.

Chapter 41

The End of the Middle

Those were tragic years for our family. Mother, more than a little put out, I must say, by Flossie's return, continued to live with us, but her reign was ended. In 1930, one Monday on the way to the Woman's Club, she fell and broke her hip. Poor Mother, she was very proud of the small size of her feet. She had worn a size one shoe all during her young ladyhood, had been a "famous" dancer, and could run like the wind. It was this vanity that led to her death.

The day before the accident the sidewalks were icy, but she had insisted on going to church without rubbers. It was to show her feet, though she'd be furious if we said it. Coming out of church Mr. Tufts, who had a car there, had seen her start for home and stopped her.

"It's dangerous," he said. "Get in with us and we'll take you home."

That was just enough to nettle her; to imply that she didn't know how to walk on ice was an insult. She refused to go with him, but he was insistent and forced her against her will to get into his car. Before our house he got out, took her arm and accompanied her up the stone front steps. She was boiling mad at it.

I begged her next day to take a taxi to the club, which was at least four long blocks away.

"At least walk in the middle of the street," I said.

That's what she had done, but her heel hit a small ice patch and down she went. She couldn't move, but just lay there, unobserved, in the middle of the street like a wounded sparrow until a taxi passing that way stopped. The man lifted her and brought her home. It was her finish, for though she lived almost twenty years longer, she was always a cripple. For years I helped her up and downstairs and carried her meals up to her daily. It went on for eighteen years in all.

While Mother was in the hospital from this first fall, around the first of March the same year I received a telephone call while I was taking care of a patient in my office in Passaic. Floss had heard disturbing news by phone from her mother, in Monroe: her father had gone out with a gun to clean out a woodchuck that had a burrow next to the well-house and had been hurt badly. Floss was beside herself in her haste to get off. I had a patient on the table. She called me again in five minutes. I dropped my case and ran. When we got to Monroe, an hour's ride, her father was dead. I went down alone to see the body. Floss couldn't bear to look at it, for he had been her lifelong god and protector.

He was dead all right. Shot in the belly with a load from a twelve-gauge shell. He seemed, from the marks on the rocks, to have been poking about the hole, the dogs with him, when the gun was discharged. He had died instantly in a way similar to his only son a year or two before him. Fortunately we had got there in time to keep off the dogs.

We took trips in summer, mostly to New England. Then in 1931, while Paul was in his last year at camp, Enajerog as they called it, we took a two weeks' cruise, one of our happiest, from Montreal, past Quebec, out the Gulf of Saint Lawrence, past Anticosti, through the Straits of Belle Isle to Doctor Grenfell's mission hospital at Saint Anthony, Newfoundland. Many of the people and places I saw there have deeply influenced my later writing: it was this that I had first desired, to quit the urban life and go out into the wilderness. There, facing me, it was, stretch-

ing away from the north shore, from Godbou, from Seven Isles, to
the North Pole if I wanted to follow.

The small vessel, the *S.S. North Voyageur*, seemed
like a plaything, three feet below the dock's edge, when we
boarded it at Montreal. But when we went ashore, at Forteau
Bay, to post letters before passing through the Straits, it looked
as big as the *Leviathan*.

The very day we arrived at Forteau a child had been lost over
the stern of a skiff on the way back from a picnic at one of the
small islands a little way offshore. The parents took it with a
curious, hopeless calm that I have never forgotten.

Scotch and Irish, they are an isolated people who hole up
winter long and can hardly walk a hundred feet when the sun
returns. But in a month, the sun having hit them, they are
hardy as seals again.

A few days later as the ship entered Saint Anthony's small
harbor to anchor, its siren was sounded. From the rocks, where
they are penned, hundreds of huskies let out their desolate
howls. They are fed the scum from the tops of the hogsheads in
which the crude cod livers are brought in from the boats. Savage
beasts not easy to handle.

I never saw monkshood of a deeper blue.

In the ward of the hospital there was a young Eskimo mother
and her three-week-old infant.

How shall such impressions be described? We live in filth, we
eat, drink and bathe in it; as we can we thrive on it. We are
suffocated by the primitive and the pure.

So on our return when, a little ahead of schedule, we arrived
at Greely Island, where the first east-west transatlantic fliers had
been grounded, we found two children of the lighthouse keeper
there, our social-service worker on board tried to teach them the
game of hide and seek, but could make no headway with them.
They could see no point in it, only stood and stared: Why hide?
you could almost hear them say, when we spend our lives only
to find?

The flight had been organized by the German Count so-and-so,
dying of cancer. He had a German pilot and the Irishman he
had taken along for luck, as the newspaper stories had it, and

had come down at mid-winter in a blinding fog and landed, by pure luck, upon the only level spot for fifty miles around beyond the rocks.

The ground now in summer was covered in places with *molte*, as the Scandinavians call them, "bake-apple," as they called them there: a raspberrylike berry on a single stem. It stood no more than two to three inches above the ground, was flesh-colored and tasted delicious. There were dark "crow berries" also, everywhere, as I walked alone over the rocks looking for a possible place to get into the water, having sworn to a group of fellow passengers that I'd go swimming somehow, somewhere on the trip come what might. I found blanched sea-urchin shells everywhere over the terrain, which the gulls had dropped from the air to crack them for eating.

Having arrived at the far north side of the island at last I stripped down and went in, with two or three puffins looking at me beyond the rocks. It was desperately cold and the bottom too shell-covered for bathing; but I got in up to my waist and dipped under enough to give my belly a foot-long cut on a shelly rock. At least I had evidence that I was in the water. It is strange to bathe alone in an Arctic sea.

Part Three

"Old though I am, for lady's love unfit,
the power of the beauty I remember yet."

Chapter 42

A Look Back

When I look at Rutherford today with its neon-lighted drug stores and real-estate offices, jowl to jowl, down the main street, it's hard to recall the small village in which I grew up.

Imagine! No sewers, no water supply, no gas, even. Certainly no electricity; no telephone, not even a trolley car. The sidewalks were of wood, crosspieces nailed to two-by-fours laid on the ground; cracks between the boards in which yellow-jackets nested to swarm out as we walked over them. It's astonishing how the sting of those insects hurt. The streets were not paved at all in most places; a macadam road was a novelty.

Instead of those "improvements" we had cesspools in the back yard and outhouses as on any farm—all this within ten miles of the metropolis. Our drinking water was rain water collected from the roof down leaders which drained into a cistern. From the cistern the water was pumped by a hand pump in the kitchen into a tin-lined wooden tank in the attic. Ed and I got a dime apiece for an hour's pumping when it was needed.

The rooms were lit by kerosene oil lamps—am I *that* old?—held in cast-iron brackets in the bedrooms and large, handsome glass and porcelain lamps, especially over the dining-room table, that pulled down on chains when they were to be filled, cleaned and lighted.

I slept in the room next to my parents. There was one lamp in a bracket between my room and theirs. I liked the light to go to sleep with. There, pretending to be asleep, night after night, I heard Pop read *Trilby* to mother as she lay in bed and he sat up to see the text. I heard of Svengali, the mesmerist, of Little Billee and of Trilby herself. In fact, I named my pet white mice after them: Trilby, pure white, and Little Billee, a black head and white and black body.

The streets were always being ripped up for water, for sewers, for gas. When the Iveson mansion was finally completed across the street from us, and on the night of the wedding of the son or daughter, I forget which, the worm of gaslights from the house to the street was lighted, the house ablaze with lights, the guests arriving from the railroad station—a continuous row of carriages—it was the finest sight I ever saw.

The whole town could not have comprised more than five thousand people: the Deans, the Hollisters, the Cummingses, the Ivesons themselves. Once, a good many years later, on one of the darker streets, a man was seen descending from a ground-floor window. The cop on the beat yelled to him to halt—there had been several robberies at the time in that neighborhood, but he ran to get among the shrubbery. The officer fired and killed him. When they rolled him over he was found to be X, a neighbor of the woman, her lover.

Once old man Roseman, who used to drive as a boy for one of the old-time doctors, a morphine addict, was coming across the sand lot near Spring Dell, when he heard a crash and saw a bare-legged man, his trousers in one hand, blood streaming from his knees, run madly down the hill toward Orient Way and disappear. Roseman fairly rolled on the ground laughing. Having recognized the fellow at the moment, he realized what had occurred: he himself had been mistaken for the returning husband, and the lover had taken the kitchen window in one leap, glass and all.

Once Pop told me of the organization of the Union Club. They needed money. Someone suggested that they each put up a dollar, when before a further move could be made, Mr. Weaver—now dead half a century or more—a big, cigar-smoking man who had a good-looking daughter, got up and made a little speech.

"Gentlemen," he said, "there were two farmers who had adjoining acres. One of them was a pious man, so that when the field had been plowed and harrowed in the spring he went into his field with his bag of rye and this is what he did: He picked up a handful of the seed and scattered it around like this (a mere pinch of seed held between two fingers) as he said, dropping the seed to the ground: God bless the good seed. God bless the good seed.

"His neighbor across the fence also went out to plant his seed. He scooped it up by the handful, and as he threw it around him, strode along saying: And to hell with it. To hell with it!

"Now, gentlemen, which of these farmers do you think got the crop? I make a motion that we all contribute five dollars to the founding of the club."

Pop was a good storyteller but too abstemious and modest a man for his own happiness.

The town was, a good half of it, grown to oaks and chestnut trees. On the way to school in the fall we kids could always count on a small pocketful of nuts, delicious really, on our way down almost any street in the place. Mother on her way down to the stores would start at least half a mile up the Passaic Avenue hill across from the Episcopal Church and take a path striking off to the left and go nearly half the distance through the trees.

Recently, oh, within the last three or four years, my old fourth-grade teacher met Floss downtown and told her this story:

She, Helen Walcot, was a small girl then. She lived on Home Avenue just where the path through the woods came out not far from the front yard where as a girl she would be playing. She was used to seeing Mrs. Williams come past at various times during the week on her way to make her purchases. She had noted, as a little girl will, that Mrs. Williams was in not too many weeks to have a baby, and she wondered, she told Floss, what it would be, a girl or a boy.

It was I.

Perhaps that explained my love of trees and that my first wish was to be a forester.

Ed and I, Jim Hyslop and Lest Maxwell, my special friend,

went through the primary and middle ages of childhood together
—before women touched us—as one. We loved and hated each
other with fierçest intensity, though Jim, the naturalist, may not
have hated as much as we others. Ed and I were brothers, that
made it savage at times. I can remember the most minor turns of
their moods as shown in their faces, looking down or up, the way
they turned their toes in walking, how they sat or ran. Jim's very
open-mindedness no doubt determined his career.

Between the ages of seven and nine, sitting on the round seat
about the great oak in the Copeland's lot, I proposed marriage
to Ada, Lester's sister—only a hundred feet from the spot (such
is fate) where, twenty years later, I proposed marriage to Flossie,
who had not been born at the time of the first proposal. Thus
there may be a fate in places whose laws escape us. There was a
great white oak prominent on the farm at Monroe, too, and in
front of our house there is today a white oak beginning to grow
venerable.

Jim and I combed Kipp's woods, behind our back fences—*as
I write this there sounds in my ears the kick of my shoes as I
went over Maxwell's back fence directly across the lot as I went
to pick up Lester on my way to sylvan school.* One day I killed
a robin in the apple tree at Rice's. I almost cried at the sight
of it lying out of shape and bloodied on the ground. In the
sumacs near there, we killed a kitten, most unhappily and once
with our guns we shot at a red squirrel on a high limb in the
woods until it too dropped to the ground, dead. I didn't enjoy it.

Kipp's woods was my magic forest. I wanted to be a forester,
but the only schools with courses on the subject were at Cornell
and Yale. They were post-graduate courses. Jim went to Massachusetts Agricultural College where he majored in entomology.
He ended as Chief of the Extension Bureau of the United States
Department of Agriculture, writing for twenty years at his
encyclopedia of noxious insects—only to be met at the end by a
refusal on all sides to publish his magnum opus.

"Yes, it's needed. Of course it's needed. But how can we
finance it?"

So there it stands in manuscript form, filling a side of the
room where they have set up his bed.

He is almost blind.

I have tried in every way at my disposal to get the money to have his great work published. No one, no university, no institution will undertake it.

The Meadows, the marshland separating the ridge where Rutherford lies from the next ridge, a continuation of the Palisades in Weehawken, was romantic ground for us growing boys. We didn't dare go into the dense cedar-swamps that flourished there in which blueberry pickers in the fall were often lost; the mosquitos were so thick you could almost grasp in the air at random about your head and kill a half-dozen of them. Large flocks of egrets had their nests there, and once in a while a stray deer would be tracked through the trees.

I remember once when the boys were small taking them in along an old wood road in our boots from Paterson Avenue among the trees to dig up a wild azalea. I found a bush and carried it out, the roots and a good hunk of wet sod resting, in a burlap bag, across my shoulders.

The last of the cedar swamps died when the water level of the swamp was changed by the crisscrossing highways and ditches dug everywhere for various drainage projects. Fire did the rest.

For a time black duck and teal, occasionally a Canada goose would fly in during the hunting season, but now even the cattails have disappeared, their place having been taken by the "caneys" as the boys call them, rather beautiful with their purple plumes filling the fields between ditches. But the whole character of the place has been altered.

There is one house in the town—it's strange to go into houses along a street over a period of over thirty years, meeting different people from those formerly living there—where tragedy has never failed to take a stand. It's a large house on a fairly high terrace with oaks, beeches and a hundred-foot-high tulip tree standing about it.

The first owner, I believe, was a tall, gangling German who got to be mayor of the town and was liked and admired by everyone. Yet he was most unfortunate in that, though he had

four children, a brilliant son and a lovely daughter, he had also
two other boys who were mentally retarded. The brilliant son
died young, and the other two became a lifelong care.

After he died and his musical and cultured wife moved with
her daughter to a smaller place, a second family took possession
of the house. This was an executive of a large New York commercial house, whose wife had been something of an invalid for
years. A large, benevolent woman who often sent Flossie and me
baskets of vegetables and fruit from what must have been a
luxuriant farm in South Jersey.

To repay her in some sense for this small favor she asked me
in return if I would not now and then give her a prescription
for a few ounces of camphorated tincture of opium—paregoric,
in short. She had some obscure gastric disability for which a
physician in Philadelphia had prescribed the tincture. She acknowledged it probably wasn't very good for her, but as she was
often in great pain and that this seemed the only thing that
relieved it . . . And so forth and so forth. She was, however,
extremely anxious that her husband should not know about the
weakness, and so I gave her the stated amount of the drug,
notifying the proper authorities that she was an addict.

This was all before she moved to the house of which I am
speaking. After she moved there she became extremely ill, fell,
hurt herself and was bedridden. But worse than that she had
developed an atrophy of one forearm accompanied by considerable pain. I looked, looked at the pupils of her eyes, knew I
hadn't given her any opium recently, but decided she was suffering, nevertheless, from a toxic neuritis induced by the drug and
that I had no right to keep what I knew from her husband any
longer.

So I went downstairs with him, but before I could open my
mouth, he began to confess. He had been giving his wife opiates
for years. He knew he was doing wrong but . . . Then I told him
my part in the deal.

We went upstairs together and told the big, imposing woman
the result of our colloquy, and I added that as far as I was concerned I was through. I was a young man and wanted to get out
of the mess. Then she let me have it. I tell you I never was so

cursed in my life. Blasphemy, filth, threats of suit didn't move me, however. She died not long after.

The third family, descendants of one of the oldest families in the state, were no less affected, and quit the house after the daughter's unfortunate marriage. Perhaps that completes the cycle, since the present occupants are apparently normal, well-adjusted citizens.

Chapter 43

Of Medicine and Poetry

When they ask me, as of late they frequently do, how I have for so many years continued an equal interest in medicine and the poem, I reply that they amount for me to nearly the same thing. Any worth-his-salt physician knows that no one is "cured." We recover from some somatic, some bodily "fever" where as observers we have seen various engagements between our battalions of cells playing at this or that lethal maneuver with other natural elements. It has been interesting. Various sewers or feed-mains have given way here or there under pressure: various new patterns have been thrown up for us upon the screen of our knowledge. But a cure is absurd, as absurd as calling these deployments "diseases." Sometimes the home team wins, sometimes the visitors. Great excitement. It is noteworthy that the sulfonamids, penicillin, came in about simultaneously with Ted Williams, Ralph Kiner and the rubber ball. We want home runs, antibiotics to "cure" man with a single shot in the buttocks.

But after you've knocked the ball into the center-field bleachers and won the game, you still have to go home to supper. So what? The ball park lies empty-eyed until the next game, the next season, the next bomb. Peanuts.

Medicine, as an art, never had much attraction for me, though it fascinated me, especially the physiology of the nervous system. That's something. Surgery always seemed to me particularly unsatisfying. What is there to cut off or out that will "cure" us? And to stand there for a lifetime sawing away! You'd better be a chef, if not a butcher. There is a joy in it, I realize, to know that you've really cut the cancer out and that the guy will come in to score, but I never wanted to be a surgeon. Marvelous men— I take off my hat to them. I knew one once who whenever he'd get into a malignant growth would take a hunk of it and rub it into his armpit afterward. Never knew why. It never hurt him, and he lived to a great old age. He had imagination, curiosity and a sense of humor, I suppose.

The cured man, I want to say, is no different from any other. It is a trivial business unless you add the zest, whatever that is, to the picture. That's how I came to find writing such a necessity, to relieve me from such a dilemma. I found by practice, by trial and error, that to treat a man as something to which surgery, drugs and hoodoo applied was an indifferent matter; to treat him as material for a work of art made him somehow come alive to me.

What I wanted to do with him (or her, or it) fascinated me. And it didn't make any difference, apparently, that he was in himself distinguished or otherwise. It wasn't that I wanted to save him because he was a good and useful member of society. Death had no respect for him for that reason, neither does the artist, neither did I. As far as I can tell that kind of "use" doesn't enter into it; I am myself curious as to what I do find. The attraction is bizarre.

Thus I have said "the mind." And the mind? I can't say that I have ever been interested in a completely mindless person. But I have known one or two that are close to mindless, certainly useless, even fatal to their families, or what remains of their families, whom yet I find far more interesting than plenty of others whom I serve.

These are the matters which obsess me so that I cannot stop writing. I can recall many from the past, boys and girls, bad pupils, renegades, dirty-minded and -fisted, that I miss keenly. When some old woman tells me of her daughter now happily married to a handicapper at the Garden City track, that she has two fine sons, I want to sing and dance. I am happy. I am stimulated. She is still alive. Why should I feel that way? She almost caused me to flunk out of grammar school. I almost ruined my young days over her.

But I didn't. I love her, ignorant, fulsome bit of flesh that she was, and some other really vicious bits of childhood who ruined the record of the whole class—dead of their excesses, most of them. They flatter my memory. The thing, the thing, of which I am in chase. The thing I cannot quite name was there then. My writing, the necessity for a continued assertion, the need for me to go on will not let me stop. To this day I am in pursuit of it, actually—not there, in the academies, nor even in the pursuit of a remote and difficult knowledge or skill.

They had no knowledge and no skill at all. They flunked out, got jailed, got "Mamie" with child, and fell away, if they survived, from their perfections.

There again, a word: their perfections. They were perfect, they seem to have been born perfect, to need nothing else. They were there, living before me, and I lived beside them, associated with them. Their very presence denied the need of "study," that is study by degrees to elucidate them. They were, living, the theme that all my life I have labored to elucidate, and when I could not elucidate them I have tried to put them down, to lay them upon the paper to record them: for to do that is, after all, a sort of elucidation.

It isn't because they fascinated me by their evildoings that they were "bad" boys or girls. Not at all. It was because they were there full of a perfection of the longest leap, the most unmitigated daring, the longest chances.

This immediacy, the thing, as I went on writing, living as I could, thinking a secret life I wanted to tell openly—if only I could—how it lives, secretly about us as much now as ever. It is the history, the anatomy of this, not subject to surgery, plumbing or cures, that I wanted to tell. I don't know why. Why tell that which no one wants to hear? But I saw that when I was successful in portraying something, by accident, of that secret world of perfection, that they did want to listen. Definitely. And my "medicine" was the thing which gained me entrance to these secret gardens of the self. It lay there, another world, in the self. I was permitted by my medical badge to follow the poor, defeated body into those gulfs and grottos. And the astonishing thing is that at such times and in such places—foul as they may be with the stinking ischio-rectal abscesses of our comings and goings—just there, the thing, in all its greatest beauty, may for a moment be freed to fly for a moment guiltily about the room. In illness, in the permission I as a physician have had to be present at deaths and births, at the tormented battles between daughter and diabolic mother, shattered by a gone brain—just there—for a split second—from one side or the other, it has fluttered before me for a moment, a phrase which I quickly write down on anything at hand, any piece of paper I can grab.

It is an identifiable thing, and its characteristic, its chief character is that it is sure, all of a piece and, as I have said, instant and perfect: it comes, it is there, and it vanishes. But I have seen it, clearly. I have seen it. I know it because there it is. I have been possessed by it just as I was in the fifth grade—when she leaned over the back of the seat before me and greeted me with some obscene remarks—which I cannot repeat even if made by a child forty years ago, because no one would or could understand what I am saying that then, there, it had appeared.

The great world never much interested me (except at the back of my head) since its effects, from what I observed, were so disastrously trivial—other than in their bulk; smelled the same as most public places. As Bob McAlmon said after the well-dressed Spanish woman passed us in Juarez (I had said, Wow! there's perfume for you!):

"You mean that?" he said. "That's not perfume, I just call that whores."

Chapter 44

The City of the Hospital

The city of the hospital is my final home. You bring into it what you are, what your forebears were before you, first-generation Americans in many cases, who bring Europe with them also, peasant Europe with all its kindness, greed, cupidity and its despair.

There are good doctors and bad doctors: you can't tell them by their names; thieves, even murderers, with the most respectable names. On the other hand there are the most painstaking and humane priests of healing whose names show their origin to have been the ghettos of Poland or Sicily's stricken villages. There are financial geniuses whose parents not so many years back started operations at some corner fruit stand, men who could well give our Morgans and Rockefellers points on how to improve the complexion of a nickel. They are just what you might expect from their heritage, those who prey on others of their own kind. But there are also men and women who pain over every dollar they charge the sick for their cure and live virtually poverty-stricken lives of devoted service to mankind—which doesn't on the other hand make them the best doctors by any means.

It's a strange thing how many phases go into the making of a good, serviceable physician. Some have hands, just good surgeon's hands, and if by luck they have a head and a heart to go with them, they can reach the heights. Others are a menace to the community they inhabit. How are you going to tell them apart?

Most of their fellows know them. But the human animal is an untrustworthy self-seeker, and the worst doctors know how to make themselves attractive. They are usually popular.

Who, when he has to pay his rent or his office nurse's salary, would hesitate to take out a pair of tonsils if he is offered the opportunity to do so? No matter what the contours of the pharynx will look like afterward, he's licensed to do it and he'll go ahead. He doesn't even know the significance of the anatomical picture, much less care about the end results.

My own conception of the job has been to consider myself a man in the front line, in the trenches. It's the only way I can respect myself and go on treating what comes to me, men, women and children. I don't know everything about medicine and surgery but I *must* know well what I do know, besides which I must be thoroughly aware of what I do not know. I can't handle everything but I must never miss anything. I must play the game to win every time, often by referring a case with the greatest possible speed to someone else, get for the patient the finest service I can find in my region, at the least possible cost consistent with his ability to pay.

By and large we couldn't live in the world today were it not for the medical profession, and I mean just that. We'd plain die, masses of us, tomorrow, if medical techniques were not kept up no matter what our fractional beliefs might be. On the other hand we may be populating the world with idiots. No one knows the answer.

I am grateful at least that I studied medicine (which is an idea: to study medicine but not to practice it) that I might know what goes on in myself as well as others. Gertrude Stein spoke of this clearly in her own life. She took it from the top down. She began with the psychic factors under William James and was, according to his testimony, a brilliant student. Then finding she did not want to limit herself to the abstractions but preferred rather the study of the whole man, went to Johns Hopkins for the somatic factor, the study of the physical body to make her knowledge whole. For the practice of letters concerns the whole man no matter what the stylistic variants may be. What better then than to know your subject thoroughly in all its aspects before beginning to exploit it? That was, at least, Gertrude Stein's conception of the advantages of knowing medicine if you wish to be a writer.

Obviously enough, the entire world today is a hospital so that, one thing canceling the other, that makes the hospital a very normal environment. It is only incidentally concerned with illness: quite casually, to itself, it measures, with some indifference, the decay of flesh, its excreta, bad odors and even its ecstasies of birth and cure. Cure to a physician is a pure accident, to the pathologist in his laboratory almost a disappointment. The real thing is the excitement of the chase, the opportunity for exercise of precise talents, the occasion for batting down a rival to supersede him, to strut, to boast and get on with one's fellows. Discovery is the great goal—and the accumulation of wealth.

Today the hospital is part of the fairgrounds for the commercial racket carried on by the big pharmaceutical houses. Almost every day there are exhibits of the latest drugs put on by the sales force of this or that manufacturer in the doctor's waiting room. It is a place as busy as the city editor's desk of a big newspaper, for the latest cures are front-page stuff today. If the physician does not hand out the latest variant of the popular cure-all, he will fast lose his practice. Rightly so. The practice of medicine and surgery is close to the realm of necromancy today; miracles are being looked for and performed; knowledge *has* increased at such a rate that one should be ashamed to die of anything short of decapitation over the edge of a windshield.

Then we have the managerial staff, and after them the nursing staff—which has many occupations apart from techniques. They are women, they are young women, they are for the most part intelligent young women and frequently, in their crisp and becoming uniforms, they appear as beautiful young women with whom the distresses of mankind have little to do directly. It is their own backgrounds out of which the "call" comes to serve humanity that determine their lives. Fine eyes, velvet skin (or coarse), arms built for love, breasts casqued in starched linen, never to be pictured or kissed.

What shall they do? The discipline is rigid. I have long listened to their stories.

"She has decided to stay there."

"Where?"

"Where she is now, at Grasslands."

"The insane?"

"Yes, she loves it. The only one in her class. They get two hundred and fifty a month. Of course thirty-five dollars of it is taken out for meals."

"You mean little Audrey?"

"She has signed up to go on from two to eleven."

"They get a day off?"

"Two days, up there. But she doesn't want the women. She only wants to take care of the men. She can't stand the women."

"Good for her."

"Do you know Nellie De Graff is up there?"

"You mean . . . ?"

"Yes. She is in a private cottage."

"I did hear that she's been hitting the bottle recently."

"A hopeless case. Her children signed her in. I'm sorry for her husband. Three to five hundred a week, the poor man, he can't stand it."

One New Year's morning I wasn't too steady myself when a little redhead came up to me.

"What time is it?"

"11:15."

"O God, if I can only hold out till noon."

"What's the matter with your eye?"

"Fell downstairs this morning—at four A.M."

This was the same one whom her friends had dragged in soused to the gills through the dormitory window while they were serving their time at the Contagious Hospital in Newark. They undressed her, pushed her under the shower to get her on duty at seven.

Some of them (one is all I remember) are so well-made they can land a job, let's say, as "hostess" at some night club. But that's not the only type. There are the ones with powerful legs, hair to entice a Botticelli or a Modigliani to draw them. They are lost or almost lost in most cases.

These are the necessities that drive them to decide on their choice of service.

And what becomes of them? Some stay on, think of Alaska or Korea, but never get there. A few with wit or the intelligence or the stomachs to do it, marry the medical men, still unattached, who serve as interns in the places. Good marriages. But most marry men, good fellows who cannot hope to afford their wives the sorts of associations they have grown used to in their three years of hospital service, in the private rooms and among the older men on the attending staff. These are individuals of far greater culture in many cases than the girls have been used to, far greater wealth and talent also than is usually available to them. The girls are tempted. The prospect is at times a glittering one. They are deeply affected. Shall they deny themselves this last chance at distinction before the plunge into mediocrity and the raising of a family?

And the older men? Here is often charm, loyalty, devotion to very love itself—shown in a roseate cloud—offered not crudely if hesitatingly, but even courageously. The opportunities are manifold, the late time of duty, the freedom from restraint at strange hours, the very intimate character of the occupation with the human carcass, at times under great stress, the complete (but not complete) knowledge of its processes. The girls have to witness everything there is to see and to know. Surgery is complete knowledge, and witnessing births gives detailed plans of what they themselves are built for.

The only thing the girls lack is the practice of the physiology of love. Its knowledge is old-hat to them before they have been two years out of high school, and they themselves are ripe, in fact, sadly enough, overripe. That intensifies the loss: the knowledge, the opportunities denied, the constant attack they are under from all sides leave them worn out often before they have started. They have caught a glimpse of love, have been offered endless opportunities for its physical fulfillment but, in the end, come away, ignorant, their fine bodies wasted and their minds unsatisfied. Not that all of them have minds or even sensibilities, but at least the hospital has swallowed them.

One day I was coming out of the cloakroom when I ran into

a young surgeon whom I very much like, a really good guy. I greeted him affectionately and received a gruff reply. This was unlike the man.

"Hey," I said, grabbing him by the shoulder as he was passing me, "what's the idea?"

"Oh, nothing," he said.

But I kept hold of him and continued. "Don't give me that stuff," I said. "What's biting you? Come on, give."

"You wanna know?"

"Sure, that's why I asked you." We were standing in the passage to the lobby.

"I was over at the other hospital this morning. I had an operation scheduled since yesterday. But when I got there at eight o'clock, somebody else had the place sewed up."

"And . . . ?"

"I went to the scrub room to find what was up. There he was, the whole place was crowded with them." He paused a moment and I waited.

"So, I said to him, 'What have you got this morning, a gall bladder?' "

" 'No, just an appendix,' he told me. That made me mad. You know him."

"Yes, I know him," I said.

"Well, I stood there a minute, the whole room was listening. Then I said to him, 'You know, I got an idea: The next man that comes into your office, when you look at him and decide you want to take out his gall bladder, you have a little gun in the top drawer of your desk and point it at his belly and you say to him, "For two hundred and fifty dollars I won't take out your gall bladder." He looks at you and he sees you mean business'—they were all scrubbing up and all listening to me. 'Then he gives you the money.' "

"Did you really say that to him?" I asked, fascinated and gleefully chuckling to myself, thinking of this cocky little chap standing behind the first, twice his size, who had stopped scrubbing as had all the others to listen.

" 'In that way,' " went on my friend, " 'you accomplish three things: first, you get the money; two, you save a lot of time for everyone; and third, your patient escapes a needless operation.' "

Men at operating tables drop dead, sometimes, at their tasks. The young are always pushing their elders, as in all corporate work. Brilliant work gets done and is often never acclaimed. There is much genius among physicians, as in any occupation to which a man or woman can devote himself, great work done casually in the course of duty for which no praise is asked and none given other than a nurse's smile or a friend's nod of the head, superb accomplishments. For what? For a few bucks? But that, the crown of the physician, is not today the thing most recognized.

An old friend of my father's once said to me when I was one day raving against a flagrant miscarriage of justice in our local courts, "Willie, what do you think you can get in a court of law?"

"Why the least you can ask for," I said, "is common justice."

"Oh, no," he replied, "you won't get justice, that's impossible. All you'll get is the best that is available in your locality."

It's no different with medicine, a rat race, if there ever was one, in which the ones most devoted to humanity often come in second best. But it can't be helped. If a man brings me his son, saying to me that the boy has "an appendix" which the father wants out and I tell him the boy is perfectly well and shouldn't be touched, what does the father do? He goes to the next man down the block who takes on the job without even looking. Who's the sucker? Why, I am, of course. Multiply that by a thousand times and add to it the fact that in the end all cases are lost, while the postponement of the evil is all we hope for, and you'll grasp at once the money that's in the racket.

The doctor is admitted to all houses. Often a man will say, "I'm leaving the front door open, Doc, you'll find her in bed. Go ahead in. She's looking for you." It's a great ticket of admission to a lot of things.

When the girls come up for their nurse's graduation and stand on the platform in their starched uniforms to receive their diplomas, some of them will appear to the onlookers as the most beautiful women in the world, which they are.

And then the grinning head of the Board of Governors will stand at the front, as I have often seen it done, with a list in his hand and call the girls up one by one, each to receive her scroll. He may start in, "Miss Adams"—but then, as he goes on, he will begin to arrive at a sticker (the fool could have studied the name previously), he hesitates: "Miss—tch"—he laughs, the audience is howling and the girl, recognizing what he is trying to say, comes red-faced to the front. That's the mark of her condition. She is embarrassed by the offensive snobbery of the man.

Chapter 45

White Mule

In 1932 Angel Flores broke a different ice by publishing a book of short stories of mine which he had solicited for his Dragon Press. Nothing of mine had sold. I was resigned to it. I was, however, glad to have the man take the stories which I had been jotting down for a year or more during the depression. It made an attractive little collection with which I felt rather pleased; but that was the end of it. Few books were sold and I never heard of Angel Flores again.

Several months later a doctor friend of mine from the hospital came up to me and said, "Doc, I've been down to the convention at Atlantic City."

"Tha' so?"

"Yeah. Saw some of your books down there for sale on the boardwalk."

"You did? What books?"

"Book of short stories. *Knife of the Times.* Is that it?"

"Yeah. How many of them?"

"Oh, they had a big stack. Maybe a hundred or more."

"How much were they selling for?"

He smiled. "How much?" I insisted.

"You wanna know?"

"What am I asking you for?"

"You won't be sore?"

"No."

"Fifteen cents apiece."

"Wow! How can I get at 'em?"

"I'm going down next week. If they're still there I'll get them for you. How many do you want?"

"All of them."

So I got a crate of them a few weeks later, but unfortunately let them slip through my fingers as usual.

Mrs. John, my typist, had moved to Paterson. Another friend, Mrs. George Heath, an excellent office woman before her marriage, had taken her place for me. Plays, stories and whatnot began to appeal again. The depression had struck us. Fred Miller was out of employment: a tool designer living precariously over a garage in Brooklyn, he had started a magazine *Blast* (not after Pound's London adventure in Vorticism) to which I was contributing the short stories that later went into *Life Along the Passaic River*.

A strange person named (an alias, I think) Ronald Lane Latimer, of Columbia University, at the same time started to issue a few books under the insigne, The Alcestis Press. And John Coffee was being thrown out of basement bars when he began to prate his social sermons there. He had been a fur thief working the big department stores, selling the furs afterward to give to charity and his impoverished friends.

It was the depression, I'll say!

Latimer published for me *An Early Martyr,* superbly, lavishly printed on rag paper, dedicated to John Coffee, who had been arrested and sent to Matteawan Hospital for the criminally insane—without trial—to prevent him from getting up in court and saying his say as he had intended to do, that he was not insane, but that he was robbing to feed the poor since the city was doing nothing for them. I visited him there. Later he was let go in charge of his brother. The place was overcrowded.

Then in '36 Latimer brought out my *Adam and Eve & The City*. But still nothing sold. I think Latimer did a Stevens book before he went broke and quit.

Surely around these years sometime, maybe as late as '39, Ford Madox Ford came to New York with his wife, Biala, the painter, to establish residence here and become an American citizen. He lived at Ten Fifth Avenue, and was really, at that time, a sick man—gasping often for breath on mild exertion—though he'd never if possible let you know it. One night, trying to get into a taxi, I thought his end had come.

For some reason, unapparent to me, Ford had decided to back me up. He founded a group, "The Friends of William Carlos Williams," which, though it horribly embarrassed me, was an honor I had to accept out of courtesy to him. We met several times in some small restaurant in the Village (somebody must have had some coin, though when dinner was served the invited guests donated a dollar each, I think) and various speeches were given. I couldn't see it, didn't want it, other than as a courtesy to him, but so it went. He came several times to see us in Rutherford and tried hard to sell us one of his wife's pictures; but again, I couldn't see it. Maybe I hurt him. It couldn't be helped.

One day we were invited to a supper to be cooked by the old boy himself, who always reminded me of my father, on the third floor over a commercial establishment on East Twenty-eighth Street—the apartment of Carl Van Doren, who never admired me. But that night, the fried plantain was fine, and we had a good time of it.

The World's Fair of 1939-1940 in New York was over. I had again wanted to write the libretto for an opera on the theme of the heroic life of George Washington. Tibor Serly had half-agreed to do the music, and since the theme of this World's Fair was, in fact, Washington's life, with a heroic statue of Washington himself featured on the esplanade, I thought this was my opportunity. Grover Whalen couldn't see it!

After Serly backed out, I went to Virgil Thomson, whose music to Gertrude Stein's *Four Saints in Three Acts* had been so superlatively good.

I met Thomson at lunch in the restaurant of the famous old Hotel Chelsea on West Twenty-third Street. He was really very nice.

"You don't know anything about the stage, do you?" he said.

"No."

"Then what the hell do you bother with it for? All these scenes and directions . . . You're a poet, aren't you?"

"Yes."

"Then write your poem and forget it. But what about this ballet? All these 'snow maidens' you've got here."

"Well, that's a ballet of the snow at Valley Forge."

He laughed. "Imagine me doing a ballet of snow maidens!" he said and snorted. "What would they say of me?"

I said nothing.

"Who is this Washington? Who is he?" he said.

"I am Washington," I told him.

"That's different." And he cooled down a bit. "Well, write your poem then and when you're ready with it I'll do the music."

Maybe someday I'll take him up, if we're not both dead or incapacitated by that time—*it'll be good, too, the way I have reconceived it—without snow maidens!*

James Laughlin at that time published my second novel, *White Mule,* and when the book appeared had gone skiing in New Zealand as a member of the American team.

That it was a hit of a day with the critics was at least a compliment to us both—my first real success. But with the publisher away and not enough books printed, there was a problem.

Laughlin *père* had me up to New Milford, Connecticut, to consult me as to what to do.

"What are you going to do about this situation?" he asked me.

"What am I going to do? I have no authority to order more books printed," I said. "All I did for the book was to write it..."

But he printed a second edition.

Sometime during the thirties—I have forgotten when exactly or where—I got to know Nathanael West. It may have been through John Herrmann, I don't know. I can't remember the man's face because I confuse him with someone else, a lawyer, but he was a thin, slightly stooped individual with the same half-embarrassed black eyes. West was a big fellow who had had a tryout with the Giants at one time as an outfielder because of his hitting. But he lost interest. That wasn't his line.

I asked him, "How did you get that name?"

"Horace Greeley said, 'Go west, young man.' So I did."

That was Pep West to the core; a talent as fine as any of his day. He was at the time I met him front man at the Hotel Sutton in East Fifty-eighth Street, and we planned a revival of *Contact.* He was writing his novel, *Miss Lonelyhearts* then, or had written it. I was a firm admirer of it and of the man himself. Together we published three issues of the new *Contact.* But I couldn't keep up the pace. The scripts that came in were not distinguished. I remember a short poem by Ilya Ehrenburg, who later made such a name for himself in Moscow. I think we finally accepted it. It wasn't bad.

Then Pep took up pheasant hunting at Erwinna in eastern Pennsylvania, though it consisted mostly in wearing the costume and hat (resembling Sherlock Holmes's famous double earflap chapeau) and buying expensive guns. I doubt if he ever shot anything. Then he married his Irish beauty—with a head on her shoulders to please him, be it said—and *Contact* died in that contact. He was a great guy. His novel *The Day of the Locust* is the only piece about Hollywood that can be ranked, as far as I know, as *belles lettres.* He and the lady were killed one night at a crossroads, returning from a deer hunt in Mexico, having shot nothing, I imagine, but those "shots" to fill the eye such as Hollywood always seems to be approaching but never quite achieves.

Chapter 46

Storm

In the fall of '38 Mother, lame as she was, was just finishing her summer at the little cottage at "the shore." My cousin Bill had written that it was getting dampish and chilly, evenings, and that he thought I'd better come up for her, though she didn't want to leave.

When I arrived there it was a beautiful, quiet day. There were rumors of a hurricane coming up the coast, but there had not been a hurricane along that shore for a hundred years, literally. It would burn out beyond Nantucket, as usual. The weather that day confirmed it. We had lunch. While Mother was getting her few things together, I wandered out onto the beach to pick up shells and a few interesting stones for our rock garden. Not a breath of air was stirring when, at three o'clock in the afternoon, we pulled out of the wooded driveway and started for home. And yet, within two hours, seawater was three feet deep where Mother's bed stood.

We hadn't reached much beyond Milford when we began to find heavy elms blocking the roadway and wires down. I tried to get some gas to make sure I had enough for the eighty-mile trip. All the pumps were stalled. No power. On the Merritt Parkway, the rain sweeping us in streams, a cop gesticulated at us as we went by—"The reservoir!" but I didn't stop. I found later it was threatening at that time to break over the right of way. Even so I didn't quite grasp the situation, though so many roads were blocked, necessitating detours, that I should have been more aware. Near White Plains I particularly remember a group of high-school students standing in the rain waiting for a bus, long past caring for their condition. At the parkway below Port Chester there were sewer entrances from which geysers of muddy water were spouting. I was so thrilled and amazed at it, as was Mother, and so taken up with finding a way to keep moving forward—at times difficult to discover—that we hardly noticed how the time was passing.

It took us six hours to complete the trip, a trip that usually took two hours. But when we arrived in Rutherford we at last got a grasp of what had been going on. Trees were down all about our house. The place was a wreck.

Flossie told me of how the trees leaned up against our front windows and the leaves were torn to shreds.

Some years later, in 1946, I think, a novel upon the far more devastating effects of the storm along the shore of Rhode Island appeared: *Sudden Guest,* by Christopher La Farge. Floss and I read it with delight. She particularly was moved by the picture of the old woman in the house on her private domain who was really moved, but not shaken, only battered and revealed by the storm. Floss liked the book so much that I had a copy of it bound in blue morocco for her.

As a special distinction I thought I'd send to La Farge, whom I do not know, and ask him to inscribe it with his name to her from me. So I wrote asking him for that favor. After a week or two I received a letter from his secretary telling me that Mr. La Farge did not make a practice of inscribing books except for his intimate friends—otherwise what distinction would there be in it? I told Floss what I had intended and what result I had gotten.

"I never wanted you to have the book bound for me. Why did you do it?"

It was a lesson.

The Second World War had begun in Europe, but we had not yet entered it. After printing the *Collected Poems*, Laughlin stopped for a while, but he continued to publish my plays, articles and poems in the anthology *New Directions,* and did a paper-bound collection of poems, *The Broken Span.*

It was again the play which once more attracted me but, as usual, there seemed small hope of getting a production. But ideas were crowding my head and pretty soon I began to put down the scenes as they occurred to me.

Kitty Hoagland asked me to do something in 1939 or 1940 for the local Little Theatre. They had put on a dramatization by Kitty of my short story, "To Fall Asleep," thereby losing the support of some influential but conservative subscribers. I wrote one-act plays, but nothing came of them. Not only were they difficult to produce, emotionally steep (and sophisticated) but the draft drew the most versatile male actors away, and then the war on top of that caused lack of workers, money and audience, which in turn closed up the Little Theatre.

So with three one-act plays on my hands—I rather liked the plays—and nothing to do with them, I put them together with an over-all story to tie them up, calling the whole, "Many Loves or Trial Horse #1."

The war being on, my boys had joined the Navy. Bill, the physician, was in the far Pacific, Paul on a destroyer on Atlantic patrol. Paul Herman's estate at Harriman had to be sold at a tenth of its original cost, and we quit going there week-ends and in summer forever. Florence's mother came back to Rutherford a mere shadow of her former self to live at the end in a nearby sanatorium until she died, within a month of the passing away of my little mother in 1949.

Mother's last years were ruinous for her by almost total loss of sight and hearing. This, together with her unhealed broken hip, made her life miserable. As usual we had been away, to visit the Sheelers at Irvington, New York, that day, when on our return Mrs. Taylor who had her in her nursing home phoned to tell me that she had suddenly become pretty bad.

Floss offered to go with me to see her. She was already unconscious. Two pressing cases called me away. Floss sat beside the old woman. When I returned she was gone, quietly, without regaining consciousness, as though she had fallen asleep. Those last few years I learned to know my mother pretty well. Her mind, a torture of conflicting reflections, led her through all perils. At the last when she could see almost nothing, the mind saw for her—to the minutest details.

A Mr. E. J. Luce, one of the founders of the Unitarian Church with Mother and Father and a few others, a man who had been dead for twenty or more years, came to visit her one day, she said. He was hemming a small tablecloth. Mother had always been a little in awe of him, an awkward left-handed sort of man—an excellent, stubborn lawyer and organist at the church—also an ex-ballplayer at Williams College fifty years before. Mr. Luce came and sat down before Mother and looking down, talking occasionally, went on with his sewing. She was fascinated by the care he gave to his needlework.

They were tiny little stitches, extremely neat and competently well done. He went on systematically as they talked. Mother asked him about his son who had died surely sixty years before as an infant—Mr. Luce had painted the infant's portrait, a circular plaque, which hung over the fireplace in his front room. He told her that the child was with its grandmother and very happy, etc. And all the while Mother watched the needlework with the greatest interest and satisfaction. To make sure she was not being deceived, she also glanced at the man's clothes, even to his shoes, which she described in the minutest detail.

"He was here," she said defiantly to my comments. Who was I to contradict her? She could see again as she had seen in her youth, to the last detail.

When Laughlin ran out of paper for a new book, I was fortunate in finding two young men, Harry Duncan and Paul Williams, associates of the Cummington Press, to rescue me once more. I had a script of twenty or thirty poems.

—*Were you up here last night?*
Yes.
What were you doing?
Writing.

What did you write?
The story of my life—

Sometimes during the war, when the boys were at sea—as at other times of stress—it would be comforting to be carrying a poem in my head, searching for an aberrant structure—and unable for the whole day to get it down. The ideas for a prose statement would keep me warm. A whole play would work itself out and not a moment for its scribbling. Then the great moment would come, it got jotted down. Meanwhile the medical case in hand took up the entire energy and brought the forgetfulness that comes with all labor.

The really curious thing to me is that from complete occupation with either a poem or the delivery of a child, I come away, not fatigued, but rested. That's the secret. I suppose it's the same with an athletic team that has gone stale, when the coach advises them to go out and drink a pail of suds. That lets them down. The same for me. I don't admire work for work's sake. I believe heartily what Dallam Simpson has said or quoted that: "The whole aim of the gang that runs Russia, U.S.A., Britain and France, is to destroy the contemplative life altogether, to its last vestige, and to create 'WORK' until no one shall be left with time to think about anything."

But for me the work is the interim when I think best—relieved of all tensions. In fact, it is only then that I am blissfully happy.

To drive the streets at all seasons is also my delight, alone in my car, though it is only to return home at the end of an hour. It is not unexciting, either. It is a formal game. It is also moderately dangerous. The duels with the other guy—or woman—who takes a wide swing into the right of way are a test of skill. Any moment's heedlessness is a potential accident. I pride myself on my escapes. No cowboy on the range could be happier in the chances he takes. Once a car and a coal truck were coming down Union Avenue abreast, over the crest of the hill. I was coming up at a good speed. There was no chance, apparently, to avoid a crash. I was lucky, of course, but it gave me a big kick to drive in over the gutter to my left, dodge between two trees, ride twenty feet up the sidewalk, duck out again between trees and skim past a police car following the coal truck.

"Hi, Doc!" is all they said.

Chapter 47

Lectures

The war was on, the Second World War. I was in my middle fifties and the Pediatric Department of the hospital called for much of my time. About then schools and colleges began to want me to talk and to read my poetry to the students. Dartmouth, Pennsylvania State College, Cooper Union, Vassar, Mt. Holyoke, Buffalo, Middlebury, Harvard, N. Y. U., Bard, Brandeis, Salt Lake City, Puerto Rico all invited me. The fee was usually twenty-five to fifty dollars, not including expenses. I read at Barnard College to a small group, with a basketball game going on across the corridor. Possibly there and at Columbia I was not paid at all.

One of the first longer trips was to Dartmouth, by the White Mountain Express in the dead of winter, all day long on the train, for a three o'clock appointment. On the way I picked up a copy of Conrad Aiken's early anthology of American Poems only to find that my name had been omitted. I spoke of this to him later. He was confused. I had hoped he might be confident, so I might be enlightened as to his motives. No luck. At Dartmouth I think thirteen students, as well as three of the faculty, came out to hear me. I enjoyed the Orozco decorations in the library.

When Bob Brittain was in the graduate school at Princeton he had me down to tea one day to be looked over. It was very charming. There was a remark made that I might be invited there for a reading or a lecture sometime. It didn't come off. I was chagrined. A year or so later Babette Deutsch and I were there as judges in an intercollegiate poetry conference. We got snagged, or maybe it was only I, in a discussion with two of the giggling English instructors on whether or not a painting by Rembrandt of a side of beef in a butcher shop could be as beautiful as a portrait of the artist's wife, Saskia. Babette went on with the gang to an informal pow-wow at the Inn, but I cut across campus and, after watching some lacrosse players awhile, came home.

At Penn State College, one year, bidden by Ted Roethke and Bob Wetterau, Ted gave Floss and me a steak and trimmings with an excellent Chambertin that nearly ruined me. I remember that talk (it was one of my first): for the first fifteen minutes of it I heard myself discoursing pleasantly, but what I was talking about was not at all what I had intended to say. At that moment my wits returned. It was a valuable experience. I found that from then on I should never be at a loss for words.

It was sometime in April in 1942 or '43 I spoke and read my poems in the Great Hall of Cooper Union. There were four of us performing: Auden, Kreymborg, Malcolm Cowley and myself. Houston Peterson, the Director of the Forums—held in the Great Hall nightly during the winter months—introduced us. The occasion was of great interest to Floss, for her father had organized meetings in this hall with Gompers, etc. in the early days when he was active in unionization.

On the evening we read, there was an audience of more than a thousand persons, and someone remarked that they had never seen so many poets held silent in one place. And afterward, when we came out on the square, I was startled to see everything covered with snow—there had been torrential rains all afternoon and early evening. Snow in April!

The readings and talks at various universities have taken us all over the U. S. finally. But at that point it was Dartmouth again (much more successful this time), Middlebury College, Harvard, Vassar, Holyoke—where I had a lucky day and was held up as a model of clear diction and impromptu resourcefulness of thought by the mother of Norman Macleod of the English faculty. New York University has been very generous. At City College, New York, at a luncheon speaking engagement, I was defining our right as Americans to our own language, saying that English, its development from Shakespeare's day to this, does not primarily concern us.

"But this language of yours," said one of the instructors, himself an obvious Britisher, "where does it come from?"

"From the mouths of Polish mothers," I replied.

At the Brooklyn Polytechnic Institute a class of men showed arresting interest in verse construction when I showed them something of its mechanics and explained the rationale governing my proposals for making a comprehensive change from the older modes.

At Rutgers my reading was held in the physics laboratory, a lucky break for me, giving me a running start for my proposals. Last year, 1950, I received an honorary degree of Litt. D. from the same school, and was declared by the president to be the Poet Laureate of New Jersey, the significance of which must largely have escaped him, I think. It is seldom, arguing from the general to the particular, that any but a laborer can follow the trend of thought I espouse, which goes mostly—if it goes at all and seldom in professional minds does it go at all—from the particular, soon abandoned, to the general, its origins then forgot.

At Bard College at Annandale-on-Hudson, the same year, I was given another honorary degree, standing under the trees in the campus bare-headed. At such times I look about me wondering if they know what they are honoring. The basic meaning is confused.

I have read at Brandeis where Professor Lewisohn felt sure that the Fitts-Fitzgerald translation of *Antigone* must be cast in some newfangled verse form having nothing akin to the formal thunder of the Greek. They gave me a communal supper just before my appearance on the platform, a bad thing for me, and there were accounts of the Welsh bardic poet, who had just preceded me, arriving late, completely drunk, but acquitting himself with distinction.

But the first to honor me had been Buffalo with an LL.D. They plan to honor the recipients of such awards only once in a hundred years and always with the same distinction. It is pleasant to meet such men as I have met at these formalities.

In 1946 Floss and I attended a two-weeks English conference at Salt Lake City, Utah. We drove out, Charlotte, Flossie's sister, dividing the chore with me. I had never but once before that been west of the Mississippi River. Literature, finally, was paying off. At Salt Lake Allen Tate, whom I had always despised, and who in his turn had always considered me of the lunatic fringe, and I learned mutually to respect, even to like each other. He plays the violin rather well and had once been a pupil of the renowned Ysaye. He and Eric Bentley were at Mozart's sonatas whenever they could get off together.

Walter Van Tilburg Clark, Caroline Gordon, Mark Schorer, all swam with us in a nearby pool evenings, and at Alta we rode in the ski-lift (specially connected for us) over the snowless ground now blossoming profusely on the slopes between the tall firs: columbine, with which I was familiar, and other blooms I cannot name. Thrilling to be lifted that way above the mountainside, feet dangling, high over the earth to the shoulder of the slope, while far below was a Greyhound Bus full of visiting governors of the states who leaned out to stare up at us enviously, I can imagine. There were patches of rotten snow all about us.

Later we heard the story of the famous "Emma" mine and talked with its guardian, the guardian rather of its ghost, its faithful lover and suitor, George Watson.

Walter Clark and Maia disappeared higher while we walked slowly about or lay gasping from the altitude. Later they told us that they had gone to the northern summit.

On our return from Salt Lake, Florence, Charlotte and I drove the "Million-Dollar Highway," a name given it because of the gold quartz with which it had been inadvertently paved.

That day we saw too the miraculous relics of the cliff-dwellers at Mesa Verde—far more extensive than I had imagined.

And now four years later we have just returned, by grace of the Poem, from a tour of the West-Coast states. Seattle to

Los Angeles, to El Paso (Juarez to visit Bob McAlmon), to New Orleans, for the first time, to fly home.

Once before we had flown, only once, to San Juan, Puerto Rico, to a conference at the University at Rio Piedras—that was in 1941.

That was a trip!—our first by air. We hadn't even the slightest idea which way the plane would be heading until we got to the field—not out to sea but inland over a sea of lights to Philadelphia, another light sea, Washington, Richmond, then with a full moon coming up over a livid cloud-shelf to the east to palm trees at dawn and the Miami airport. Breakfast and down the ramp to a blue bay and the clipper lying waiting for a handful of us under a clear morning sky.

The roar and a rush of water, three screaming girls and at once we were above the clouds—the most delightful part of the whole journey—puffs of white cloud, their shadows ten thousand feet below us on the turquoise sea, definitely turquoise above the reefs invading the ultramarine of the deeper water. That flight had for us the surprising reality of all dreams of flying, leaping, sometimes to music, which both Floss and I had known in sleep during infancy and childhood—now realized. I had the additional excitement of visiting, at a wish, by enormous leaps, the place where my family, as I knew it, had originated, the West Indies. I thought of Hart Crane and his abortive visit to such Carib seas, and my own *In the American Grain*.

It was a small group in our flying boat, including a nervous priest and another writer—though he got on only at San Pedro in Cuba. Cuba, the far eastern point of it, was our first landfall, the grayish hills scudding under us crisscrossed by lines of goat trails which seemed to be everywhere. We came down easily, over the water, to the Spanish of those at the pier.

At Port au Prince, Haiti, an hour later, it was blowing half a gale. We cut into it but the waves were high. When we hit the first one hard! we rebounded fifty feet into the air, then down, up and down again. All in brilliant sunshine along a green mountain to our right, immaculately primitive.

At the dock we were allowed to alight upon a narrow boardwalk which had a high fence at the end, beyond which we were not permitted to go.

The pavilion, or covered dock space at our left was crowded by natives of the better class, the political class, in holiday dress, come to cheer their white-haired president on his way by special plane to Washington with his retinue to negotiate a loan. After he had zoomed out of the harbor we were permitted to follow.

It was from this city of small low houses my Uncle Carlos had fled in the early 1880's to an American gunboat before the revolutionists coming in at the far end of the street. They had been at the midday meal—the food on the table—the paintings of my grandmother and grandfather on the wall above them.

"Doctor Hoheb," the American officer had announced, suddenly poking his head in at the door, "we're pulling out. They're coming in at the far end of the street. It's your last chance. You'd better come with us."

The doctor sent his wife and nine children ahead of him, went into his small pharmacy and office, swept the cash from the till into his pocket and ran after them as the firing began. Everything had been left just as it lay, food, silver, clothes, surgical equipment, everything. And so to Panama where they spent the rest of their lives. That is what comes of an amorous disposition! For had his wife Rita not objected to Carlos' popularity with the ladies, he would not have left Santa Isabel to go to Haiti out of spite, and so, first-rate surgeon that he was, he would not have had to subject them all to such outrages. No doubt but for the fact that he was more French than Spanish and adored the language of his beloved Paris, he would not have been attracted there—a chapter which someday must be written in full. All these thoughts passed through my head as I stood there at the little pier looking down into the water. There was also a young girl who sold chewing gum and postcards and who, in her person, made some of our shows seem tawdry. How do we impress ourselves with substitutes when the originals of our moods are missing?

At Trujillo we landed in the river among tropical foliage on both banks. Here only for a moment. Spanish again. I thought of my family, my father's foster-father, Wellcome, the itinerant photographer of Puerto Plata of those days, and the print of the "new pier" of 1880 which I still keep in an old trunk in the attic. It is hard to think of old things surrounded by the affections of a noonday sun in the tropics. Trujillo the tyrant, hard to know what to think in view of the benefits he has occasioned— and even here, back in the hills, there is talk of warfare across a trivial border.

At San Juan, Puerto Rico, we landed behind the city in the lagoon, tied to the dock, and were, at once, offered by the aviation officers about the best daiquiri cocktails I have ever tasted. My cousins were there to greet us.

Chapter 48

The F.B.I. and Ezra Pound

Ezra had written me, just before Hitler invaded France, his opinion that Mussolini's assistance to Franco after his, Franco's, violation of the Spanish Constitution, was no more than a gesture toward cleaning out a mosquito swamp in darkest Africa. I replied with a furious blast: That he, Ezra, was a hell of an American and more in the same vein. The war was on and that was the end of our correspondence for a number of years.

Then one day Floss came home to tell me that one of the tellers at the bank had asked her if I knew a person in Italy called Ezra Pound.

"He was talking about something on the radio last night."

"Ezra Pound?" said Floss.

"Something about ol' Doc Williams of Rutherford, New Jersey, would understand. Something like that—but I couldn't get the rest of it."

"What the hell right has he to drag me into his dirty messes?"

"I'm just reporting what I heard," said Floss. "You're always getting mixed up in something through your 'friends,'" she said.

I questioned the teller about it later, but that's all he knew. It was just a chance contact; he never heard the broadcast again.

Then one day I was approached by a young chap at my office door who showed me his credentials, then proceeded to ask me if I had heard the broadcasts then going on from the mouth of Ezra Pound in Italy.

I told him, No, though I had heard about them.

Would I be able to identify the voice if I did hear it?

No. I didn't think that would be possible though I might be fairly certain that it was he who was talking.

"He is a friend of yours and has been in the past for many years?"

"Yes. From college days."

"Would you have any objections to testifying that the voice you heard was his voice?"

"Certainly not, if I can feel sure that it is actually he talking, but how can I be absolutely sure?"

"We will bring records of his broadcasts here to your office with a machine to reproduce them."

"I should be most interested to hear them."

"All we ask is that you identify the voice as that of Ezra Pound."

"I can say that the recording I hear sounds like the voice of Ezra Pound. I can't say more than that."

"Are you a loyal American citizen?" he said looking me steadily in the eye. I was embarrassed.

"Of course I'm a loyal American citizen. I—I—I've spent my whole life, generally speaking, for my country, trying to serve it in every way I know how. I've even written a book about it."

"What book?"

"It's called *In the American Grain*—and many articles and critical essays—I am William Carlos Williams, the author. I'll get you the book if you want it."

"It won't be necessary. We have to establish that these broadcasts against our government at this time are authentically by Ezra Pound. You as an intimate of his of long standing could be of material assistance to the government's case in identifying the man. We shan't inconvenience you in any way. The records will be brought here to you in your own house. You would have no objections to this on personal grounds, I suppose, if you felt that the records we play for you were actually the voice of Ezra Pound?"

"Not in the least."

"You have two sons, Doctor Williams?"

"Yes. They are both in the Navy, one, the doctor, in the Pacific, and the other on a destroyer on patrol duty between this country and Europe."

"That's fair enough. So it'll be all right for us to bring you the records for you to listen to?"

"Certainly."

But he never did. I had two visits from the F.B.I. during the war, but I never heard the records. I heard later from a friend who had, in fact, had an opportunity to hear the records in Washington. He said they were divided into two parts, the first half seeming to be Pound, all right, but to amount to little more than vituperation against President Roosevelt, his family and the international Jew upon whom Pound blamed everything. The second part, according to my informant, seemed to be by someone else, a different voice, raving about a variety of proposals and quiddities that were more histrionic than treasonable.

A year after the war was over I received the letter I had written Ezra cursing him out over the Franco matter. I had been chairman of the local Committee for Medical Help to Loyalist Spain; the letter had been opened by the authorities. Pound at least never saw it. That is how, I suppose, my name had been identified with his from the beginning.

So here is Pound confined to a hospital for the insane in Washington; Bob McAlmon working for his brothers in El Paso; Hemingway a popular novelist; Joyce dead; Gertrude Stein dead; Picasso doing ceramics; Soupault married to a wealthy (?) American; Skip Cannell—who after divorcing Kitty married a French woman, *disparu!*; Nancy Cunard still alive, thin as paper as she is; Bill and Sally Bird, unable to stand the Paris weather any longer, removed to Tangier; Sylvia Beach, who had been cleaned out by the Germans, living upstairs from her famous Twelve rue de l'Odéon. Clotilde Vail dead; Brancusi too old to work; Stieglitz dead; Hart Crane dead; Juan Gris—at one time my favorite painter—long since dead; Charles Demuth dead; Marsden Hartley dead; Marcel Duchamp idling in a telephoneless Fourteenth Street garret in New York; the Baroness dead; Jane Heap dead; Margaret Anderson, I don't know where; Peggy Guggenheim, active at least, in Venice keeping a gallery for modern pictures in which it is said she hardly believes; Steichen a director at the Modern Museum; Norman Douglas writing— but I think not; T. S. Eliot a successful playwright; Auden, E. E. Cummings, Wallace Stevens—alive and working; Marianne Moore translating *Les Fables* of La Fontaine. I saw her recently at a supper of the National Institute of Arts and Letters. She has done the fables over three times, each time with a different critical objective in view, twenty books of I don't know how many pieces in all.

She says that Ezra Pound has been of great assistance to her in the work which must be finished by June 1951.

Harold Loeb—where?—but back in Wall Street; Ford Madox Ford dead; Henry Miller married and living with his wife and children on a half-mile-high mountain near Carmel, California, from which he seldom descends. Lola Ridge dead; Djuna Barnes living in poverty somewhere, not, at least, writing; Bob Brown, having lost his money, surviving in Brazil; Carl Sandburg turned long since from the poem; Alfred Kreymborg a member of the Institute of Arts and Letters; Mina Loy, Eugene O'Neill—more or less silent.

Chapter 49

Friendship

Without absolute friends no man or marriage can last long. By absolute I mean a full confessional—a room—a Pennsylvania Station waiting room of a place, a precinct, private to him alone: A marriage the same, a space where it may thrive. Two such friendships have been our privilege in these years.

It may be a treasured religion or personal and lifelong intimacy between individuals, very close, as a marriage itself may be close. But in this case I mean something else. I mean between marriages to make the marriage possible.

It should be dangerous—uncertain—made of many questionable crossties, I think, that might fail it. But, while they last, give it a good cellular structure—paths, private connections between the members—full of versatility.

If a man and a woman are friends with another pair and one of each is left alone with one of the other pair, crossed any way you like, anything might result: that sort of risky relationship is refreshing only so long as it is uncertain.

We'd sit sometimes with Charles and Katherine Sheeler after discussing someone's pictures and open the bilge cocks, and some evenings obey the drunk's gossip to our heart's content—that kind of friends.

Katherine was of the earthy type—wistful as all such women are of the esthetic—small hands and feet but generous at heart. She was a gifted raconteur. One of her Pennsylvania stories was of a masterful and beautiful woman, no longer young, who dominated a small city west of Philadelphia, call it Allentown, in the last century—that age of chivalry—who was the madam of a prosperous bawdy house there.

This beautiful woman of whom Kate was speaking had her place on one of the side streets though it was indistinguishable otherwise from some of the best residences in town just as she, in her own person, was not to be distinguished on her daily rounds at the markets from the ladies of any of the better families. She attended church regularly, but there the resemblance to the well-to-do society of the place ended, for she had no female friends. She dealt at the best shops, in fact to all outward appearances, she was a lady. Her lawns were mowed regularly, her flower beds were always in order: cannas, coleas, geraniums.

Inside as well as out her house was in order. The girls, though not seen in the streets, were charming and well instructed. They had better manners than the daughters of the rich. The clientele of the place was a constant source of satisfaction to all concerned. You could see the woman, as Kate told it, virtually giving the girls the best that could be got in any of the better finishing schools of New York or New England. I don't think they had any classes, but certainly their speech and dress were bettered while she kept them in her charge. Several married well after her instruction. And they had to be ladies since they were visited by the most courteous and generous gentlemen of the town.

As time went on this well-ordered business of the city only increased in popularity, and the tone of it grew more chaste.

The madam had no difficulty in maintaining her social position either, until the test came when a prominent citizen of the town died. As a token of esteem for his many benefits to local charities, it was suggested that a special testimonial dinner be given to raise money for a monument in his name.

The madam of the house begged to be permitted to add her mite, but her name was not included on the list of the sponsors. But in the end by the sheer size of her check—a thousand dollars, which in those days was such that it could not be refused—she publicly placed herself on the honor roll. Katie would never repeat this story; we never could get her to say why.

Charles had had to give up his old Bucks County house, of which they were both very fond. There he had done so much of his early, well-known work. They looked around for something as fine but finding nothing, made the New York move, toward a living at least, by photography.

They had when we first knew them an apartment where the Whitney Museum is now located on Eighth Street. When that property was purchased for the Museum, Charles and Katherine went across the street to the apartment just vacated by Tex Guinan.

But the best was when, fed up with the city they went up to South Salem, New York, a bungalowlike building out in the hills by an old church and graveyard surrounded by a stone wall, with a convenient bootlegger down the road. Applejack was about the best you could buy in those days.

We weren't young any more. We weren't looking for parties—Cézanne still seemed a god—Steichen was an intimate. In fact after a year or two when Charles and Kate moved to Ridgefield to more comfortable quarters, it was a good deal, I suppose, because of Steichen who had his experimental farm in the neighborhood.

But the country today is always deceiving. There Katherine was found to have a malignant disease, sickened and died. For nine years Charles lived alone in that house.

In the summer of 1948, having had a mild anginal attack a few months earlier, when I went to Seattle to lecture at the English Conference there, I carried a small bottle of Hennessy's Three Star which Floss had slid in my suitcase under my pajamas. I didn't open it until one day approaching Butte, Montana. I couldn't tell what was the matter with me and got a little scared until, on the timetable, I noticed the altitude was over 6,000 feet; then I understood. I went into the men's room at the end of the car, opened the bottle, found a paper cup and saw a soldier in uniform looking at me across from the windows.

"How about it," I said. "Do you want to join me?"

"What is it?" he asked.

"Brandy, good brandy. Get yourself a cup, or is it against the law to offer a man in uniform a drink?"

"No," he said, "nothing like that. But that's too strong for me. Beer's my poison."

So we fell into conversation. He told me he was from somewhere in upstate New York, had just been home on a furlough and was returning to San Francisco expecting to be shipped abroad.

Butte, just at sunset, was a strangely beautiful city; a single street like a flight of giant steps ascending the mountain side, brightly lit, as if some temple site to the deity, the smelters flaming about the mines high upon both sides. It impressed me as of an overwhelming grandeur in that barren country.

It was a good conference, too, that at Washington. It was there I began to find for myself a little confidence on the platform, helped, no doubt, by Granville Hicks's statement that it had been an arousing experience for him to hear me read. Before that, as Floss had always told me, I kept fighting my audiences. But why not? I always had the feeling that they were only listening out of a cynical curiosity, wanting to grin at an unintended obscenity—to get a commonplace titillation. I had nothing for the most part but contempt for them. I was angry and resentful, or laughing at them, generally. But if someone whom I respected wanted to hear me read my poems, that was something else again. Besides I was just beginning to learn how to read, which made a great difference.

The last night, at the round table when we were all there, S—, John van Druten, Hicks, and myself, along with a representative from the faculty, it was discovered that S— was lit to the gills. Quite a party. One gathers together to save a brother from the wolves in such cases. He didn't need it.

Charles Abbott came to see us one winter's day about ten years ago. We sat in our front room all afternoon, Floss, he and I, over a highball or two, staring into a wood fire in our grate, letting the light fade. We hardly moved other than to refill our glasses. The phone didn't ring once. We thought we were in heaven.

He told us of his project: to collect manuscripts of the living poets, English and American—whatever could be had—material that as often was thrown away or lost that could be used later to piece out an understanding of their lives and methods of work. He had written asking me if I had anything of the sort lying around about the house that I could give him for the Lockwood Memorial Library at the University of Buffalo where a room had been set aside for the collection. We talked, using that as our hint, of writing, American writing, especially, of his Oxford days, exchanging opinions and confidences. He asked us if we would not visit him at Gratwick Highlands the coming summer and told us something of the old farm east of Buffalo where he lived with his family, on what had been, before the disastrous recent depression, a wealthy man's estate.

They occupied the old coachman's house near the entrance to the estate, the barn and greenhouses, aided by Nora, Mrs. Abbott's own nurse when she had been a child and still the mainstay of the new establishment. Charles commuted every day sixty miles to Buffalo, to his duties at the University.

But there was and is another family, Bill's family. Bill, Mrs. Abbott's brother, the youngest of the male Gratwicks, manages what interests him of the old farm. In short, he breeds sheep, Dorsets I think they call them, sheep with curled horns (he must have fifty of them in one pasture or another about the place) and grows for sale tree peonies of distinction which he hybridizes successfully. His wife, Harriet, a Saltonstall, abets him in his enterprises, dividing her time otherwise between her three girls (one recently married) and a passion, an active passion, for the arts, her chief interest being a music school which she has founded there.

The whole farm as it is now, a hundred and fifty acres of cultivated land and forest, cut by a miniature if deep ravine, a narrow brook at the bottom, does in fact, however, still center about the wreck of the big house, the former summer residence of the Gratwicks which employed in its day a staff of twenty to thirty servants, farmers and attendants.

The night Floss and I arrived there, after batting around Buffalo a while, finding our way, Wyndham Lewis, his young wife and a little dog were being entertained at the Abbotts' where he had been in residence while painting an official portrait of the president of the college, a commission which Charles had secured for him. He had not wanted to give up his apartment

on the book-filled enclosure, really the old back porch, where
he had been living for a month or more. So we were invited
by the Bill Gratwicks to spend the first night there.

It was a beautiful evening in June. Charles took Lewis and
me for a moonlight walk about the place just after sundown.
We wandered about in a place completely unknown to me, down
sheep paths and across a tennis enclosure, pushing aside a
section of iron grille-work to enter the abandoned formal garden
of the old estate, through masonry arches unbelievably romantic
in their semi-decay.

Vines, especially the stonecrop, climbed in massive waves
matted about the tops of the walls in which robins, catbirds,
thrushes, the brown thrashers were fluttering and singing. I
thought I had never in my life experienced such a luxury of
sound and rustic profusion. The moon was up, we walked about,
Lewis asking me a question or two. I virtually speechless.

The next evening, the eve of Lewis' departure, we were to
have supper at the Gratwicks, where we had been staying that
first twenty-four hours.

He told us that he was really an American, that in fact he had
been born just over the hill in the Genesee Valley beyond the
dark garden where I had walked the night before.

Harriet had prepared a good roast for us, at which Lewis
asked if there were not wine to go with it, that he was used
to having wine with his meals. Bill said he did think they had
one bottle of something left from a case they had opened at
Christmas.

"Get it," said Lewis.

Bill did so, a sauterne, I think, but that didn't bother Lewis,
though it was not red. It was opened.

The next night we spent at the Abbotts', where we were to
stay. A thunderstorm came up toward evening. Floss was upstairs, but my own bed was in a narrow place at the west end
of the first-floor porch, just room enough for a single bed. As
the storm grew heavier a leader from the roof just a foot or
two from my ear rushed with water beside me as I lay there
dry and comfortable. I will always remember the noise of that
water as one of the most soothing sounds I have ever known.

The next summer, Nassos, the painter, a small Greek, gentle and industrious, was there, installed in the old and abandoned chicken coop where Theresa, Mrs. Abbott, was also painting in her spare moments. He had come originally to illustrate and to celebrate the tree peonies—hybrids with such names as White Coiling Dragon (Hakubanryo), Dance for the Gathering Clouds (Skinkagura) and Billow of Crimson Smoke (Nissho), whose fragile but luxuriant bursts of white, pink and crimson petals in woody stems put them among the most beautiful flowers in the world.

Bill Gratwick, taking his inspiration from that plant whose leaves open like the fingers of a delicate hand, has done some creditable pieces of sculpture on this theme.

So Nassos had painted a number of studies of the peonies, the four colors white, pink, red and yellow, about which he had woven exotic and semi-abstract landscapes. What better then, as Bill suggested, than that I should write poems also celebrating the flowers.

To clinch the bargain Bill suggested a ceremony during which I was to be crowned Poet Laureate of the Tree Peonies— so that one day I heard a great whooping and hollering, not understanding what was going on. I had been reading, in French, Paul Valéry's address to the French Academy on his election to membership in that august body—a speech which greatly impressed me by its logical force and simplicity. Then I woke up to what was going on. Back of the Abbotts' house I heard Bill shouting as he approached mounted on a Ford tractor, the throttle wide open charging across the furrows of the garden patch. He had placed a two-foot square concrete block on the open chassis of the farm machine, on which when he approached and stopped, he bade me mount. As I did so Harriet squeezed up beside me on one side—it wasn't very wide—and was it Floss or Theresa on the other? Nassos climbed up somewhere behind, the children ran after us with the dogs, while Floss perhaps with Charles walked in the rear.

With Bill at the wheel and everyone laughing and screaming, we charged away again. I thought someone was going to be killed. I didn't as yet know what Bill had in mind, but he brought us all safely to the lily pond. Everybody climbed down, I was placed at a favorable spot on the embankment about the circular pond while everyone applauded, and I was crowned by Harriet with a garland of Siberian Olive, gray green, new plucked and woven for the occasion.

"Speech, speech!"

What could have occurred to me but the beginning in French of Valéry's speech before the French Academy which had so impressed me that I had learned it by heart? I threw out my chest and, frowning like a Caesar, let fly. I shan't forget little Lucy's face, nor Neil's beside her. She was half-scared, looking up at me, her mouth open as if it had indeed been a demigod come to earth.

But I couldn't keep up the mood. So with a libation of lemonade and a dispensation of cake and ice cream, the party returned to the world of the Genesee Valley, the sheep, and the wrens in the hollow fences. Nassos took pictures of the proceedings, but in his excitement kept a finger or thumb over the aperture of the camera, leaving the film blank for posterity.

I did write one poem, I think, as proof of my new office, but other interests that involved us all intervened.

One day a summer or two ago, so I was told, at one of the Grange parties Bill, whose genius for the impromptu is never at a loss for expression, had got their young into a square dance, when he saw Agnes, Charles's daughter, outside. She had been riding, at night, in the woods, as the girls there love to do, and had come up to find out the why of the festivities.

Seeing the girl, Bill opened a window of the big room and taking her hand conducted her gallantly through it. It was a hot night, she had next to nothing on, a loose open shirt of some sort, shorts of the sort worn about the house and for tennis by young girls. Everyone was relaxed, loose-limbed from the dancing when Bill and Agnes began to do a *pas de deux*—he soon quitting to watch her as she for once in her life forgot herself to the music and let go.

The twenty or thirty Grange people from the farms thereabouts, as well as the musicians and others from Rochester, were spellbound as she went into a spontaneous pantomimic expression of her youthful desires—half-realized, unknown to herself—weaving to the music, whirling, bending hips, knees and shoulders, arms waving to the musical phrase.

Finally, after a long work-out she seemed to come to herself, frightened, glanced about her half-laughing, and ran off through the window as she had come.

The third summer Harriet asked me to write what she called a hymn for Rogation Sunday to celebrate the planting of the crops. Canning, one of the teachers of harmony at Rochester, wrote a musical setting, for brasses, for it. It was performed at the lily pool, at the end of a long program. I read the poem first to the assembled audience, which was stretched out at ease on the grass.

At supper with the conductor, Mr. Hollenbeck, our composer, we, the children, the Abbotts and Gratwicks, at the long table in the broad dining room, Bill, looking out the big French windows, unexpectedly remarked: "There go the girls!"—as his sheep, their heads bobbing, wandered by toward the home pasture. I tried to write a libretto for an operetta for them at Bill's request—but it didn't come out.

The trouble was the lightness that sort of composition requires is quickly submerged in the serious implications that, for me, surround it. Looking for a theme, I hit on the witch-hunt trials now or at that time prevalent in Washington and saw, naturally, the analogy between those and the others that had such a tragic end in Salem, Massachusetts, in 1696.

The history fascinated me. I did the libretto—a voluminous affair—with an historical sweep that would have done honor to Tolstoy.

"A major work," said Charles Abbott.

About as suitable for singing, said others, as Veblen's *The Theory of the Leisure Class*.

At Yaddo, where I finally showed it to a composer, Ben Weber, he seized it eagerly, but it burned a hole through the floor in the end. No contemporary problem may be touched in that mode!

Chapter 50

Projective Verse

Until we have reorganized the basis of our thinking in any category we cannot understand our errors. An advance of estimable proportions is made by looking at the poems as a field rather than an assembly of more or less ankylosed lines— well illustrated by Charles Olson in the following:

PROJECTIVE VERSE
(projectile
(percussive
(prospective

vs.

The NON-Projective

Charles Olson

(or what a French critic calls "closed" verse, that verse which print bred and which is pretty much what we have had, in English and American, and have still got, despite the work of Pound & Williams:
it led Keats, already a hundred years ago, to see it (Wordsworth's, Milton's) in the light of "the Egotistical Sublime"; and it persists, at this latter day, as what you might call the private-soul-at-any-public-wall)

Verse now, 1950, if it is to go ahead, if it is to be of *essential* use, must, I take it, catch up and put into itself certain laws and possibilities of the breath, of the breathing of the man who writes as well as of his listenings. (The revolution of the ear, 1910, the trochee's heave, asks it of the younger poets.) . . .

I

First, some simplicities that a man learns, if he works in OPEN, or what can also be called COMPOSITION BY FIELD, as opposed to inherited line, stanza, over-all form, what is the "old" base of the non-projective.

(1) the *kinetics* of the thing. A poem is energy transferred from where the poet got it (he will have some several causations), by way of the poem itself to, all the way over to, the reader. Okay. Then the poem itself must, at all points, be a high energy-construct and, at all points, an energy-discharge. So: how is the poet to accomplish same energy, how is he, what is the process by which a poet gets in, at all points energy at least the equivalent of the energy which propelled him in the first place, yet an energy which is peculiar to verse alone and which will be, obviously, also different from the energy which the reader, because he is a third term, will take away?

This is the problem which any poet who departs from closed form is specially confronted by. And it involves a whole series of new recognitions. From the moment he ventures into FIELD COMPOSITION— puts himself in the open—he can go by no track other than the one the poem under hand declares for itself. Thus he has to behave, and be, instant by instant, aware of some several forces just now beginning to be examined. (It is much more, for example, this push, than simply such a one as Pound put, so wisely, to get us started: "the musical phrase," go by it, boys, rather than by, the metronome.)

(2) is the *principle*, the law which presides conspicuously over such composition, and, when obeyed, is the reason why a projective poem can come into being. It is this: FORM IS NEVER MORE THAN AN EXTENSION OF CONTENT. (Or so it got phrased by one, R. Creeley, and it makes absolute sense to me, with this possible corollary, that right form, in any given poem, is the only and exclusively possible extension of content under hand.) There it is, brothers, sitting there, for USE.

Now (3) the *process* of the thing, how the principle can be made so to shape the energies that the form is accomplished. And I think it can be boiled down to one statement (first pounded into my head by Edward Dahlberg): ONE PERCEPTION MUST IMMEDIATELY AND DIRECTLY LEAD TO A FURTHER PERCEPTION. It means exactly what it says, is a matter of, at *all* points (even, I should say, of our management of daily reality as of the daily work) get on with it, keep moving, keep in, speed, the nerves, their speed, the perceptions, theirs, the acts, the split-second acts, the whole business, keep it moving as fast as you can, citizen. And if you also set up as a poet, USE USE USE the process at all points, in any given poem always, always one perception must must must MOVE, INSTANTER, ON ANOTHER! . . .

Let's start from the smallest particle of all, the syllable. It is the king and pin of versification, what rules and holds together the lines, the larger forms, of a poem. I would suggest that verse here and in England dropped this secret from the late Elizabethans to Ezra Pound, lost it, in the sweetness of meter and rime, in a honey-head. (The syllable is one way to distinguish the original success of blank verse, and its falling off, with Milton.) . . .

It would do no harm, as an act of correction, to both prose and verse as now written, if both rime and meter, and, in the quantity words, both sense and sound, were less in the forefront of the mind than the syllable, if the syllable, that fine creature, were more allowed to lead the harmony on. With this warning, to those who would try: to step back here to this place of the elements and minims of language, is to engage speech where it is least careless—and least logical. Listening for the syllables must be so constant and so scrupulous, the exaction must be so complete, that the assurance of the ear is purchased at the highest—forty-hour-a-day—price. . . .

But the syllable is only the first child of the incest of verse (always, that Egyptian thing, it produces twins!) The other child is the LINE. And together, these two, the syllable *and* the line, they make a poem, they make that thing, the—what shall we call it, the Boss of all, the "Single Intelligence." And the line comes (I swear it) from the breath, from the breathing of the man who writes, at the moment that he writes, and thus is, it is here that, the daily work, the WORK, gets in, for only he, the man who writes, can declare, at every moment, the line, its metric and its ending—where its breathings shall come to, termination.

The trouble with most work, to my taking, since the breaking away from the traditional lines and stanzas, and from such wholes, as, say, Chaucer's *Troilu*s or S's *Lear*, is: contemporary workers go lazy RIGHT HERE WHERE THE LINE IS BORN.

Let me put it badly, The two halves are:

      the HEAD, by way of the EAR, to the SYLLABLE

      the HEART, by way of the BREATH, to the LINE

. . . I am dogmatic, that the head shows in the syllable. The dance of the intellect is there, among them, prose or verse. Consider the best minds you know in this here business: where does the head show, is it not, precise, here, in the swift currents of the syllable? It is true, what the master says he picked up from Confusion: all the thoughts men are capable of can be entered on the back of a postage stamp. So, is it not the PLAY of a mind we are after, is not that that shows whether a mind is there at all? . . .

In presenting the reconstruction of the poem as one of the major occupations of the intelligence in our day, take the following example:

After nine years Charles Sheeler had married again. His bride was Musya Sokolova, a dancer who at the age of fifteen had been driven from Russia by the Revolutionists.

He abandoned the place at Ridgefield where he had taken her, and came to live in the Hudson River Valley near New York. He had got hold of the gardener's cottage of the former Lowe estate, a miniature mansion of gray stone, mansard-roof style, deep-set French windows that was perfect to his purpose.

We have the location: a wilfully destroyed Hudson River estate, a former home of the "aristocracy" of American Colonial history with subsequent wealth engrafted upon it to make it lovelier, Washington Irving's country, the country of the early Dutch and English—the Livingstons, the Phillipses, the woman who might have married George Washington and made him a New York State instead of a Virginia planter, with all that is implied in that.

The main building of sixty or more rooms had been torn down, out of very spite, it seemed, toward Franklin Roosevelt, leaving only the small cottage, the voluminous barns, and the remains of as beautiful a grove of trees, maples, purple beeches, basswoods, Japanese ginkos to be found in the eastern part of the country. Many of them were over seventy years old when Charles and Musya moved in.

The poem is our objective, the secret at the heart of the matter—as Sheeler's small house, reorganized, is the heart of the gone estate of the Lowes—the effect of a fortune founded on tobacco or chicle or whatever it was.

Charles Sheeler, artist, has taken the one rare object remaining more or less intact (I omit the spacious wooden barn) a stone unit of real merit stylistically and proceeded to live in it—with

Musya, a Russian of a tragic past but vigorous integrities, and make a poem (a painting) of it; made it a cell, a seed of intelligent and feeling security. It is ourselves we organize in this way not against the past or for the future or even for survival but for integrity of understanding to insure persistence, to give the mind its stay.

The poem (in Charles's case the painting) is the construction in understandable limits of his life. That is Sheeler; that, lucky for him, partial or possible, is also music. It is called also a marriage. All these terms have to be redefined, a marriage has to be seen as a thing. The poem is made of things—on a field.

The poem, the small house (gray stone, a wisteria vine big around as a leg, the association of the broken-down estate peopled by the perfect trees) has been seized by Charles difficultly, not easily, and made into an expression—as well as he can, which he paints—as well as he can! (Not realistically.)

But the thing, the make-up of their house, is a continuation of the earlier life, of Sheeler the artist, of his old Welsh father, his Pennsylvania background, even of the fact that his uncle planned when he was a boy to make him a pitcher for the old Athletics and took him to the field to induce him to go in that direction.

The house that they have set up (I continue to refer to the construction, the reconstitution of the poem as my major theme) is the present-day necessity.

Charles admires his friends like the Greens and others for their tastes and abilities against which he places his own valid reasons, consciously, appraising what they offer and offering his own values. If they are friends they will see that against the advantages of Paris, of Italy, of whatever place it may be, he must lay his own poem, fully conscious of their Brancusis, their Picassos, their Cézannes, to which I add, their Lorcas, even their British.

And what has he had to give? Bucks County barns? How shall we in this region of the mind which is all we can tactically, sensually know, organize our history other than as Shaker furniture is organized? It is a past, totally uninfluenced by anything but the necessity, the total worth of the thing itself, the relationship of the parts to the whole. The Shakers made furniture for their own simple ritualistic use, of white pine, applewood, birch—what they had. Sheeler has a remarkable collection of this furniture. He has quilts, rugs, glass, early paintings in use about him.

Musya, his wife, has the solid Russian sense of a present-day quality not overshadowed by an overwhelming Western European past. She has been able with Sheeler's assistance to transfer herself to this environment—like her great, really great friend and admiration, the daughter of Leo Tolstoy, who also lives in the Hudson River Valley just across the river.

That is a feat of the intelligence, to transfer an understanding from an aristocratic past and from another context of thoughts to this context, the context of Shaker pieces, a New York Modern Museum, bad as it can be at times. To transfer values into a new context, to make a poem again.

I have seen men and women run off from the pressing necessity of making a new construction. This woman, full of strong qualities, has come bringing qualities for a new construction here. It is of great value to me to have these factors before me when I come to composition. They are the essentials of my work in making the poem.

Once, after Willie Hansen had been let go from the now despoiled Lowe estate, he took a job as gardener for the Princesse de Talleyrand, née Gould, who had a much larger place at Tarrytown, which we were privileged to visit. (In the orchid houses hardly a soul cuts a flower.) One never knows what is of use in rebuilding the poem. One uses what one finds. Willie didn't last long there.

Nothing can grow unless it taps into the soil.

Chapter 51

Ezra Pound at St. Elizabeth's

When I go to see Ezra Pound today it is at St. Elizabeth's Hospital in Washington, the District of Columbia, where he has been confined since his arrest following the last war: a gray stone building, designed and constructed not more recently than before the turn of the century, I am sure, with high, barred windows and long, broad halls. At the end of one of these there is a table protected by a simple movable screen beyond which, in the corner, Ezra has his reclining chair and holds what state may be had. From one until four o'clock daily he may, if he wishes to, receive visitors. When I have been there his wife Dorothy has always been present. In fact, I believe she has not missed a single day to be at his side since the first day of his incarceration. On fine days in summer he is privileged to sit outdoors in the parklike grounds with her all during the afternoons. He has been an exemplary patient, according to the official directly responsible for his care. What will come of the situation only the future can tell.

But the first time I was a visitor at the place I was much more disturbed; the disturbed mind has always been a territory from which I shrank instinctively as before the unknown. Ezra's first weeks or months of close confinement among more or less desperate cases—his only exercise having been in a small concrete court surrounded by a high wall—had profoundly affected me, when I heard of it. I took a taxi out of Washington after a meeting of

335

the Fellows of the Library of Congress, a twenty-minute ride, not knowing what I was going to find. We went in at one of the gates, apparently unguarded. It was a fine afternoon and I began to inquire where the building was that I had been told he was in. I don't know how many acres the institution occupies, but we must have covered them all when finally I got to the right one and, telling the taxi to wait, I went in for my visitor's permit.

"You'll find him sitting out there under the trees with his wife," said the man.

There he was, sure enough, in a brand-new beach chair, Dorothy before him reading aloud to him as I approached through a group of the other inmates who looked at me curiously. He didn't know I was coming, so that when I was almost up to him and he saw who I was, he leaped out of his chair and grabbed my outstretched hand—then embraced me.

"Well," said Dorothy, "it's Bill Williams. Isn't it?"

We talked at random for an hour that day. He looked much as I had always found him, the same beard and restless twitching of the hands, shifting his shoulders about as he lay back in the chair studying me, the same bantering smile, screwing up his eyes, the half-coughing laugh and short, swift words, no sentence structure worth mentioning. I was of course happy to find him looking so well.

We talked mostly of the situation of letters in our world—not good; of personalities and the lack of initiative in those who should be active—myself among the others, implied.

Naturally we could not avoid the perennial subject, economics and the convictions shared by many with Ezra—that it is international finance that brings us all at always shorter and shorter periods to our ruin. That wars are made by the international gang which runs Russia, England, France, Germany, the United States and what others. They are identifiable, have a known complexion—fool many but not all—and that in the present instance F.D.R. was the prime criminal. All I could do was to listen.

Dorothy listened too. This is her husband whose hardship she devotedly shares: a tall, ascetic Englishwoman for whom all who see and know her have a deep respect and affection. The

Pounds have no money. For the first winter Dorothy lived in a third-floor unheated room adjacent to the hospital. We invited her to come for a rest and visit at our home near New York but she refused.

We talked that day under the trees of Nancy Cunard, I remember, and of her experiences during the German occupation of France and many other such things; of Wyndham Lewis over whom both Dorothy and Ezra laughed when I mentioned some of our experiences with him at Buffalo the summer before. Ezra believes Lewis a bit mad but thinks him one of the very few informed people of the world, quite excusably eccentric when you consider the blithering idiots who rule us from high places.

It is elementary to Pound that if anybody knew anything at all that really goes on among governments, it would be child's play to get on a solid basis of government and bring about peace. But he thinks not more than five men in Washington know a single thing that is basically important—he considered Tinkham of Massachusetts one—so that if anything worthwhile gets done, it is by the purest accident.

For instance Ezra is convinced that after twenty minutes' instruction in the Georgian dialect, if at the beginning of our difficulties with Russia, Stalin would have given him a five-minute interview, he could have shown the man the error in his thinking, made him see, comprehend, and act on it, and all the subsequent confusion and disaster could have been avoided.

Marx never mentions in the *Kapital* one word of money, never knew anything of the true situation now governing the world. He was a product of the middle of the nineteenth century —all his libertarian dialectic goes back to that—and . . .

A dialectic, of whatever sort, is merely a premise, in this case false, logically followed to its verbal terminations, whereat we close our eyes and commit logical murder.

Why in a world dominated by such a theme look for love's subleties or even its absence or presence?

Do we have to be idiots dreaming in the semi-obscurities of a twilight mood to be poets? The culmination of our human achievement, all that we desire, can't be achieved by closing our eyes to a veritable wall barring our path. The theme of the poem must at such a point be the removal of the block to everything we might achieve once that barrier is removed. If we are to be taxed out of existence to feed private loans, the revenue from which is used by an international gang to perpetuate armed conflicts, at private profit—to further enrich the same gang—that, the inferno of the *Cantos*, must be one of the poet's nearest concern.

So we talked, of who is in the know, as against the self-interested mob of "legislators," the pitiful but grossly ignorant big-shots who play in with the criminals—in city, state and nations; of our first duty as artists, the only semi-informed men of the community, whose sweep is the whole field of knowledge. It is our duty at all costs to speak; at all costs, even imprisonment in such isolation, such quarantine, from the spread of information as a St. Elizabeth's affords.

I don't say that Ez *said* all this, but from his halting broken jabs and ripostes of conversation, it is what I inferred. On the way back to Washington this last time when he had stood up to bid me good-bye and I had got to the gate, thinking of many things, I hailed a taxi and when I got in found the driver was a colored man.

We started to talk, as I always do with these important messengers, saying something about the climate of the place and so forth and so forth. When I told him that I was a physician out to the hospital on a visit to an old friend who was confined there, he, as anyone might be, was interested mostly in himself.

"So you're a doctor. Look Doc, I got a bad back. As long as I'm sitting here driving, I do all right but as soon as I start to do any lifting, I'm no good."

"Sounds to me like you might have a dislocated interverte-bral disc," I said. "How long has it been bothering you?"

"Oh, about two years."

"How did it come on? Suddenly after an accident or some heavy lifting?"

"It came on about a week after I was out with a woman friend of mine. We done about everything in the book. About a week later it began to bother me. I think it was that."

"Too much for you, huh?"

"Well, I think I strained myself."

"Perfectly possible. Have you done anything about it?"

"Oh yeah, I got a doctor, but he wants me to be operated on and I'm not hankering for it."

"How old are you?"

"Forty-eight years old. I knew a friend had it done, a woman, and she didn't come out so well. It's over a year now and she still can't do anything. Think I ought to go through with it?"

"It's just according to how much it bothers you," I said. "If it isn't bad, you might even get over it by leaving it alone, as long as you're symptom-free. But if it really bothers you, I think you ought to look into it. Surgery is the only sure cure—if you've got the right man."

"Oh he's a good man, all right. How long would it lay me up?"

"Well, they got to get the crushed pieces out of there, clean the edges up good and fuse the bones. I don't know too much about the technique but it'll be a minimum of six weeks, I'd think, before you're on your feet again, though it may be that they'll slap a plaster cast on you and get you going sooner."

We were silent awhile at one point at an intersection, then I went on—something about the present world situation on which he had some firm convictions: about what a fool Stalin would be to sit around the next two or three years until we had the mines all planted under him to blow him to kingdom come and not be readying himself to get the jump on us if he can.

I was a little surprised to hear such talk in Washington, D. C., from a man so *au courant* with public opinion.

"Maybe you're right," I said.

"Sure I'm right, wouldn't you do the same thing if you were in his position. We got to best him but it stands to reason that's what's in his mind."

"And what can we do about it?" I said.

"Not a thing, not a thing, except we can think—as long as we keep in line."

"That's what my friend is sitting out there in the hospital for, thinking things like that."

"Is that right. What did he do?"

"He broadcast against this country, from Italy, while we were at war."

"That's bad, you can't do that. What did he say?"

Then I went on to give a brief outline of Ezra's international opinions, the emphasis he lays on the exchange, the international gang, what Ezra calls F.D.R.'s failure to eradicate the basic evil at the critical point, his indictment of the international bankers, their history and their personnel in our day. My man listened closely as we drove through Washington traffic toward my hotel. As I got to the close of my little exposition, he stopped his taxi and turned to me.

"And that's what they got him locked up for," he said.

"Yes, substantially that's what it amounts to."

The man looked at me. "He ain't crazy," he said. "He just talk too much."

My occasions for visiting Ezra are not frequent. I go when I can as I did this last time in mid-winter when we cannot be outdoors but must remain by the big windows adjacent to the old round wooden table with the battered screen making a small room of it at the end of the corridor. I have never been in his cell where he is permitted to receive books and other small gifts of various sorts. The man is sixty-five now and has grown heavier during the past year. His reddish hair, beard and moustaches have been permitted to grow wildly at random—the long hairs framing his unchanged features half-ludicrously, half-frighteningly to resemble the face of the beast in Cocteau's well-known film—and as I speak of it, there is an even deeper resemblance there between the two creatures, Pound in actual life and the imaginative creature of the French film artist. Pound greatly admires Cocteau, and Dorothy during the last year sent me Cocteau's recent poems.

I had heard of a move that had been made to re-open the case, if the charge is still valid, in an attempt to have Pound removed from St. Elizabeth's for treatment under more favorable surroundings. But Pound had refused to entertain the idea, stating that he knew he would be shot by an agent of the "international crew" the moment he stood outside the hospital gates. Maybe he's right, for one thing is certain: he'd never stop talking.

All my life has been one steady bawling out from this old intimate over my sluggishness in appreciating the gravity of the world situation in the terms of his dialectic. In many cases I can see the justice of his views, both in that particular, regarding the criminal abuse of the functions of money, as well as the place of the poem in our attack; it is a basic agent in putting pressure on the blackguards who compel servitude, abetted by the various English Departments of "the university" with their "sacred" regard for a debased precedent. Formally it plays right into the hands of the criminals in charge of government that alone can compel obedience.

"Attack at that level!" screams Pound.

But we do not see, as he points out, that in the formalisms of the poem itself the criminal sits secure, embedded there so that plaintive officialdom—with all their rewards and prizes, work for the very gang they would destroy. The poem (not "poetry," that sop) is the capsule where only, at times in the intelligence, the facts of the case may be made secure.

Hence the hatred of the poem, the vicious and violent attempt to suppress it—the shock that it at times occasions—and the constant attempt to defame any who is brushed by its flame—when it is a flame, which isn't, it must be said, often the case. The poem is the active agent, sometimes of a basic attack. In it the world may, and often has, to live in hiding.

They burn books, they suppress their freedom, incarcerate their perpetrators, even attempt to burn a picture, in the same mood, such as the "Guernica". This confirms Pound's reasons in using the poem as his take-off, as an oak uses an acorn for the same purpose, or mustard will cover a field with blossom.

A year ago, in the same month of February, when I quitted Ez and was walking toward the exit in the cold rain through the mud of the hospital grounds, I had to go past one of the old buildings. I felt now that I had begun to know the place, my first terror, physician though I am, at the total implications of the place having subsided. At first I had gone cold as I entered the narrow door in the tower which leads up by a winding stone stairway round and around to his floor. I had gone up two flights instead of one to the wrong level. I pressed the button of the bell and was admitted by a wary attendant. All about me were the inmates, lining the walls on both sides, some standing, some sitting, some lying on the stones. I followed the attendant who after identifying me by phone from the main office let me out again telling me to go a floor below and lean on the bell if no one answered the first time.

This I had grown used to. Some sense of humanity had returned to me as I walked along, taking a short cut to the exit which brought me within fifty feet of the building adjacent to the one Pound was occupying. A regularly spaced scream coming from somewhere in the building I was passing caught my ear, then as I came out beyond the edge of an angle in the wall, I saw a figure from which I could not remove my eyes. It is surprising how open and apparently unguarded the whole grounds of the institution present themselves to a visitor: you walk about, you go in and out apparently unobserved and certainly unobstructed, but as I looked up from the mud where I was somewhat carefully stepping, I saw this man, naked, full-on and immobile, his arms up as though climbing a wall, plastered against one of the high windows of the old building like a great sea slug against the inside of a glass aquarium, his belly as though stuck to the glass that looked dulled or splattered from the bad weather. I didn't stop, but kept looking up from time to time. I glanced around to see if there were any women about. There was no one on the grounds at that point but myself. The man's genitals were hard against the cold (it must have been cold) glass, plastered there in that posture of despair. When would they come and take him down? After all it was glass, window glass, bars though there were beyond it. The white flesh like a slug's white belly separated from the outside world, without frenzy, stuck silent on the glass.

I can't understand how Pound has been so apparently unmoved by his incarceration, guilty or essentially innocent as he may be. His mind has not budged a hair's breadth from his basic position, he has even entrenched himself more securely in it—recently finding precedents in the writings of a certain Controller of the Currency sixty or seventy-five years ago, who held similar views on our official perfidies. Pound has privileges, it must be acknowledged, and is kindly treated by the hospital personnel. But he does not waste them. He works constantly, reads interminably. The curator of the Oriental Library in Washington brings him the texts he is interested in when he wants them; he has the Greek of whoever it may be to decipher and understand. He may translate; he has his typewriter: his erudition is become more and more fearsome as time passes, whatever the outcome is to be.

And it must be said of a life of confinement, if he survives it, that much of the world's greatest writing has waited on a removal from the world of affairs for its doing. Concentration is what a man needs to bring his mind to harvest. We may and he will, whoever he may be, change ourselves by our contacts, but to drain off the good we must find quietude. The monk's cell is ideal for the purpose, though it has limitations in its narrowing orthodoxy or partisanship of outlook. Nevertheless it represents quiet, relief from economic pressures: one can write then. Prison, though, is better, or seems to have been so in the past. Aesop was a slave; many a Greek did his best work in exile to Sicily or even the next city. Sappho must have felt mightily confined by Lesbos; Raleigh wrote well in prison: *Pilgrim's Progress* came from confinement—as birth does also—but the best of all was *Don Quixote*, when Cervantes was put in jail. There are other examples.

The poem is a capsule where we wrap up our punishable secrets. And as they confine in themselves the only "life," the ability to sprout at a more favorable time, to come true in their secret structure to the very minutest details of our thoughts, so they get their specific virtue.

We write for this, that the seed come true, and it appears to be this which makes the poem the toughest certainty of continued life that experience acknowledges. Pound is writing and say what you will of government, our own in particular in this case, it is permitting him, to the limit of his ability, to avail himself of the stores of knowledge found in the national capital.

"Yes," I said to him as we were about to part again this last time, "what you say is quite true, but what you forget, Ez, is

William Carlos Williams   **344**

that logical as your elucidations may be, logic, mere logic, convinces no one."

For once he didn't reply, but Dorothy looked up suddenly and pointed a finger at him, opening her eyes and smiling, as much as to say, "there you are." He never said a word.

But when I reached home he sent me the usual semi-abusive letter—having regained his breath—followed by another letter a week or two later. He had smiled when I spoke of the autobiography, saying, "You can say anything you please about me with perfect safety, since I have no legal status in the country."

Chapter 52

Yaddo

In 1950 the Corporation of Yaddo, through Elizabeth Ames, the director, invited Floss and me to visit the estate at Saratoga Springs, New York. We had been invited the year before but couldn't go. This time we accepted. It was unusual for a husband and wife to be invited to Yaddo together. We had a fine big room and old-fashioned bath on the first floor of the West Cottage. Other wives who wished to see their husbands when in residence at the Foundation could do so only during the day, or week-ends. It cost the poor (?) artists ten dollars a night if they wished to spend a night with their wives in Saratoga Springs.

I'd heard of Yaddo, next to the racing track at Saratoga, and Josephine Herbst had told me, "You can walk through a hedge and stand at the very rail on the back stretch."

It was on these premises that Edgar Allan Poe completed the last stanza of his popular poem *The Raven*, while still the well-to-do foster child of the Allens—visiting the baths and eating trout dinners with the fashion of the day.

The atmosphere of the present establishment is somewhat that of the cloister, but completely secular: a big old mansion in the style of an English country house where for the past half-century writers, painters, musicians and sculptors are invited to come for visits among pine forests, lawns, a formal rose garden of an acre or two in graded terraces to write, paint, or whatever it may be, at their ease.

Above us, at one end of the second floor of the West Cottage resided Ben Weber, the composer, who had been enjoying for a year a grant from the National Institute of Arts and Letters. One day as he, Floss and I were walking slapping deer flies on our way to breakfast, we got talking about opera and the libretto, the relationship of one to the other—which preceded the other and so forth.

Weber is a short, almost inarticulate, red-headed, round-headed and soft-voiced man, who seldom appeared at the infrequent after-working-hours parties in the various studios, and when he did he drank preferably only beer. I told him I had a libretto or the makings of a libretto for an opera I had been working on. He looked at me, said every composer was looking for a libretto and that he had been scouring the country for one for at least two years. I could see he was watching me. I asked him if he'd care to look at mine, which I delivered to him that evening in his room which I saw then for the first time.

That is the way Yaddo works. Floss went upstairs with me. This was the cottage Mrs. Peabody had built when the main building was out of use at one time. This had been her boudoir —still in the original style. Weber had his piano there. For days, he said, he'd do nothing but stare out through the rain, perhaps over the lawns between the stands of towering spruces improvising on the keys as the mood might strike him. He had been there a month or more. We had cocktails after which he played us an unfinished song suite—if it was a suite and not single songs— music to two of Blake's poems which he had been commissioned to finish before the end of summer.

My own studio, to which I had been assigned, was on the top floor of the main building. It was vaulted high under the roof with wide high windows filling the whole east side of it, over- looking the main eastward sloping pasture, grown to creeping thyme an eighth of a mile to the Italianate fountain basins and the paths to the rose garden. In the distance you could see Bemis Heights in Vermont. The glass of the side window was etched with the scratched-in names of poets who had used the room in the past. It was too much for me. Instead, I asked for a small studio cabin beyond the garden with a fireplace and a pile of split cordwood.

It was cold last August at Yaddo as I worked to finish *Paterson, Book IV* from my voluminous notes of at least a hundred and twenty-five pages, bringing them down to a scant twenty-two. I had to burn all the wood assigned to me. The place smelled of ashes and aromatic decay.

I worked steadily, seven days a week from right after breakfast until noon, and from one to four P.M. without a break for two weeks. It was just about all I could do.

At Yaddo the meals are served strictly according to schedule. The first day I asked for bacon and eggs. There was no bacon served with the eggs at breakfast. At the proper time at the end of each meal a bell is struck and the guests carry their soiled dishes to the carts to be wheeled into the kitchen. But as Nicolas Calas, whom I was delighted to see there after so many years, told me, Where in the civilized world—after you got over the mild discipline of such minor rules—where could a man or woman find such kindness and freedom to work as one might please? No questions are asked. No record is kept. The artist is generously supported without limit, well-fed, well-housed in superbly adjusted and pleasing surroundings. He is likewise protected from his fellows: no visiting between studios is permitted before teatime each day.

Calas was working on a commentary upon or an exact deciphering of the symbolism depicted in the Hieronymus Bosch triptych the *Garden of Delights*. In any case it is one of his main works. I was privileged to be shown Calas' working papers in the text. Every detail of the picture is being studied with a microscope; the scholarship is appalling. I'd go crazy. But when the work is finally printed nothing that I have seen as revelatory of the mind of the Middle Ages, in the Low Countries especially, would seem to approach it, at least in intentions. But the very nature, the painstaking nature of the work made Calas practically a recluse.

John Husband, there from Tulane, Harvey Shapiro, Richard Eberhart and his kites, Jessamyn West, the brothers Pierre and Philippe Marcelin from Haiti writing their latest novel in collaboration, Mitsu who had followed her husband Taro, painters who, because Christians, had gone through hell as conscientious objectors in Japan during the last war. Mitsu had a toothache! and never let out a peep.

The day after I had shown Weber my libretto he spoke enthusiastically of it. But my play, *A Dream of Love*, in spite of enthusiasms, is still a dream.

There are several books still to be written: a biography of my mother, the continuation of the *White Mule* series; the prose, essays, prefaces and miscellaneous comment should be collected, and so forth. That will all come.

Chapter 53

Translations

I have always wanted to do some translations from Spanish. It was my mother's native language as well as one which my father spoke from childhood. But more than that the language has a strong appeal to me, temperamentally, as a relief from the classic mood of both French and Italian. Spanish is not, in the sense to which I refer, a literary language. It has a place of its own, an independent place very sympathetic to the New World.

This independence, this lack of integration with our British past gives us an opportunity, facing Spanish literature, to make new appraisals, especially in attempting translations, which should permit us to use our language with unlimited freshness. In such attempts we will not have to follow precedent but can branch off into a new diction, adapting new forms, even discovering new forms in our attempts to find accurate equivalents for the felicities of the past. That at least has been my thought—especially in attacking Spanish poems. It still remains my ambition.

There is a noteworthy body of verse for us to work upon. It isn't as rich as English in the multiplicity of its achievements, but there are lyrics in the *Romancero* of distinguished beauty. We have scarcely touched them. I tried to bring over a few when I was just beginning to find myself, but I was not ready for them.

My first attempts with the language were rather upon prose

than the poem. My father, when he was in his last days, helped me do a short story by Rafael Arevalo Martinez of Guatemala. It was called "The Man Who Resembled a Horse." We had a lot of fun with it. Later there was a collection of poems from Loyalist Spain called, *And Spain Sings*. I did some of those and found them exciting.

But the chief challenge to us today is Lorca and through him Gongora, of whom he was beginning to speak more and more toward the end of his life. It looks to me as though in Lorca and Gongora, putting them over into our language, we have almost an ideal opportunity for trying out new modes entirely separate from anything either English or French. I must confess I have done nothing yet to carry this work on, but it strongly attracts me and someday soon I shall begin.

But when Mother was in her eighties, and we looked about for something to do to amuse her, I hit upon an old book that Pound must have left here on one of his visits. We started to translate it, and we found ourselves richly entertained. *El Perro y la Calentura*, literally, *The Dog and the Fever*, it was the work of the famous Don Francisco Quevedo, a contemporary of Lope de Vega and of Shakespeare. He called it a *novela peregrina,* a country novel, and wrote it during one of the periods when he was exiled from Madrid, perhaps not during the first exile—which was for having killed a man whom he had seen insulting a woman in the cathedral while she was at prayer— but the second or third, the result of a political struggle with intriguers at court for whom his hatred was intense.

To me the novel is unique and fascinating. It was translated into English during the early eighteenth century but not completely—or with any accuracy; whoever did it didn't at all get the feeling. The scheme of it is a putting down of the facts about the corrupt court, but not openly, which Quevedo couldn't afford. Instead we have a story told in terms of proverbs of the people, among the scene and sounds of the farm where he then was staying. It is all by implication, nothing is directly stated— very much as might be done today.

The surface is bucolic but the undertone is vicious, violent in its attack upon those persons in power at court whom Quevedo hated. Mother and I began the work casually, but before long we grew engrossed in it as we attempted to find in English equivalents for the old Spanish. For it was old Spanish, which increased the difficulty and the charm. It had its bawdy side also, which never discouraged Mother; she loved it.

In fact, that's one of the things that attracted me when I saw the name Quevedo in the first place. Mother has always had questionable stories about Quevedo to tell me; Spanish literary tradition is shot with them. You'll find them here, especially toward the end of the brief account when, under cover of a device he uses, covering the facts more and more, he goes into a wild account of an affair in a garden during which the old church dignitary, who is leading a double life, is himself cuckolded.

After a year or more Mother and I completed the job under great difficulties multiplied by the language which finally baffled us almost completely. The writing is in slang, an early seventeenth-century slang full of obscure references which, I confess, were sometimes impossible to interpret. The first translators didn't even attempt that part. But there is enough that can be understood to make that particular part of the work the most amusing. We finally got even that in one way or another. I sent one page that we couldn't even get started on to a Professor Salinas of Johns Hopkins to see if he wouldn't give us a hint or two. But he wouldn't even look at it, sent it back with the helpful comment, however, that the text was probably corrupt along with the other difficulties, which was really quite an aid. One or two passages which made no sense whatever became fairly intelligible when the spelling was somewhat changed.

No one has, of course, printed this work for us though I have several times offered it. But someday I hope to make it attractive by doing a running commentary to accompany and interpret the text. I don't want a scholarly exhibit. I want something that can be read by anyone looking for amusement, someone who will sit down with the whole story and give himself to the entertainment it offers.

In her last years, when it was impossible for us to keep her at home any longer we had to find a place where Mother could stay. By the greatest of good fortune, or bad fortune, if I must tell the truth, she was able to move into the very bed that Nana Herman, Flossie's mother, had just vacated. It was a most unfortunate series of circumstances. But in the end nothing could have turned out better for me or the whole family.

For it brought us the friendship of a remarkable woman and that of her equally devoted and entertaining husband who, whatever his drawbacks, made all our lives the gayer for his presence. Mrs. Taylor is British; so is Harry. No one not reared in the school that taught her could have done for Mother what she did. At first Mother looked at her with suspicion, but that was Mother. She resented going to live with Mrs. Taylor, she hated the food, she fought the hospital bed she had to lie in, she wouldn't use the bed-pan that was necessary for her until at last— and this continued for over ten years—Mrs. Taylor picked her up bodily every night toward three A.M. to sit her on the pot. And this with a never failing smile even while my mother fought and squirmed and told her how clumsy she was and how she was hurting her. Occasionally, when Mother was bad, Mr. Taylor would have to help his wife. Those times it would be a riot. Year after year this went on. I never heard a complaint from Mrs. Taylor, something that just doesn't occur in these degenerate times in this environment. Besides which you've got to be strong. Mrs. Taylor was strong.

Meanwhile Harry did the cooking, his hair standing on end, his undershirt buttoned to the neck, his pants all but falling off, unshaved and with half a load on whenever he could get the opportunity. I don't think he would deny it, it was part of his life, something in which he believed and still believes.

"When Harry starts a bottle, of no matter what," his wife would say, "he has to finish it."

She shrugged her shoulders, smiled, as much as to say, What can you do? and interfered as little as possible. She merely kept his finances at an absolute ebb. He instinctively accepted it, so that they got along without brawls. She wasn't the kind to brawl, and he carried on his work as cook with his usual liberal hand.

"They give me too much!" Mother used to complain bitterly. But Harry didn't pay too much attention to her so all she could do was to leave it. He'd come in occasionally while she was eating and watch her, asking her how she was doing. She'd look at him with her bleary vision and say nothing. What was the use? She liked the man. She liked anything that wore pants, and she liked Harry far more than Mrs. Taylor, who really did everything for her. More than that she liked Harry Taylor because he was far subtler than his wife; he was in short an artist *manqué*. Mother knew this and spoke to me of it several times. Mrs. Taylor knew it also and it was that, something unusual in the man, which held her respect. He had been a dancer. You could see it by the calves of his legs when you were permitted to look at them; they were extraordinarily developed.

Harry Taylor had not been, as was his wife, from poor parents. Mrs. Taylor's father was postmaster in a small town north of London. But the family of her husband was wealthy or at least well-to-do. They were bankers and it was to his father's bank that Harry Taylor was apprenticed when he had come of age. It bored the young man to tears. For, however he had arranged it—perhaps he had been given a few dancing lessons as part of his social upbringing—he had acquired sufficient skill as a dancer to want to have a fling at the stage. He must have got to show his ability in some manner or another, for his parents got wind of it and sat down hard on his ambitions. It broke the young man's heart.

"They couldn't permit it," was what Mrs. Taylor told me, "not stage dancing!" Such a thing could not be tolerated in banking circles such as he would be expected to frequent. Impossible. It would have to be given up and at once. So that settled that. Harry went back to the bank.

It didn't last long for, since he couldn't dance, since he had been frustrated in his life's ambition to be a dancer, to exhibit his flamboyant, happy person behind the footlights where he belonged, since he was trapped, defeated, without hope of escape, he took it out the only way which appeared open to him, in dreams abetted by the drinking of anything alcoholic he could lay his hands on. And with that he did all right. He became such a souse that when the First World War came along and he saw an opportunity to get away from the bank which he hated, he enlisted in the Navy, as a cook! His parents were glad to let him go.

It's a long story and I don't know the half of it, but with his ability as a galley-cook some years after the War, Harry landed in this country, seeking his fortune. He landed in the West, in the general region of the Rocky Mountains where the dime novel had at one time instructed all good younger sons of British aristocracy to go. Particularly he was cook in a large Salt Lake City hospital. The girls were attractive there and the liquor was supreme. But things became serious in the case of one of the young ladies, a Mormon, and Harry wrote home asking them what they thought of the fact that she belonged to that unusual religious belief. He may have been hoping they'd object and that he would then be able to tell her that he couldn't go through with it. For when he received a reply that as long as she was a nice girl, from a good family, his family could see no objection to his marrying her, he one night hopped a freight and got out of town.

In Canada, where he landed, he took a job with Ringling Brothers Circus. He was with the outfit, a galley cook, when in Victoria one day he met the future Mrs. Taylor, married her and finally, after many changes of fortune landed with her in Rutherford.

It's all over now as far as we are concerned, but I cannot forget those obscure kindnesses showered so selflessly by both those people upon the difficult and unforgiving woman that Mother was in her old age. I'll never forget how she laughed the day the canary fell in the dish water. Mr. Taylor dried it as best he could and then put it in the oven to warm up and get its feathers thoroughly into condition. When Mrs. Taylor finally rescued the bird, though it had been the boon companion of its boss up to then, it wouldn't go near him but perched on top of the kitchen door, where Mother would see it from her chair, and cursed him. Try as he might he couldn't coax the bird back to its former friendly habits; Mother laughed until she cried over it.

One day when I went to visit her I could see she was full of something she wanted to tell me.

"You must get him to dance for you," she said. "But he is

good, really good," she said. "Get him to show you. It is something to see. You must see it." But the man only smiled and wouldn't repeat the act. It seems that, being well liquored up the day before and feeling tip-top, he had found Mother gloomy and depressed. He wanted to liven her up and had started a pirouette. She opened her eyes, she knew it was good, and gave her whole attention. At that, the two there alone in the room, he went on with the routine until, with a final burst of virtuosity, he completed it with an entrechat that had Mother enthralled and applauding.

Chapter 54

The Practice

It's the humdrum, day-in, day-out, everyday work that is the real satisfaction of the practice of medicine; the million and a half patients a man has seen on his daily visits over a forty-year period of weekdays and Sundays that make up his life. I have never had a money practice; it would have been impossible for me. But the actual calling on people, at all times and under all conditions, the coming to grips with the intimate conditions of their lives, when they were being born, when they were dying, watching them die, watching them get well when they were ill, has always absorbed me.

I lost myself in the very properties of their minds: for the moment at least I actually became *them*, whoever they should be, so that when I detached myself from them at the end of a half-hour of intense concentration over some illness which was affecting them, it was as though I were reawakening from a sleep. For the moment I myself did not exist, nothing of myself affected me. As a consequence I came back to myself, as from any other sleep, rested.

Time after time I have gone out into my office in the evening feeling as if I couldn't keep my eyes open a moment longer. I would start out on my morning calls after only a few hours' sleep, sit in front of some house waiting to get the courage to climb the steps and push the front-door bell. But once I saw the patient all that would disappear. In a flash the details of the case would begin to formulate themselves into a recognizable outline, the diagnosis would unravel itself, or would refuse to make itself plain, and the hunt was on. Along with that the patient himself would shape up into something that called for attention, his peculiarities, her reticences or candors. And though I might be attracted or repelled, the professional attitude which every physician must call on would steady me, dictate the terms on which I was to proceed. Many a time a man must watch the patient's mind as it watches him, distrusting him, ready to fly off at a tangent at the first opportunity; sees himself distrusted, sees the patient turn to someone else, rejecting him.

More than once we have all seen ourselves rejected, seen some hard-pressed mother or husband go to some other adviser when we know that the advice we have given him has been correct. That too is part of the game. But in general it is the rest, the peace of mind that comes from adopting the patient's condition as one's own to be struggled with toward a solution during those few minutes or that hour or those trying days when we are searching for causes, trying to relate this to that to build a reasonable basis for action which really gives us our peace. As I say, often after I have gone into my office harassed by personal perplexities of whatever sort, fatigued physically and mentally, after two hours of intense application to the work, I came out at the finish completely rested (and I mean rested) ready to smile and to laugh as if the day were just starting.

That is why as a writer I have never felt that medicine interfered with me but rather that it was my very food and drink, the very thing which made it possible for me to write. Was I not interested in man? There the thing was, right in front of me. I could touch it, smell it. It was myself, naked, just as it was, without a lie telling itself to me in its own terms. Oh, I knew it wasn't for the most part giving me anything very profound, but it was giving me terms, basic terms with which I could spell out matters as profound as I cared to think of.

I knew it was an elementary world that I was facing, but I have always been amazed at the authenticity with which the simple-minded often face that world when compared with the tawdriness of the public viewpoint exhibited in reports from the world at large. The public view which affects the behavior of so many is a very shabby thing when compared with what I see every day in my practice of medicine. I can almost say it is the interference of the public view of their lives with what I see which makes the difficulty, in most instances, between sham and a satisfactory basis of thought.

I don't care much about that, however. I don't care a rap what people are or believe. They come to me. I care for them and either they become my friends or they don't. That is their business. My business, aside from the mere physical diagnosis, is to make a different sort of diagnosis concerning them as individuals, quite apart from anything for which they seek my advice. That fascinates me. From the very beginning that fascinated me even more than I myself knew. For no matter where I might find myself, every sort of individual that it is possible to imagine in some phase of his development, from the highest to the lowest, at some time exhibited himself to me. I am sure I have seen them all. And all have contributed to my pie. Let the successful carry off their blue ribbons; I have known the unsuccessful, far better persons than their more lucky brothers. One can laugh at them both, whatever the costumes they adopt. And when one is able to reveal them to themselves, high or low, they are always grateful as they are surprised that one can so have revealed the inner secrets of another's private motives. To do this is what makes a writer worth heeding: that somehow or other, whatever the source may be, he has gone to the base of the matter to lay it bare before us in terms which, try as we may, we cannot in the end escape. There is no choice then but to accept him and make him a hero.

All day long the doctor carries on this work, observing, weighing, comparing values of which neither he nor his patients may know the significance. He may be insensitive. But if in addition to actually being an accurate craftsman and a man of insight he has the added quality of—some distress of mind, a restless concern with the . . . If he is not satisfied with mere cures, if he lacks ambition, if he is content to . . . If there is no content in him and likely to be none; if in other words, without wishing to force it, since that would interfere with his lifelong observation, he allows himself to be called a name! What can one think of him?

He is half-ashamed to have people suspect him of carrying

on a clandestine, a sort of underhand piece of spying on the public at large. They naively ask him, "How do you do it? How can you carry on an active business like that and at the same time find time to write? You must be superhuman. You must have at the very least the energy of two men." But they do not grasp that one occupation complements the other, that they are two parts of a whole, that it is not two jobs at all, that one rests the man when the other fatigues him. The only person to feel sorry for is his wife. She practically becomes a recluse. His only fear is that the source of his interest, his daily going about among human beings of all sorts, all ages, all conditions will be terminated. That he will be found out.

As far as the writing itself is concerned it takes next to no time at all. Much too much is written every day of our lives. We are overwhelmed by it. But when at times we see through the welter of evasive or interested patter, when by chance we penetrate to some moving detail of a life, there is always time to bang out a few pages. The thing isn't to find the time for it— we waste hours every day doing absolutely nothing at all—the difficulty is to catch the evasive life of the thing, to phrase the words in such a way that stereotype will yield a moment of insight. That is where the difficulty lies. We are lucky when that underground current can be tapped and the secret spring of all our lives will send up its pure water. It seldom happens. A thousand trivialities push themselves to the front, our lying habits of everyday speech and thought are foremost, telling us that *that* is what "they" want to hear. Tell them something else. You know you want to be a successful writer. This sort of chit-chat the daily practice of medicine tends drastically to cure.

Forget writing, it's a trivial matter. But day in day out, when the inarticulate patient struggles to lay himself bare for you, or with nothing more than a boil on his back is so caught off balance that he reveals some secret twist of a whole community's pathetic way of thought, a man is suddenly seized again with a desire to speak of the underground stream which for a moment has come up just under the surface. It is just a glimpse, an intimation of all that which the daily print misses or deliberately hides, but the excitement is intense and the rush to write is on again. It is then we see, by this constant feeling for a meaning, from the unselected nature of the material, just as it comes in over the phone or at the office door, that there is no better way to get an intimation of what is going on in the world.

We catch a glimpse of something, from time to time, which shows us that a presence has just brushed past us, some rare thing—just when the smiling little Italian woman has left us. For a moment we are dazzled. What was that? We can't name it; we know it never gets into any recognizable avenue of expression; men will be long dead before they can have so much as ever approached it. Whole lives are spent in the tremendous affairs of daily events without even approaching the great sights that I see every day. My patients do not know what is about them among their very husbands and children, their wives and acquaintances. But there is no need for us to be such strangers to each other, saving alone laziness, indifference and age-old besotted ignorance.

So for me the practice of medicine has become the pursuit of a rare element which may appear at any time, at any place, at a glance. It can be most embarrassing. Mutual recognition is likely to flare up at a moment's notice. The relationship between physician and patient, if it were literally followed, would give us a world of extraordinary fertility of the imagination which we can hardly afford. There's no use trying to multiply cases, it is there, it is magnificent, it fills my thoughts, it reaches to the farthest limits of our lives.

What is the use of reading the common news of the day, the tragic deaths and abuses of daily living, when for over half a lifetime we have known that they must have occurred just as they have occurred given the conditions that cause them? There is no light in it. It is trivial fill-gap. We know the plane will crash, the train be derailed. And we know why. No one cares, no one can care. We get the news and discount it, we are quite right in doing so. It is trivial. But the hunted news I get from some obscure patients' eyes is not trivial. It is profound: whole academies of learning, whole ecclesiastical hierarchies are founded upon it and have developed what they call their dialectic upon nothing else, their lying dialectics. A dialectic is any arbitrary system, which, since all systems are mere inventions, is necessarily in each case a false premise, upon which a closed system is built shutting those who confine themselves to it from the rest of the world. All men one way or another use a dialectic of some sort into which they are shut, whether it be an Argentina or a Japan. So each group is maimed. Each is enclosed in a dialectic cloud, incommunicado, and for that reason we rush into wars and prides of the most superficial natures.

Do we not see that we are inarticulate? That is what defeats us. It is our inability to communicate to another how we are locked within ourselves, unable to say the simplest thing of importance to one another, any of us, even the most valuable, that makes our lives like those of a litter of kittens in a wood-pile. That gives the physician, and I don't mean the high-priced psychoanalyst, his opportunity; psychoanalysis amounts to no more than another dialectic into which to be locked.

The physician enjoys a wonderful opportunity actually to witness the words being born. Their actual colors and shapes are laid before him carrying their tiny burdens which he is privileged to take into his care with their unspoiled newness. He may see the difficulty with which they have been born and what they are destined to do. No one else is present but the speaker and ourselves, we have been the words' very parents. Nothing is more moving.

But after we have run the gamut of the simple meanings that come to one over the years, a change gradually occurs. We have grown used to the range of communication which is likely to reach us. The girl who comes to me breathless, staggering into my office, in her underwear a still breathing infant, asking me to lock her mother out of the room; the man whose mind is gone—all of them finally say the same thing. And then a new meaning begins to intervene. For under that language to which we have been listening all our lives a new, a more profound language, underlying all the dialectics offers itself. It is what they call poetry. That is the final phase.

It is that, we realize, which beyond all they have been saying is what they have been trying to say. They laugh (For are they not laughable?); they can think of nothing more useless (What else are they but the same?); something made of words (Have they not been trying to use words all their lives?). We begin to

see that the underlying meaning of all they want to tell us
and have always failed to communicate is the poem, the poem
which their lives are being lived to realize. No one will believe
it. And it is the actual words, as we hear them spoken under all
circumstances, which contain it. It is actually there, in the life
before us, every minute that we are listening, a rarest element—
not in our imaginations but there, there in fact. It is that essence
which is hidden in the very words which are going in at our ears
and from which we must recover underlying meaning as
realistically as we recover metal out of ore.

The poem that each is trying actually to communicate to us
lies in the words. It is at least the words that make it articulate. It
has always been so. Occasionally that named person is born who
catches a rumor of it, a Homer, a Villon, and his race and the
world perpetuates his memory. Is it not plain why? The physician,
listening from day to day, catches a hint of it in his preoccupation. By listening to the minutest variations of the speech we
begin to detect that today, as always, the essence is also to be
found, hidden under the verbiage, seeking to be realized.

But one of the characteristics of this rare presence is that
it is jealous of exposure and that it is shy and revengeful. It
is not a name that is bandied about in the market place, no
more than it is something that can be captured and exploited
by the academy. Its face is a particular face, it is likely to appear under the most unlikely disguises. You cannot recognize
it from past appearances—in fact it is always a new face. It
knows all that we are in the habit of describing. It will not use
the same appearance for any new materialization. And it is our
very life. It is we ourselves, at our rarest moments, but inarticulate for the most part except when in the poem one man,
every five or six hundred years, escapes to formulate a few gifted
sentences.

The poem springs from the half-spoken words of such patients
as the physician sees from day to day. He observes it in the
peculiar, actual conformations in which its life is hid. Humbly
he presents himself before it and by long practice he strives
as best he can to interpret the manner of its speech. In that
the secret lies. This, in the end, comes perhaps to be the occupation of the physician after a lifetime of careful listening.

Chapter 55

West: 1950

On our way to the West in 1950, our first stop was Chicago, which Floss had never seen. We got a taxi with a fat driver who took us out along the lake front. Floss didn't think I had tipped him sufficiently after the trip, so I ran after him, catching him when he made the turn to pick up his next fare inside the station enclosure. He was just leaving, opened his window just enough to admit my hand and say thank you to me. I told him it was my wife's idea. He smiled and nodded. I hadn't noticed how shabby the sleeve of *my* overcoat had become.

The upper Mississippi caught our imaginations as we approached Minneapolis and St. Paul at sundown. —*I have never seen the picture* The River. *Must get Steichen to have it put on for us at the Modern Museum*— The dairy country. No wonder.

Next morning crossing the Dakotas we began to see the ducks, and evidence of the hunters—from the lake cities. It was opening day. Every small pool along the right of way had its brood— half fledged. I watched them all day long. They looked like teal.

You'd see miles and miles of fenced land, brown as an old coat, absolutely abandoned, the back house tilted by the wind, not even a dog around the place. It was late October. We had had a piddling sleet storm that morning but it had stopped. The young ducks were everywhere there was water. None on the wing, except short flights from our intrusion.

I had seen all this once before:

"What's it like here in winter?" I asked the trainman when I was traveling out West alone in 1948.

"Frightful!" was his word for it. I stood on the back platform and watched the barrenness unreeling.

Returning that time with a light load, only three pay customers on this run, the porter had told me. "You, that other man and a woman. I bin away from home a week," he continued, "and I had to borrow five dollars from the conductor so I could eat during the lay-off in Seattle."

The porter was a tall, aging man, a big fellow with a heavily featured, seamed face. He eased himself gratefully into the seat beside me when I made room for him.

"My home's Chicago. I don't get paid till I get back at the Pullman office. I got a young wife and two small children. I never know what I'm going to find when I get there. We got a nice little house, but you never know."

"You originally from Chicago?"

"No. New York is my home, but I grew up in Chicago. It's a good city. I got two brothers there. One has a restaurant business over near the lake. Fine place. He employs white and colored girls about fifty-fifty. He's making money. Wants me to come in with him. Not me. I'm satisfied—or would be, but for a few things."

"What about your other brother?"

"Oh, him. If you saw him you'd think he owned the world. He's the biggest and best-looking of us all—I got another brother in New York, but I never see him."

"You say this one in Chicago is making money, too?"

"Oh yes, he's making money. He drives a Cadillac car and wears hundred-and-fifty-dollar clothes. (I could see him! I have always envied colored men the way they can wear their pants! Nothing like it.) Shoes: Shirts—everything to match—a pocketful of money. But he hasn't got a nickel he can really call his own. No sir, not for me. He makes a big splash but I don't want nothing of that in my life."

"How come?"

"They own him."

"Who?"

"City Hall. He has to report back there every two hours all
day long. He works for them. Everything he does comes from
those people. Everything he owns too, if they just say the word
he won't have nothin'! The one in New York owns a line of
taxis. They all made good in my family—if I could just be sure
what I was coming home to on this trip I wouldn't have a thing
to complain about."

"We got nothing to do," I said. "Can't you tell me a little
more about it?"

"Sure, I'll tell you. The trip before the last when I got home
I got held up and lost all my pay. You see we get in late, just
about dark. We get paid off at the main office and then we go
home. They know that and they lay for us. I wasn't a block
from the house when two of them walked up to me. One stuck
a gun into my ribs and told me not to yell, while the other one
reached in and took every cent I had in my pockets. That's the
third time it happened to me."

"Did you get it back?"

"How am I going to get it back?"

"There must be cops around."

"Once I got it back. A young man come up behind me and
grabbed me. I started to yell and fought him back. He hit me
with his gun but I hung onto him and kept on yelling. Just
then a taxi cab pulled up to the curb and the driver climbed
out.

" 'What's going on here?' he asked.

" 'This man is drunk and I'm taking him home.'

" 'I'm not drunk,' I said. 'He's trying to rob me.' With that
he started to run with my money in his hand.

"So the taxi driver grabs him and we kept on fighting and
yellin' until a cop come and pulled us all in."

"A good guy, huh?" I commented.

"He was a good guy. Maybe he recognized me from my
brother."

"What happened?"

"Well, I didn't want to make any charges. I knew my wife
would be waiting and I wanted to go home.

" 'All I want is to get back my pay,' I told them. But they

wouldn't hear of that—the Court had my pay—so I had to make charges against the man and they locked him up. My wallet was in the Court's hands. When it came to the trial the judge took me into his room and asked me what I was going to sue for.

" 'I don't want nothin',' I said, 'I just don't want to have him take my money.'

" 'How much did he take?' the judge asked.

"I told him how much it was and he said it wasn't enough, I should sue him for $250. The boy's mother and father was in court crying and saying they was poor and that they didn't have that much money and that he had always been a good boy. But the judge told them to get it and to get it quick. So they got it and paid it to the Court. They sent the boy up for five years."

"Did you finally get your money back?" I asked.

"Oh, I got it back all right, about ninety dollars. The rest went to the judge. He just kept it. And three months after that I was riding on the street car . . . There next to me on the seat . . . was my man."

"Who?"

"The one who held me up. Right next to me!"

"But I thought . . ."

"Yes sir, three months after they sent him up for five years. He recognized me too and he called me a name and said he had a good mind to blow my guts out right there where I sat. I don't know how I got out of that car."

"You say your wife is a young woman?"

"Yes. She's twenty years younger than I am. I never was married before. She's a good wife and I got two fine children. Clean and pretty."

I waited, feeling that he hadn't finished something he wanted to tell me.

"Last time but one," he said then, "my wife told me two men came to sell her a vacuum cleaner.

" 'I got one,' she told them.

" 'Oh, but you must see this one,' they said, 'it's a new model.' They pushed their way in and told her they wanted to demonstrate how it worked. So while one was plugging in the machine the other one took her and then they cleaned me out. Took all the money she had and raped her and went away."

"But didn't she scream or yell?"

"What good would that do? She might have got worse."

"Probably true," I said.

"Yes, sir, it's true. That's what can happen to us—I'm through with that city. I want to get out and go somewhere else."

"But why don't they pay you with a check instead of the cash?"

"That wouldn't do no good, they'd get you anyhow."

"Tell me," I said, for I wasn't sure, "what you consider a fair tip for a three-day trip like this?"

He laughed. "You remember that last stop? That woman with the little girl? Well, she got off and I put her bags down and walked away. Then she sent the little girl back to me with a ten-cent piece."

"Look, honey," I said to her, "you go buy yourself some candy with that." He laughed again. "Sometimes it's nothing and sometimes we find a wallet under the pillow when we go to make up the beds. Why, I found one last summer with seven hundred and fifty dollars in it. That man was telephoning all over the place for it. I turned it in at the office in Seattle . . . and what do you think happened?"

"Reward?"

"Nothin', not a cent. But suppose somebody else found it but me. Most likely I'd lose my job."

"Hey!" he said as one of the dining-car waiters walked by where we were sitting, "You get out of here!" Then he turned to me. "They're not supposed to be in these cars," he said. "We gotta watch them every minute. They're the ones."

"Wouldn't five dollars be a fair tip?" I asked him.

"Not fair, but generous. I'd be glad to get it."

"You're sure it's enough?"

"That's a big tip. I don't get that but once in a while, sometimes not all year."

Approaching the Blackfoot Reservation, the mist and sleet had subsided. The sun began to come out. I lay down awhile.

I had a bellyache and felt a little uneasy. Floss was keeping her eye out for the Clark Memorial, a small obelisk near the right of way, to commemorate his famous journey through these parts in 1804-5. She saw it and right afterward told me that we were apparently coming into a new oil field just being exploited at Cliffedge, the tanks and pumps blossoming on the hills everywhere. I particularly noticed a long shed and the name, Jones & Laughlin, Supplies.

So that's how good books get published, I thought to myself. The Blackfoot Agency was a few miles off, a small village, with a narrow macadam road leading to it from the railroad switch at our right. And towering beyond that, after the snowstorm, the peaks of the Rockies in brilliant sunshine above the empty hotel of Glacier National Park. What could we think as the train climbed laboriously through the ravine of Marias Pass until dark? A lonely world.

Rain greeted us at dawn. All we could see of Puget Sound was a curtain of mist and the ducks, punctuated by herons, on a stump perhaps, and the usual harbor gulls, a few fish crows and an occasional hawk.

Professor Heilman and his wife met us. The week was a strenuous one. Almost the first thing he said to me was, "Wednesday evening you will talk on the novel."

Knowing nothing of the novel, I had to think quick. Accordingly I developed a theory in my dreams that night which proved very useful during the trip: The novel, a form I have never respected, is in effect a strip-tease. You take off the garments a chapter at a time, beginning with the front. As you get deeper your subject begins more and more to reveal itself—a Becky Sharp for instance—but at the last, the form being not serious but a romantic subterfuge, there is a blackout, the war is won or lost or someone loses his life one way or another and that's the end.

"Oh, no!"

"Oh, yes!" I replied. "But if and when you get down to nothing more than the sheer (nylon) panties, or shall we say, jock strap, slip a finger under the edge and snap it off—we have, hopefully, the poem."

"But what about *War and Peace?* What about . . . ?"

"Horatio Alger?"

"Well, what about Horatio Alger?"

"In a novel something is always bared—to a point. The hidden talent, the hidden crime—Raskolnikov—the unapparent firmness not at first disclosed. But never the fact, never the underlying nudity of patriotic or economic stress, or reality of other sort. It can't be so. This is a novel, a romantic, subtle frieze."

"I object."

(Though the crowd liked the notion they thought it quite shocking.)

"You see," I went on, "there are no primitive novels. It began, barely, with the poem. You do not get the novel until you begin to hide the cruel nudity; until you get clothes. Carlyle saw this and gave it out (as much as he dared, poor man, in his Victorian world) in *Sartor Resartus,* his awful image of a nude Parliament. Can you possibly imagine Henry James without an accompaniment of corsets and Prince Alberts with striped trousers? I can't. We must, in a novel to begin with, have clothes, clothes to strip off—almost. The occasion of the novel is when as time passes our clothed men develop at last into clothes horses. There is a famous cartoon by Tenniel, it may be, showing Louis, a skinny-legged, bald and toothless old man; next Rex, a huge, curled wig supporting a hat with plumes, an embroidered coat, below pads for the legs, and finally—Louis Rex, in full regalia, the king himself—Louis XV.

"So that the novel is most at home and occupies its greatest esteem when nothing but the clothes remain, which, when stripped off reveal—a cipher. The iconoclast at work. It should, as did Henry James's work, usher in the classic age, the poem.

"But the poem had better be a body of some firmness or the novel will again overtake it. The short story is another attack."

I was expected to talk for three weeks, in sequence, on the novel, the short story and the modern poem, with an elucidating lecture to the general public between, on the "Creative Process." There were also seminars, conferences, occasional lectures, and manuscripts to be examined and individually elucidated to their creators. Four novels (in five days), etc., the first stop. I had to remember that though a heretic, I was a teacher and was paid to go there (to Flossie's benefit) for that.

A culture is a rich and wonderful thing. I had often to plough ahead, in the hour, to win out even at some cost of intelligibility: had not Washington lost the battle of Germantown by his field commanders' ignoring that very thing?

And at this very Washington University had I not heard of one guest lecturer who made it a practice to lie on the floor at dinner parties when he felt bored and who finally quit the place two weeks before he had finished giving his course? He had not left the questions from which to make up a final examination and so his pupils lost their time and credits. But he was a Princeton man, which should have excused him. I didn't want to be like that.

And then short stories and five poems or groups of poems. Floss read the novel scripts (I couldn't do it all), told me the stories and advised on certain chapters.

Ted Roethke was there, Matthews, Jerry Willis and Heilman himself. I have forgotten the name of the young poet, a most unpromising-looking young man, a major, as it turned out, in music; he had on a grimy corduroy, leather-lined coat, a dirty face, hands that looked as if they hadn't been washed for a month. He showed me an (imperfect) poem about self-destruction—the best I had read on the trip—involving a kitten that brushed against his ankle at a critical moment and turned him off.

I pointed out to him that the poem, well-made if one were up to it, ended about ten lines above the point where he came to a stop. He would not accept my criticism.

"But, look," I said, and read the passage over to him. He still shook his head.

"I understand, of course," he told me, "but that isn't the kind of ending I want. I want it to die off like a refrain in music that gradually fails."

I looked again and learned something about myself, that I am often too abrupt.

"Yes, I see what you mean," I said, "but you'll have to go

about it some other way. Take some lines out from up here (I pointed out a premature passage) and insert it below."

He looked. "Well, perhaps. I'll have to study it." He added that some in the group of which he was a part criticized him because they thought his work too much influenced by William Carlos Williams.

"Do you think it stands in your way?" I said. I can't remember that he answered.

They have a museum of Oriental art in Seattle that presents some statues of action, figures in wood, full size, that are among the finest examples of Chinese carving that I have ever beheld. The Greeks seem frozen beside them. There is one particular painting too, or screen, of a hundred crows in flight, nothing more, that might open our minds, were we before it, to many worlds. I think of Shapley of the Harvard Observatory and his active wish for many crossing cultures in a truly enlightened world to ease our plight.

We made or renewed many friendships at Seattle. Carmen Lopez, Helen Russel, her husband, Jim, a most patient man. We took a taxi out there to supper one evening. It was almost six o'clock. The young man, the driver, looked at me when I gave him the address.

"Where?" he said.

It was ten miles off to the south and east of our New Jersey address.

Chapter 56

The College Life

At Reed College, our next stop, we were met by Jones and Mac-Rae. There was a flood on. Rain had fallen continuously for a month. They got a room for us at the old Portland Hotel designed by Stanford White, a replica, it was said, of the old Murray Hill of New York. There Floss observed the waiter peeling my soft-boiled egg at breakfast, holding the spineless ovule in his fingers afterward and with the other hand pouring a spoonful of hot water over it before gently depositing it in the cup. It went with the height of the ceilings and the formal old-style lobby.

There are nearly as many on the faculty at Reed as there are students, a mere six hundred. There at a small reception luncheon at the Faculty Union I inadvertently got myself off to a bad start by saying that all editors are liars (my experience), before an editor of the august Portland *Observer*, assistant to its proprietor and the kindly President of the College itself.

Later I said that I had suffered at my lectures.

"You're not alone," said MacRae, "we of the faculty also suffer before you."

"Is that so?" I said.

"Only because we are not sure how much you will omit," he reassured me.

The students showed me their work, some of it advanced, at interviews. I locked myself into MacRae's office one day with a

young woman in blue jeans. When someone came hammering at
the door and couldn't get in she told me it was against the law
to lock oneself in with a student.

I saw a boy and girl talking obliviously together as our group
passed from one hall to another. She, pretty as a baby, flushed
crimson as she became aware of us passing.

Stanly Moore, teacher of philosophy, Reynolds, Jones particularly, I took to. In my talks, after all, I had to say *something*,
kind, kind as they were all, so again I was reduced to inventing a
theory upon the creative process, the origin of art, a Freudian
offset.

"There is one thing God Himself cannot do," I said. "He cannot raise the arm and lower it at the same time."

"He could if He wanted to," said Stanly.

"No, He couldn't. Not at the same time. Not at once raise the
arm and lower it at the same time. Therefore duality, therefore
the sexes. Sex is at the bottom of all art. He is unity, but to
accomplish simultaneity we must have had two, multiplicity,
the male and the female, man and woman—acting together, the
fecundating principle."

"Go on," he said.

"Therefore" (it was a thrill to be talking to the most intelligent
philosopher I ever met, one who eschews awkward words—and
smiled) "therefore, everything we do is an effort to achieve conjunction, not to say unity, and the stronger our sex, as men, the
stronger our actions, the more heat, the more physiologic oxygen
we drive to our brains the better the work of art we shall or are
likely to perform."

"That's Heraclitus," he advised me. "The arrow and the bow;
the string is pulled back and as the fingers release it the arrow
is driven forward: action and reaction."

"That will do," I said, "but we are more articulate today.
Duality. Woman for her part no less willing in her search for a
conjunction, a unity of the impossible union, lends herself to
the drive. She wastes to nothing if she is not, on her part, able
to complete the act, the original act, to make it one. And so can
be measured as she drives, she also, toward that. I think women
are neglected in the arts."

He cautioned that I underrated them. So the time passed.

I was gradually learning how to read my poems aloud. I found that audiences listened attentively and applauded. It was a strange experience. One young man brought a volume of my *Collected Poems 1938* for me to autograph.

"Where did you get this?" I asked.

"At the University of Oregon Co-op," he said to me.

"Are there any more there?" because I was bound there over the week-end.

"No," he said, "this was the last one."

"How much did you pay for it?"

"Seventy-five cents."

I offered him ten dollars for it. In New York it was unobtainable at any price, but he refused. It was a perfect copy.

The last evening we had a party at MacRae's—other nights at other places. Next day was Sunday. Reynolds picked me up for a special view of the North Shore Indian culture as shown by the superb collection at the museum.

I was impressed by a wooden sculptured feast bowl or series of bowls in the form of a giant painted in formal patterns by those primitive peoples. The man, in conventional costume of furs and beads, was on his back, black and red and white, with his knees drawn up, his head raised on a log. His belly was hollowed for the main course, the hollowed-out places in the chest and head were smaller and in and on the knees and thighs another cavity was for the tid-bits or special favors. The chiefs designed what patterns were to be used and the women of the tribe executed the work.

The tribe, a term I borrowed from the ethnologists, was the theme· of much that I had to say of the arts. Culture, that martyred word of the subjectivists, came more and more to be my thought. Frustration, we have been told, is the origin of the dream of art, that fantasy—something to make us laugh. Frustrated over what? Over the impossibility of raising and lowering the arm at the same instant? What else can it be? And who is not, I said, frustrated?

It is the theme of all the novels of the Northwest, I told them: a beautiful young girl, preferably Norwegian, blond and wellfetlocked; she is brought up by her pioneer grandmother who has been knocked down more than likely by her worthy lord on more than one drunken occasion. This reputable primitive has taken charge of her beautiful granddaughter, taught her never to undress even alone at bedtime without keeping her pants on until she has dropped her nightgown over them from above. This the child has done—to keep her mind and herself uncorrupted until her wedding day—that cannot come too soon. But finding herself unexplained and maybe inexplicable to herself in her loveliness, which she has perceived as well as might another (she isn't dumb), at the first opportunity, at the age of fifteen perhaps—she is a big, full-blown girl—she, breathless, strips herself bare before the first pier glass she finds and stands there astonished. After which she finds and marries the first narcissistic athlete she can discover and hell breaks loose.

"But where do all the phonies come from?" asked one young man.

Just reverse the process, the pioneer woodman against whom it is impossible for the son to compete (in the Freudian manner): the old boy holds the bed as well as the floor; and the guy, not a five-footer by any means, finds his carcass, shaped to fell trees, a considerable hardship and handicap. What is it called—a transvestist?—he admires, as he should, ladies' underwear. He's ready-made for the girl to hop off with.

This comedy, shaped after fact as well as upon the Oedipus complex—the impossibility of winning the mother's affection—we see it as often in New England with as disastrous results where the churlish ship master would come home and possess his wife over the heads of his sons, who had had her among them for a month, a year, two years sometimes.

So there is, inevitably, harmless frustration for us all, grapes on a branch (out of reach) for everyone and as he chooses. This is the primitive. A culture is measured as it gives us that. Find a shard in the desert about Tucson. Upon it there are regularly ordered black brush strokes. By that you know that men have had release there from boredom, from the lives of hogs, that war has been somewhat restricted long enough at least for them to develop for respite a culture in art.

Thus we find out the function of art, since no one knows anything at all for certain. Frustrated, the measure of a culture is its depth, its thickness, its opportunities for employment of the faculties. The end of life may be to penetrate the female or to be completed in the reverse of that. Right. But what female? There are females of too many coverings and wishes to explore them all. By finding only one pocket for relief we bore our women to the point of frustration, indeed, our own.

But a culture allows us to beat our enemy, the husband—as Homer, the Troubadours, Shelley, Browning (not Shakespeare) never tired of telling us, and Pound in youth never tired of repeating. The magician, the sorcerer, who was no mean competitor for the chief and all his women: even youth had his head cut off or even more than that. In a cultured environment there were many resources for abler men, many layers of achievement in the arts.

The artist is not by any means a frustrated man, never has been. Don't blush to write a poem, stand up to it, *provided* it is a structure, a structure built upon your own ground to assert it, your ground where you stand on your own feet, in every man's despite.

A bridge builder builds a construction over a stream or a mountain gorge—which he then crosses—what's he going to do when he gets there? Cross back again (usefulness is no answer) to carry over a peck of beans? There is no more useful occupation, if it comes to that, than the poem: it shows us a way out.

Take, for example, a girl, I said, taller than usual. She lived across the side street from us facing our cherry tree, the last of two still standing. Sometimes, when cherries were ripe the kids about the block used to go up the tree for a few cherries that could be found in our semi-soot-starved side yard.

One day I saw Ruth, a full-grown woman, perched up that tree reading a book.

"What the hell you doing up there?" I said.

"Reading."

"Good," I told her. "Go to it," and went on my way. I realized afterward what it was. She wanted to get out of the house because she had a brother there, few knew of him, a cripple and an idiot, twenty-one years of age. She had nowhere else at the moment to go. The family was secretive about the true situation and never let on.

They moved away and Ruth was found one morning dead in the garage, the engine dead also, run out of gas. Carbon monoxide poisoning. She'd been out the night before. She wasn't pregnant, but had maybe had a proposal of marriage and felt forced to refuse it because of the brother at home or something like that. Maybe he turned her down because of it. She had run out of resources. A culture might easily have taken up that sort of thing. Nobody ever had the guts even to condone the youthful Pound at his first minor indiscretion in taking an unfortunate woman from the streets and giving her his bed to sleep in.

These are the things I talked to them about: A lecturer for the English Department who had followed Spender to Reed College. I told them rhyming wasn't worth much. I saw one of the best short stories there by a man who was a conscientious objector and had been sentenced to serve a three-year term because of it. Another had a good novel half-done—he lives with two grandmothers—his parents not being apparent—and wrote as an old woman talks. I found another chap with a first-rate essay on Gertrude Stein, one of the most lucid I have yet encountered. Good kids, all of them, doing solid work.

The Columbia River was flooded as usual approaching Eugene. The University of Oregon was kind to us in one way: we had a room, the guest room at the woman's dormitory. It is said that when it was opened the year before the superintendent, Miss Turnipseed, carried the first girl in over the portal. They were beautiful to look at, three hundred and fifty of them—no dungarees allowed—in their multicolored skirts and blouses. We saw them every day—a few Japanese, a few Negroes—big girls some of them. I don't think I ever saw so many big girls in one place —enough to frighten you. Very lovely, though, and possibly as mild as kittens, but they didn't look it.

And roses! They really have them in that country, bushes six feet tall with twenty blossoms upon them, mostly pink, and somewhat rainwashed but big as plates in diameter. The plant

life in Oregon, the evergreens, the hollies are a delight to the
eye, but the rain that causes them and the great forests of
Douglas firs to flourish is not always so alluring. It rained and
rained. The timber raids of generations have depleted the forests.
It still goes on and the Weyerhauser interests and mills are far
from popular, so much so that when the man's small daughter
was kidnapped several years ago there was little sympathy for him.

I forgot to tell of an experience at Seattle. That too is a
fabulous place for the luxuriance of its vegetation. In spite of
the rains, the "dry rains of the Northwest" they call them, Floss
and I after breakfast always took a short walk.

This day we turned back of the hotel, going in a new direction,
admiring the flowers blooming in the small gardens—it was not
a rich street—until we came to a fine holly tree in full berry.
We stopped to admire it.

As we stood there looking at that and some roses which it
surprised us to see so luxuriant at that time of year we were
approached by an old fellow in a ragged-looking shirt and dis-
reputable-looking pants.

"You like flowers?" he asked. "Come around in my back yard
and I'll show you some of the finest in Seattle."

We looked at each other, smiled, and, having nothing else to
do, decided to humor the old fellow. So we followed him around
his little place a little downhill to the rear thinking to see something really unusual. The whole back of his property could not
have taken in an area twenty feet square. There were some naked
grapevines, a small patch of what he told us were loganberries,
the remains of some tomato vines and the chrysanthemums of
which he had spoken.

"What do you think of those?"

The only thing noteworthy about them that I could see was
their stems.

"Did you ever see anything finer?" he questioned me. "Look at
those stems!" And then I understood what he was driving at: the
length of stem was his criterion. For the flowers he seemed to
care nothing at all, but that there were stems nearly five feet
long, or longer, made them extraordinary in his eyes.

His whole horticultural world was concentrated into this small
back-yard patch. He told us that he had lived, a bachelor, in that

house for nearly fifty years, that of the grapes which grew on
that vine which we could see beside his back door he every year
made wine, some of which he gave to his friends, pressing the
juice from the grapes with a press of his own design and manufacture.

"Come inside a minute, will you?" he said, opening the back
door, "and I'll show it to you."

Again we hesitated, but again we yielded, entering a low
cellarway into the basement of the house; it was filled with paraphernalia of all sorts—garden tools, old furniture, a work table
—from among which he produced a small wine press in perfect
working order and showing evidence of having been recently used.

"Look at that," he said. "I made one like that last year and
gave it to one of my friends so that this year I had to make
another. I'm sorry the wine isn't fit to drink yet or I'd let you
taste some of it. It's very good.

"That's my furnace. You see that bin full of wood. That's what
I burn in the fall, packing boxes I break up. Got a lot of time,
haven't I? But that goes pretty fast. Underneath I've got my coal.
Right under there. See."

"You've got everything you need," I said, "to be quite comfortable."

"Look over there on the wall."

I looked and saw the frame of a bicycle with the wheels, lacking
tires, on a nail beside it. "That's the finest bicycle that was ever
made, as good today as when it was first put on the market.
That's a Columbia. Did you ever hear of that?"

"Did I? I should say I did. That was the bicycle they used to
sell when I was a boy."

"That's it. I've had that bicycle since 1898, over fifty years.
Come upstairs a minute."

There was nothing to do now but follow.

"This is my kitchen. I'm sorry to have to show it to you this
way with the dishes in the sink. This is my bedroom. And does
your wife play the piano? Try that keyboard. There isn't a finer
tone in the city. I used to have a woman here that played it once
in a while but she died and I haven't had anyone around that
plays it recently. Try it. That's a fine piano."

Standing there in that cluttered room the old fellow sketched

his family history for us since he left Boston; I think it was in
1883. His name was Kaufman, had a brother in Dallas, Texas,
and so on and on until we had to leave.

Later that day the young lady who took Floss about the city
while I was lecturing pricked up her ears when Floss spoke of
our experience.

She immediately identified our friend and said he was well
known to her, had in fact more than once, meeting her in the
street before his house, as he met us, tried to induce her to view
his various possessions of which he was so proud. Often when
she leaves her car in the parking place near the hotel and across
from where he lives she finds it washed and polished when she
returns for it after business hours—for she helps her mother in
a flower shop hard by.

"Sometimes in the fall, as at present, in the middle of all our
flowers, he will bring me a bunch of his chrysanthemums—with
their long stems. He is one of the richest men in Seattle! Owns
property all over the city."

Most have never made the progression, I told all of them,
indeed very few have ever made it (and today in the poem they
have begun to fall back from even the insignificant advances that
were made)—the progression from the sentiment, the thought
(philosophy) or the concept to the poem itself—from the concern
with Hamlet to *Hamlet,* the play. That was the secret meaning
inside the term "transition" during the years when the painters
following Cézanne began to talk of sheer paint: a picture a
matter of pigments upon a piece of cloth stretched on a frame.
I told them the Hartpence story.

It is the making of that step, to come over into the tactile
qualities, the words themselves beyond the mere thought expressed that distinguishes the modern, or distinguished the
modern of that time from the period before the turn of the
century. And it is the reason why painting and the poem became
so closely allied at that time. It was the work of the painters
following Cézanne and the Impressionists that, critically, opened
up the age of Stein, Joyce and a good many others. It is in the
taking of that step over from feeling to the imaginative object,

on the cloth, on the page, that defined the term, the modern term—a work of art, what it meant to them. It is a step that must take place inside the mind before the concept, like an egg, can be laid. It is to *play,* I told them, not fall in among the strings. That's where it begins. As Ed, my brother, once quoted some Frenchman as saying *"L'architecture, c'est poser un caillou sur un autre."*

This is a hard climb—it was for me—a hard thing to accomplish, but it is that which must be accomplished before sentimentality can be abolished and the thing itself emerge, liberating the man.

That, I said, was the primary understanding before you could understand what followed. The key, the master-key to the age was that jump from the feeling to the word itself: that which had been got down, the thing to be judged and valued accordingly. Everything else followed that. Without that step having been taken nothing was understandable.

The gyrations in trying to "understand" cubism, for instance, the "false" perspectives of somebody's view inside Chartres, the distortions—finally Picasso's horse-faced women, etc., etc.— the . . . No sense.

—and then, to go write a sonnet! Where's the thought or invention or initiative of any sort in that? Even Eliot knew enough not to do it, I told them, nor had any who thought during the past fifty years.

One day Professor Maas, the poet laureate of Australia, took us for a long auto ride back of Eugene, the center of the new boom in lumber. It was no pleasure. For a fact, I fell asleep beside Flossie, who sat on the front seat between us. Depressing to witness the carnage among the trees, long sections of their massive trunks flying past us on heavy trucks, the bark torn by the mauling they had received in the struggle to get them out of the gullies where they had grown for a century.

Chapter 57

The Ocean, The Orient

We made the trip to San Francisco by night in order to have more time in that metropolis before leaving for Los Angeles (the fabulous) with Eyvind, Flossie's nephew, who was on his way north via Carmel to pick us up.

Crossing on the ferry from Oakland I was astonished to see the rock of Alcatraz so near shore occupying the center in that amphitheater of enormous bridges between the islands. It seemed somehow the chief actor in the tragedy of the place; no wonder they want to get rid of it. Its fame must be embarrassing. We saw Telegraph Hill from which in the old days the arrival of a ship through the Golden Gate—gold with the sun setting behind it—was signaled.

But the outstanding thing that I was aware of among all the West Coast cities was that they faced the Orient; that Europe had no more than a legendary hold on them; that airplanes or no airplanes they were remote from ancient, Occidental cultures; and that they were still in the hands of predatory interests. They are isolated between the Sierras and the sea, with such estates as San Simeon perched upon the coastal range. Such colonies as Carmel and Pt. Lobos sliding off into the water imitative as all hell, and the tide building behind them backward areas, letting the present Barbary Coast of the mind rape them supinely. It is nostalgic, for they don't go there to adventure, but to hang on, to hang on to the past, not to get rid of it, and the fine weather just makes so much more for a long day for regression for the old who believe that to be young is to be princely. A sad deceit is waiting.

The Orient, which they fear, is their opportunity; to *embrace that "new."* But they cling to worn-out Europe as though the feudal were their king. The young in the colleges yearn for France, for New York, Boston, for that "culture," and look (through the eyes of New England teachers) to a past, feeling themselves yokels.

While Japan, China and Korea lie across the water from them to their ruin. At Eugene they have an Oriental collection brought from China as a result of the Boxer Rebellion. Someone bought it cheap from someone who had come into possession of it at that time. On the first floor they have tapestries a lifetime might be spent in studying, such brilliance of color and skill has been lavished upon them. At the top of the formal stairway is a massive marble just where the steps turn back upon themselves and reach, at either side of that landing. It is the figure of some personage or ruler (though no name is given) more than full scale, a draped figure in repose. The eyes are bemused, the face tranquil. The man is standing, as I remember it, a leather belt about his belly, the folds of his gown slightly caught at one point. They have at least given the figure the whole platform! We sat on the bench opposite and were lost in admiration. The stained marble seemed to make the whole campus outside us an absurdity.

Alcatraz in San Francisco harbor had that same effect upon me: a comment in rock, disturbingly unequivocal in its statement— not of the place. Definitely not wanted.

We didn't go down the coast road but took Highway 101 back of the coastal range down the inner valley, four hundred and twenty miles. San Francisco was the last mission of the Spanish intruders coming north, among all the missions from Monterey up, at a day's walk apart. The eucalyptus trees hereabouts were exceptionally vigorous.

The Sunday at San Francisco we spent taking a drive over the Golden Gate bridge and twenty miles beyond into the open country to the top of Mount Tamalpais, open country facing the Pacific, empty of legend, past redwood patches, regrowth beginning again.

The best were the ranches here and there almost on the coast. Small dairy farms at long distances from each other. It might have been Arcadia. It wasn't. A very puzzling effect: the bay four thousand feet below the summit, the city in the distance in a half-haze.

We stayed in the Los Angeles area, the San Fernando Valley, a small one-story house among a hundred similar—at Van Nuys —facing to the East—the low mountains—across orange groves. Where one year ago not a house other than a half-neglected rancho had been standing.

In the small yard—it was middle November—there were calla lilies, though the fig trees had been frost-nipped the night before we arrived. There were chrysanthemums, roses; the new grass was thick and green, repeated up and down the street. We went to the corner to a lumber-yard to pick up bits of clapboard, etc., for the open fire. Charlotte told us that it had been up to 94 three days before our arrival.

One day she took us for a drive to the San Fernando Mission. Hum, hum, hum, hum, hum, hum, hum! and told us of a night twenty years before when the place was still a ruin, before its restoration as a girls' school, that she and Ramon Navarro had visited it by moonlight—he had his guitar along. The place was guarded by barbed-wire fences.

They climbed through the wire, sat at the portico among the old stones before the chapel and sang songs. The day we were there the mimosa tree in the small garden was in flower. I pulled down a small branch for Floss to smell it. We walked into the crooked chapel decorated in red and blue, the wood panels irregularly formed, the whole establishment out of alignment. Very old and broken, never having been more than mediocre, it had its own difficult logic.

We had avoided the crowd of visiting schoolchildren, and a few others who had obviously come in a bus from the city—the boys being yelled at by the—whatever he was—a Christian Brother, I think, with a shabby overcoat covering his black clothes.

"Get your hands off those things. Come on over here where I can watch you. . . . You see this carved woodwork. They brought it from the other side, but it was too big, so they had to cut it in half. This is the upper part of it. . . . This was the main altar. The lower half is at the other end of the room around that doorway. . . ."

We went down the broad stairs, with a shallow well beside it in the stones. The clumsy copper of the old still lay at one side. They knew how to live.

Across the road in the small public park were two pomegranate trees, some of the fruit split open with a late ripeness, though it was cold in the park. The caretaker must have picked up any fallen fruit earlier. Seeing no one about, I gave the small tree a vigorous shake or two, but nothing came down. Further along there was a white star-jasmine in bloom. Indian labor had no doubt been the sole thing that had made such things possible.

Here was I a visiting lecturer in English, with a "new" theory of the art to propound, looking at this decay, somewhat affected by its perverse logic. It had a difficult justice about it. What should be new is intent upon one thing, the metaphor—the metaphor is the poem. There is for them only one metaphor: Europe—the past. All metaphor for them, inevitably so, is the past: that is the poem. That is what they think a poem is: metaphor.

But their opportunity is to be unhandcuffed from that closest of all ties: the metaphoric. They don't live, they metaphorize. But they can't metaphorize upon that of which they have never heard. Except one old man in San Francisco, Philip Pye, M. A., who had the greatest difficulty to get a publisher for his translation of the classic—*The Natural Economic Order*. It is a plan to secure an uninterrupted exchange of the products of labor, free from bureaucratic interference, usury and exploitation, by Silvio Gesell. Finally the Free Economy Publishing Company, San Antonio, Texas, did print it. I wish to record the fact here.

The young people at the colleges find themselves on the edge of a metaphor from which not only they cannot escape but which their teachers re-enforce for them. Though they did invite me to talk.

I told them: Your great advantage is that your minds face

the Orient. You are relatively unencumbered by the past. . . . Go to your museums. The North Coast Indians who made all their livelihood fishing. They were induced by the British to put *all* their resources into it. Then their market was denied them. They starved.

Sometimes, like kids who don't know their lessons, they are embarrassed because they can't complete the metaphor. Or when they find triumphantly that they can do so (win a prize at the Juilliard School or so) they are fifty times thrilled at it, a blinding triumph.

Then one day I had somewhat of a shock. I had finished my talks and had had enough of it. But I had been asked to give one more on the campus at the University of California in Los Angeles, at three o'clock one Wednesday. The usual thing. They told me that Dylan Thomas had had close to a hundred people come out to hear him a month or two before.

"About forty or fifty, I suppose," I said.

"You never can tell."

I was bored. They asked me what I wanted to do.

"Just one thing. I don't want to stand."

They moved up a big table about twenty feet long and I found a chair for it. They placed the microphone, I threw my rather ratty-looking coat on the grand piano at the back and got my books out. I hadn't been paying much attention to the audience. When I looked up the place was jammed to the doors and others were trying to get in.

Professor So-and-so said, "We might as well get started."

"Sure. Why not?"

So he stood before the crowd below me and said the usual ten words. I told them this: "Do you want to hear me read—because that's what I've been asked to do—or do you want me to talk?"

"Talk," said some.

"Read," said others.

"All right, I'll talk and read"—I hadn't prepared a damn thing. "The first thing to do in hearing poems is not to try to understand them at the start at least, but to *listen*. The arts are sensual in their intention to impress. Let the poem come to you.

Put all you have into trying to hear the poem, hear it. Otherwise, how can you know it is a poem? Later, perhaps, if you are
superlatively able and perspicacious you may discover what it
means"—or something like that. They took it in complete
silence. So I read, and talked and talked between what I read.
You could have heard a feather fly. Once or twice they laughed,
heartily. I surely felt no restraint. Then I quit. They almost
took the roof off: there was no temple mood to that crowd. It
brought the blood to my head. I thanked them and closed with
the poem about the sea elephant.

Later I got a letter: "I never thought to see the poem so
appreciated. When my son told me—I had tears in my eyes."
With the stuff *I* write. It was an ovation. The newspapers
next day commented on my youthful voice. The Prof came to
Bob Wetterau's party at Flax bookstore in Los Angeles next
day and bought three books.

That was a good party at Flax. I read to five ladies in the
corner. Anais Nin was there and Man Ray and his wife, Don
Paquette, Charlotte, Eyvind Earle. Later Bob had invited us to
his house for supper—volaille à la Bob with Armagnac poured
over it and lighted at the table.

He had, let me see, five pullets, pretty good-sized birds they
were; we waited and waited and waited, looking round the room,
the front room that had a high barreled ceiling as though a
Swede had built. We had cocktails, peanuts and so on, then he
said to come in. He wanted to do it all himself, his wife said.

Then we waited some more. We could smell something roast-
ing—in sweet butter, he told us afterward. Then he brought
them in hot in a pan and poured the Armagnac over it, and
tried to light it and it wouldn't light. Then he tried again, two
or three times, then it lit and a big blue flame stood up out of
the pan all around the chickens, and he served us each one with
mushrooms and wild rice and poured gravy over it.

Then Charlotte and Eyvind, Alice and the little girl Kristin
came in and had to sit for almost an hour in the other room
while we ate and talked and laughed. He opened bottles of an
excellent white wine—Californian. Then we had a green salad
in a big wooden bowl, well savored. At last we went into the

other room for coffee and dessert. Kristin, Eyvind's daughter, was
half-asleep and cried and they tried to make her lie down. She
wouldn't.

At last the Browns came in with a big dish of fruit. Pears and
persimmons. They said they had trees loaded with them, though
they were not yet quite ripe.

Then a queer thing happened. Mrs. Miner, Mrs. Wetterau's
mother, mentioned that she was from Texas. Mrs. Wetterau, her
daughter, had gone to the Texas Industrial College for Women.

"Then you must have heard of my cousin, Jack Hubbard,"
I said.

"What was that?" said Mrs. Miner, who was not at first listening. "Did I hear the name Hubbard?"

"Yes. My cousin, Jack Hubbard. President of the Texas Industrial College for . . ."

"Good Lord! Why he's our best friend in the world. My
husband was speaker of the Texas House and Jack and he . . .
Why do I *know* him? Why, yes, his mother's name was Hurrard."

"Yes, and her sister was my grandmother on my mother's side."

"You don't mean it!"

The last night Eyvind insisted that I record some reading of
my poems on his excellent wire machine. I did, for an hour. I
didn't want to do it then but we did—while Floss and Charlotte patiently listened and Alice, Eyvind's wife, slept soundly
on the couch.

We drove next day to the station in Los Angeles. I had never
succeeded in getting there the whole time of our visit, though
we had been all around it through the various narrow canyons,
visiting the Hollywood Bowl, even passing George Antheil's
house number once, though we didn't stop. We almost missed
the train, having miscalculated the time of its departure.

At dawn I saw the sign Tucson on a station platform and the
same day at three, after crossing the desert miles near the Mexican
border, left the beautiful train (if anything is beautiful) to meet
Bob McAlmon coming grinning up the platform at El Paso
where the Hubbards had lived in the old days.

Juarez, across the bridge. Three cents the trip. *Sur le pont d'Avignon*—is all I could think of. The sparrows at night in the park—Bob and his brothers, George and Alec and their wives—tequilla at five cents a glass, a quail dinner and the Mexicans, the poor Indians—one huddled into a lump against the ironwork of the bridge at night—safe perhaps from both sides, incredibly compressed into a shapeless obstruction—asleep.

Next day the desert, across from the cotton fields, the railroad track dividing them. Copper, the smoke of the smelter stretching out across the desert miles—the endless waste of rubble—nightfall on the desert and the train gradually ascending in slow curves a thousand feet in a few miles. *Cholla, Okeechoya*. The moon coming up.

Next day Louisiana sugar-cane. New Orleans. Cold. Bourbon Street, the Cathedral. The excuses by the sexton:

A new organ. A good one. It ought to be. It cost over twenty-two thousand dollars.

Chapter 58

The Poem Paterson

Even though the greatest boon a poet grants the world is to reveal that secret and sacred presence, they will not know what he is talking about. Surgery cannot assist him, nor cures. The surgeon must himself know that his surgery is idle. But the object of this continuous scribbling comes to him also, I can see by his eyes that he acknowledges it.

That is why I started to write *Paterson*: a man is indeed a city, and for the poet there are no ideas but in things. But the critics would have it that I, the poet, am not profound and go on with their profundities, sometimes affecting to write poems in their very zeal as thinkers. It all depends on what you call profound. For I acknowledge it would, in dealing with man and city, require one to go to some depth in the form for the purpose.

The thinkers, the scholars, thereupon propound questions upon the nature of verse, answering themselves or at least creating tension between thoughts. They think, and to think, they believe, is to be profound. A curious idea, if what they think is profitable to their thinking they are rewarded—as thinkers.

But who, if he chose, could not touch the bottom of thought? The poet does not, however, permit himself to go beyond the thought to be discovered in the context of that with which he is dealing: no ideas but in things. The poet thinks with his poem, in that lies his thought, and that in itself is the profundity. The thought is *Paterson*, to be discovered there.

Therefore the thinker tries to capture the poem for his purpose, using his "thought" as the net to put his thoughts into. Absurd. They are not profound enough to discover that by this they commit a philosophic solecism. They have jumped the track, slipped out of category; no matter what the thought or the value, the poem will be bad, to make a pigeon roar.

The first idea centering upon the poem, *Paterson*, came alive early: to find an image large enough to embody the whole knowable world about me. The longer I lived in my place, among the details of my life, I realized that these isolated observations and experiences needed pulling together to gain "profundity." I already had the river. Flossie is always astonished when she realizes that we live on a river, that we are a river town. New York City was far out of my perspective; I wanted, if I was to write in a larger way than of the birds and flowers, to write about the people close about me: to know in detail, minutely what I was talking about—to the whites of their eyes, to their very smells.

That is the poet's business. Not to talk in vague categories but to write particularly, as a physician works, upon a patient, upon the thing before him, in the particular to discover the universal. John Dewey had said (I discovered it quite by chance), "The local is the only universal, upon that all art builds." Keyserling had said the same in different words. I had no wish, nor did I have the opportunity to know New York in that way, and I felt no loss in that.

I thought of other places upon the Passaic River, but, in the end, the city, Paterson, with its rich colonial history, upstream, where the water was less heavily polluted, won out. The falls, vocal, seasonally vociferous, associated with many of the ideas upon which our fiscal colonial policy shaped us through Alexander Hamilton, interested me profoundly—and what has resulted therefrom. Even today a fruitful locale for study. I knew of these things. I had heard. I had taken part in some of the incidents that made up the place. I had heard Billy Sunday: I had talked with John Reed: I had in my hospital experiences got to know many of the women: I had tramped Garret Mountain as a youngster, swum in its ponds, appeared in court there, looked at its charred ruins, its flooded streets, read of its past in Nelson's history of Paterson, read of the Dutch who settled it.

I took the city as my "case" to work up, really to work it up. It called for a poetry such as I did not know, it was my duty to discover or make such a context on the "thought." To *make* a poem, fulfilling the requirements of the art, and yet new, in the sense that in the very lay of the syllables Paterson as Paterson would be discovered, perfect, perfect in the special sense of the poem, to have it—if it rose to flutter into life awhile— it would be as itself, locally, and so like every other place in the world. For it is in that, that it be particular to its own idiom, that it lives.

The Falls let out a roar as it crashed upon the rocks at its base. In the imagination this roar is a speech or a voice, a speech in particular; it is the poem itself that is the answer.

In the end the man rises from the sea where the river appears to have lost its identity and accompanied by his faithful bitch, obviously a Chesapeake Bay retriever, turns inland toward Camden where Walt Whitman, much traduced, lived the latter years of his life and died. He always said that his poems, which had broken the dominance of the iambic pentameter in English prosody, had only begun his theme. I agree. It is up to us, in the new dialect, to continue it by a new construction upon the syllables.

Yesterday, with my guest John Husband and little Paul, my grandson—who was surely coming down with something—we took a ride out to see the terrain of Paterson. We started around eleven o'clock. Paul sat in the back alone. He wanted to know how fast the car would go. Eighty, I said. Then do it. Hmm.

We saw the spring at Great Notch coming out of the rock. I told John that Rutherford had been called Boiling Springs by the Indians because of the water boiling up out of the sands everywhere along the edge of the higher land approaching the swamps.

"Where are they now?" he asked.

"This is the last one that I know of. The others—one was running near home up to a year ago—have been diverted into sewers or filled up."

"Amazing!" said he. "Not a thing left of them in the whole country. But why?"

"Well, there was one across the tracks from us, a woman owned the property and kept it up beautifully, had a little pool there with goldfish and all that, open to the public. There was a standpipe with a good faucet—the water running continuously the year round."

"And . . . ?"

"You know. The people that went there fouled it up, actually shat in it, stole the pipe, killed the fish, dumped garbage, tramped the grass, the usual thing."

John, living in the flat New Orleans country, was thrilled even at that mild lift of the rocks, at least a *little* rise of ground. When we came to the peak and could look down, a sheer two hundred feet, he gasped at what he saw.

"Is that New York?"

"No, New York is ten to fifteen miles over there beyond the mist. This is Paterson."

"You don't mean it. Is that why? Did you know about this before you started to write?"

"No, not clearly but I had seen it—at one time or another."

"I mean," he went on, "something you could visualize so distinctly, practically hold it in the hollow of your hand."

"No. I was just lucky, that's all. I wanted a city. I thought of Newark, that's on the river too, but Paterson was upstream, nearer the source, and it had the falls—that was the big thing." We didn't get out of the car.

"Shall we go down the back way, Paul?"

"Yes. Is it dangerous?" The roadway was covered with melting ice but someone had put ashes on it.

"Look at that little house," pointed out John. It was on the very peak of the adjacent rocks outside the park area.

"Some artist," I said. "It's always an artist that does such intelligent things. Probably an Italian—they love the hilltops."

"Oh, it might be a writer, though," said John.

"Is *this* dangerous?" asked Paul, as we came to a sharp icy turn on a steep turn of the road.

"Look," I said, "it's not very dangerous, but don't always wish for something dangerous," I warned him. "Some day you might get it when you don't want it."

At the falls, not a soul. Little water going over it. Mud, fortunately shallow, adjacent to an area where the road circled at the parking place. From the spray, the brink was covered with a curious ice formation, globes, as big as your head, or larger, of smooth ice, hundreds of them, a field of hell-cabbages, you might say, some of which could be kicked loose, others impossible to move.

I went forward to the edge near the narrow bridge. The ground was glassy, but an iron grille at the lookout made it safe enough.

John watched us from about ten feet back while Paul managed to free one of the peculiar ice-heads.

"Good," I said, "now throw it over the edge."

But it was too heavy for him. He asked me to heave it. He clung to me as I went to the grille and threw it. It rose a little, then plunged downward and disappeared from our view to be followed almost at once by an explosive bang as it hit the ice below.

The experiment was a great success. Paul was delighted and immediately went about to get another bomb.

"This must have been about the spot where Mrs. Cummins stood before she fell or jumped into the stream below."

"Yes, that was a story," said John.

"And over there is where Sam Patch must have stood—that's the point."

"Where?" said Paul.

"There."

"Did he jump from there?"

"Yes, to retrieve the roller when they were running the bridge across."

"Quite a story, quite a story."

"You can't blame me for picking it up, can you?"

"How deep is the water?" asked Paul. "I mean at the deepest place?"

Index

395

Index